MICHAEL CURTIS is Professor of Political Science at Rutgers University, and has taught at several other institutions, including Yale University, Cornell University, Oberlin College and the University of Massachusetts. Dr. Curtis has written and edited over fifteen books in the fields of comparative politics, political theory, and Middle East affairs.

Other Avon Books by
Michael Curtis

THE GREAT POLITICAL THEORIES, VOL. 2

THE GREAT POLITICAL THEORIES VOLUME 1

FROM PLATO AND ARISTOTLE TO LOCKE AND MONTESQUIEU

*Edited, with introduction
and commentary, by*
MICHAEL CURTIS
Professor of Political Science
Rutgers University

AVON BOOKS ◆ NEW YORK

AVON BOOKS
A division of
The Hearst Corporation
1350 Avenue of the Americas
New York, New York 10019

Copyright © 1981 by Michael Curtis
Copyright © 1961 by Avon Books
Published by arrangement with the author
Library of Congress Catalog Card Number: 80-70020
ISBN: 0-380-00785-1

First Avon Books Printing: April 1961

AVON BOOKS TRADEMARK REG. U.S. PAT. OFF. AND IN OTHER COUNTRIES, MARCA REGISTRADA, HECHO EN U.S.A

Printed in the U.S.A.

OPM 25 24 23 22 21

Acknowledgments

Extracts from Seneca's writings taken from *The Stoic Philosophy of Seneca* by Moses Madas. Copyright © 1958 by Moses Hadas. Reprinted by permission of Doubleday & Company, Inc.

Extracts from Aquinas' writings taken from *The Political Ideas of St. Thomas Aquinas* by Dino Bigongiari. Copyright ©, 1953 by Hafner Publishing Company. Reprinted by permission of Hafner Publishing Company, Inc.

Extracts from Augustine's writings taken from *The City of God*, translated by Marcus Dods. Copyright, ©, 1950 by Random House, Inc. Reprinted by permission of Random House, Inc.

Extracts from Spinoza's writings taken from *Writings on Political Philosophy*, edited by A.G.A. Balz. Copyright ©, 1937 by D. Appleton-Century Company, Inc. Reprinted by permission of G. Bell & Sons.

TABLE OF CONTENTS

-⫸-⫸-⫸-⫸-⫸-⫸-⫸-⫸

Preface... 11
Introduction... 13

Section I: The Greeks.. 23
Section II: Hellenism and Roman Stoicism........... 102
Section III: Rome.. 120
Section IV: Early Christianity.................................. 140
Section V: Medieval Life and Thought 157
Section VI: The Two Realms: the Last Phase 175
Section VII: The Renaissance................................... 215
Section VIII: The Reformation 234
Section IX: The Right of Resistance....................... 263
Section X: Sovereignty and Divine Right.............. 301
Section XI: Hobbes and Spinoza............................. 326
Section XII: The Development of
        Constitutionalism 357
Section XIII: Vico and Hume................................... 390
Section XIV: French Thought in the Late
        17th and 18th Centuries.................................... 412

Selected Bibliography.. 441
Index... 453

THE GREAT POLITICAL THEORIES
1

From Plato and Aristotle to
Locke and Montesquieu

PREFACE

->>>->>>->>>->>>->>>->>>->>>->>>

      This book, and its companion volume, seek to introduce the student of political ideas directly to some of the major writers, from Plato to our contemporaries. I have tried to extract some of the important theories and arguments found in these writers, and have linked them with all-too-brief commentaries. The titles of the subheadings within each extract are mine and are not usually those of the author of the works. The choice of the works and extracts, especially of what to omit, has been partly determined by physical limitation, as well as by their value in illustrating the changing themes in political thought. I have tried to provide, where possible, continuous extracts from an author; in other cases, I have used a number of works of the writer to present an integrated section. I have found in my voyage of discovery, as did Voltaire's Candide, that only the unwise value every word in an author of repute.

MICHAEL CURTIS
New Brunswick,
New Jersey

INTRODUCTION

->>->>->>->>->>->>->>->>

Speculation on politics can take a variety of forms, from the preoccupation with the operational and manipulative aspects of public affairs to the creation of philosophic systems. Inquiry of the first type—on the correct number of members of a cabinet, the most desirable size and form of electoral area, the manner in which the legislative process should operate—is associated with the world of practical political activity and with journalistic commentary on it. The latter type, concerned with the nature of man, social relationships and political institutions, is normally elaborated in political treatises. Like Lear we all delight to hear:

> poor rogues
> Talk of court news; and we'll talk with them too,
> Who loses, and who wins: who's in, who's out.

Politics in this sense is almost the oldest profession in the world. It was tales of this kind that Herodotus, the first historian, delighted to relate. But politics is more than a sordid, if exciting, story of personal intrigue and machination, more than the spectacle of a multitude of ambitious politicians trampling on one another's egos. It is also the history of strong, differing conceptions of the desirability of public policies, and of beliefs on the right kind of political structure and behavior. It is therefore with the great treatises of political philosophy, which deal with problems of this kind, that we are primarily interested in this book.

Political philosophy is reflection on political phenomena, the attempt to understand them and the discussion of their significance. It is distinguished from more empirical forms of investigation of politics, such as how a certain geographical area has voted and why, or an analysis of decisions reached by a court, or the influences on a policy-maker when he is making a decision—not so much by rigid lines, as by the greater stress and reliance on the reflective and less on the descriptive and analytical element of study. Political philosophy makes use of and contains analytical, descriptive and historical material, but it subordinates these to philosophical or ethical considerations. For ultimately, political philosophy is reflection on the right or the best kind of political order, which is only one part of the larger and more fundamental question, the right or best kind of life man should lead.

There is no inevitable or necessary antagonism between political philosophy and what is generally called political science, only a difference, perhaps a misunderstanding, about jurisdictional boundaries. Students of both subjects are engaged in a common enterprise of political enlightenment. In this task, political philosophy furnishes a basis on which empirical investigation can more correctly and more usefully be carried out. It does this by trying to elucidate the premises and assumptions implicitly accepted by all political investigators as they undertake their task of description and analysis, by relating their empirical findings and conclusions to a wider area of knowledge, and by commenting critically, if it be necessary, on the all too frequent art of the sustained platitude. Political philosophy attempts to clarify ideas on political behavior and institutions; at its most ambitious, it proposes an ideal or the best possible regime for the age.

The Chinese have a curse: may you live in interesting times. Historically, political thought has been formulated in periods of crisis—economic, military, cultural or spiritual. It is sobering to recall how many of the great classics of political thought, drawn on in this book, were written by political exiles, as were those of Machiavelli, Grotius, Fortescue, Hobbes and Locke. In a broad sense, the aphorism of Sir Leslie Stephen, that political thought is the offspring of a revolution or the symptom of an approaching one, remains a valid, historical remark.

Plato and Aristotle made their monumental contributions to political thought in an era when the city-state, about which they were concerned, was on the point of disappearing, with the attempt of Alexander, the pupil of Aristotle, to conquer the known world. In the 14th century, Marsiglio of Padua, and in the 15th century Nicholas of Cusa suggested the need for representation of the community in both ecclesiastical and temporal organizations at a time when clerical domination of society was becoming subject to increasing challenge. The appeal of Hobbes for a strong sovereign power was the response to a state of civil war endangering both political institutions and personal security. The classical definitions of democracy in the 17th century were the outcome of a period in which the cutting off of ears, not to mention heads, for political reasons was not uncommon, and in which bills of attainder, impeachment processes, and judgment by a Court of Star Chamber, a familiar occurrence. Marx's analysis of class conflict in society and his prophecy of an impending revolution was an expression of his distaste for the social conditions produced by developing industrialism. T. H. Green's modification of British liberalism occurred with the realization that a laissez-faire philosophy was no longer adequate to satisfy demands and aspirations of the late 19th century. Oakeshott's modern conservative approach to politics is an outcome of deep skepticism about the value of any nontraditional behavior and the advisability of long-range planning in an age of rapid, unpredictable change.

No important political theorist has yet written a "Thoughts on the Causes of our Present Content." Indeed, contemporary defenders of the American experience and way of life like Daniel Boorstin argue that the very absence of systematic political thought in the United States is not a cause for lamentation, as many have suggested, but rather that this is the best possible tribute to the success of the American experiment. If the decline of political theory has been one of the intellectual characteristics of the contemporary Western world, it is primarily the result of the fulfillment of many of those aspirations that have given impetus to theory. Perhaps the narrowness of perspective adopted by the West, as well as the increasing complexity of world problems, has blinded theorists to the grave issues that remain or has blunted their acuteness of vision. For, as Adlai Stevenson has suggested, "The engine of progress has run out of the fuel of discontent." An alternative intellectual irritant to provoke discussion of social problems has yet to be found.

The advice of Lord Acton in his inaugural lecture was to study problems, not periods. The soundness of his advice is apparent once the history of political philosophy is seen not as a series of answers to the same question, but as the history of a problem that is constantly changing. "The one thing we cannot do with the *Summa* of Aquinas," wrote Carl Becker, "is to meet its arguments on their own ground." The political philosophy of any writer, in so far as it has significance, is his response to the conditions of his environment; it is both the biography of his era and his own autobiography. The theorist may be a conscious defender of the institutions of his time, as was Locke, justifying the English Revolution, or Burke defending the British Constitution against the French Revolution, or he may attack those institutions and their practices openly as did Marx, or surreptitiously, as did Spinoza. How effective he will be depends on the conditions of his age as much as on himself. The path of history is strewn with the tracts of neglected prophets. The history of political theory, McIlwain has said, is not the history of a few isolated political classics: it is the study of a stream of influence which has flowed down from age to age. The test of political theory ought to be historical, rather than metaphysical.

Yet influential or not, a classic in political theory, as in other fields, enriches the cumulative store of wisdom and ideas. The great theorist is the man who expresses with rigor, internal logic and insight, the dilemmas of his age, and discusses most effectively the problems with which his generation is preoccupied. He stands out above his contemporaries not so much by his originality, which is rare enough in human thought, as by the force and vigor with which he expounds his doctrine.

Political thought results from the immersion of the writer in the political phenomena of his times, but this is not a deterministic process. Subjective impressions—Hitler's envy of successful Jews in Vienna; psychological characteristics—Hobbes' self-confessed natural timidity; and national predispositions—Burke's belief that things British were little short of perfect—all affect theory. The study of personality may help explain the origin, if not the validity or merit, of theory. Even if it is no longer true

> That every boy and every gal
> That's born into the world alive
> Is either a little Liberal
> Or else a little Conservative

the history of theory, as William James remarked, is to a great extent that of the clash of human temperaments.

Like any intellectual inquiry, political philosophy is partly a process of communion with the past involving familiarity with the great writers, a continuing discourse with history. This can be both a disillusioning and a disconcerting process, as Stephen Spender has indicated in what he called the Obstacle Race way of studying philosophy. The whole field of human thought is set out with logical obstructions, and the students watch the philosophers race around it. Some of them get further than others, but they all fall sooner or later into the traps that language sets for them. Yet, without a familiarity with the great intellectual political inheritance, one might repeat the error of Herbert Spencer, who expressed familiar ideas in the belief they were original, purely out of ignorance that they had previously been discussed.

But political philosophy is more than merely intellectual gymnastics on political themes. Every age emphasizes different aspects of its inheritance depending on its own problems. In medieval theory, it is impossible to separate entirely the political and religious elements. Machiavelli's attempt to establish purely political criteria for institutions, almost totally neglects the religious inheritance except as it supported those institutions. The 19th century writers, in a broadly optimistic climate of opinion, tended to emphasize the rationalism and progressive attitude of previous writers. Contemporary thought, with its overtones of pessimism, and preoccupied with the difficulties rather than the successes of modern life, has picked out of the 19th century certain thinkers, Kierkegaard, Burckhardt, de Tocqueville, who swam against the main current and whose vision of politics is similar to our own. Fashions in political ideas are almost as ephemeral as in women's clothes.

Apart from its value as continuation of the intellectual inheritance of civilization, political philosophy serves to clarify and make precise political concepts, to redefine and reanalyze the political terminology of every age. The idea of "the consent of the people" is one thing in Locke; it has quite different implications today, when the possession of property is no longer the key to political participation. The concept of "sovereignty" was valuable for Bodin and Hobbes in periods of civil disorder; in united or homogeneous communities its appropriateness as an explanation of the legitimacy of command and of obedience can be questioned. Political philosophy examines customary beliefs and practices in the possibility that what has been accepted as an imponderable may, as Veblen suggested, be only "an article of make-believe, axiomatic by force of settled habit." In this way, political philosophy helps to evaluate the present correctly, and shows that historical analogies may be dangerous as well as helpful.

Political philosophy is a search for understanding. It can provide no panacea for social problems nor give final answers to questions. Indeed, to search for final answers is to presume a purpose or final cause about which such answers can be made, an assumption that might be justified theologically, but not politically. Few political thinkers today would talk, as did Aristotle, in teleological terms about the nature and behavior of political institutions. The role of political philosophy is more modest. It talks in terms of probability, not of certainty.

It can suggest, it cannot prove. The great theorist, like the great artist, is the person who with sympathy, understanding and imagination, gains insight into the needs of his time. He can influence but he cannot manipulate the human beings who make up his field of study; he cannot consciously control them as the scientist controls the ingredients and the conditions of his experiment. Indeed the very impact of his ideas may make them a self-denying prophesy if men seek to escape the ends forecast by him. Marx's theory of the inevitable increase in the misery of the workers has been rendered invalid partly because of the conscious efforts of governments in the field of social security to prevent such an outcome.

Political philosophy is abstraction, and abstraction is meaningful only when it is related to concrete example and actual behavior. Political philosophy is grounded in the acquisition of empirical data if it has valid meaning as distinct from emotional impact. It is true that the study of politics cannot be expected to produce the same degree of certainty as can the study of natural science. The search for a political science in the sense of a series of definite laws explaining political phenomena may be unrewarding and fruitless if the political scientist engages in research with an eye more on his status relative to the natural sciences than on the inevitable limitations of his subject. But it is clear that the search for political understanding is advanced by a rigorous analysis of political behavior and inter-relationships.

The fact that moral values cannot be proved in any scientific fashion does not prevent the theorist from searching for or holding them. At the same time the significance of moral values is in no way reduced by methodological clarification of political statements. Such clarification implies only that these values are not capable of being tested or are not meaningful in the same way as an analytical statement. It does not imply that the values themselves are thereby reduced in significance or in importance.

To search for political values so that they may be presented in a comprehensible form is a laudable purpose. But it does not provide information about political activity that is based on scientific probability. Political philosophy neglects at its peril the genuine research performed by political scientists, including those who concentrate on political behavior and who have sometimes been wrongly regarded as its enemies. Appeals to self-evident principles, or to eternal law or divine providence, or to metaphysical abstraction cannot by themselves illuminate political activity with meaningful propositions.

This is not denying the previous argument that speculation plays a useful role in understanding political phenomena. But speculation is limited and a scientific, methodological approach can be valuable in clarifying both the meaning of values, and also the consequences of actions based on those values. Epistemological questions—such as "How does one go about acquiring knowledge?"—need answering if speculation is not to degenerate into idle curiosity. At the same time, political philosophy, like all attempts to understand, is built on commonsense assumptions. For example, an individual recognizes that others have similar experiences to his, causality or regularity is accepted as a general phenomenon, a degree of freedom of will is granted by almost all thinkers, observations can disclose "facts" acceptable to everyone. Such general ideas and statements are basic to all political study, but they show that the scientific method too has certain limitations.

Political philosophy is related directly to political life. Not all political theorists offer specific suggestions, as did Machiavelli, on how a usurper should act to maintain power or how he can best be overthrown, or Bodin, who advocated a council for the king. But all political philosophy is concerned with providing theoretical formulae on the basis of which political activity may take place. The political philosopher, said Ernest Barker, must study the busy hum of affairs in the cave before he can move into the upper light of contemplation.

Most thinkers are interested in the implementation of their theories: Machiavelli, Grotius, Locke, Rousseau, Saint-Simon, address their work to a particular person or group. Even Spinoza, who pleaded for understanding rather than praise or condemnation, stands as a symbol for resistance to communal intolerance. Not all, like the 19th century positivist or the contemporary Marxist, have the conviction that history is on their side, that its laws can be predicted, and that it is well to accept the inevitable. But this does not reduce them to pessimistic indifference or lessen their interest in the political outcome of their ideas. Political activity is the result of the actions of human beings, and not of the General Will, the Dialectical Process, the Collective Unconscious, the Racial Blood or the Spirit of Consciousness: political theorists are aware that their ideas can affect the nature of that activity. Yet if there is merit in this, there is danger too. Political theorists, like practicing politicians, do well to be aware of the tendency of all political activity to treat men as objects.

Political philosophy studies political phenomena. But what is regarded as "political" is decided by convenience rather than nature. The core of political philosophy has always been the study of those central institutions, organizations and personnel that have the power to issue directions and rules, and the relationship of the governed to government. The recurring problems of political philosophy are those concerning the nature of society, law, obligation, rights, duties, command, responsibility and obedience. In modern theory, there has been a preoccupation with sovereignty, power, influence and groups.

Though all thinkers would agree that these bodies and concepts are legitimate subjects for investigation by political philosophy, not all agree on the inclusion of religious, educational, moral, cultural or sexual matters. Yet on many occasions these subjects must be included in the scope of political philosophy. The problem of whether a Catholic President of the United States will owe prior loyalty to the Pope or to his office has been of some practical, as well as theoretical, recent significance. The democratic concept of government remains a myth and not a reality when the educational system is inadequate or the electorate ill-informed. Free speech is largely a meaningless abstraction if one has nothing to say. Similarly, morals are properly subject to political inquiry. From Plato to the present the problem of censorship continues and is immersed in aesthetic, as well as moral and political, implications. Similarly, one cannot talk coherently of the good or the right kind of life without examining the cultural and aesthetic setting of society. The amount of work to be performed, the use made of leisure time, the style of housing, public buildings and cities, the quality of entertainment available, all play their part in the determination of what Aristotle called the mature man, the man whose character is formed by the aggregate of experience. Even the most intimate of human relations, the sexual, has political implications. Birth control is more than a simple religious problem. Students of demography and of the relation between land productivity and population, especially in the underdeveloped nations of the world, may well consider this the most important contemporary single factor in politics.

Part of the reason why there can be no final answers in political philosophy is the very fact of the changing nature of the subject matter with which it deals. The task of inquiry is made even more complex, the answers are made more indeterminate, by the degree of change in the thing studied. One need not be a determinist in order to hold that certain trends of social life are cumulative and irreversible. It is unlikely that the processes of industrialism or of science will ever be deliberately turned back. The problems which they have produced, and with which political philosophy must deal, multiply with increasing rapidity.

All theories of society are based on a particular hierarchy of values, overtly expressed or implicit. Without the value judgments of a thinker, his work becomes limited at best, sterile at worst. He must be concerned about correct ends, not simply means. The slogan of Maurras, *"Politique d'abord,"* becomes valid only if the ends are assumed, and the problems are those of technique only. It neglects the discussion of the purpose of politics, and its place in the totality of human experience. Political philosophy cannot escape philosophic arguments about the nature of man, free will or determinism, rational and instinctive behavior, the meaning of progress and of change, the quality of human life.

SECTION I

THE GREEKS

Political philosophy proper began with the Greeks. It may be true that all succeeding political philosophy is a footnote to and a commentary on Plato. This does not deny the importance of other civilizations: the Egyptian, the Hebrew, the Persian, the Hittite. Historical research has shown that Greek science owes a considerable debt to Babylonia; a much more understanding view has been recently taken on Persian institutions. Yet while in pre-Greek writings there are fragments of a political nature and discussion of some political problems—a written code of law, a tribal God, God as the source of political authority, bureaucracy and, above all, the nature of the absolute ruler or despot—there are no systematic or exhaustive expositions.

In Homer there are four different examples of political organization, but no coherent view of the operation of politics. It is the Greeks of the 5th and 4th centuries B.C. who created the terminology of politics, taking the words from everyday usage and applied thought to political action. Politics was inseparable from life in the *polis,* a city possessing common habits, military strength, a myth of its origin, its own god and religion, and citizens. It is this last characteristic that differentiates the *polis* and future political organizations from associations based on blood and religious ties.

The city-state of Athens in the 5th and 4th centuries B.C., with its 1,000 square miles of territory, its 40,000 citizens and 400,000 mixed population, remains one of the pinnacles of human civilization. Its basis was not so much individual material welfare or comfort as communal pride, communal magnificence and dedication. Indeed, material comforts were modest. The Greeks were badly clothed and ill shod; there

were no such magnificent road or drainage systems as were
notable in Persia or Rome. Public affairs were regarded a
more important and significant than private matters—the op
posite of *polites* is *idiotes* (those who are uninterested in
public affairs).

Leisure, "that most exquisite of delights," love of conversa
tion, admiration of physical beauty of both men and women
delight in the theater and the great trio of dramatists, Aeschy
lus, Sophocles and Euripides, participation in communa
affairs—all these are different aspects of a sophisticated cul
ture that has been so prolific in influence in the arts of litera
ture and architecture, philosophy and political behavior. Ver
satility was the hallmark of the citizen. Education, as Pericles
said, should mold a person "capable of the most varied forms
of activity and able to adapt himself to different circum
stances with versatility and grace." The dangers of such ama
teurism and dilettantism are obvious, as can be seen in the
remark of Aristotle that a gentleman should play the flute, but
not too well.

Yet if Athens had great art and literature, had its Academy
and Lyceum, put great stress on education and proclaimed the
value of government by discussion, its history was marred by
examples of military aggression and intolerance, and by its
economic base of slavery. Its heyday was short. In 490 and
480, the Athenians had beaten the Persians at Marathon and
at Salamis, in 432 they began the disastrous 27-year war with
Sparta which ruined their liberal civilization, and in 332 they
fell to the Macedonians. Athens' intolerance was shown by
the killing of Socrates, the banishing of Themistocles and the
imprisonment of Miltiades; Critias, one of the pupils of Socra
tes, became one of the Thirty Tyrants. The whole economy
rested on slavery, since there was no occupation except that of
politics which was not performed by slaves. Even those who
argued against Aristotle's view of slavery as natural, did not
propose its abolition.

If we are more familiar with the rationalism of the Greeks,
their pride in human reason and confidence in the cosmos,
permeated by reason, we must also note that Greece produced
the Orphic-Pythagorean myths with their emphasis on the
sinful body, idea of guilt and the world as a place of punish
ment.

The *polis* contained a community, the sole source of au
thority, dedicated to the purpose of achieving the good life.
This purpose would be accomplished through individual par
ticipation in communal affairs, a duty the individual volun-

tarily accepted and which was desirable both for the community and for his own development. The general object was the creation of social balance and harmony, which meant not totalitarian control, but a reconciliation of individual differences, based on the premise that the desire for individual fulfillment need not end in anarchy. State, or social, action was needed, but there was no claim that the state had an existence of its own, apart from the individuals who made up its citizen body. The best kind of self-realization and society was the goal; doing well or living well was the aim of inquiry and action. Politics, therefore, became a proper subject of inquiry, a process concerned with the meaning of *nomos*—law and custom—and with the wisdom of social organization.

Sophocles

Antigone, written in 441 B.C. by Sophocles, is the immortal drama in which the order of the ruler Creon forbidding the burial of Polyneices is defied by his niece Antigone, the sister of the slain man. The play embodies the conflict between opposing points of view and principles on a number of basic issues confronting all political systems.

At the core of the conflict is the issue of the nature of law and justice. Differences exist between the claims of divine law, the unwritten laws of God, and natural law on the one hand and the laws made by the existing rulers. The expression of individual conscience and will conflicts with the demands of the ruler. The ties of blood relationships are opposed to the impersonal loyalty to the state. The struggle exists between men and women, and between young and older people. *Antigone* is a timeless drama in its discussion of the problem of disobedience by an individual of the state and its ruler and the effect of that disobedience on the parties involved.

Sophists

The first important group of political thinkers were the Sophists, of whom Gorgias, Protagoras, Prodicus, Hippias and Thrasymachus are the most familiar. They were teachers who created subjects by inventing definitions and concepts, and who were paid for teaching them. Not endowed with university chairs, not attached to any particular culture or *polis*, they traveled everywhere to deliver their lectures, helping their students to practical success. Versatile in their interests and varied in their background, they introduced ideas of cosmopolitanism, skepticism and free thinking, education for all and academic freedom. They had no single doctrine; they shared a common intellectual attitude and manner of life. They taught *sophia,* the wisdom, knowledge and skill that was necessary for the successful conduct of life as individual or citizen. Above all, the study of man was important. For Protagoras, "man is the measure of all things," for Gorgias, the proper study of mankind was man.

From their ranks came Socrates (470–399 B.C.). Soldier, sculptor, renowned for his heavy drinking as well as his love of inquiry, he wrote nothing himself, and contemporaries have left conflicting accounts of him and his work. For Plato, Socrates was the great example of intellectual integrity, the man always prepared to discuss, the professor who sought not to profess, the teacher who refused to indoctrinate, who aimed to make men think. His method of achieving knowledge was through the dialectical process of question and answer, which would lead to precise definition and to understanding. Socrates criticized the Sophists as a group for professing false knowledge, not in the sense of misleading or incorrect information, but in not penetrating sufficiently the significance of the subjects they were treating.

Plato

The greatness of the teacher is best shown by the caliber of his students. The most distinguished of the pupils of Socrates was the aristocratic Athenian, Plato (427–347 B.C.), founder of the first college, the Academy, in 388, and the first great systematic political theorist. No political writer can completely ignore or neglect the *Republic,* the book devoted to the meaning and implementation of justice both by the individual and the state. Its political ideas, as expounded by the spokesman Socrates, are still attacked and defended with genuine passion.

Plato concerned himself with fundamental questions: the meaning of justice, the right kind of life, the makeup of the human personality, the purpose of political association, the best type of political structure, the classification of constitutions, the need for trained rulers, the meaning of knowledge. The *Republic* is a book on politics, but it is also on psychology, morality, education and eugenics.

Plato was critical of the accepted Athenian idea of all citizens participating in politics. The exercise of political power was as skilled a profession as any other, requiring long apprenticeship and dedication. Ruling was a distinct craft, needing a group of trained rulers. This involves drawing distinctions between human beings on the basis, not of their possession of material wealth, but on what part of the soul was dominant in their character. The three elements of the soul—appetite, courage and reason—were related to class and to function in the state. If appetite, or the satisfaction of physical desires, dominated, the individual would be in the laboring class, if it was spirit or courage, he would be a warrior, if it was reason, or the faculty of possessing true knowledge, he would be a ruler. Constitutions were thus related to the character of the citizen body. The good state, like the good man, possessed the characteristics of temperance, courage, wisdom and justice.

Although there was provision for children born in one class to reach a higher, this was an exceptional rather than a typical procedure. Plato's society was not only ordered, but structured and hierarchical, with everyone in his allotted, proper place. Interrelated therefore with the political structure was an educational system, which prepared individuals for their function, and a science of eugenics which prepared the individuals themselves.

Plato was largely interested in the class of rulers or guardians: how they could be obtained, what education was necessary for them, how their life was to be organized, the way in which they could acquire real knowledge, their methods of control over the rest of society, the way in which they could create the necessary feeling of unity and community interest. This group of learned ascetics was to be a communal body, renouncing both private property and individual wives, both of which might induce them to act in their individual, rather than the general, interests.

Most important of all, members of this group were not simply rulers, they were philosophers. They alone could understand what was of permanent value, had knowledge of the dialectic and the Forms of goodness and justice. Their very reluctance to govern was an illustration of their fitness to do so. In order to govern, they had to leave the realm of true knowledge and philosophical inquiry, as Plato suggested in the striking allegory of the cave in Book 7, to descend to the dark realm of ordinary life.

The *Republic* presented an ideal regime, the feasibility or likelihood of which was not clear. In his other major political work, *Laws*, Plato seemed to have abandoned the possibility of realizing such a regime, for he proposed an impersonal code of law as a substitute for the reason of the ruler, and approved the possession of private property by the rulers as well as the ruled. Certainly, Plato was pessimistic in his view of inevitable, progressive deterioration of government from the starting point of timocracy until the final form of tyranny.

The ideal state was an ordered state, in which all fulfilled their function and worked for the good of the whole, and in which education prepared the individual for his function and for citizenship. But it was also a structure of rigid control, static social position, censorship of literature and art, limitation of power to an elite capable of grasping the definitive body of knowledge necessary for ruling.

Plato's favorite analogies, with which the work is full, are taken from ordinary life. But the master-slave, shepherd-flock relationships of automatic and inevitable command and obedience are not a valid picture of the ruler-citizen relationship. The ruler, unless he is divine, cannot "make the city" as the sculptor makes a statue or the painter fills his canvas. But Plato and his ideas have been a model for all succeeding utopian projects.

Aristotle

Unlike Plato, Aristotle (384–322 B.C.) was born not in Athens but at Stagira. After studying under Plato, and tutoring Alexander the Great between 342 and 334, he founded his own school, the Lyceum, in Athens. He taught there until 322 when he was accused of impiety and fled. Aristotle was familiar with life at court. His father was court physician to the King of Macedonia (which perhaps explains the large number of medical metaphors in his work); he knew several rulers as well as Alexander. He was versed in an extraordinary variety and number of subjects: biology, physics, psychology, logic, aesthetics, as well as ethics and politics. As teacher, he was also director of what must have been the first task force of graduate students engaging in the process known as research.

The temper of Aristotle's *Politics* is different from that of the *Republic*. It is cool, quiet, reasonable, not so ambitious, lacking in strong enthusiasm or advocacy. Much of the disordered logical presentation of the book is due to the fact that it is more a series of lecture notes and a number of independent essays than a polished treatise.

Aristotle is the cool, dispassionate, moderate observer, the empirical investigator of political institutions and behavior. His was the first exhaustive analysis of existing constitutions, and he thus created political science. His classification of political regimes has been either repeated or has been the starting point of most succeeding discussion of governmental systems. His discussion in Book 5 of revolutions and the methods of preserving a political system is still a fount from which contemporaries draw. His definition of citizenship, if not his defense of slavery, is still a challenging one.

Observation was necessary to study phenomena and the way they changed, in order to find the real nature of anything. Plato's conception of change had been of degeneration from the ideal; Aristotle believed that change was teleological, movement toward the natural, predetermined end. The end of man's actions was happiness, which is achieved by the correct control of his desire by his reason. The end of the state was self-sufficiency, which was achieved by moderation, in its wealth, its size, its constitution and its ruling group. The best human being was the one in whom the "nature" of the person had been most realized. The best form of regime was the one in which the "nature" of the *polis* had been realized the most.

Man and state were linked together. Man was by nature a political animal who reached perfection and became civilized as a citizen. The state was a natural phenomenon, since it was the means by which man could reach his end. It was natural because it was the end to which associations, the household and the tribe, moved, and because this end provided the good life.

Aristotle was concerned with the most important topic of political inquiry, the best form of political association or constitution. His classification of states was determined partly by the number of rulers and partly by their aim, whether they acted for the good of the whole or only for themselves. His discussion of democracy is still pertinent today. He presented fairly the advantages—collective judgments are more satisfactory than individual ones, and the many should rule (as shown in his metaphor that those who wear the shoe know best where it pinches)—and the drawbacks, especially the problem of what to do with the outstanding man.

His argument on the supremacy of law, which provides both stability and reason freed from all passion, his distinction between numerical and proportional equality, distributive and corrective justice, his discussion of the mixed regime guided by moderation as the means of maintaining stability, his argument for the limitation of material wealth, his views on liberal education, the function of leisure, the nature of citizenship, the happy life, all have been immensely influential.

Aristotle bequeathed a great legacy to political thought, but not to any one school. If he stressed the desirability of moderation and of respect for the law, he was not yet the counterpart of the modern constitutionalist. If he argued for limitation of wealth, he was no socialist. If he tended to suggest at

times that monarchy was the best form of government, he was
no devoted advocate of unrestricted, hereditary monarchy.
His emphasis was on the need for constitutional stability—to
be secured by stable foundation of economic power, by education and breeding—for this was the great virtue of the good
polis. Above all, Aristotle is important for his belief in the
possibility of a political science, and for his investigations of
the ends of states and of the activities of men making up those
states.

SOPHOCLES

Antigone

The Need for Obedience and the Case for Disobedience

CREON

My friends, the very gods who shook the state
with mighty surge have set it straight again.
So now I sent for you, chosen from all,
first that I knew you constant in respect
to Laius' royal power; and again
when Oedipus had set the state to rights,
and when he perished, you were faithful still
in mind to the descendants of the dead.
When they two perished by a double fate,
on one day struck and striking and defiled
each by his own hand, now it comes that I
hold all the power and the royal throne
through close connection with the perished men.
You cannot learn of any man the soul,
the mind, and the intent until he shows
his practise of the government and law.
For I believe that who controls the state
and does not hold to the best plans of all,
but locks his tongue up through some kind of fear,
that he is worst of all who are or were.
And he who counts another greater friend
than his own fatherland, I put him nowhere.
So I—may Zeus all-seeing always know it—
could not keep silent as disaster crept
upon the town, destroying hope of safety.
Nor could I count the enemy of the land
friend to myself, not I who know so well
that she it is who saves us, sailing straight,
and only so can we have friends at all.

With such good rules shall I enlarge our state.
And now I have proclaimed their brother-edict.
In the matter of the sons of Oedipus,
citizens, know: Eteocles who died,
defending this our town with champion spear,
is to be covered in the grave and granted
all holy rites we give the noble dead.
But his brother Polyneices whom I name
the exile who came back and sought to burn
his fatherland, the gods who were his kin,
who tried to gorge on blood he shared, and lead
the rest of us as slaves—
it is announced that no one in this town
may give him burial or mourn for him.
Leave him unburied, leave his corpse disgraced,
a dinner for the birds and for the dogs.
Such is my mind. Never shall I, myself,
honor the wicked and reject the just.
The man who is well-minded to the state
from me in death and life shall have his honor. . . .

CREON
Stop now, before you fill me up with rage,
or you'll prove yourself insane as well as old.
Unbearable, your saying that the gods
take any kindly forethought for this corpse.
Would it be they had hidden him away,
honoring his good service, his who came
to burn their pillared temples and their wealth,
even their land, and break apart their laws?
Or have you seen them honor wicked men?
It isn't so.
No, from the first there were some men in town
who took the edict hard, and growled against me,
who hid the fact that they were rearing back,
not rightly in the yoke, no way my friends.
These are the people—oh it's clear to me—
who have bribed these men and brought about the deed.
No current custom among men as bad
as silver currency. This destroys the state;
this drives men from their homes; this wicked teacher
drives solid citizens to acts of shame.
It shows men how to practise infamy
and know the deeds of all unholiness.
Every least hireling who helped in this
brought about then the sentence he shall have.

But further, as I still revere great Zeus,
understand this, I tell you under oath,
if you don't find the very man whose hands
buried the corpse, bring him for me to see,
not death alone shall be enough for you
till living, hanging, you make clear the crime.
For any future grabbings you'll have learned
where to get pay, and that it doesn't pay
to squeeze a profit out of every source.
For you'll have felt that more men come to doom
through dirty profits than are kept by them. . . .

CREON
You there, whose head is drooping to the ground,
do you admit this, or deny you did it?

ANTIGONE
I say I did it and I don't deny it. . . .

CREON
You—tell me not at length but in a word.
You knew the order not to do this thing?

ANTIGONE
I knew, of course I knew. The word was plain.

CREON
And still you dared to overstep these laws?

ANTIGONE
For me it was not Zeus who made that order.
Nor did that Justice who lives with the gods below
mark out such laws to hold among mankind.
Nor did I think your orders were so strong
that you, a mortal man, could over-run
the gods' unwritten and unfailing laws.
Not now, nor yesterday's, they always live,
and no one knows their origin in time.
So not through fear of any man's proud spirit
would I be likely to neglect these laws,
draw on myself the gods' sure punishment.
I knew that I must die; how could I not?
even without your warning. If I die
before my time, I say it is a gain.
Who lives in sorrows many as are mine

how shall he not be glad to gain his death?
And so, for me to meet this fate, no grief.
But if I left that corpse, my mother's son,
dead and unburied I'd have cause to grieve
as now I grieve not.
And if you think my acts are foolishness
the foolishness may be in a fool's eye. . . .

CREON
These rigid spirits are the first to fall.
The strongest iron, hardened in the fire,
most often ends in scraps and shatterings.
Small curbs bring raging horses back to terms.
Slave to his neighbor, who can think of pride?
This girl was expert in her insolence
when she broke bounds beyond established law.
Once she had done it, insolence the second,
to boast her doing, and to laugh in it.
I am no man and she the man instead
if she can have this conquest without pain.
She is my sister's child, but were she child
of closer kin than any at my hearth,
she and her sister should not so escape
their death and doom. . . .
If I allow disorder in my house
I'd surely have to licence it abroad.
A man who deals in fairness with his own,
he can make manifest justice in the state.
But he who crosses law, or forces it,
or hopes to bring the rulers under him,
shall never have a word of praise from me.
The man the state has put in place must have
obedient hearing to his least command
when it is right, and even when it's not.
He who accepts this teaching I can trust,
ruler, or ruled, to function in his place,
to stand his ground even in the storm of spears,
a mate to trust in battle at one's side.
There is no greater wrong than disobedience.
This ruins cities, this tears down our homes,
this breaks the battle-front in panic-rout.
If men live decently it is because
discipline saves their very lives for them.
So I must guard the men who yield to order,
not let myself be beaten by a woman.

Better, if it must happen, that a man
should overset me.
I won't be called weaker than womankind.

PLATO

The Republic

The Basis of Social Organization
Socrates is Talking to Adeimantus

Imagine a rather short-sighted person told to read an inscription in small letters from some way off. He would think it
a godsend if someone pointed out that the same inscription
was written up elsewhere on a bigger scale, so that he could
first read the larger characters and then make out whether the
smaller ones were the same.

We think of justice as a quality that may exist in a whole
community as well as in an individual, and the community is
the bigger of the two. Possibly, then, we may find justice there
in larger proportions, easier to make out. So I suggest that we
should begin by inquiring what justice means in a state. Then
we can go on to look for its counterpart on a smaller scale in
the individual.

Well then, I continued, suppose we imagine a state coming
into being before our eyes. We might then be able to watch
the growth of justice or of injustice within it. When that is
done, we may hope it will be easier to find what we are looking for.

A state comes into existence because no individual is self-
sufficing; we all have many needs.

We call in one another's help to satisfy our various requirements; and when we have collected a number of helpers and
associates to live together in one place, we call that settlement
a state.

If one man gives another what he has to give in exchange
for what he can get, it is because each finds that to do so is
for his own advantage.

Very well, said I. Now let us build up our imaginary state
from the beginning. Apparently, it will owe its existence to
our needs, the first and greatest need being the provision of
food to keep us alive. Next we shall want a house; and thirdly,
such things as clothing.

How will our state be able to supply all these demands? We
shall need at least one man to be a farmer, another a builder,
and a third a weaver. Will that do, or shall we add a shoe-

maker and one or two more to provide for our personal wants?

The minimum state, then, will consist of four or five men.

Now here is a further point. Is each one of them to bring the product of his work into a common stock? Should our one farmer, for example, provide food enough for four people and spend the whole of his working time in producing corn, so as to share with the rest; or should he take no notice of them and spend only a quarter of his time on growing just enough corn for himself, and divide the other three-quarters between building his house, weaving his clothes, and making his shoes, so as to save the trouble of sharing with others and attend himself to all his own concerns?

The first plan might be easier, replied Adeimantus.

That may very well be so, said I; for, as you spoke, it occurred to me, for one thing, that no two people are born exactly alike. There are innate differences which fit them for different occupations.

And will a man do better working at many trades, or keeping to one only?

Keeping to one.

And there is another point: obviously work may be ruined, if you let the right time go by. The workman must wait upon the work; it will not wait upon his leisure and allow itself to be done in a spare moment. So the conclusion is that more things will be produced and the work be more easily and better done, when every man is set free from all other occupations to do, at the right time, the one thing for which he is naturally fitted.

We shall need more than four citizens, then, to supply all those necessaries we mentioned. You see, Adeimantus, if the farmer is to have a good plough and spade and other tools, he will not make them himself. No more will the builder and weaver and shoemaker make all the many implements they need. So quite a number of carpenters and smiths and other craftsmen must be enlisted. Our miniature state is beginning to grow.

Still, it will not be very large, even when we have added cowherds and shepherds to provide the farmers with oxen for the plough, and the builders as well as the farmers with draught-animals, and the weavers and shoemakers with wool and leather.

And yet, again, it will be next to impossible to plant our city in a territory where it will need no imports. So there will have to be still another set of people, to fetch what it needs from other countries.

Moreover, if these agents take with them nothing that those other countries require in exchange, they will return as empty-handed as they went. So, besides everything wanted for consumption at home, we must produce enough goods of the right kind for the foreigners whom we depend on to supply us. That will mean increasing the number of farmers and craftsmen.

And then, there are these agents who are to import and export all kinds of goods—merchants, as we call them. We must have them; and if they are to do business overseas, we shall need quite a number of ship-owners and others who know about that branch of trading.

Again, in the city itself how are the various sets of producers to exchange their products? That was our object, you will remember, in forming a community and so laying the foundation of our state.

Obviously, they must buy and sell.

That will mean having a market-place, and a currency to serve as a token for purposes of exchange.

Now suppose a farmer, or an artisan, brings some of his produce to market at a time when no one is there who wants to exchange with him. Is he to sit there idle, when he might be at work?

No, he replied; there are people who have seen an opening here for their services. In well-ordered communities they are generally men not strong enough to be of use in any other occupation. They have to stay where they are in the market-place and take goods for money from those who want to sell, and money for goods from those who want to buy.

That, then, is the reason why our city must include a class of shopkeepers—so we call these people who sit still in the marketplace to buy and sell, in contrast with merchants who travel to other countries.

There are also the services of yet another class, who have the physical strength for heavy work, though on intellectual grounds they are hardly worth including in our society—hired labourers, as we call them, because they sell the use of their strength for wages. They will go to make up our population.

Well, Adeimantus, has our state now grown to its full size?

Perhaps.

Then, where in it shall we find justice or injustice?

If we are to have enough pasture and plough land, we shall have to cut off a slice of our neighbours' territory; and if they too are not content with necessaries, but give themselves up to getting unlimited wealth, they will want a slice of ours.

So the next thing will be that we shall be at war . . . we

have discovered the origin of war in desires which are the
most fruitful source of evils both to individuals and to states.

Quite true.

This will mean a considerable addition to our community—
a whole army, to go out to battle with any invader, in defence
of all this property and of the citizens we have been describ-
ing. . . .

These guardians of our state, inasmuch as their work is the
most important of all, will need the most complete freedom
from other occupations and the greatest amount of skill and
practice . . . And also a native aptitude for their calling. . . .

So it is our business to define, if we can, the natural gifts
that fit men to be guardians of a commonwealth, and to select
them accordingly.

The nature required to make a really noble Guardian of our
commonwealth will be swift and strong, spirited, and philosophic.

Who Should Rule?

It is obvious that the elder must have authority over the
young, and that the rulers must be the best.

And as among farmers the best are those with a natural
turn for farming, so, if we want the best among our Guardians, we must take those naturally fitted to watch over a
commonwealth. They must have the right sort of intelligence
and ability; and also they must look upon the commonwealth
as their special concern—the sort of concern that is felt for
something so closely bound up with oneself that its interests
and fortunes, for good or ill, are held to be identical with
one's own.

[They must be] full of zeal to do whatever they believe is
for the good of the commonwealth and never willing to act
against its interest.

They must be capable of preserving this conviction, never
forgetting it or allowing themselves to be either forced or
bewitched into throwing it over.

We shall choose only those whose memory holds firm and
who are proof against delusion.

We must also subject them to ordeals of toil and pain and
watch for the same qualities there. And we must observe them
when exposed to the test of yet a third kind of bewitchment.
As people lead colts up to alarming noises to see whether they
are timid, so these young men must be brought into terrifying
situations and then into scenes of pleasure, which will put

them to severer proof than gold tried in the furnace. If we find one bearing himself well in all these trials and resisting every enchantment, a true guardian of himself, preserving always that perfect rhythm and harmony of being which he has acquired from his training in music and poetry, such a one will be of the greatest service to the commonwealth as well as to himself. Whenever we find one who has come unscathed through every test in childhood, youth, and manhood, we shall set him as a Ruler to watch over the commonwealth; he will be honoured in life, and after death receive the highest tribute of funeral rites and other memorials. All who do not reach this standard we must reject.

These, then, may properly be called Guardians in the fullest sense, who will ensure that neither foes without shall have the power, nor friends within the wish, to do harm. Those young men whom up to now we have been speaking of as Guardians, will be better described as Auxiliaries, who will enforce the decisions of the Rulers.

Now, said I, can we devise something in the way of those convenient fictions we spoke of earlier, a single bold flight of invention, which we may induce the community in general, and if possible the Rulers themselves, to accept?

I shall try to convince, first the Rulers and the soldiers, and then the whole community, that all that nurture and education which we gave them was only something they seemed to experience as it were in a dream. In reality they were the whole time down inside the earth, being moulded and fostered while their arms and all their equipment were being fashioned also; and at last, when they were complete, the earth sent them up from her womb into the light of day. So now they must think of the land they dwell in as a mother and nurse, whom they must take thought for and defend against any attack, and of their fellow citizens as brothers born of the same soil.

It is true, we shall tell our people in this fable, that all of you in this land are brothers; but the god who fashioned you mixed gold in the composition of those among you who are fit to rule, so that they are of the most precious quality; and he put silver in the Auxiliaries, and iron and brass in the farmers and craftsmen. Now, since you are all of one stock, although your children will generally be like their parents, sometimes a golden parent may have a silver child or a silver parent a golden one, and so on with all the other combinations. So the first and chief injunction laid by heaven upon the Rulers is that, among all the things of which they must show themselves good guardians, there is none that needs to be so carefully watched as the mixture of metals in the souls of the children. If a child of their own is born with an alloy of iron or brass, they must, without the smallest pity, assign him the station proper to his nature and thrust him out among the craftsmen or the farmers. If, on the contrary, these classes produce a child with gold or silver in his composition, they will promote him, according to his value, to be a Guardian or an Auxiliary. They will appeal to a prophecy that ruin will come upon the state when it passes into the keeping of a man of iron or brass. [This story, might not be believed by] the first generation; but their sons and descendants might believe it, and finally the rest of mankind. . . .

We must take every precaution against our Auxiliaries treating the citizens in any such way and, because they are stronger, turning into savage tyrants instead of friendly allies; and they will have been furnished with the best of safeguards, if they have really been educated in the right way. . . .

Then besides that education, it is only common sense to say that the dwellings and other belongings provided for them must be such as will neither make them less perfect Guardians nor encourage them to maltreat their fellow citizens.

With that end in view, let us consider how they should live and be housed. First, none of them must possess any private property beyond the barest necessaries. Next, no one is to have any dwelling or store-house that is not open for all to enter at will. Their food, in the quantities required by men of temperance and courage who are in training for war, they will receive from the other citizens as the wages of their guardianship, fixed so that there shall be just enough for the year with nothing over; and they will have meals in common and all live together like soldiers in a camp. Gold and silver, we shall tell them, they will not need, having the divine counterparts of those metals always in their souls as a god-given possession, whose purity it is not lawful to sully by the acquisition of that mortal dross, current among mankind, which has been the occasion of so many unholy deeds. They alone of all the citizens are forbidden to touch and handle silver or gold, or to come under the same roof with them, or wear them as ornaments, or drink from vessels made of them. This manner of life will be their salvation and make them the saviours of the commonwealth. If ever they should come to possess land of their own and houses and money, they will give up their guardianship for the management of their farms and households and become tyrants at enmity with their fellow citizens instead of allies. And so they will pass all their lives in hating and being hated, plotting and being plotted against, in much greater fear of their enemies at home than of any foreign foe, and fast heading for the destruction that will soon overwhelm their country with themselves. For all these reasons let us say that this is how our Guardians are to be housed and otherwise provided for, and let us make laws accordingly.

Here Adeimantus interposed. Socrates, he said, how would you meet the objection that you are not making these people particularly happy? It is their own fault too, if they are not; for they are really masters of the state, and yet they get no good out of it as other rulers do, who own lands, build themselves fine houses with handsome furniture, offer private sacrifices to the gods, and entertain visitors from abroad; who possess, in fact, that gold and silver you spoke of, with everything else that is usually thought necessary for happiness. These people seem like nothing so much as a garrison of mercenaries posted in the city and perpetually mounting guard.

Yes, I said, and what is more they will serve for their food only without getting a mercenary's pay, so that they will not be able to travel on their own account or to make presents to a mistress or to spend as they please in other ways, like the people who are commonly thought happy. You have forgotten to include these counts in your indictment, and many more to the same effect.

Well, take them as included now.

And you want to hear the answer?

Yes.

We shall find one, I think, by keeping to the line we have followed so far. We shall say that, though it would not be surprising if even these people were perfectly happy under such conditions, our aim in founding the commonwealth was not to make any one class specially happy, but to secure the greatest possible happiness for the community as a whole. We thought we should have the best chance of finding justice in a state so constituted, just as we should find injustice where the constitution was of the worst possible type; we could then decide the question which has been before us all this time. For the moment, we are constructing, as we believe, the state which will be happy as a whole, not trying to secure the well-being of a select few; we shall study a state of the opposite kind presently. It is as if we were colouring a statue and someone came up and blamed us for not putting the most beautiful colours on the noblest parts of the figure; the eyes, for instance, should be painted crimson, but we had made them black. We should think it a fair answer to say: Really, you must not expect us to paint eyes so handsome as not to look like eyes at all. This applies to all the parts: the question is whether, by giving each its proper colour, we make the whole beautiful. So too, in the present case, you must not press us to endow our Guardians with a happiness that will make them anything rather than guardians. We could quite easily clothe our farmers in gorgeous robes, crown them with gold, and invite them to till the soil at their pleasure; or we might set our potters to lie on couches by their fire, passing round the wine and making merry, with their wheel at hand to work at whenever they felt so inclined. We could make all the rest happy in the same sort of way, and so spread this well-being through the whole community. But you must not put that idea into our heads; if we take your advice, the farmer will be no farmer, the potter no longer a potter; none of the elements that make up the community will keep its character. In many cases this does not matter so much: if a cobbler goes to the bad and pretends to be what he is not, he is not a danger to the state; but, as you must surely see, men who make only a vain show of being guardians of the laws and of the commonwealth bring the whole state to utter ruin, just as, on the other hand, its good government and well-being depend entirely on them. We, in fact, are making genuine Guardians who will be the last to bring harm upon the commonwealth; if our critic aims rather at producing a happiness like that of a party of peasants feasting at a fair, what he has in mind is something other than a civic community. So we must consider whether our aim in establishing Guardians is to secure the greatest possible happiness for them, or happiness is something of which we should watch the development in the whole commonwealth. If so, we must compel these Guardians and Auxiliaries of ours to second our efforts; and they, and all the rest with them, must be induced to make themselves perfect masters each of his own craft. In that way, as the community grows into a well-ordered whole, the several classes may be allowed such measure of happiness as their nature will compass.

The Function of Rulers

. . . our Rulers will find the best principle for determining the size of the state and the proportionate amount of territory, beyond which they will not go: the state should be allowed to grow only so far as it can increase in size without loss of unity.

So we must lay yet another command on our Guardians: they are to take all possible care that the state shall neither be too small nor yet one that seems great but has no unity.

Not so hard as the duty we mentioned earlier, of moving down any inferior child born to the Guardians into the other classes and promoting from those classes any child who is good enough to be a Guardian. Our intention there was to set the other citizens to work, one man at one task for which his nature fitted him, so that by keeping to that one business he might come to be a single man and not many. In that way the state as a whole would grow to be a single community, and not many.

It will all be easy enough, if only they will see to 'the one great thing,' as the saying goes, though I would rather call it the one thing that is sufficient: education and nurture. If a sound education has made them reasonable men, they will easily see their way through all these matters as well as others which we will pass over for the moment, such as the possession of wives, marriage, and child-bearing, and the principle that here we should follow, as far as possible, the proverb which says that friends have all things in common.

Moreover, when a community has once made a good start, its growth proceeds in a sort of cycle. If a sound system of nurture and education is maintained, it produces men of a good disposition; and these in their turn, taking advantage of such education, develop into better men than their forebears, and their breeding qualities improve among the rest, as may be seen in animals.

In short, then, those who keep watch over our commonwealth must take the greatest care not to overlook the least infraction of the rule against any innovation upon the established system of education either of the body or of the mind.

. . . Our children's pastimes, then, as I began by saying, must be kept from the first within stricter bounds; if any licence be admitted, they will catch the spirit and will never grow into law-abiding and well-conducted men. And so, when children have made a good beginning in their play and musical education has instilled a spirit of order, this reverence for law will attend them in all their doings and foster their growth, restoring any institutions that may earlier have fallen into decay.

As a consequence, they will rediscover rules of behaviour which their predecessors have let fall into disuse, including matters supposed to be of little importance . . . It is probable that the bent given by education will determine the quality of later life, by that sort of attraction which like things always

have for one another, till they finally mount up to one imposing result, whether for good or ill. For that reason I should
not myself be inclined to push legislation to that length..... .

[Similarly] there will be no need to dictate to men of good
breeding about business matters. They will soon find out for
themselves what regulations are needed.

There is something very like invalids in some states with a
bad form of government, which forbid their citizens, under
pain of death, to make any radical change in the constitution,
and at the same time honour as a good and profoundly wise
person any obsequious flatterer who, without attempting such
drastic treatment, can minister agreeably to their humours,
which he is clever enough to anticipate.

Surely there is something very amusing in the way [the
ministers in these invalid states] go on enacting their petty
laws and amending them, always imagining they will find
some way to put an end to fraud in business and in all those
other transactions I was speaking of. They have no idea that
really they are cutting off the heads of a hydra.

I should have thought that laws and institutions of that
order do not deserve the attention of a law-giver worthy of the
name, no matter whether the constitution be good or bad. If it
is bad, they are useless and effect nothing; if good, some are
such as anyone could devise, and the rest will follow of themselves from the practices we have already instituted. . . .

There are institutions of the highest worth and importance
that must be left to the Delphian Apollo.

The founding of temples, sacrifices, and the cults of gods,
demigods, and heroes; the burial of the dead, and services to
propitiate the powers of the other world. These are matters we
do not understand ourselves, and in founding our commonwealth we shall be wise to consult no other religious authority
than our national divinity.

The Composition of a State

I take it that our state, having been founded and built up
on the right lines, is good in the complete sense of the word.

Obviously, then, it is wise, brave, temperate, and just.

To begin then: the first quality to come into view in our
state seems to be its wisdom.

. . . But there are many and various kinds of knowledge in
our commonwealth. There is the knowledge possessed by the
carpenters or the smiths, and the knowledge how to raise

crops. Are we to call the state wise and prudent on the strength of these forms of skill?

Is there any form of knowledge, possessed by some among the citizens of our new-founded commonwealth, which will enable it to take thought, not for some particular interest, but for the best possible conduct of the state as a whole in its internal and external relations?

It is that art of guardianship which resides in those Rulers whom we just now called Guardians in the full sense.

So, if a state is constituted on natural principles, the wisdom it possesses as a whole will be due to the knowledge residing in the smallest part, the one which takes the lead and governs the rest. Such knowledge is the only kind that deserves the name of wisdom, and it appears to be ordained by nature that the class privileged to possess it should be the smallest of all.

Next there is courage. It is not hard to discern that quality or the part of the community in which it resides so as to entitle the whole to be called brave.

Because anyone who speaks of a state as either brave or cowardly can only be thinking of that part of it which takes the field and fights in its defence.

Courage is another quality which a community owes to a certain part of itself. And its being brave will mean that, in this part, it possesses the power of preserving, in all circumstances, a conviction about the sort of things that it is right to be afraid of—the conviction implanted by the education which the lawgiver has established.

Two qualities still remain to be made out in our state, temperance and the object of our whole inquiry, justice. Can we discover justice without troubling ourselves further about temperance?

At first sight, temperance seems more like some sort of concord or harmony than the other qualities did.

Temperance surely means a kind of orderliness, a control of certain pleasures and appetites. People use the expression, "master of oneself," whatever that means, and various other phrases that point the same way.

Is not "master of oneself" an absurd expression? A man who was master of himself would presumably be also subject to himself, and the subject would be master; for all these terms apply to the same person.

I think, however, the phrase means that within the man himself, in his soul, there is a better part and a worse; and that he is his own master when the part which is better by nature has the worse under its control. It is certainly a term of praise; whereas it is considered a disgrace, when, through bad breeding or bad company, the better part is overwhelmed by the worse, like a small force outnumbered by a multitude. A man in that condition is called a slave to himself and intemperate.

Then now look at our newly founded state and you will find one of these two conditions realized there. It deserves to be called master of itself, if temperance and self-mastery exist where the better part rules the worse.

It is also true that the great mass of multifarious appetites and pleasures and pains will be found to occur chiefly in children and women and slaves, and, among free men so called, in the inferior multitude; whereas the simple and moderate desires which, with the aid of reason and right belief, are guided by reflection, you will find only in a few, and those with the best inborn dispositions and the best educated.

Do you see that this state of things will exist in your commonwealth, where the desires of the inferior multitude will be controlled by the desires and wisdom of the superior few? Hence, if any society can be called master of itself and in control of pleasures and desires, it will be ours.

On all these grounds, then, we may describe it as temperate.

Furthermore, in our state, if anywhere, the governors and the governed will share the same conviction on the question who ought to rule.

Temperance will reside in both the governors and in the governed.

Temperance works in a different way from courage and wisdom: it extends throughout the whole gamut of the state, producing a consonance of all its elements from the weakest to the strongest as measured by any standard you like to take—wisdom, bodily strength, numbers, or wealth. So we are entirely justified in identifying with temperance this unanimity or harmonious agreement between the naturally superior and inferior elements on the question which of the two should govern, whether in the state or in the individual.

Good, said I. We have discovered in our commonwealth three out of our four qualities, to the best of our present judgement. What is the remaining one, required to make up its full complement of goodness? For clearly this will be justice. . . .

You remember how, when we first began to establish our commonwealth and several times since, we have laid down, as a universal principle, that everyone ought to perform the one function in the community for which his nature best suited him. Well, I believe that that principle, or some form of it, i justice. . . .

Surely we have often heard people say that justice means minding one's own business and not meddling with other men's concerns; and we have often said so ourselves.

Well, my friend, it may be that this minding of one's own business, when it takes a certain form, is actually the same thing as justice. . . .

I think that this quality which makes it possible for the three we have already considered, wisdom, courage, and temperance, to take their place in the commonwealth, and so long as it remains present secures their continuance, must be the remaining one. And we said that, when three of the four were found, the one left over would be justice.

Well now, if we had to decide which of these qualities will contribute most to the excellence of our commonwealth, i would be hard to say whether it was the unanimity of ruler and subjects, or the soldier's fidelity to the established conviction about what is, or is not, to be feared, or the watchful intelligence of the Rulers; or whether its excellence were not above all due to the observance by everyone, child or woman slave or freeman or artisan, ruler or ruled, of this principle that each one should do his own proper work without interfering with others.

It seems, then, that this principle can at any rate claim to rival wisdom, temperance, and courage as conducing to the excellence of a state. The only possible competitor of these qualities must be justice.

No great harm would be done to the community by a general interchange of most forms of work, the carpenter and the cobbler exchanging their positions and their tools and taking on each other's jobs, or even the same man undertaking both.

But another kind of interchange would be disastrous. Suppose, for instance, someone whom nature designed to be an artisan or tradesman should be emboldened by some advantage, such as wealth or command of votes or bodily strength, to try to enter the order of fighting men; or some member of that order should aspire, beyond his merits, to a seat in the council-chamber of the Guardians. Such interference and exchange of social positions and tools, or the attempt to combine all these forms of work in the same person, would be fatal to the commonwealth.

Where there are three orders, then, any plurality of functions or shifting from one order to another is not merely ut

erly harmful to the community, but one might fairly call it
the extreme of wrongdoing.

This is injustice. And, conversely, let us repeat that when
each order—tradesman, Auxiliary, Guardian—keeps to its
own proper business in the commonwealth and does its own
work, that is justice and what makes a just society.

Now if two things, one large, the other small, are called by
the same name, they will be alike in that respect to which the
common name applies. Accordingly, in so far as the quality of
justice is concerned, there will be no difference between a just
man and a just society.

Well, but we decided that a society was just when each of
the three types of human character it contained performed its
own function; and again, it was temperate and brave and wise
by virtue of certain other affections and states of mind of
those same types.

Accordingly if we are to be justified in attributing those
same virtues to the individual, we shall expect to find that the
individual soul contains the same three elements and that they
are affected in the same way as are the corresponding types in
society.

Here, then, we have stumbled upon another little problem:
Does the soul contain these three elements or not?

Surely we must admit that the same elements and charac-
ers (reason, appetite and spirit) that appear in the state must
exist in every one of us; where else could they have come
from? It would be absurd to imagine that among peoples with
a reputation for a high-spirited character, like the Thracians
and Scythians and northerners generally, the states have not
derived that character from their individual members; or that
it is otherwise with the love of knowledge, which would be
ascribed chiefly to our own part of the world, or with the love
of money, which one would specially connect with Phoenicia
and Egypt.

The Composition of the Soul

The same three elements exist alike in the state and in the
individual soul.

Does it not follow at once that state and individual will be
wise or brave by virtue of the same element in each and in the
same way? Both will possess in the same manner any quality
that makes for excellence.

Then it applies to justice: we shall conclude that a man is
just in the same way that a state was just. And we have surely

not forgotten that justice in the state meant that each of the three orders in it was doing its own proper work. So we may henceforth bear in mind that each one of us likewise will be a just person, fulfilling his proper function, only if the several parts of our nature fulfill theirs.

And it will be the business of reason to rule with wisdom and forethought on behalf of the entire soul; while the spirited element ought to act as its subordinate and ally. The two will be brought into accord, as we said earlier, by that combination of mental and bodily training which will tune up one string of the instrument and relax the other, nourishing the reasoning part on the study of noble literature and allaying the other's wildness by harmony and rhythm. When both have been thus nurtured and trained to know their own true functions, they must be set in command over the appetites, which form the greater part of each man's soul and are by nature insatiably covetous. They must keep watch lest this part, by battening on the pleasures that are called bodily, should grow so great and powerful that it will no longer keep to its own work, but will try to enslave the others and usurp a dominion to which it has no right, thus turning the whole of life upside down. At the same time, those two together will be the best of guardians for the entire soul and for the body against all enemies from without: the one will take counsel, while the other will do battle, following its ruler's commands and by its own bravery giving effect to the ruler's designs.

And so we call an individual brave in virtue of this spirited part of his nature, when, in spite of pain or pleasure, it holds fast to the injunctions of reason about what he ought or ought not to be afraid of.

And wise in virtue of that small part which rules and issues these injunctions, possessing as it does the knowledge of what is good for each of the three elements and for all of them in common.

And, again, temperate by reason of the unanimity and concord of all three, when there is no internal conflict between the ruling element and its two subjects, but all are agreed that reason should be ruler.

Finally, a man will be just by observing the principle we have so often stated. . . .

Each part of his nature is exercising its proper function, of ruling or of being ruled. . . .

Our principle that the born shoemaker or carpenter had better stick to his trade turns out to have been an adumbration of justice; and that is why it has helped us. But in reality justice, though evidently analogous to this principle, is not a matter of external behaviour, but of the inward self and of attending to all that is, in the fullest sense, a man's proper concern. The just man does not allow the several elements in his soul to usurp one another's functions; he is indeed one who sets his house in order, by self-mastery and discipline coming to be at peace with himself, and bringing into tune those three parts, like the terms in the proportion of a musical scale, the highest and lowest notes and the mean between them, with all the intermediate intervals. Only when he has linked these parts together in well-tempered harmony and has made himself one man instead of many, will he be ready to go about whatever he may have to do, whether it be making money and satisfying bodily wants, or business transactions, or the affairs of state. In all these fields when he speaks of just and honourable conduct, he will mean the behaviour that helps to produce and to preserve this habit of mind; and by wisdom he will mean the knowledge which presides over such conduct. Any action which tends to break down this habit will be for him unjust; and the notions governing it he will call ignorance and folly.

We have to consider injustice.

This must surely be a sort of civil strife among the three elements, whereby they usurp and encroach upon one another's functions and some one part of the soul rises up in rebellion against the whole, claiming a supremacy to which it has no right because its nature fits it only to be the servant of the ruling principle. Such turmoil and aberration we shall, I think, identify with injustice, intemperance, cowardice, ignorance, and in a word with all wickedness.

And now that we know the nature of justice and injustice, we can be equally clear about what is meant by acting justly and again by unjust action and wrongdoing.

How do you mean?

Plainly, they are exactly analogous to those wholesome and unwholesome activities which respectively produce a healthy or unhealthy condition in the body; in the same way just and unjust conduct produce a just or unjust character. Justice is produced in the soul, like health in the body, by establishing the elements concerned in their natural relations of control and subordination, whereas injustice is like disease and means that this natural order is inverted.

It appears, then, that virtue is as it were the health and comeliness and well-being of the soul, as wickedness is disease, deformity, and weakness.

And also that virtue and wickedness are brought about by one's way of life, honourable or disgraceful.

The Three Waves

a) Equality of Women

Women are expected to take their full share, except that we treat them as not quite so strong. . . .

If we are to set women to the same tasks as men, we must teach them the same things. They must have the same two branches of training for mind and body and also be taught the art of war, and they must receive the same treatment.

Possibly, if these proposals were carried out, they might be ridiculed as involving a good many breaches of custom. . . .

We must not be frightened of the many witticisms that might be aimed at such a revolution, not only in the matter of bodily exercise but in the training of women's minds, and not least when it comes to their bearing arms.

The first thing to be settled, then, is whether these proposals are feasible; and it must be open to anyone, whether a humorist or serious-minded, to raise the question whether, in the case of mankind, the feminine nature is capable of taking part with the other sex in all occupations, or in none at all, or in some only; and in particular under which of these heads this business of military service falls.

. . . We did agree that different natures should have different occupations, and that the natures of man and woman are different; and yet we are now saying that these different natures are to have the same occupations. . . .

If, then, we find that either the male sex or the female is specially qualified for any particular form of occupation, then that occupation ought to be assigned to one sex or the other. But if the only difference appears to be that the male begets and the female brings forth, we shall conclude that no difference between man and woman has yet been produced that is relevant to our purpose. We shall continue to think it proper for our Guardians and their wives to share in the same pursuits.

The next thing will be to ask if there is any profession or occupation in civic life for the purposes of which woman's nature is different from man's. . . .

Natural gifts are to be found here and there in both creatures alike; and every occupation is open to both, so far as their natures are concerned, though woman is for all purposes the weaker. . . .

. . . for the purpose of producing a woman fit to be a

Guardian, we shall not have one education for men and another for women, precisely because the nature to be taken in hand is the same.

It follows that one woman will be fitted by nature to be a Guardian, another will not; depending on whether they possess the qualities for which we selected our men Guardians. So for the purpose of keeping watch over the commonwealth, woman has the same nature as man, save in so far as she is weaker.

It follows that women of this type must be selected to share the life and duties of Guardians with men of the same type, since they are competent and of a like nature, and the same natures must be allowed the same pursuits.

There is nothing contrary to nature in giving our Guardians' wives the same training for mind and body.

b) The Abolition of the Family

From the principle that male and female Guardians shall have occupations in common, it follows that, for them, no one man and one woman are to set up house together privately: wives are to be held in common by all; so too are the children, and no parent is to know his own child, nor any child his parent.

I imagine no one would deny the immense advantage of wives and children being held in common, provided it can be done. I should expect dispute to arise chiefly over the question whether it is possible. . . .

Well, if our Rulers are worthy of the name, and their Auxiliaries likewise, these latter will be ready to do what they are told, and the Rulers, in giving their commands, will themselves obey our laws and will be faithful to their spirit in any details we leave to their discretion.

It is for you, then, as their law-giver, who have already selected the men, to select for association with them women who are so far as possible of the same natural capacity. Now since none of them will have any private home of his own, but they will share the same dwelling and eat at common tables, the two sexes will be together; and meeting without restriction for exercise and all through their upbringing, they will surely be drawn towards union with one another by a necessity of their nature.

Anything like unregulated unions would be a profanation in a state whose citizens lead the good life. The Rulers will not allow such a thing. . . .

We must have marriages, as sacred as we can make them;

and this sanctity will attach to those who yield the best results. . . .

If we are to keep our flock at the highest pitch of excellence, there should be as many unions of the best of both sexes, and as few of the inferior, as possible, and only the offspring of the better unions should be kept. And again, no one but the Rulers must know how all this is being effected; otherwise our herd of Guardians may become rebellious.

We must, then, institute certain festivals at which we shall bring together the brides and the bridegrooms. There will be sacrifices, and our poets will write songs befitting the occasion. The number of marriages we shall leave to the Rulers' discretion. They will aim at keeping the number of the citizens as constant as possible, having regard to losses caused by war, epidemics, and so on; and they must do their best to see that our state does not become either great or small.

I think they will have to invent some ingenious system of drawing lots, so that, at each pairing off, the inferior candidate may blame his luck rather than the Rulers.

Moreover, young men who acquit themselves well in war and other duties, should be given, among other rewards and privileges, more liberal opportunities to sleep with a wife, for the further purpose that, with good excuse, as many as possible of the children may be begotten of such fathers.

As soon as children are born, they will be taken in charge by officers appointed for the purpose, who may be men or women or both, since offices are to be shared by both sexes. The children of the better parents they will carry to the crèche to be reared in the care of nurses living apart in a certain quarter of the city. Those of the inferior parents and any children of the rest that are born defective will be hidden away, in some appropriate manner that must be kept secret.

These officers will also superintend the nursing of the children. They will bring the mothers to the crèche when their breasts are full, while taking every precaution that no mother shall know her own child; and if the mothers have not enough milk, they will provide wet-nurses. They will limit the time during which the mothers will suckle their children, and hand over all the hard work and sitting up at night to nurses and attendants.

Guardians must hold their wives and children in common. It is consistent with our other institutions and also by far the best plan.

What is the greatest good at which the lawgiver should aim in laying down the constitution of a state, and what is the worst evil?

Does not the worst evil for a state arise from anything that tends to rend it asunder and destroy its unity, while nothing does it more good than whatever tends to bind it together and make it one?

And are not citizens bound together by sharing in the same pleasures and pains, all feeling glad or grieved on the same occasions of gain or loss; whereas the bond is broken when such feelings are no longer universal, but any event of public or personal concern fills some with joy and others with distress?

And this disunion comes about when the words "mine" and "not mine," "another's" and "not another's" are not applied to the same things throughout the community. The best ordered state will be the one in which the largest number of persons use these terms in the same sense, and which accordingly most nearly resembles a single person. When one of us hurts his finger, the whole extent of those bodily connexions which are gathered up in the soul and unified by its ruling element is made aware and it all shares as a whole in the pain of the suffering part; hence we say that the man has a pain in his finger. The same thing is true of the pain or pleasure felt when any other part of the person suffers or is relieved.

The best organized community comes nearest to that condition, and it will recognize as a part of itself the individual citizen to whom good or evil happens, and will share as a whole in his joy or sorrow.

A Guardian must regard everyone whom he meets as brother or sister, father or mother, son or daughter, grandchild or grandparent.

They behave as a real family. They must show towards all whom they call "father" the customary reverence, care, and obedience due to a parent, if they look for any favour from gods or men, since to act otherwise is contrary to divine and human law.

In our community when things go well or ill with any individual everyone will use that word "mine" in the same sense and say that all is going well or ill with him and his.

This way of speaking and thinking goes with fellow-feeling; so that our citizens, sharing as they do in a common interest which each will call his own, will have all their feelings of pleasure or pain in common.

A result that will be due to our institutions, and in particular to our Guardians' holding their wives and children in common.

But you will remember how, when we compared a well-ordered community to the body which shares in the pleasures and pains of any member, we saw in this unity the greatest good that a state can enjoy. So the conclusion is that our commonwealth owes to this sharing of wives and children by its protectors its enjoyment of the greatest of all goods.

Moreover, this agrees with our principle that they were not to have houses or lands or any property of their own, but to receive sustenance from the other citizens, as wages for their guardianship, and to consume it in common. Only so will they keep to their true character; and our present proposals will do still more to make them genuine Guardians. They will not rend the community asunder by each applying that word "mine" to different things and dragging off whatever he can get for himself into a private home, where he will have his separate family, forming a centre of exclusive joys and sorrows. Rather they will all, so far as may be, feel together and aim at the same ends, because they are convinced that all their interests are identical.

Rid of cares, they will live a more enviable life than the Olympic victor, who is counted happy on the strength of far fewer blessings than our Guardians will enjoy. Their victory is the nobler, since by their success the whole commonwealth is preserved; and their reward of maintenance at the public cost is more complete, since their prize is to have every need of life supplied for themselves and for their children; their country honours them while they live, and when they die they receive a worthy burial.

c) Philosophers Must Be Kings

. . . our next attempt, it seems, must be to point out what defect in the working of existing states prevents them from being so organized, and what is the least change that would effect a transformation into this type of government—a single change if possible, or perhaps two; at any rate let us make the changes as few and insignificant as may be.

Well, there is one change which, as I believe we can show, would bring about this revolution—not a small change, certainly, nor an easy one, but possible.

Unless either philosophers become kings in their countries or those who are now called kings and rulers come to be sufficiently inspired with a genuine desire for wisdom; unless, that is to say, political power and philosophy meet together, while the many natures who now go their several ways in the one or the other direction are forcibly debarred from doing so, there can be no rest from troubles for states, nor yet, as I believe, for all mankind; nor can this commonwealth which we have imagined ever till then see the light of day and grow to its full stature.

. . . the philosopher, with his passion for wisdom, will be one who desires all wisdom, not only some part of it. If a student is particular about his studies, especially while he is too young to know which are useful and which are not, we shall say he is no lover of learning or of wisdom; just as, if he were dainty about his food, we should say he was not hungry or fond of eating, but had a poor appetite. Only the man who has a taste for every sort of knowledge and throws himself into acquiring it with an insatiable curiosity will deserve to be called a philosopher.

. . . the genuine philosophers are those whose passion it is to see the truth. . . . The amateurs of the arts and men of action can be distinguished from the philosophers we are concerned with, who are alone worthy of the name.

Your lovers of sights and sounds delight in beautiful tones and colours and shapes and in all the works of art into which these enter; but they have not the power of thought to behold and to take delight in the nature of Beauty itself. That power to approach Beauty and behold it as it is in itself, is rare indeed.

Now if a man believes in the existence of beautiful things, but not of Beauty itself, and cannot follow a guide who would lead him to a knowledge of it, is he not living in a dream? Consider: does not dreaming, whether one is awake or asleep, consist in mistaking a semblance for the reality it resembles?

Contrast with him the man who holds that there is such a thing as Beauty itself and can discern that essence as well as the things that partake of its character, without ever confusing the one with the other. . . .

We may say that he knows, while the other has only a belief in appearances; and we might call their states of mind knowledge and belief.

The perfectly real is perfectly knowable, and the utterly unreal is entirely unknowable.

Now if there is something so constituted that it both *is* and *is not*, it will lie between the purely real and the utterly unreal.

Well then, as knowledge corresponds to the real, and absence of knowledge necessarily to the unreal, so, to correspond to this intermediate thing, we must look for something between ignorance and knowledge.

This we call belief, a different power from knowledge.

Knowledge and belief, then, must have different objects, answering to their respective powers.

And knowledge has for its natural object the real—to know the truth about reality, . . . and has the power of knowing the real as it is. Whereas belief is the power of believing.

If a man has a belief, there must be something before his mind; he cannot be believing nothing.

Now we said that ignorance must correspond to the unreal, knowledge to the real. So what he is believing cannot be real nor yet unreal.

Belief, then, cannot be either ignorance or knowledge.

It rather seems to be something more obscure than knowledge, but not so dark as ignorance, and so to lie between the two extremes.

Well, we said earlier that if some object could be found such that it both *is* and at same time *is not*, that object would lie between the perfectly real and the utterly unreal; and that the corresponding faculty would be neither knowledge nor ignorance, but a faculty to be found situated between the two.

And now what we have found between the two is the faculty we call belief.

It seems, then, that what remains to be discovered is that object which can be said both to be and not to be and cannot properly be called either purely real or purely unreal. If that can be found, we may justly call it the object of belief, and so give the intermediate faculty the intermediate object, while the two extreme objects will fall to the extreme faculties.

On these assumptions, then, I shall call for an answer from our friend who denies the existence of Beauty itself or of anything that can be called an essential Form of Beauty remaining unchangeably in the same state for ever, though he does recognize the existence of beautiful things as a plurality —that lover of things seen who will not listen to anyone who says that Beauty is one, Justice is one, and so on. I shall say to him, Be so good as to tell us: of all these many beautiful things is there one which will not appear ugly? Or of these many just or righteous actions, is there one that will not appear unjust or unrighteous?

They must inevitably appear to be in some way both beautiful and ugly.

And again the many things which are doubles are just as much halves as they are doubles. And the things we call large or heavy have just as much right to be called small or light.

Then, whatever any one of these many things may be said to be, can you say that it absolutely *is* that, any more than that it *is not* that?

Can you think of any better way of disposing of them than by placing them between reality and unreality?

It seems, then, we have discovered that the many conventional notions of the mass of mankind about what is beautiful or honourable or just and so on are adrift in a sort of twilight between pure reality and pure unreality.

And we agreed earlier that, if any such object were discovered, it should be called the object of belief and not of knowledge. Fluctuating in that half-way region, it would be seized upon by the intermediate faculty.

So when people have an eye for the multitude of beautiful things or of just actions or whatever it may be, but can neither behold Beauty or Justice itself nor follow a guide who would lead them to it, we shall say that all they have is beliefs, without any real knowledge of the objects of their belief.

But what of those who contemplate the realities themselves as they are for ever in the same unchanging state? Shall we not say that they have, not mere belief, but knowledge?

And, further, that their affection goes out to the objects of knowledge, whereas the others set their affections on the objects of belief; for it was they, you remember, who had a passion for the spectacle of beautiful colours and sounds, but would not hear of Beauty itself being a real thing.

So we may fairly call them lovers of belief rather than of wisdom—not philosophical, in fact, but philodoxical.

The name of philosopher, then, will be reserved for those whose affections are set, in every case, on the reality.

Since the philosophers are those who can apprehend the eternal and unchanging, while those who cannot do so, but are lost in the mazes of multiplicity and change, are not philosophers, which of the two ought to be in control of a state?

Guardians should be competent to guard the laws and ways of life in society.

Well, there can be no question whether a guardian who is to keep watch over anything needs to be keen-sighted or blind. And is not blindness precisely the condition of men who are entirely cut off from knowledge of any reality, and have in their soul no clear pattern of perfect truth, which they might study in every detail and constantly refer to, as a painter looks at his model, before they procede to embody notions of justice, honour, and goodness in earthly institutions or, in their character of Guardians, to preserve such institutions as already exist?

It would be absurd not to choose the philosophers, whose knowledge is perhaps their greatest point of superiority, provided they do not lack those other qualifications of experience and excellence of character.

What we have to explain, then, is how those qualifications can be combined in the same persons with philosophy.

Certainly.

The first thing, as we said at the outset, is to get a clear view of their inborn disposition. One trait of the philosophic nature we may take as already granted: a constant passion for any knowledge that will reveal to them something of that reality which endures for ever and is not always passing into and out of existence. And, we may add, their desire is to know the whole of that reality; they will not willingly renounce any part of it as relatively small and insignificant.

Another trait is truthfulness, a love of truth and a hatred of falsehood that will not tolerate untruth in any form.

Now we surely know that when a man's desires set strongly in one direction, in every other channel they flow more feebly, like a stream diverted into another bed. So when the current has set towards knowledge and all that goes with it, desire will abandon those pleasures of which the body is the instrument and be concerned only with the pleasure which the soul enjoys independently—if, that is to say, the love of wisdom is more than a mere pretence. Accordingly, such a one will be temperate and no lover of money; for he will be the last person to care about the things for the sake of which money is eagerly sought and lavishly spent.

Again, in seeking to distinguish the philosophic nature, you must not overlook the least touch of meanness. Nothing could be more contrary than pettiness to a mind constantly bent on grasping the whole of things, both divine and human.

And do you suppose that one who is so high-minded and whose thought can contemplate all time and all existence will count this life of man a matter of much concern?

For such a man death will have no terrors.

A mean and cowardly nature can have no part in the genuine pursuit of wisdom.

And if a man is temperate and free from the love of money, meanness, pretentiousness, and cowardice, he will not be hard to deal with or dishonest. So, as another indication of the philosophic temper, you will observe whether, from youth up, he is fair-minded, gentle, and sociable.

Also you will not fail to notice whether he is quick or slow to learn. No one can be expected to take a reasonable delight in a task in which much painful effort makes little headway.

And if he cannot retain what he learns, his forgetfulness will leave no room in his head for knowledge; and so, having all his toil for nothing, he can only end by hating himself as well as his fruitless occupation. We must not, then, count a forgetful mind as competent to pursue wisdom; we must require a good memory.

Further, there is in some natures a crudity and awkwardness that can only tend to a lack of measure and proportion; and there is a close affinity between proportion and truth. Hence, besides our other requirements, we shall look for a mind endowed with measure and grace, which will be instinctively drawn to see every reality in its true light.

Our philosopher will be quick to learn and to remember, magnanimous and gracious, the friend and kinsman of truth, justice, courage, temperance.

Is the Philosopher Useless?

(A parable will illustrate the attitude of existing states towards the philosopher.)

Imagine this state of affairs on board a ship or a number of ships. The master is bigger and burlier than any of the crew, but a little deaf and short-sighted and no less deficient in seamanship. The sailors are quarrelling over the control of the helm; each thinks he ought to be steering the vessel, though he has never learnt navigation and cannot point to any teacher under whom he has served his apprenticeship; what is more, they assert that navigation is a thing that cannot be taught at all, and are ready to tear in pieces anyone who says it can. Meanwhile they besiege the master himself, begging him urgently to trust them with the helm; and sometimes, when others have been more successful in gaining his ear, they kill them or throw them overboard, and, after somehow stupefying the worthy master with strong drink or an opiate, take control of the ship, make free with its stores, and turn the voyage, as might be expected of such a crew, into a drunken carousal. Besides all this, they cry up as a skilled navigator and master of seamanship anyone clever enough to lend a hand in persuading or forcing the master to set them in command. Every other kind of man they condemn as useless. They do not understand that the genuine navigator can only make himself fit to command a ship by studying the seasons of the year, sky, stars, and winds, and all that belongs to his craft; and they have no idea that, along with the science of navigation, it is possible for him to gain, by instruction or practice, the skill to keep control of the helm whether some of them like it or not. If a ship were managed in that way, would not those on board be likely to call the expert in navigation a mere star-gazer, who spent his time in idle talk and was useless to them?

The critic is right in calling the best sort of philosophers useless to the public; but for that he must rather blame those who make no use of them. It is not in the natural course of things for the pilot to beg the crew to take his orders. What is natural is that the sick man, whether rich or poor, should wait at the door of the physician, and that all who need to be governed should seek out the man who can govern them; it is not for him to beg them to accept his rule, if there is really any help in him. But our present rulers may fairly be compared to the sailors in our parable, and the useless visionaries, as the politicians call them, to the real masters of navigation.

Under these conditions, the noblest of pursuits can hardly be thought much of by men whose own way of life runs counter to it. But by far the most formidable reproach is brought upon philosophy by those professed followers whom your critic no doubt had in mind when he denounced almost all of its votaries as utterly worthless and the best of them as of no use.

So it is, then, with this temperament we have postulated for the philosopher: given the right instruction, it must grow to the full flower of excellence; but if the plant is sown and reared in the wrong soil, it will develop every contrary defect, unless saved by some miracle. Or do you hold the popular belief that, here and there, certain young men are demoralized by the private instructions of some individual sophist? Does that sort of influence amount to much? Is not the public itself the greatest of all sophists, training up young and old, men and women alike, into the most accomplished specimens of the character it desires to produce?

Whenever the populace crowds together at any public gathering, in the Assembly, the law-courts, the theater, or the camp, and sits there clamouring its approval or disapproval, both alike excessive, of whatever is being said or done; booing and clapping till the rocks ring and the whole place redoubles the noise of their applause and outcries. In such a scene what do you suppose will be a young man's state of mind? What sort of private instruction will have given him the strength to hold out against the force of such a torrent, or will save him from being swept away down the stream, until he accepts all their notions of right and wrong, does as they do, and comes to be just such a man as they are?

And I have said nothing of the most powerful engines of persuasion which the masters in this school of wisdom bring to bear when words have no effect. As you know, they punish the recalcitrant with disfranchisement, fines, and death.

Every one of these individuals who make a living by teaching in private and whom the public are pleased to call sophists and to regard as their rivals, is teaching nothing else than the opinions and beliefs expressed by the public itself when it meets on any occasion; and that is what he calls wisdom. It is as if the keeper of some huge and powerful creature should make a study of its moods and desires, how it may best be approached and handled, when it is most savage or gentle and what makes it so, the meaning of its various cries and the tones of voice that will soothe or provoke its anger; and, having mastered all this by long familiarity, should call it wisdom, reduce it to a system, and set up a school. Not in the least knowing which of these humours and desires is good or bad, right or wrong, he will fit all these terms to the fancies of the great beast and call what it enjoys good and what vexes it bad. He has no other account to give of their meaning; for him any action will be "just" and "right" that is done under necessity, since he is too blind to tell how great is the real difference between what must be and what ought to be. It would be a queer sort of education that such a person could offer.

And is there anything to choose between him and one who thinks it is wisdom to have studied the moods and tastes of the assembled multitude, either in painting and music or in politics? They will fall under the fatal necessity to give them whatever they like and do whatever they approve.

It is inconceivable that the multitude should ever believe in the existence of any real essence, as distinct from its many manifestations, or listen to anyone who asserts such a reality.

The multitude can never be philosophical. It is bound to disapprove of all who pursue wisdom; and so also, of course, are those individuals who associate with the mob and set their hearts on pleasing it.

What hope can you see, then, that a philosophic nature should be saved to persevere in the pursuit until the goal is reached? Remember how we agreed that the born philosopher will be distinguished by quickness of understanding, good memory, courage, and generosity. With such gifts, already as a boy he will stand out above all his companions, especially if his person be a match for his mind; and when he grows older, his friends and his fellow citizens will no doubt want to make use of him for their own purposes. They will fawn upon him with their entreaties and promises of advancement, flattering beforehand the power that will some day be his.

What will become of a youth so circumstanced, above all if he belongs to a great country and is conspicuous there for his birth and wealth, as well as for a tall and handsome person? Will he not be filled with unbounded ambition, believing himself well able to manage the affairs of all the world, at home and abroad, and thereupon give himself airs and be puffed up with senseless self-conceit? . . .

Therefore in a way, the very qualities which make up the philosopher's nature may, with a bad upbringing, be the cause of his falling away, no less than wealth and all other so-called advantages.

These, then, are the dangers which threaten the noblest natures, rare enough in any case, and spoil them for the highest of all pursuits. And among men of this type will be found those who do the greatest harm or, if the current should chance to set the other way, the greatest good, to society and to individuals; whereas no great good or harm will come to either from a little mind. . . .

The remnant who are worthy to consort with Philosophy will be small indeed: perhaps some noble and well-nurtured character, saved by exile from those influences which would have impaired his natural impulse to be constant in her service; or it may be a great mind born in a petty state whose affairs are beneath its notice; and, possibly, a gifted few who have turned to philosophy from some other calling which they rightly disdain.

Is the Philosopher-King Possible?

There never will be a perfect state or constitution, nor yet a perfect man, until some happy circumstance compels these few philosophers who have escaped corruption but are now called useless, to take charge, whether they like it or not, of a state which will submit to their authority; or else until kings and rulers or their sons are divinely inspired with a genuine passion for true philosophy. If either alternative or both were impossible, we might justly be laughed at as idle dreamers; but, as I maintain, there is no ground for saying so. Accordingly, if ever in the infinity of time, past or future, or even today in some foreign region far beyond our horizon, men of the highest gifts for philosophy are constrained to take charge of a commonwealth, we are ready to maintain that, then and there, the constitution we have described has been realized, or will be realized when once the philosophic muse becomes mistress of a state. For that might happen. Our plan is difficult—we have admitted as much—but not impossible.

The public will change their opinion, if you avoid controversy and try gently to remove their prejudice against the love of learning. It is only ill-temper and malice in oneself that call out those qualities in others who are not that way inclined; in my belief, the public with a few exceptions is not of such an unyielding temper.

If it is ill-disposed towards philosophy, the blame must fall on that noisy crew of interlopers who are always bandying abuse and spiteful personalities—the last thing of which a philosopher can be guilty. A man whose thoughts are fixed on true reality has no leisure to look downwards on the affairs of men, to take part in their quarrels, and to catch the infection of their jealousies and hates. He contemplates a world of unchanging and harmonious order, where reason governs and nothing can do or suffer wrong; and, like one who imitates an admired companion, he cannot fail to fashion himself in its likeness. So the philosopher, in constant companionship with the divine order of the world, will reproduce that order in his soul and, so far as man may, become godlike; though here, as everywhere, there will be scope for detraction.

Suppose, then, he should find himself compelled to mould other characters besides his own and to shape the pattern of public and private life into conformity with his vision of the ideal, he will not lack the skill to produce such counterparts of temperance, justice, and all the virtues as can exist in the ordinary man. And the public, when they see that we have described him truly, will be reconciled to the philosopher and no longer disbelieve our assertion that happiness can only come to a state when its lineaments are traced by an artist working after the divine pattern.

He will take society and human character as his canvas, and begin by scraping it clean. That is no easy matter; but, as you know, unlike other reformers, he will not consent to take in hand either an individual or a state or to draft laws, until he is given a clean surface to work on or has cleansed it himself.

Next, he will sketch in the outline of the constitution. Then, as the work goes on, he will frequently refer to his model, the ideals of justice, goodness, temperance, and the rest, and compared with them the copy of those qualities which he is trying to create in human society. Combining the various elements of social life as a painter mixes his colours, he will reproduce the complexion of true humanity, guided by that divine pattern whose likeness Homer saw in the men he called godlike. He will rub out and paint in again this or that feature, until he has produced, so far as may be, a type of human character that heaven can approve.

Until philosophers hold power, neither states nor individuals will have rest from trouble, and the commonwealth we have imagined will never be realized.

Kings and hereditary rulers might have sons with a philosophic nature, and these might conceivably escape corruption. It would be hard to save them, we admit; but can anyone say that, in the whole course of time, not a single one could be saved?

Well, one would be enough to effect all this reform that now seems so incredible, if he had subjects disposed to obey; for it is surely not impossible that they should consent to carry out our laws and customs when laid down by a ruler. It would be no miracle if others should think as we do; and we have, I believe, sufficiently shown that our plan, if practicable, is the best. So, to conclude: our institutions would be the best, if they could be realized, and to realize them, though hard, is not impossible.

ARISTOTLE
The Politics

The Political Association

All associations aim at some good; and the particular association which is the most sovereign of all, and includes all the rest, will pursue this aim most, and will thus be directed to the most sovereign of all goods. This most sovereign and inclusive association is the polis, as it is called, or the political association. . . .

First of all, there must necessarily be a union or pairing of those who cannot exist without one another. Male and female must unite for the reproduction of the species—not from deliberate intention, but from the natural impulse, which exists in animals generally as it also exists in plants, to leave behind them something of the same nature as themselves. Next, there must necessarily be a union of the naturally ruling element with the element which is naturally ruled, for the preservation of both. The element which is able, by virtue of its intelligence, to exercise forethought, is naturally a ruling and master element; the element which is able, by virtue of its bodily power, to do what the other element plans, is a ruled element, which is naturally in a state of slavery; and master and slave have accordingly a common interest. . . .

The first result of these two elementary associations [of male and female, and of master and slave] is the household or family, . . . naturally instituted for the satisfaction of daily recurrent needs. The next form of association—which is also the *first* to be formed from more households than one, and for the satisfaction of something more than daily recurrent needs —is the village. The most natural form of the village appears to be that of a colony or offshoot from a family. . . . This is the reason why each Greek polis was originally ruled—as the peoples of the barbarian world still are—by kings. They were formed of persons who were already monarchically governed.

The fact that men generally were governed by kings in ancient times, and that some still contiune to be governed in that way, is the reason that leads us all to assert that the gods are also governed by a king. We make the lives of the gods in the likeness of our own—as we also make their shapes. . . .

The final and perfect association, formed from a number of villages, is the polis—an association which may be said to have reached the height of full self-sufficiency; or rather we may say that while it *grows* for the sake of mere life, it *exists* for the sake of a good life.

The State is Natural

Because it is the completion of associations existing by nature, every polis exists by nature, having itself the same quality as the earlier associations from which it grew. It is the end or consummation to which those associations move, and the "nature" of things consists in their end or consummation; for what each thing is when its growth is completed we call the nature of that thing, whether it be a man or a horse or a family . . . the end, or final cause, is the best. Now self-sufficiency is the end, and so the best.

From these considerations it is evident that the polis belongs to the class of things that exist by nature, and that man is by nature an animal intended to live in a polis. He who is without a polis, by reason of his own nature and not of some accident, is either a poor sort of being, or a being higher than man: he is like the man of whom Homer wrote in denunciation:

"Clanless and lawless and heartless is he."

The man who is such by nature at once plunges into a passion for war; he is in the position of a solitary advanced piece in a game of draughts.

The reason why man is a being meant for political association, in a higher degree than bees or other gregarious animals can ever associate, is evident. Nature, according to our theory, makes nothing in vain; and man alone of the animals is furnished with the faculty of language. The mere making of sounds serves to indicate pleasure and pain, and is thus a faculty that belongs to animals in general: their nature enables them to attain the point at which they have perceptions of pleasure and pain, and can signify those perceptions to one another. But language serves to declare what is advantageous and what is the reverse, and it therefore serves to declare what is just and what is unjust. It is the peculiarity of man, in comparison with the rest of the animal world, that he alone possesses a perception of good and evil, of the just and the unjust, and of other similar qualities; and it is association in these things which makes a family and a polis. . . .

The polis is prior in the order of nature to the family and the individual, since the whole is necessarily prior to the part. If the whole body be destroyed, there will not be a foot or a hand . . .

We thus see that the polis exists by nature and that it is prior to the individual. Not being self-sufficient when they are isolated, all individuals are so many parts all equally depending on the whole. The man who is isolated—who is unable to share in the benefits of political association, or has no need to share because he is already self-sufficient—is no part of the polis, and must therefore be either a beast or a god.

There is therefore an immanent impulse in all men towards an association of this order. But the man who first *constructed* such an association was none the less the greatest of benefactors. Man, when perfected, is the best of animals; but if he be isolated from law and justice he is the worst of all. If man be without virtue, he is a most unholy and savage being, and worse than all others in the indulgence of lust and gluttony. Justice belongs to the polis; for justice, which is the determination of what is just, is an ordering of the political association.

. . . Every state is composed of households. The parts of household management will correspond to the parts of which the household itself is constituted. A complete household consists of slaves and freemen. But every subject of inquiry should first be examined in its simplest elements; and the primary and simplest elements of the household are the connexion of master and slave, that of the husband and wife, and that of parents and children. The factors to be examined are therefore three—first, the association of master and slave; next, the marital association; and lastly, what may be called the parental association. But besides the three factors which thus present themselves for examination there is also a fourth, which some regard as identical with the whole of household management, and others as its principal part. This is the element called "the art of acquisition."

We may first speak of master and slave. There are some who hold that the exercise of authority over slaves is a form of science. They believe that the management of a household, the control of slaves, the authority of the statesman, and the rule of the monarch, are all the same. There are others, however, who regard the control of slaves by a master as contrary to nature. In their view the distinction of master and slave is due to law or convention; there is no natural difference between them; the relation of master and slave is based on force, and being so based has no warrant in justice.

Defense of Slavery

We may make the assumption that property is part of the household, and that the art of acquiring property is a part of household management; and we may do so because it is impossible to live well, or indeed to live at all, unless the necessary conditions are present. We may further assume that, just as each art which has a definite sphere must necessarily be furnished with the appropriate instruments if its function is to be discharged, so the same holds good in the sphere of household management. Finally, we may also assume that instruments are partly inanimate and partly animate: the pilot, for instance, has an inanimate instrument in the rudder, and an animate instrument in the look-out man. On the basis of these assumptions we may conclude that each article of property is an instrument for the purpose of life; that property in general is the sum of such instruments; that the slave is an animate article of property; and that subordinates, or servants, in general may be described as animate instruments which are prior to other inanimate instruments. There are instruments of *production;* but articles of household property [such as the slave or other chattels] are instruments of *action*. Life is action and not production; and therefore the slave [being an instrument for the purpose of life] is a servant in the sphere of action . . .

An "article of property" is a term that is used in the same sense in which the term "part" is also used. Now a part is not only a part of something other than itself: it also belongs entirely to that other thing. It is the same with an article of property as it is with a part. Accordingly, while the master is merely the master of the slave, and does not belong to him, the slave is not only the slave of his master; he also belongs entirely to him.

From these considerations we can see clearly what is the nature of the slave and what is his capacity. We attain these definitions—first, that "anybody who by his nature is not his own man, but another's, is by his nature a slave"; secondly, that "anybody who, being a man, is an article of property, is another's man"; and thirdly, that "an article of property is an instrument intended for the purpose of action and separable from its possession."

Ruling and being ruled not only belongs to the category of things necessary, but also to that of things expedient; and there are species in which a distinction is already marked, immediately at birth, between those of its members who are intended for being ruled and those who are intended to rule. . . . There are also many kinds both of ruling and ruled elements. This being the case, the rule which is exercised over the better sort of ruled elements is a better sort of rule—as, for example, rule exercised over a man is better than rule over an animal. The reason is that a function is a higher and better function when the elements which go to its discharge are higher and better elements; and where one element rules and another is ruled, we may speak of those elements as going together to discharge a function. . . . In *all* cases where there is a compound, constituted of more than one part but forming one common entity—whether the parts be continuous or discrete—a ruling element and a ruled can always be traced. This characteristic is present in animate beings by virtue of the whole constitution of nature, inanimate as well as animate; for even in things which are inanimate there is a sort of ruling principle, such as is to be found, for example, in a musical harmony.

Whatever may be said of inanimate things, it is certainly possible, as we have said, to observe in animate things—and to observe there first—the presence of a ruling authority, both of the sort exercised by a master over slaves and of the sort exercised by a statesman over fellow citizens. The soul rules the body with the sort of authority of a master: mind rules the appetite with the sort of authority of a statesman or a monarch. . . . It is clearly natural and beneficial to the body that it should be ruled by the soul, and again it is natural and beneficial to the affective part of the soul that it should be ruled by the mind and the rational part; whereas the equality of the two elements, or their reverse relation, is always detrimental. What holds good in man's inner life also holds good outside it; and the same principle is true of the relation of man to animals as is true of the relation of his soul to his body. Tame animals have a better nature than wild, and it is better for all such animals that they should be ruled by man because they then get the benefit of preservation. Again, the relation of male to female is naturally that of the superior to the inferior—of the ruling to the ruled. This general principle must similarly hold good of all human beings generally.

We may thus conclude that all men who differ from others as much as the body differs from the soul, or an animal from a man—all such are by nature slaves, and it is better for them, on the very same principle as in the other cases just mentioned, to be ruled by a master. A man is thus by nature a slave if he is capable of becoming the property of another, and if he participates in reason to the extent of apprehending it in another, though destitute of it himself. Herein he differs from animals, which do not apprehend reason, but simply obey their instincts. But the use which is made of the slave diverges but little from the use made of tame animals; both he and they supply their owner with bodily help in meeting his daily requirements. . . .

It is nature's intention also to erect a physical difference between the body of the freeman and that of the slave, giving the latter strength for the menial duties of life, but making the former upright in carriage and useful for the various purposes of civic life—a life which tends, as it develops, to be divided into military service and the occupations of peace.

. . . It is thus clear that, just as some are by nature free, so others are by nature slaves, and for these latter the condition of slavery is both beneficial and just.

But it is easy to see that those who hold an opposite view are also in a way correct. There is also a kind of slave, and of slavery, which exists by law or convention. The law in virtue of which those vanquished in war are held to belong to the victor is in effect a sort of convention. That slavery can be justified by such a convention is a principle against which a number of jurists bring what may be called an "indictment of illegality." They regard it as a detestable notion that anyone who is subjugated by superior power should become the slave and subject of the person who has the power to subjugate him, and who is his superior in power. Some, however, support it. . . . The cause of this divergence of view is to be found in the following consideration. There is a sense in which goodness, when it is furnished with material resources, has the greatest power to subjugate; and a victor is always preeminent in respect of *some* sort of good. This connexion of power with goodness or some sort of good leads to the idea that "power goes with goodness"; . . . the dispute between the two sides thus comes to turn exclusively on the point of justice. On this point, one side holds that justice is a relation of mutual goodwill . . . ; the other side holds that the rule of a superior is in itself, and by itself, justice. . . . If the divergent views are pitted separately against one another . . . , neither view has any cogency, or even plausibility, against the view that the superior *in goodness* ought to rule over, and be the master of, his inferiors. . . .

There are some who, clinging, as they think, to a sort of justice, assume that slavery in war is always and everywhere just. Simultaneously, however, they contradict that assumption; for in the first place it is possible that the original cause of a war may not be just, and in the second place no one would ever say that a person who does not deserve to be in a condition of slavery is really a slave. If such a view were accepted, the result would be that men reputed to be of the highest rank would be turned into slaves or the children of slaves, if it happened to them or their parents to be captured and sold into slavery. This is the reason why Greeks do not like to call such persons slaves, but prefer to confine the term to barbarians. They are driven, in effect, to admit that there are some who are everywhere and inherently slaves, and others who are everywhere and inherently free. The same line of thought is followed in regard to nobility, as well as slavery. Greeks regard themselves as noble not only in their own country, but absolutely and in all places; but they regard barbarians as noble only in their own country—thus assuming that there is one sort of nobility and freedom which is absolute, and another which is only relative.

. . . It is thus clear that there is some reason for the divergence of view which has been discussed, and that not all those who are actually slaves, or actually freemen, are natural slaves or natural freemen. It is also clear that there are cases where such a distinction exists, and that here it is beneficial and just that the former should actually be a slave and the latter a master—the one being ruled, and the other exercising the kind of rule for which he is naturally intended and therefore acting as master. But a wrong exercise of his rule by a master is a thing which is disadvantageous for both master and slave. The part and the whole, like the body and the soul, have an identical interest; and the slave is a part of the master, in the sense of being a living but separate part of his body. There is thus a community of interest, and a relation of friendship, between master and slave, when both of them naturally merit the position in which they stand. But the reverse is true when matters are otherwise and slavery rests merely on legal sanction and superior *power*.

The authority of the master and that of the statesman are different from one another, and it is *not* the case that all kinds of authority are, as some thinkers hold, identical. The authority of the statesman is exercised over men who are naturally free; that of the master over men who are slaves; and again the authority generally exercised over a household by its head is that of a monarch, while the authority of the statesman is an authority over freemen and equals. But there *may be* a science [of ruling] which belongs to masters, and another [of serving] which belongs to slaves.

Paternal Rule

. . . The head of the household rules over both wife and children, and rules over both as free members of the household, he exercises a different sort of rule in either case. His rule over his wife is like that of a statesman over fellow citizens; his rule over his children is like that of a monarch over subjects. The male is naturally fitter to command than the female, except where there is some departure from nature; and age and maturity are similarly fitter to command than youth and immaturity. In most cases where rule of the statesman's sort is exercised there is an interchange of ruling and being ruled: the members of a political association aim by their very nature at being equal and differing in nothing. Even so, and in spite of this aim, it is none the less true that when one body of citizens is ruling, and the other is being ruled, the former desires to establish a difference—in outward forms, in modes of address, and in titles of respect. The relation of the male to the female is permanently that in which the statesman stands to his fellow-citizens. Paternal rule over children, on the other hand, is like that of a king over his subjects. The male parent is in a position of authority both in virtue of the affection to which he is entitled and by right of his seniority; and his position is thus in the nature of royal authority. Homer, therefore, was right and proper in using the invocation

Father of Gods and of men

to address Zeus, who is king of them all. A king ought to be naturally superior to his subjects, and yet of the same stock as they are; and this is the case with the relation of age to youth, and of parent to child.

. . . Is the goodness of those who naturally rule the same as the goodness of those who are naturally ruled, or does it differ? If we say that both of them ought to share in the nobility of goodness, why should one of them permanently rule, and the other be permanently ruled? The difference between them cannot be simply a difference of degree . . . the difference between ruler and ruled is one of kind. If, on the other hand, we say that one of them ought, and the other ought not, to share, we commit ourselves to a strange view. How can the ruler rule properly, or the subject be properly ruled, unless they are both temperate and just? Anyone who is licentious or cowardly will utterly fail to do his duty. The conclusion which clearly emerges is that both classes must share in goodness, but that there must be different kinds of goodness for them—just as there are also different kinds of goodness among different classes of the ruled.

The soul has naturally two elements, a ruling and a ruled; and each has its different goodness, one belonging to the rational and ruling element, and the other to the irrational and ruled. . . . it is a general law that there should be naturally ruling elements and elements naturally ruled. . . . The rule of the freeman over the slave is one kind of rule; that of the male over the female another; that of the grown man over the child another still. It is true that all these persons possess in common the different parts of the soul; but they possess them in different ways. . . . they must all share in moral goodness but not in the same way—each sharing only to the extent required for the discharge of his or her function. The ruler, accordingly, must possess moral goodness in its full and perfect form because his function, regarded absolutely and in its full nature, demands a master-artificer, and reason is such a master-artificer; but all other persons need only possess moral goodness to the extent required of them.

The Nature of Citizenship

A polis or state belongs to the order of "compounds," in the same way as all other things which form a single "whole," but a "whole" composed, none the less, of a number of different parts. . . . A state is a compound made up of citizens; and this compels us to consider who should properly be called a citizen and what a citizen really is. The nature of citizenship, like that of the state, is a question which is often disputed: there is no general agreement on a single definition: the man who is a citizen in a democracy is often not one in an oligarchy. . . . A citizen is not one by virtue of residence in a given place: resident aliens and slaves share with them a common place of residence. Nor can the name of citizen be given to those who share in civic rights only to the extent of being entitled to sue and be sued in the courts. This is a right which belongs also to aliens who share its enjoyment by virtue of a treaty. . . . Also we may also dismiss children who are still too young to be entered on the roll of citizens, or men who are old enough to have been excused from civic duties. There is a sense in which the young and the old may both be called citizens, but it is not altogether an unqualified sense: we must add the reservation that the young are undeveloped, and the old superannuated citizens.

What we have to define is the citizen in the strict and unqualified sense, who has no defect that has to be made good before he can bear the name—no defect such as youth or age, or such as those attaching to disfranchised or exiled citizens. The citizen in this strict sense is best defined by the one criterion, "a man who shares in the administration of justice and in the holding of office."

. . . constitutions obviously differ from one another in kind, and some of them are obviously inferior and some superior in quality; for constitutions which are defective and perverted . . . are necessarily inferior to those which are free from defects. It follows that . . . the citizen under each different kind of constitution must also necessarily be different. We may thus conclude that the citizen of our definition is particularly and especially the citizen of a democracy. Citizens living under other kinds of constitution *may* possibly, but do not necessarily, correspond to the definition. There are some states, for example, in which there is no popular element: such states have no regular meetings of the assembly, but only meetings specially summoned; and [so far as membership of the courts is concerned] they remit the decision of cases to special bodies. In Sparta, for example, the Ephors take cases of contracts (not as a body, but each sitting separately); the Council of Elders take cases of homicide; and some other authority may take other cases. Much the same is also true of Carthage, where a number of bodies of magistrates have each the right to decide all cases.

But . . . in constitutions other than the democratic, members of the assembly and the courts do not hold that office for an indeterminate period. They hold it for a limited term; and it is to persons with such a tenure that the citizen's function of deliberating and judging is assigned in these constitutions. The nature of citizenship in general emerges clearly from these considerations; and our final definitions will accordingly be: (1) "he who enjoys the right of sharing in deliberative or judicial office attains thereby the status of a citizen of his state," and (2) "a state, in its simplest terms, is a body of such persons adequate in number for achieving a self-sufficient existence."

For practical purposes, it is usual to define a citizen as "one born of citizen parents on both sides," and not on the father's or mother's side only; but sometimes this requirement is carried still farther back, to the length of two, three, or more stages of ancestry. This popular and facile definition has induced some thinkers to raise the question, "How did the citizen of the third or fourth stage of ancestry himself come to be a citizen?" . . . the matter is really simple. If, in their day, they enjoyed constitutional rights in the sense of our own definition . . . they were certainly citizens. It is obviously impossible to apply the requirement of descent from a citizen father or a citizen mother to those who were the first inhabitants or original founders of a state.

A more serious difficulty is perhaps raised by the case of those who have acquired constitutional rights as the result of a revolutionary change in the constitution. . . . The question raised by such an addition to the civic body is not the question of fact, "Who is actually a citizen?" It is the question of justice, "Are men rightly or wrongly such?" It must be admitted, however, that the further question may well be raised, "Can a man who is not justly a citizen be really a citizen, and is not the unjust the same thing as the unreal?" Obviously there are holders of office who have no just title to their office; but we none the less call them office-holders, though we do not say they are justly such. Citizens too, are defined by the fact of holding a sort of office; and it follows, therefore, that those who have received this sort of office after a change in the constitution must, in practice, be called citizens.

The question whether, in justice, they are citizens or not is a different matter. . . . The problem raised by this larger question is that of deciding when a given act can, and when it cannot, be considered to be the act of the state. We may take as an example the case of an oligarchy or tyranny which changes into a democracy. In such a case there are some who are reluctant to fulfil public contracts—arguing that such contracts were made by the governing tyrant, and not by the state—and unwilling to meet other obligations of a similar nature. But the question here raised would seem to be closely allied to a question which takes us still further—"On what principles ought we to say that a state has retained its identity, or, conversely, that it has lost its identity and become a different state?"

The most obvious mode of dealing with this question is to consider simply territory and population. On this basis we may note that the territory and population of a state may be divided into two (or more) sections, with some of the population residing in one block of territory, and some of it in another. This difficulty need not be regarded as serious. The identity of a polis is not constituted by its walls.

. . . Still assuming a single population inhabiting a single territory, shall we say that the state retains its identity as long as the stock of its inhabitants continues to be the same . . . and shall we thus apply to the state the analogy of rivers and fountains, to which we ascribe a constant identity in spite of the fact that part of their water is always flowing in and a part always flowing out? Or must we take a different view, and say that while the population remains the same, for the reason already mentioned the *state* may none the less change?

. . . If a polis is a form of association, and if this form of association is an association of citizens in a polity or constitution, it would seem to follow inevitably that when the constitution suffers a change in kind, and becomes a different constitution, the polis also will cease to be the same polis, and will also change its identity. We may cite an analogy from the drama. We say that a chorus which appears at one time as a comic and at another as a tragic chorus is not continuously the same, but alters its identity—and this in spite of the fact that the members often remain the same. . . . The criterion to which we must chiefly look in determining the identity of the state is the criterion of the constitution. . . .

The Good Citizen and the Good Men

Is the excellence of a good man and that of a good citizen identical or different? . . . Citizens differ in capacity but the end which they all serve is safety in the working of their association; and this association consists in the constitution. The conclusion to which we are thus led is that the excellence of the citizen must be an excellence relative to the constitution. It follows on this that if there are several different kinds of constitution . . . there cannot be a single absolute excellence of the good citizen. But the good man is a man so called in virtue of a single absolute excellence.

It is thus clear that it is possible to be a good citizen

without possessing the excellence which is the quality of the good man. . . . In the best state the excellence of being a good citizen must belong to all citizens indifferently, because that is the condition necessary for the state being the best state; but the excellence of being a good man cannot possibly belong to all—unless, indeed, we hold that every citizen of a good state must also be a good man. . . . There is a further point to be made. Just as a living being is composed of soul and body, or the soul of the different elements of reason and appetite, or the household of man and wife, or property of master and slave, so the polis too is composed of different and unlike elements. . . . It follows upon this difference between the elements of which the polis is composed that there cannot be a single excellence common to all the citizens, any more than there can be a single excellence common to the leader of a dramatic chorus and his assistants.

It is clear from these considerations that the excellence of the good citizen and that of the good man are not in *all* cases identical. But the question may still be raised whether there are not *some* cases in which there is identity. We call a good ruler a "good" and "prudent" man, and we say of the statesman that he ought to be "prudent." We may thus assume that, in the case of the ruler, the excellence of the good citizen is identical with that of the good man. But we have to remember that subjects too are citizens. It therefore follows that the excellence of the good citizen cannot be identical with that of the good man in all cases, though it may be when he is a ruler.

Men hold in esteem the double capacity which consists in knowing both how to rule and how to obey, and they regard the excellence of a worthy citizen as consisting in a good exercise of this double capacity. Now if the excellence of the good man is in the one order of ruling, while that of the good citizen is in both orders of ruling and obeying, these two excellences cannot be held in the same esteem. The position thus being that we find men holding (1) that ruler and ruled should have different sorts of knowledge, and not one identical sort, and (2) that the citizen should have both sorts of knowledge, and share in both.

There is rule of the sort which is exercised by a master; and by this we mean the sort of rule connected with menial duties. Here it is not necessary for the ruler to know how to do, but only to know how to use the ruled: indeed the former kind of knowledge (by which we mean an ability to do menial services personally) has a servile character. In some states the working classes were once upon a time excluded from office, in the days before the institution of the extreme form of democracy. The occupations pursued by men who are subject to rule of the sort just mentioned need never be studied by the good man, or by the statesman, or by the good citizen—except occasionally and in order to satisfy some personal need. . . . But there is also rule of the sort which is exercised over persons who are similar in birth to the ruler, and are similarly free. Rule of this sort is what we call political rule; and this is the sort of rule which the ruler must begin to learn by being ruled and by obeying—just as one learns to be a commander of cavalry by serving under another commander, or to be a general of infantry by serving under another general and by acting first as colonel and, even before that, as captain. This is why it is a good saying that "you cannot be a ruler unless you have first been ruled." Ruler and ruled [under this system of political rule] have indeed different excellences; but the fact remains that the good citizen must possess the knowledge and the capacity requisite for ruling as well as for being ruled, and the excellence of a citizen may be defined as consisting in "a knowledge of rule over free men from both points of view."

A good man, like a good citizen, will need knowledge from both points of view. Accordingly, on the assumption that the temperance and justice required for ruling have a special quality, and equally that the temperance and justice required for being a subject in a free state have *their* special quality, the excellence of the good man (*e.g.* his justice) will not be one sort of excellence. It will include differt sorts—one sort which fits him to act as a ruler, and one which fits him to act as a subject. . . .

"Prudence" is the only form of goodness which is peculiar to the ruler. The other forms must, it would seem, belong equally to rulers and subjects. . . . The form of goodness peculiar to subjects cannot be "prudence," and may be defined as "right opinion." The ruled may be compared to flute-makers: rulers are like flute-players who use what the flute-makers make.

Is citizenship in the true sense to be limited to those who have the right of sharing in office, or must mechanics be also included in the ranks of citizens? If we hold that mechanics, who have no share in the offices of the state, are also to be included, we shall have some citizens who can never achieve the excellence of the good citizen since they have no experience of ruling. If, on the other hand, mechanics should not be called citizens, in what class are they to be placed? They are not resident aliens, neither are they foreigners: what is their class? The best form of state will not make the mechanic a citizen. In states where mechanics *are* admitted to citizenship we shall have to say that the citizen excellence of which we have spoken cannot be attained by every citizen, or by all who are simply free men, but can only be achieved by those who are free from menial duties.

Constitutions are various: there must thus be various kinds of citizens; more especially, there must be various kinds of citizens who are subjects. In one variety of constitution it will be necessary that mechanics and labourers should be citizens: in other varieties it will be impossible. It will be impossible, for example where there is a constitution of the type termed "aristocratic," with offices distributed on the basis of worth and excellence; for a man who lives the life of a mechanic or labourer cannot pursue the things which belong to excellence. The case is different in oligarchies. Even there, it is true, a labourer cannot be a citizen (participation in office depending on a high property qualification); but a mechanic may, for the simple reason that craftsmen often become rich men.

These considerations prove two things—that there are several different kinds of citizens, and that the name of citizen is particularly applicable to those who share in the offices and honours of the state. Homer accordingly speaks in the *Iliad* of a man being treated

> like an alien man, *without honour;*

and it is true that those who do not share in the offices and honours of the state are just like resident aliens. Two conclusions also emerge from our discussion of the question, "Is the excellence of the good man identical with that of the good citizen, or different from it?" The first is that there are some states in which the good man and the good citizen are identical, and some in which they are different. The second is that, in states of the former type, it is not all good citizens who are also good men, but only those among them who hold the position of statesmen—in other words those who direct or are capable of directing, either alone or in conjunction with others, the conduct of the public affairs.

The Classification of Constitutions

. . . A constitution (or polity) may be defined as "the organization of a polis, in respect of its offices generally, but especially in respect of that particular office which is sovereign in all issues." The civic body . . . is everywhere the sovereign of the state; in fact the civic body is the polity (or constitution) itself. In democratic states, for example, the people is sovereign: in oligarchies, on the other hand, the few have that position; and this difference of the sovereign bodies is the reason why we say that the two types of constitution differ—as we may equally apply the same reasoning to other types besides these. . . .

What is the nature of the end for which the state exists, and what are the various kinds of authority to which men and their associations are subject? . . . man is an animal impelled by his nature to live in a polis. A *natural impulse* is thus one reason why men desire to live a social life even when they stand in no need of mutual succour; but they are also drawn together by a *common interest,* in proportion as each attains a share in good life. The good life is the chief end, both for the community as a whole and for each of us individually. But men also come together, and form and maintain political associations, merely for the sake of life; for perhaps there is some element of the good even in the simple act of living, so long as the evils of existence do not preponderate too heavily. It is an evident fact that most men cling hard enough to life to be willing to endure a good deal of suffering, which implies that life has in it a sort of healthy happiness and a natural quality of pleasure. . . .

It is easy enough to distinguish the various kinds of rule or authority of which men commonly speak. . . . The rule of a master is one kind; and here, though there is really a common interest which unites the natural master and the natural slave, the fact remains that the rule is primarily exercised with a view to the master's interest, and only incidentally with a view to that of the slave, who must be preserved in existence if the rule itself is to remain. Rule over wife and children, and over the household generally, is a second kind of rule, which we have called by the name of household management. Here the rule is either exercised in the interest of the ruled or for the attainment of some advantage common to both ruler and ruled. Essentially it is exercised in the interest of the ruled, as is also plainly the case with other arts besides that of ruling, such as medicine and gymnastics—though an art may incidentally be exercised for the benefit of its practitioner, and there is nothing to prevent a trainer from becoming occasionally a member of the class he instructs, in the same sort of way as a steersman is always one of the crew. Thus a trainer or steersman primarily considers the good of those who are subject to his authority; but when he becomes one of them personally, he incidentally shares in the benefit of that good—

the steersman thus being also a member of the crew, and the trainer (though still a trainer) becoming also a member of the class which he instructs.

This principle also applies to a third kind of rule—that exercised by the holders of political office. When the constitution of a state is constructed on the principle that its members are equals and peers, the citizens think it proper that they should hold office by turns. At any rate this is the natural system, and the system which used to be followed in the days when men believed that they ought to serve by turns, and each assumed that others would take over the duty of considering his benefit, just as he had himself, during his term of office, considered the interest of others. To-day the case is altered. Moved by the profits to be derived from office and the handling of public property, men want to hold office continuously. The conclusion which follows is clear. Those constitutions which consider the common interest are *right* constitutions, judged by the standard of absolute justice. Those constitutions which consider only the personal interest of the rulers are all *wrong* constitutions, or *perversions* of the right forms. Such perverted forms are despotic . . . whereas the polis is an association of freemen . . . the term "constitution" signifies the same thing as the term "civic body." The civic body in every polis is the sovereign; and the sovereign must necessarily be either One, or Few, or Many. On this basis we may say that when the One, or the Few, or the Many rule with a view to the common interest, the constitutions under which they do so must necessarily be right constitutions. On the other hand the constitutions directed to the personal interest of the One, or the Few, or the Masses, must necessarily be perversions. . . . Among forms of government by a single person Kingship denotes the species which looks to the common interest. Among forms of government by a few persons Aristocracy is of a similar species either because the best are the rulers, or because its object is what is best for the state and its members. Finally, when the masses govern the state with a view to the common interest, the name used for this species is the generic name common to all constitutions—the name of "Polity." There is a good reason for the usage. . . . It is possible for one man, or a few, to be of outstanding excellence; but when it comes to a large number, we can hardly expect a fine edge of all the varieties of excellence. What we can expect particularly is the military kind of excellence, which is the kind that shows itself in a mass. This is the reason why the defence forces are the most sovereign body under this constitution, and those who possess arms are the persons who enjoy constitutional rights. . . .

Three perversions correspond to these three right constitutions. Tyranny is the perversion of Kingship; Oligarchy of Aristocracy; and Democracy of Polity. Tyranny is a government by a single person directed to the interest of that person; Oligarchy is directed to the interest of the well-to-do; Democracy is directed to the interest of the poorer classes. None of the three is directed to the advantage of the whole body of citizens.

Tyranny, as has just been said, is single-person government of the political association on the lines of despotism: oligarchy exists where those who have property are the sovereign authority of the constitution; and conversely democracy exists where the sovereign authority is composed of the poorer classes, and not of the owners of property. We have defined democracy as the sovereignty of numbers; but we can conceive a case in which the majority who hold the sovereignty in a state are the well-to-do. Similarly oligarchy is generally stated to be the sovereignty of a small number; but it might conceivably happen that the poorer classes were fewer in number than the well-to-do, and yet—in virtue of superior vigour— were the sovereign authority of the constitution. In neither case could the definition previously given of these constitutions be regarded as true. We might attempt to overcome the difficulty by combining both of the factors—wealth with paucity of numbers, and poverty with mass. On this basis oligarchy might be defined as the constitution under which the rich, being also few in number, hold the offices of the state; and similarly democracy might be defined as the constitution under which the poor, being also many in number, are in control. But this involves us in another difficulty. If our new definition is exhaustive, and there are no forms of oligarchy and democracy other than those enumerated in that definition, what names are we to give to the constitutions just suggested as conceivable—those where the wealthy form a majority and the poor a minority, and where the wealthy majority in the one case, and the poor minority in the other, are the sovereign authority of the constitution? The course of the argument thus appears to show that the factor of number —the small number of the sovereign body in oligarchies, or the large number in democracies—is an accidental attribute, due to the simple fact that the wealthy are generally few and the poor are generally numerous. Therefore the . . . real ground of the difference between oligarchy and democracy is poverty and riches, not numbers. It is inevitable that any constitution should be an oligarchy if the rulers under it are rulers in virtue of riches, whether they are few or many; and it is equally inevitable that a constitution under which the poor rule should be a democracy.

It happens, however, that the rich are few and the poor are numerous. . . . It is only a few who have riches, but all alike share in free status.

Justice in the State

Both oligarchs and democrats have a hold on a sort of conception of justice; but they both fail to carry it far enough, and neither of them expresses the true conception of justice in the whole of its range. In democracies, for example, justice is considered to mean equality. It does mean equality—but equality for those who are equal, and not for all. In oligarchies, again, inequality in the distribution of office is considered to be just; and indeed it is—but only for those who are unequal, and not for all. The advocates of oligarchy and democracy both refuse to consider this factor—who are the persons to whom their principles properly apply—and they both make erroneous judgements. The reason is that they are judging *in their own case;* and most men, as a rule, are bad judges where their own interests are involved. Justice is relative to persons; and a just distribution is one in which the relative values of the things given correspond to those of the persons receiving. . . . But the advocates of oligarchy and democracy, while they agree about what constitutes equality in the *thing,* disagree about what constitutes it in *persons.* The main reason for this is the reason just stated—they are judging, and judging erroneously, in their own case; but there is also another reason—they are misled by the fact that they are professing a sort of conception of justice, and professing it up to a point, into thinking that they profess one which is absolute and complete. The oligarchs think that superiority on one point—in their case wealth—means superiority on all: the democrats believe that equality in one respect—for instance, that of free birth—means equality all round.

Both sides, however, fail to mention the really cardinal factor. If property were the end for which men came together and formed an association, men's share of the state would be proportionate to their share of property; and in that case the argument of the oligarchical side—that it is not just for a man who has contributed one pound to share equally in a sum of a hundred pounds with the man who has contributed all the rest—would appear to be a strong argument. But the end of the state is not mere life; it is, rather, a good quality of life. . . . it is the cardinal issue of goodness or badness in the life of the polis which always engages the attention of any state that concerns itself to secure a system of good laws well obeyed. The conclusion which clearly follows is that any polis which is truly so called, and is not merely one in name, must devote itself to the end of encouraging goodness. Otherwise, a political association sinks into a mere alliance, which only differs in space from other forms of alliance where the members live at a distance from one another. Otherwise, too, law becomes a mere covenant—or (in the phrase of the Sophist Lycophron) "a guarantor of men's rights against one another"—instead of being, as it should be, a rule of life such as will make the members of a polis good and just.

. . . It is clear, therefore, that a polis is not an association for residence on a common site, or for the sake of preventing mutual injustice and easing exchange. These are indeed conditions which must be present before a polis can exist; but the presence of all these conditions is not enough, in itself, to constitute a polis. What constitutes a polis is an association of households and clans in a good life, for the sake of attaining a perfect and self-sufficing existence. This consummation, however, will not be reached unless the members inhabit one and the self-same place and practise intermarriage. Therefore the various institutions of a common social life—marriage-connexions, kin-groups, religious gatherings, and social pastimes generally—arose in cities. But these institutions are the business of friendship. It is friendship which consists in the pursuit of a common social life. The end and purpose of a polis is the good life, and the institutions of social life are means to that end. A polis is constituted by the association of families and villages in a perfect and self-sufficing existence; and such an existence, on our definition, consists in a life of true felicity and goodness.

It is therefore for the sake of good actions, and not for the sake of social life, that political associations must be considered to exist. . . . Those who contribute most to an association of this character have a greater share in the polis . . . than those who are equal to them (or even greater) in free birth and descent, but unequal in civic excellence, or then those who surpass them in wealth but are surpassed by them in excellence. From what has been said it is plain that both sides to the dispute about constitutions . . . profess only a partial conception of justice.

Who Should be Sovereign?

There are several alternatives: the people at large; the wealthy; the better sort of men; the one man who is best of all; the tyrant. But all these alternatives appear to involve unpleasant results: indeed, how can it be otherwise? . . . What if the poor, on the ground of their being a majority, proceed to divide among themselves the possessions of the wealthy—will not this be unjust? "No, by heaven" (a democrat may reply); "it has been justly decreed so by the sovereign." "But if this is not the extreme of injustice" (we may reply in turn), "what *is?*" Whenever a majority of any sort, irrespective of wealth or poverty, divides among its members the possessions of a minority, that majority is obviously ruining the state. . . . A tyrant uses coercion by virtue of superior power in just the same sort of way as the people coerce the wealthy. Is it just that a minority composed of the wealthy should rule? If they too behave like the others—if they plunder and confiscate the property of the people—can their action be called just? If it can, the action of the people, in the converse case, must equally be termed just. It is clear that all these acts of oppression . . . are mean and unjust. Should the better sort of men have authority and be sovereign in all matters? In that case, the rest of the citizens will necessarily be debarred from honours, since they will not enjoy the honour of holding civic office. We speak of offices as honours; and when a single set of persons hold office permanently, the rest of the community must necessarily be debarred from all honours. Is it better than any of the other alternatives that the one best man should rule? This is still more oligarchical . . . because the number of those debarred from honours is even greater. It may perhaps be urged that there is still another alternative; that it is a poor sort of policy to vest sovereignty in any person . . . subject as persons are to the passions that beset men's souls; and that it is better to vest it in law. . . . But the law itself may incline either towards oligarchy or towards democracy; and what difference will the sovereignty of law then make in the problems which have just been raised? The consequences already stated will follow just the same.

There is this to be said for the Many. Each of them by himself may not be of a good quality; but when they all come together it is possible that they may surpass—collectively and as a body, although not individually—the quality of the few best. Feasts to which many contribute may excel those provided at one man's expense. In the same way, when there are many, each can bring his share of goodness and moral prudence; and when all meet together the people may thus become something in the nature of a single person, who—as he has many feet, many hands, and many senses—may also have many qualities of character and intelligence. This is the reason why the Many are also better judges of music and the writings of poets: some appreciate one part, some another, and all together appreciate all.

. . . It is not clear, however, that this combination of qualities, which we have made the ground of distinction between the many and the few best, is true of all popular bodies and all large masses of men. Perhaps it may be said, "By heaven, it is clear that there are some bodies of which it cannot possibly be true; for if you included them, you would, by the same token, be bound to include a herd of beasts. That would be absurd; and yet what difference is there between these bodies and a herd of beasts?" All the same, and in spite of this objection, there is nothing to prevent the view we have stated from being true of *some* popular bodies. . . .

What are the *matters* over which freemen, or the general body of citizens—men of the sort who neither have wealth nor can make any claim on the ground of goodness—should properly exercise sovereignty? It may be argued, from one point of view, that it is dangerous for men of this sort to share in the highest offices, as injustice may lead them into wrongdoing, and thoughtlessness into error. But it may also be argued, from another point of view, that there is serious risk in not letting them have *some* share in the enjoyment of power; for a state with a body of disfranchised citizens who are numerous and poor must necessarily be a state which is full of enemies. The alternative left is to let them share in the deliberative and judicial functions; and we thus find Solon, and some of the other legislators, giving the people the two general functions of electing the magistrates to office and of calling them to account at the end of their tenure of office, but *not* the right of holding office themselves in their individual capacity. . . . When they all meet together, the people display a good enough gift of perception, and combined with the better class they are of service to the state (just as impure food, when it is mixed with pure, makes the whole concoction more nutritious than a small amount of the pure would be); but each of them is imperfect in the judgments he forms by himself.

But this arrangement of the constitution presents some

difficulties. The first difficulty is that . . . experts may be better at both judging and choosing . . . It would thus appear that the people should not be made sovereign, either in the matter of the election of magistrates or in that of their examination. But in the first place we have to remember our own previous argument of the combination of qualities which is to be found in the people—provided, that is to say, that they are not debased in character. Each individual may indeed, be a worse judge than the experts; but all, when they meet together, are either better than experts or at any rate no worse. In the second place, there are a number of arts in which the creative artist is not the only, or even the best, judge. These are the arts whose products can be understood and judged even by those who do not possess any skill in the art. A house, for instance, is something which can be understood by others besides the builder: indeed the user of a house—or in other words the householder—will judge it even better than he does. In the same way a pilot will judge a rudder better than a shipwright does; and the diner—not the cook—will be the best judge of a feast. . . .

There is a second difficulty still to be faced, which is connected with the first. It would seem to be absurd that persons of a poor quality should be sovereign on issues which are more important than those assigned to the better sort of citizens. The election of magistrates, and their examination at the end of their tenure, are the most important of issues; and yet there are constitutions, as we have seen, under which these issues are assigned to popular bodies, and where a popular body is sovereign in all such matters. To add to the difficulty, membership of the assembly, which carries deliberative and judicial functions, is vested in persons of little property and of any age; but a high property qualification is demanded from those who serve as treasurers or generals, or hold any of the highest offices. This difficulty too may, however, be met in the same way as the first; and the practice followed in these constitutions is perhaps, after all, correct. It is not the individual member of the judicial court, or the council, or the assembly, who is vested with office: it is the court as a whole, the council as a whole, the popular assembly as a whole, which is vested; and each individual member—whether of the council, the assembly, or the court—is simply a part of the whole. It is therefore just and proper that the people, from which the assembly, the council, and the court are constituted, should be sovereign on issues more important than those assigned to the better sort of citizens. It may be added that the collective property of the members of all these bodies is greater than that of the persons who either as individuals or as members of small bodies hold the highest offices. . . .

Above all rightly constituted laws should be the final sovereign; and personal rule, whether it be exercised by a single person or a body of persons, should be sovereign only in those matters on which law is unable, owing to the difficulty of framing general rules for all contingencies, to make an exact pronouncement. But what rightly constituted laws ought to be is a matter that is not yet clear; and here we are still confronted by the difficulty . . . that law itself may have a bias in favour of one class or another. Equally with the constitutions to which they belong . . . laws must be good or bad, just or unjust. The one clear fact is that laws must be constituted in accordance with constitutions; and if this is the case, it follows that laws which are in accordance with right constitutions must necessarily be just, and laws which are in accordance with wrong or perverted constitutions must be unjust.

What is Justice?

In all arts and sciences the end in view is some good. In the most sovereign of all the arts and sciences—and this is the art and science of politics—the end in view is the greatest good and the good which is most pursued. The good in the sphere of politics is justice; and justice consists in what tends to promote the common interest. General opinion makes it consist in some sort of equality. . . . Justice involves two factors —things, and the persons to whom things are assigned—and it considers that persons who are equal should have assigned to them equal things. But here there arises a question which must not be overlooked. Equals and unequals—yes; but equals and unequals *in what?* This is a question which raises difficulties, and involves us in philosophical speculation on politics. It is possible to argue that offices and honours ought to be distributed unequally on the basis of superiority *in any respect whatsoever*—even though there were similarity, and no shadow of any difference, in every other respect; and it may be urged, in favour of this argument, that where people differ from one another there must be a difference in what is just and proportionate to their merits. If this argument were accepted, the mere fact of a better complexion, or greater height, or any other such advantage, would establish a claim for a greater share of political rights to be given to its possessor. But is not the argument obviously wrong? To be clear that it is, we have only to study the analogy of the other arts and sciences. If you were dealing with a number of flute-players who were equal in their art, you would not assign them flutes on the principle that the better born should have a greater amount. Nobody will play the better for being better born; and it is to those who are better at the job that the better supply of tools should be given. Let us suppose a man who is superior to others in flute-playing, but far inferior in birth and beauty. Birth and beauty may be greater goods than ability to play the flute, and those who possess them may, upon balance, surpass the flute-player more in these qualities than he surpasses them in his flute-playing; but the fact remains that *he* is the man who ought to get the better supply of flutes. . . . In matters political there is no good reason for basing a claim to the exercise of authority on any and every kind of superiority. Some may be swift and others slow; but it is in athletic contests that the superiority of the swift receives its reward. Claims to political rights must be based on the ground of contribution to the elements which constitute the being of the state. There is thus good ground for the claims to honour and office which are made by persons of good descent, free birth, or wealth. Those who hold office must necessarily be free men and taxpayers: a state could not be composed entirely of men without means, any more than it could be composed entirely of slaves. But we must add that if wealth and free birth are necessary elements, the temper of justice and a martial habit are also necessary. These too are elements which must be present if men are to live together in a state. The one difference is that the first two elements are necessary to the simple existence of a state, and the last two for its good life.

If we are thinking in terms of contribution to the state's existence, all of the elements mentioned, or at any rate several of them, may properly claim to be recognized in the award of honours and office; but if we are thinking in terms of contribution to its good life, then culture and goodness may be regarded as having the justest claim. On the other hand—and following our principle that it is not right for men who are equal in one respect, and only in one, to have an equal share of all things, or for men who are superior in one respect to have a superior share of everything—we are bound to consider all constitutions which recognize such claims as perverted forms. There is a certain sense in which all the contributors of the different elements are justified in the claims they advance, though none of them is absolutely justified. (*a*) The rich are so far justified that they have a larger share of the land, which is a matter of public interest: they are also, as a rule, more reliable in matters of contract. (*b*) The free and the nobly born may claim recognition together as being closely connected. The better-born are citizens to a greater extent than the low-born; and good birth has always honour in its own country. Also good birth means goodness of the whole stock. (*c*) Similarly we may also allow that goodness of character has a just claim; for in our view the virtue of justice, which is necessarily accompanied by all the other virtues, is a virtue which acts in social relations. (*d*) But there is a further claim that may also be urged. The many may urge their claims against the few: taken together and compared with the few they are stronger, richer, and better.

Who is to govern when the claims of different groups are simultaneously present? Suppose, for example, that the good are exceedingly few in number: how are we to settle their claim? Must we only have regard to the fact that they are few for the function they have to discharge; and must we therefore inquire whether they will be able to manage a state, or numerous enough to compose one? Here there arises a difficulty which applies not only to the good, but to all the different claimants for political office and honour. It may equally be held that there is no justice in the claim of a few to rule on the ground of their greater wealth, or on that of their better birth; and there is an obvious reason for holding this view. If there is any *one* man who in turn is richer than all the rest, this one man must rule over all on the very same ground of justice; and similarly any one man who is pre-eminent in point of good birth must carry the day over those who claim on the ground of birth. The same logic may be applied in the matter of merit or goodness. If some one man be a better man than all the other good men who belong to the civic body, this one man should be sovereign on the very same ground of justice. . . . Similarly, where one man is stronger than all the rest—or a group of more than one, but fewer than the Many, is stronger—that one man or group must be sovereign instead of the Many. . . .

. . . If there is one person (or several persons, but yet not enough to form the full measure of a state) so pre-eminently superior in goodness that there can be no comparison between the goodness and political capacity which he shows (or several show, when there is more than one) and what is shown by the rest, such a person, or such persons, can no longer be treated as part of a state. Being so greatly superior to others in goodness and political capacity, they will suffer injustice if they are treated as worthy only of an equal share; for a person of this order may very well be like a god among men. They are a law in themselves. It would be a folly to attempt to legislate for them. Reasons of this nature will serve to explain why democratic states institute the rule of ostracism. Such states are held to aim at equality above anything else; and with that aim in view they used to pass a sentence of ostracism on those whom they regarded as having too much influence owing to their wealth or the number of their connexions or any other form of political strength.

If wrong or perverted forms adopt this policy of levelling with a view to their own particular interest, something the same is also true of forms which look to the common good. This rule of proportion may also be observed in the arts and sciences generally. A painter would not permit a foot which exceeded the bounds of symmetry, however beautiful it might be, to appear in a figure on his canvas. A shipwright would not tolerate a stern, or any other part of a ship, which was out of proportion. A choirmaster would not admit to a choir a singer with a greater compass and a finer voice than any of the other members. In view of this general rule, a policy of levelling need not prevent a monarch who practises it from being in harmony with his state—provided that his government is otherwise beneficial; and thus the argument in favour of ostracism possesses a kind of political justice in relation to any of the recognized forms of pre-eminence. . . . The real question is rather, "What is to be done when we meet with a man of outstanding eminence in goodness?" Nobody, we may assume, would say that such a man ought to be banished and sent into exile. But neither would any man say that he ought to be subject to others. . . . The only alternative left—and this would also appear to be the natural course—is for all others to pay a willing obedience to the man of outstanding goodness. Such men will accordingly be the permanent kings in their states.

Kingship and the Rule of Law

. . . Is it more expedient to be ruled by the one best man, or by the best laws? Those who hold that kingship is expedient argue that law can only lay down general rules; it cannot issue commands to deal with various different conjunctures; and the rule of the letter of law is therefore a folly in any and every art. It is clear that a constitution based on the letter and rules of law is not the best constitution. . . . But that from which the element of passion is wholly absent is better than that to which such an element clings. Law contains no ele-

ment of passion; but such an element must always be present
in the human mind. The rejoinder may, however, be made
that the individual mind, if it loses in this way, gains something in return: it can deliberate better, and decide better, on
particular issues. These considerations lead us to conclude
that the one best man must be a law-giver, and there must be
a body of laws, but these laws must not be sovereign where
they fail to hit the mark—though they must be so in all other
cases. There is, however, a whole class of matters which cannot be decided at all, or cannot be decided properly, by rules
of law.

   . . . Justice for equals means their being ruled as well as
their ruling, and therefore involves rotation of office. But
when we come to that, we already come to law. The rule of
law is therefore preferable to that of a single citizen. . . . If
there are a number of cases which law seems unable to determine, it is also true that a person would be equally unable to
find an answer to these cases. Law trains the holders of office
expressly in its own spirit, and then sets them to decide and
settle those residuary issues which it cannot regulate, "as
justly as in them lies." It also allows them to introduce any
improvements which may seem to them, as the result of experience, to be better than the existing laws. He who commands that law should rule may thus be regarded as commanding that God and reason alone should rule; he who
commands that a man should rule adds the character of the
beast. Appetite has that character; and high spirit, too, per-
verts the holders of office, even when they are the best of
men. Law [as the pure voice of God and reason] may thus be
defined as "Reason free from all passion."

   To seek for justice is to seek for a neutral authority; and
law is a neutral authority. But laws resting on unwritten custom are even more sovereign, and concerned with issues of
still more sovereign importance, than written laws; and this
suggests that, even if the rule of a man be safer than the rule
of written law, it need not therefore be safer than the rule of
unwritten law.

   . . . No one disputes the fact that law will be the best
ruler and judge on the issues on which it is competent. It is
because law cannot cover the whole of the ground, and there
are subjects which cannot be included in its scope, that difficulties arise and the question comes to be debated, "Is the rule
of the best law preferable to that of the best man?" Matters of
detail, which belong to the sphere of deliberation, are obviously matters on which it is not possible to lay down a law.
The advocates of the rule of law do not deny that such mat-

ters ought to be judged by men; they only claim that they ought to be judged by many men rather than one. *All* persons in office who have been trained by the law will have a good judgement; and it may well be regarded as an absurdity that a single man should do better in seeing with two eyes, judging with two ears, or acting with two hands and feet, than many could do with many. Indeed, it is actually the practice of monarchs to take to themselves, as it were, many eyes and ears and hands and feet, and to use as colleagues those who are friends of their rule and their person. The colleagues of a monarch must be his friends: otherwise they will not act in accordance with his policy. But if they are friends of his person and rule, they will also be—as a man's friends always are—his equals and peers; and in believing that his friends should have office he is also committed to the belief that his equals and peers should have office.

The Nature of Politics

The study of politics first, has to consider which is the best constitution, and what qualities a constitution must have to come closest to the ideal when there are no external factors . . . to hinder its doing so. Secondly, politics has to consider which sort of constitution suits which sort of civic body. The attainment of the best constitution is likely to be impossible for the general run of states; and the good law-giver and the true statesman must therefore have their eyes open not only to what is the absolute best, but also to what is the best in relation to actual conditions. Thirdly, politics has also to consider the sort of constitution where the student of politics must be able to study a *given* constitution, just as it stands and simply with a view to explaining how it may have arisen and how it may be made to enjoy the longest possible life. The sort of case which we have in mind is where a state has neither the ideally best constitution (or even the elementary conditions needed for it) nor the best constitution possible under the actual conditions, but has only a constitution of an inferior type. Fourthly, and in addition to all these functions, politics has also to provide a knowledge of the type of constitution which is best suited to states in general. Most of the writers who treat of politics—good as they may be in other respects—fail when they come to deal with matters of practical *utility*. We have not only to study the ideally best constitution. We have also to study the type of constitution which is practicable—and with it, and equally, the type which is easiest to work and most suitable to states generally. . . . The sort of constitutional system which ought to be proposed is one which men can be easily induced, and will be readily able, to graft onto the system they already have. It is as difficult a matter to reform an old constitution as it is to construct a new one; as hard to unlearn a lesson as it was to learn it initially. The true statesman . . . must be able to help *any* existing constitution. He cannot do so unless he knows how many different kinds of constitutions there are.

. . . The student of politics should also learn to distinguish the laws which are absolutely best from those which are appropriate to each constitution. . . . A constitution may be defined as "an organization of offices in a state, by which the method of their distribution is fixed, the sovereign authority is determined, and the nature of the end to be pursued by the association and all its members is prescribed." Laws, as distinct from the frame of the constitution, are the rules by which the magistrates should exercise their powers, and should watch and check transgressors. The same laws cannot possibly be equally beneficial to *all* oligarchies or to *all* democracies.

The Most Practicable Type of Constitution

If we adopt as true the statements made in the *Ethics*—(1) that a truly happy life is a life of goodness lived in freedom from impediments, and (2) that goodness consists in a mean —it follows that the best way of life is one which consists in a mean, and a mean of the kind attainable by every individual. Further, the same criteria which determine whether the citizen-body have a good or bad way of life must also apply to the constitution; for a constitution is the way of life of a citizen-body. In all states there may be distinguished three parts, or classes, of the citizen-body—the very rich; the very poor; and the middle class which forms the mean. Now it is admitted, as a general principle, that moderation and the mean are always best. We may therefore conclude that in the ownership of all gifts of fortune a middle condition will be the best. Men who are in this condition are the most ready to listen to reason. Those who belong to either extreme—the over-handsome, the over-strong, the over-noble, the over-wealthy; or at the opposite end the over-poor, the over-weak, the utterly ignoble— find it hard to follow the lead of reason. Men in the first class tend more to violence and serious crime: men in the second tend too much to roguery and petty offences; and most wrongdoing arises either from violence or roguery. It is a further merit of the middle class that its members suffer least from ambition, which both in the military and the civil sphere is dangerous to states. It must also be added that those who enjoy too many advantages—strength, wealth, connexions, and so forth—are both unwilling to obey and ignorant how to obey. This is a defect which appears in them from the first, during childhood and in home-life: nurtured in luxury, they never acquire a habit of discipline, even in the matter of lessons. But there are also defects in those who suffer from the opposite extreme of a lack of advantages: they are far too mean and poor-spirited. We have thus, on the one hand, people who are ignorant how to rule and only know how to obey, as if they were so many slaves, and, on the other hand, people who are ignorant how to obey any sort of authority and only know how to rule as if they were masters of slaves. The result is a state, not of freemen, but only of slaves and masters: a state of envy on the one side and on the other contempt. Nothing could be further removed from the spirit of friendship or the temper of a political community. Community depends on friendship; and when there is enmity instead of friendship, men will not even share the same path. A state aims at being, as far as it can be, a society composed of equals and peers and the middle class, more than any other, has this sort of composition. It follows that a state which is based on the middle class is bound to be the best constituted in respect of the elements of which, on our view, a state is naturally composed. The middle classes . . . enjoy a greater security themselves than any other class. They do not, like the poor, covet the goods of others; nor do others covet their possessions, as the poor covet those of the rich. Neither plotting against others, not plotted against themselves, they live in freedom from danger; and we may well approve the prayer of Phocylides

> Many things are best for the middling:
> Fain would I be of the state's middle class.

It is clear from our argument, first, that the best form of political society is one where power is vested in the middle class, and, secondly, that good government is attainable in those states where there is a large middle class—large enough, if possible, to be stronger than both of the other classes, but at any rate large enough to be stronger than either of them singly; for in that case its addition to either will suffice to turn the scale, and will prevent either of the opposing extremes

from becoming dominant. It is therefore the greatest of blessings for a state that its members should possess a moderate
and adequate property. Where some have great possessions,
and others have nothing at all, the result is either an extreme
democracy or an unmixed oligarchy; or it may even be—indirectly, and as a reaction against both of these extremes—a
tyranny.

   . . . It is clear that the middle type of constitution is best. It
is the one type free from faction; where the middle class is
large, there is least likelihood of faction and dissension among
the citizens. Large states are generally more free from faction
just because they have a large middle class. In small states, on
the other hand, it is easy for the whole population to be
divided into only two classes; nothing is left in the middle,
and all—or almost all—are either poor or rich. The reason
why democracies are generally more secure and more permanent than oligarchies is the character of their middle class,
which is more numerous, and is allowed a larger share in the
government, than it is in oligarchies. Where democracies have
no middle class, and the poor are greatly superior in number,
trouble ensues, and they are speedily ruined. It must also be
considered a proof of its value that the best legislators have
come from the middle class. Solon was one, as his own poems
prove: Lycurgus was another (and not, as is sometimes said,
a member of the royal family); and the same is true of Char-
ondas and most of the other legislators.

   . . . Most constitutions are either democratic or oligarchical. In the first place, the middle class is in most states generally small; and the result is that as soon as one or other of the
two main classes—the owners of property and the masses—
gains the advantage, it oversteps the mean, and drawing the
constitution in its own direction it institutes, as the case may
be, either a democracy or an oligarchy. In the second place,
factious disputes and struggles readily arise between the
masses and the rich; and no matter which side may win the
day, it refuses to establish a constitution based on the common interest and the principle of equality, but, preferring to
exact as the prize of victory a greater share of constitutional
rights, it institutes, according to its principles, a democracy or
an oligarchy. Thirdly, the policy of the two states which have
held the ascendancy in Greece, Athens and Sparta, has also
been to blame. Each has paid an exclusive regard to its own
type of constitution; the one has instituted democracies in the
states under its control, and the other has set up oligarchies:
each has looked to its own advantage, and neither to that of
the states it controlled. These three reasons explain why a

middle or mixed type of constitution has never been established—or, at the most, has only been established on a few occasions and in a few states.

The Three Branches of Government

a) The Deliberative

There are three elements, or "powers," in each constitution. The first of the three is the deliberative element concerned with common affairs, and its proper constitution: the second is the element of the magistracies: the third is the judicial element, and the proper constitution of that element.

The deliberative element is sovereign (1) on the issues of war and peace, and the making and breaking of alliances; (2) in the enacting of laws; (3) in cases where the penalty of death, exile, and confiscation is involved; and (4) in the appointment of magistrates and the calling of them to account on the expiration of their office. Three different arrangements of this element are possible: first, to give the decision on *all* the issues it covers to *all* the citizens; secondly, to give the decision on *all* the issues to *some* of the citizens (either by referring them all to one magistracy or combination of magistracies, or by referring different issues to different magistracies); and thirdly, to give the decision on *some issues to all* the citizens, and on *other issues to some* of them.

The first of these arrangements, which assigns all the issues of deliberation to all the citizens, is characteristic of democracies: the equality which it implies is exactly what the people desire. But there are a number of different ways in which it may be effected. First, all the citizens may meet to deliberate in relays, and not in a single body. . . . They assemble only for the purpose of enacting laws, for dealing with constitutional matters, and for hearing the announcements of the magistrates. A second way is that all the citizens should meet to deliberate in a single body, but only for the three purposes of appointing and examining the magistrates, enacting laws, and dealing with issues of war and peace. The other matters will then be left for the deliberation of the magistracies assigned to deal with each branch; but appointment to such magistracies will be open—whether it is made by election or by lot—to all the citizens. A third way is that the citizens should meet for the two purposes of appointing and examining the magistrates, and deliberating on issues of war and foreign policy, but other matters . . . should be left to the control of boards

of magistrates which, as far as possible, are kept elective—
boards to which men of experience and knowledge ought to
be appointed. A fourth way is that all should meet to deliberate on all issues, and boards of magistrates should have no
power of giving a decision on any issue, but only that of
making preliminary investigations. This is the way in which
extreme democracy—a form of democracy analogous, as we
have suggested, to the dynastic form of oligarchy and the
tyrannical form of monarchy—is nowadays conducted.

All these ways of arranging the distribution of deliberative
power are democratic. A second system of arrangement,
which may also be carried into effect in a number of different
ways, is that *some* of the citizens should deliberate on *all*
matters. This is characteristic of oligarchy. One way of carrying this second system into effect is that the members of the
deliberative body should be eligible on the basis of a moderate
property qualification, and should therefore be fairly numerous. . . . A second way of giving effect to this system is that
membership of the deliberative body should belong only to
selected persons—and not to all persons—but that these persons should act, as before, in obedience to the rules of law.
Another way of carrying this system into effect is that those
who possess the power of deliberation should recruit themselves by co-optation, or should simply succeed by heredity,
and should have the power of overruling the laws. . . .

A third system of arrangement is that *some* of the citizens
should deliberate on *some* matters—but not on all. For instance, all the citizens may exercise the deliberative power in
regard to war and peace and the examination of magistrates;
but the magistrates only may exercise that power on issues
other than these, and these magistrates may be appointed by
election. When this is the case, the constitution is an aristocracy. Another alternative is that some issues of deliberation
should go to persons appointed by election, and others to
persons appointed by lot (with the chance of the lot either
open to all or open only to candidates selected in advance),
or, again, that all issues should go to a mixed body of elected
persons and persons appointed by lot, deliberating together.
Such ways of arrangement are partly characteristic of a "polity" verging on aristocracy, and partly of a pure "polity." . . .

A democracy will do well to apply a plan of compulsory
attendance to the deliberative assembly. The results of deliberation are better when all deliberate together; when the populace is mixed with the notables and they, in their turn, with
the populace. It is also in the interest of a democracy that the

parts of the state should be represented in the deliberative body by an equal number of members, either elected for the purpose or appointed by the use of the lot. It is also in its interest, when the members of the populace largely exceed the notables who have political experience, that payment for attendance at the assembly should not be given to all the citizens, but only to so many as will balance the number of the notables or, alternatively, that the lot should be used to eliminate the excess of ordinary citizens over the notables.

The policy which is in the interest of oligarchies is to co-opt to the deliberative body some members drawn from the populace; or, alternatively, to erect an institution of the type which exists in some states, under the name of "preliminary council" or "council of legal supervision," and then to allow the citizen-body to deal with any issues which have already been considered, in advance, by the members of this institution. . . . Another line of policy which is in the interest of oligarchies is that the people should only be free to vote for measures which are identical, or at any rate in agreement, with those submitted by the government; or, alternatively, that the people as a whole should have a consultative voice, but the deliberative organ should be the body of magistrates. If the latter alternative is adopted, it should be applied in a way which is the opposite of the practice followed in "polities." The people should be sovereign for the purpose of rejecting proposals, but not for the purpose of passing them; and any proposals which they pass should be referred back to the magistrates. . . . These are our conclusions in regard to the deliberative or sovereign element in the constitution.

b) The Executive Branch

The executive element . . . like the deliberative, admits of a number of different arrangements. These differences arise on a variety of points: (1) the number of the magistracies; (2) the subjects with which they deal; and (3) the length of the tenure of each. . . . In some states the tenure is six months; in some it is a less period; in others it is a year; and in others, again, it is a longer period. We have not only to compare these periods; we have also to inquire generally whether magistracies should be held for life, or for a long term of years, or neither for life nor for a long term but only for shorter periods, and whether, in that case, the same person should hold office more than once, or each should be eligible only for a single term. . . . There is also (4) a further point to be

considered—the method of appointment; and this raises three
questions—who should be eligible; who should have the right
of election; and how should the election be conducted? We
have first to distinguish the various methods which it is possible to apply to each of these questions, and then, on that
basis, we have to determine the particular form of magistracies which will suit a particular form of constitution. . . . The
title of magistracy should, on the whole, be reserved for those
which are charged with the duty, in some given field, of
deliberating, deciding, and giving instructions—and more especially with the duty of giving instructions, which is the
special mark of the magistrate. . . . In large states it is both
possible and proper that a separate magistracy should be allotted to each separate function. The number of the citizens
makes it convenient for a number of persons to enter an
office: it permits some of the offices to be held only once in a
lifetime, and others (though held more than once) to be held
again only after a long interval; and, apart from convenience,
each function gets better attention when it is the only one
undertaken, and not one among a number of others.

In small states, on the other hand, a large number of functions have to be accumulated in the hands of but a few
persons. The small number of the citizens makes it difficult
for many persons to be in office together; and if there were,
who would be their successors? It is true that small states
sometimes need the same magistracies, and the same laws
about their tenure and duties, as large states. But it is also true
that large states need their magistracies almost continuously,
and small states only need theirs at long intervals. . . .

Which matters need the attention of different local magistracies acting in different places, and which ought to be controlled by one central magistracy acting for the whole area?
The maintenance of order is an example. It raises the question
whether we should have one person to keep order in the
market-place and another in another place, or whether we
should have a single person to keep order in every place. We
have also to consider whether to allocate duties on the basis of
the subject to be handled, or on that of the class of persons
concerned: *e.g.* should we have one officer for the whole
subject of the maintenance of order, or a separate officer for
the class of children and another for that of women? We have
also to take into account the difference of constitutions. . . .
Shall we say that the magistracies too, as well as the magistrates, differ in some respects from one constitution to another; and shall we then add, as a qualification, that in some

cases the same magistracies are suitable, but in other cases they are bound to differ?

c) The Judicial Branch

Here the three points on which differences arise are (1) the membership of the courts; (2) their competence; and (3) the machinery for appointing the members. Membership raises the question whether the courts are to be constituted from all the citizens or from a section; competence raises the question how many kinds of courts there are; the machinery of appointment raises the question whether appointment should be by vote or by lot.

. . . We must have one or other of the following systems. (1) All the citizens should be eligible to judge on all the matters we have distinguished, and should be chosen for the purpose either (a) by vote or (b) by lot. (2) All the citizens should be eligible to judge on all these matters; but for some of them the courts should be recruited by vote, and for others by lot. (3) All the citizens should be eligible to judge, but only on part of these matters; and the courts concerned with that part should all be similarly recruited, partly by vote and partly by lot. . . . There will be an equal number of systems if a sectional method be followed—i.e. if it is only a section of the citizens, and not all, who are eligible to sit in the courts. In that case we may have (1) judges drawn from a section by vote to judge on all matters; or (2) judges drawn from a section by lot to judge on all matters; or (3) judges drawn from a section by vote for some matters and by lot for others [but, together, judging on *all* matters]; or (4) judges sitting in a limited number of courts, which are similarly recruited partly by vote and partly by lot. It will be seen that these last four systems, as has just been said, correspond exactly to the previous four. In addition, we may have a conjunction of both sorts of systems; for example we may have some courts with members drawn from the whole civic body, others with members drawn from a section of the civic body, and others, again, with a mixed membership (the same court being, in that case, composed of members drawn from the whole and of members drawn from a section); and again we may have the members appointed either by vote, or by lot, or by a mixture of both.

This gives us a complete list of all the possible systems on which courts can be constituted. The first sort of system, in which the membership of the courts is drawn from all, and the courts decide on all matters, is democratic. The second sort, in which the membership is drawn from a section, and the courts decide on all matters, is oligarchical. The third sort, in which the membership of some courts is drawn from all, and that of others from a section, is characteristic of aristocracies and "polities."

SECTION II

HELLENISM AND ROMAN STOICISM

Hellenism

In 338 B.C. Athenian pride was humbled by defeat at Chaeronea at the hands of Philip. Greece paid the penalty for its failure to unite, and became part of the Macedonian Empire. The glory of the city-state vanished when the *polis* became little more than a municipality in a far-flung empire. A century later, Greece became part of expanding Rome.

Theories of politics appropriate to the city-state were no longer applicable in this Hellenistic period. Yet Greek influence remained strong and the empire tried to Hellenize itself through Greek books and teachers. The Greek language was used in business. Its artistic products, its buildings, baths, theaters, were paid the compliment of imitation. There was also an increased interest in the mystery religions, the Orphic, with its basis in the sin of man, and the Eleusinian, with its ritual of death and resurrection paralleling the agricultural cycle, and offering a refuge in a future life. This is a period, too, in which the concept of divine right, of semi-divine kings, emerges from the influence of Eastern despotic tradition.

The *polis* was no longer the end of political organization. With a large empire, including within it a variety of nations and different laws, the possibility of a universal law emerged. Moreover, the welfare of the individual was no longer inextricably bound up with that of his city. There was no obligation to participate politically, nor belief that individual self-fulfillment required such participation.

The two leading philosophies developed in this period were Epicureanism and Stoicism.

Epicureanism

The concepts of Epicureanism are largely known to us through Lucretius, rather than Epicurus. The latter, born an Athenian citizen in Samos in 341, founded his school in his garden, a symbol of retirement from the world, in 306 and died in 270 B.C.

For the Epicurean, the universe was chaotic and anarchic, composed of atoms and the void. All knowledge was acquired by sense perception; observation was therefore essential to understanding. There were an infinite number of worlds, formed by the chance combination of atoms in infinite space. The gods, unconcerned about human affairs, lived in the void between the different worlds. They were not to be regarded superstitiously or feared, only to be envied.

Man himself was made up of body and soul. Death was not to be feared. There was no such thing as immortality; after death, atoms of the soul were scattered. The aim of life therefore was pleasure, the pursuit of which brought happiness, the final end. The injunction to follow nature meant, seek pleasure. Everything was desirable insofar as it led to pleasure, but above all, the aim was absence of pain and the achievement of peace of mind. This would be obtained personally by self-control, the mastery and limitation of desires as far as possible to those that were strictly necessary. Also, it implied limitation of social relationships—"live unknown"—refusal to be involved in family or political affairs, skepticism toward religion, which the Epicureans considered largely superstition.

Yet at the same time, the Epicurean thesis was not simply one of pleasure and pain—an idea that became singularly influential—but also one of the voluntary creation of society and of law. Society was not a natural phenomenon, but rather a deliberate creation aimed at bringing order out of chaos. Indeed, pleasure was augmented by the presence of law, provision for punishment and preservation of order. It was this stress on the opportunity for man to make his own environment that led Marx to choose Epicurus as one of two writers on whom to do his doctoral dissertation.

Stoicism

"Stoicism" is derived from "stoa" or porch, where Zeno, originally a Phoenician, began teaching about 300 B.C. The theory started from the premise of a natural order of the universe, which included the process of change, and which was at the same time divine. Man, a part of this divine order, was capable of understanding it and its laws through the reason possessed by all men. Virtue depended on knowledge, and knowledge was obtained through reason. The golden rule was "follow nature," live consistently with nature, obey the universal law of nature.

Happiness was the result of internal harmony. Nothing ought to disturb one's peace of mind. Man, living through reason, ought to suppress emotions like fear, lust or anxiety, to reach the desired state of *apathia*, or inner tranquillity.

But if Hellenistic Stoicism stressed self-control of the individual, it also had far-reaching social implications. The state was no longer the end through which man reached his fulfillment. Since all men possessed reason, since the law of nature applied to all, a universal society with cosmopolitan citizenship existed. The natural law theory, touched on by Sophocles, entered political theory permanently, with the Stoic belief that there was a natural law capable of being understood by man and providing a basis for political organization.

No matter what the laws of their individual states might be, men were all members of a universal brotherhood, for they all possessed equally a share of the stock of reason. Stoicism therefore implied equality, certainly between the sexes, and in the spiritual sphere. And it provided a beginning for interstate relations as a means of settling disputes. The belief in a universal brotherhood is only the political aspect of the view that the universe is a unity, pervaded by reason. This view, in turn, is the rationalization of the perplexity of man, seeking security and certainty in the face of a mighty empire.

Roman Stoicism

Stoicism was formulated by the Hellenists, but it was adopted by the Romans who merged some of their conservative, chauvinistic characteristics with it. It provided them with a civilized ethic in theory, often belied in practice. They emphasized, in particular, the emotional self-restraint, the refusal to give vent to pity or grief, the display of courage, especially in the face of death, the heroic virtue—qualities that Shakespeare has portrayed so magnificently in his Volumnia in *Coriolanus.*

If the theory had radical implications for the Hellenists, it was a quietistic philosophy for the Roman upper class who adopted it, perhaps as a rationalization of the need to live under oppressive rule in a period with little cultural, philosophical or agricultural development. Stoicism for them implied limitation rather than fulfillment. Happiness depended on the absence of desires. Their advocacy of the brotherhood of man did not extend to abolition of slavery, even if it sometimes led to amelioration of the lot of slaves—and even the last is not certain.

It was a personal rather than a social philosophy. It took for granted the hierarchical static order of society, and the performance by each individual of his allotted function. If there was commitment to anything, it was to maintenance of conditions as they were. "Stoicism," remarked Baudelaire, "is a religion with only one sacrament, suicide."

Extracts are presented here from two Roman Stoics, Seneca and Marcus Aurelius.

Seneca, born of a wealthy Spanish family in Córdoba, Spain, about 5 B.C., represents the elegant Stoicism fashionable in Rome during some of the most infamous days of the monarchy. His life was no illustration of his writings. A teacher of a tyrant, a time-server and fawner on the despicable Nero, nothing became his life so much as the leaving of it, with his suicide in 65 A.D., on being ordered to take his life. He advocated the simple life, disdain for material wealth, the self-sufficiency of the philosopher, the need for spiritual discipline, the necessity for the wise man to serve society.

Seneca also illustrates the growing cult of monarchy that had infiltrated from the East: the worship of the king as a god on earth and the divinity of the monarchy—views that were adopted by Augustus and Caligula and that were to become more important in the 3rd century. Seneca rationalized his support by the idea of the monarch as father of his people, the person who held the country united, the man who was a god to his subjects.

Marcus Aurelius was emperor of Rome between 161 and 180 A.D., continuously occupied by war and ruthless in waging it. His *Meditations* are notes made while resting in his campaigns rather than the treatise expected of a philosopher-king. He was not concerned with political or social reform. His writing is permeated by a mood of resignation, a view that all is for the best. The book gives little indication that he was ruler of a world empire; it is primarily an exploration of his own spiritual experience and of the need to face death courageously. He was preoccupied with the problem of the individual soul, but he accepted the Stoic view of a world state, a law of nature and equality of men.

SENECA

Stoic Philosophy

(Extracts have been selected from these works: *On Providence, On the Shortness of Life, On Tranquillity, Consolation of Helvia*, and the *Letters*.)

Avoid luxury, avoid debilitating prosperity which makes men's minds soggy and which, unless something intervenes to remind them of the human condition, renders them comatose as in unending inebriation. If a man has always been protected from the wind by glass windows, if his feet have been kept warm by constant relays of poultices, if the temperature of his dining room has been maintained by hot air circulating under the floor and through the walls, he will be dangerously susceptible to a slight breeze. All excesses are injurious, but immoderate prosperity is the most dangerous of all. It affects the brain, it conjures empty fantasies up in the mind, and it befogs the distinction between true and false with a confusing cloud. Is it not better to endure everlasting misfortune, with virtue's help, than to burst with endless and immoderate prosperity? . . . You can surpass god: he is exempt from enduring evil, you rise superior to it. Scorn poverty: no one is as poor as he was at birth. Scorn pain: either it will go away or you will. Scorn death: either it finishes you or it transforms you. Scorn Fortune: I have given her no weapon with which to strike your soul. Above all, I have taken pains that nothing should detain you against your will: the way out lies open. If you do not wish to fight you may escape. Of all the things which I deemed necessary for you, therefore, I have made none easier than dying. . . . Let every occasion and every situation teach you how easy it is to renounce Nature and throw her gift in her face. At the very altars and the solemn rites of sacrifice, even as you pray for life, study death. . . .

. . . Honors, monuments, all that ambition has blazoned in inscriptions or piled high in stone will speedily sink to ruin; there is nothing that the lapse of time does not dilapidate and exterminate. But the dedications of philosophy are impregnable; age cannot erase their memory or diminish their force. Each succeeding generation will hold them in ever higher reverence; what is close at hand is subject to envy, whereas the distant we can admire without prejudice. The philosopher's life is therefore spacious; he is not hemmed in and constricted like others. He alone is exempt from the limitations of hu-

manity; all ages are at his service as at a god's. Has time gone
by? He holds it fast in recollection. Is time now present? He
utilizes it. Is it still to come? He anticipates it. The amalgama-
tion of all time into one makes his life long. . . . If Fortune
gets the upper hand and interdicts action, he should not at
once turn his back and fly defenseless to seek a hiding place,
as if there were any place where Fortune could not reach him;
let him rather participate in public affairs more discreetly and
carefully choose some capacity in which he can be useful to
the state. . . . Has he lost the functions of a citizen? Let him
exercise those of a man.

The reason we Stoics have high-heartedly refused to confine
ourselves within the walls of a single city but have sought
relations with the whole earth and claimed the whole world
for our fatherland was to afford virtue a broader scope. Look
at the great populations and broad countries stretching out
behind you; never can so large a portion be barred to you but
that an even larger will be left open. . . .

If Fortune has removed you from the first rank in public
affairs, stand your ground anyhow and help with the shouting.
The efforts of a good citizen are never useless; by being heard
and seen, by his expression, gesture, silent determination, by
his very gait he is of service. Just as certain medicines work
by odor without taste or touch, so Virtue, at a distance and
unseen, radiates usefulness. . . . Whenever chance impediments or the political situation makes our active career impossible, far the best course is to season your leisure with activity; for never can all pursuits be so blocked off that there is no
room left for honorable action. . . .

We shall be content if we have learned to be content with
thrift, without which no amount of wealth can satisfy and
with which any amount suffices, especially since a remedy is
available: even poverty can transform itself into wealth by
applying thrift. We must habituate ourselves to reject ostenta-
tion and value things by their utility, not by their trappings.
The function of victuals is to subdue hunger; of drink to
quench thirst; of the sexual urge, its essential discharge. We
must learn to lean on our own members, to conform our dress
and food not to the latest style but to the modes our ancestors
recommend. We must learn to strengthen self-restraint, curb
luxury, temper ambition, moderate anger, view poverty
calmly, cultivate frugality, use readily available remedies for
natural desires, keep restive aspirations and a mind intent
upon the future under lock and key, and make it our business
to get our riches from ourselves rather than from Fortune.

It is never possible to erect defenses against the diversity and malignity of events strong enough to prevent a great spread of sail from being blasted by gales. We must compress our affairs into a narrow compass, to frustrate missiles; that is why exile and other disasters have sometimes proved salutary and have cured serious maladies with slight inconveniences. When a mind is deaf to instruction and cannot be cured by milder measures, is it not wholesome to apply poverty, disgrace, financial ruin, and to counter evil with evil? We must therefore learn the capacity to dine without a mob, to enslave ourselves to fewer slaves, to get clothes for the purpose they were invented for, to live less spaciously. The inside track is the one to take not only in foot races and horse races but also in the arena of life. . . .

We are all chained to Fortune. . . . All life is bondage. Man must therefore habituate himself to his condition, complain of it as little as possible, and grasp whatever good lies within his reach. No situation is so harsh that a dispassionate mind cannot find some consolation in it. . . . Apply good sense to your problems; the hard can be softened, the narrow widened, and the heavy made lighter by the skillful bearer.

Our desires, moreover, must not be set wandering far afield; since they cannot be wholly confined, we may give them an airing in the immediate vicinity. What cannot be or can hardly be we should leave alone, and follow what is near at hand and in reach of hope, but in the knowledge that all alike are trivial. Nor should we envy men in higher place; what looks lofty is precipitous.

Those, again, whom an unkind lot has placed in an equivocal position will be safer if they eliminate the pride from a situation inherently proud and, so far as they can, reduce their fortune to the common level. . . . They may balance on their perch more securely if they prepare safeguards for a successful descent by justice, gentleness, mercy, and generous and kindly administration. But the surest deliverance from these alternations of hope and despair is to fix a limit to our advancement; we should not leave the decision to Fortune, but ourselves come to a halt far this side the reaches suggested by precedent. The aspirations a man may entertain will keep the mind alert, but because they are limited they will not lead him into uncharted and ambiguous regions. . . .

Our next point is avoidance of labor for empty ends or out of empty motivation. That is to say, we must not covet what we cannot attain, or what, when we have attained it, will make us realize too late and shamefacedly the vanity of our desires. In other words, labor should not be vain in the sense that it produces no result, nor should the result, if it produces any, be unworthy of the labor; whether the attainment is nil or embarrassing, the consequence is melancholy.

We must cut down on gadding about. Many people lead an antlike existence; restless indolence would not be a bad name for it. Some of these wretches dashing as to a fire make a pitiful spectacle; they crash into people going the other way and go sprawling with their victims, and all this hurry is to pay a morning call on a man who will never return it, or attend the funeral of a man they do not know, or the trial of some litigious pettifogger, or the engagement reception of a much-married lady. . . . Every exertion must have some rationale and some objective. Industry does not reduce men to nervousness; false ideas drive them to insanity. Even the latter are actuated by some hope; an attractive surface excites them, and their bemused minds cannot penetrate the emptiness within. . . . A man who keeps himself within the bounds of nature will not feel poverty; but one who exceeds those bounds will be pursued by poverty even in the greatest opulence. For necessities even exile is sufficient, for superfluities not even kingdoms are. It is the mind which makes men rich. . . . The mind has no more to do with money than have the immortal gods. All those objects revered by untutored intellects enslaved to their own bodies—marbles, gold, silver, polished round tables of great size—are earthly dross which an unflawed mind aware of its own nature cannot love, for it is itself light and unencumbered, ready to soar aloft as soon as it shall be released. In the meantime, so far as the curbs of the members and the heavy load of body which surrounds it allow, it contemplates things divine in swift and airy thought. . . . This trivial body, the prison and fetter of the soul, is tossed hither and yon; upon it tortures, brigandage, diseases, do their worst. But the mind itself is sacred and everlasting, and not subject to violence. . . .

. . . Philosophy's first promise is a sense of participation, of belonging to mankind, being a member of society. We must be careful that our efforts to awaken admiration are not ludicrous or odious. Our principle, you remember, is "life according to nature"; but it is against Nature to torment one's body, to loathe neatness easily come by, to make a point of squalor, to use victuals that are not only cheap but loathsome and repulsive. To desire dainties is a mark of luxury; it is just as much a mark of lunacy to avoid ordinary food that is not expensive. It is frugality that philosophy asks, not affliction, and frugality need not be slovenly. This I hold is the correct mode: life should be steered between good mores and public mores; men should respect our way of life, but they should find it recognizable. . . .

. . . The wise man and the devotee of wisdom is indeed attached to his body, but in his better part he is elsewhere; his thoughts are directed to lofty matters. He is bound, as it were, by a military oath, and regards his life span as his term of enlistment. He is disciplined neither to love life nor hate it; he puts up with mortality, though he knows there is a fuller kind of existence. . . .

. . . My body I oppose to Fortune; upon it she may spend her force, but I will allow no wound to penetrate through it to myself. My body is the part of me that is subject to injury, my soul dwells in this vulnerable domicile. Never shall this flesh drive me to fear, never to assume a posture unworthy of a good man; never shall I lie out of consideration for this paltry body. When it seems right I shall sever my partnership with it, and even now, while the attachment holds, we are not equal partners; the soul can claim complete jurisdiction. Contempt of body is unqualified freedom. . . .

. . . Train your soul against poverty, and you may stay rich. Arm yourself to scorn pain; your health may continue safe and sound and never put your virtue to the test. Teach yourself to bear the loss of loved ones bravely, and all of them will happily survive you. This one training *must* one day be put to use.

Do not imagine that only great men have had the toughness to break through the trammels of human bondage. . . . Men of the meanest condition have made a mighty effort to break through to deliverance, and when they were not allowed to die at their discretion or choose their instruments for dying they snatched up whatever was ready to hand, and by their own strength transformed implements naturally harmless into weapons. . . . Nothing stands in the way of a man who wants to break loose and get away. Nature's corral is an open space, and when pressure reaches the allowable point a man can look around for an easy exit. . . . The wise man was adaptable in his mode of living—of course he was, for even in these days he would wish to be as unencumbered as possible. How, I ask you, can you consistently admire both Diogenes and Daedalus? Which do you consider a sage, the man who thought up the saw, or the man who took his cup from his wallet and smashed it as soon as he saw a boy drinking water out of the hollow of his hand? And today which would you count the wiser, the man who invents a process for spraying saffron from hidden pipes to an enormous height, who fills or empties decorative pools with a sudden rush of water, who fits assorted ceiling coffers of dining halls so ingeniously that one pattern follows close upon another and the roof changes as often as the courses, or the man who demonstrates to himself and others that Nature makes no harsh and difficult demands upon us, that we can live without the marble-worker and engineer, that we can be clothed without the silk trade, that we can have the necessities we require if we are content with what earth carries on its surface? And if the human race would hearken to this sage it would realize that the cook is as superfluous as the soldier. The men whose physical needs were simple were sages or very like sages. Necessities require little care; it is luxury that costs labor. Follow Nature and you will not wish for artificers. . . .

The essential soul has an irrational factor and also a rational. The irrational serves the rational and is the one element which is not referred to something else but refers all things to itself. For the divine reason, too, is sovereign over all things and subordinate to none, and our reason possesses the same quality because it is derived from the divine. . . . The happy life depends solely on our reason being perfect. Only perfect reason keeps the soul from being submissive and stands firm against Fortune; it assures self-sufficiency in whatever situation. It is the one good which can never be impinged upon. A man is happy when no circumstance can reduce him; he keeps to the heights and uses no buttress but himself, for a man sustained by a bolster is liable to fall. If this is not so, then many factors outside ourselves will begin to have power over us. But who wishes Fortune to be paramount, or what prudent man preens himself on what is not his?

What is the happy life? Self-sufficiency and abiding tranquillity. This is the gift of greatness of soul, the gift of constancy which perseveres in a course judged right. How can these attitudes be attained? By surveying truth in its entirety, by safeguarding in every action order, measure, decorum, a will that is without malice and benign, focused undeviatingly upon reason, at once amiable and admirable. The wise man's soul should have the quality of a god's. What can a man desire if he possesses everything that is honorable? If the dishonorable can contribute to the optimum state, then the happy life will be comprised of elements other than honorable. And what could be meaner or stupider than to weave the good of the rational soul out of irrational strands? . . .

. . . If the honorable alone does not satisfy you, then you must desiderate either the repose which the Greeks call *aokhlesia* ("undisturbedness") or else pleasure. But the first can be had in any case: when the mind is at liberty to survey the universe and nothing distracts it from the contemplation of nature it is free of disturbance. The second, pleasure, is the good of cattle; this is to add the irrational to the rational, the dishonorable to the honorable. . . . Would you count as a human being . . . one whose supreme good consists of flavors and colors and sounds? He should be crossed off the roster of the noblest of all living species, which is second only to the gods; an animal whose delight is in fodder should herd with cattle.

The irrational part of the soul has two divisions: one spirited, ambitious, headstrong, swayed by passion, and the other passive, unforceful, devoted to pleasure. The former, which is unbridled but yet of better quality and at least more stalwart and virile, these philosophers have neglected, and have deemed the latter, nerveless and abject as it is, essential to the happy life. They have put reason under its orders and have made the supreme good of the noblest of creatures a thing spineless and ignoble, a monstrous hybrid, moreover, compounded of ill-assorted and badly joined members. . . .

We assert that "happy" is what is in accordance with nature, and what is in accordance with nature is directly obvious, just as wholeness is obvious. The endowment according to nature which comes to us at birth I call not a good but the inception of good. . . . As far as perception of good and evil is concerned, both are equally mature; an infant is no more capable of the good than is a tree or some dumb animal.

And why is the good not present in tree or dumb animal? Because reason is not. Hence the good is not present in an infant because it lacks reason. It will attain to the good only when it attains to reason. There is the irrational animal, the not yet rational, and the imperfectly rational; in none of these is the good present, because the good comes with reason. . . . In the irrational there cannot be good ever; in the not yet rational there cannot be good now; in the imperfectly rational there can be good now, but there is not. . . .

And what is this good? It is a free and upstanding mind which subjects other things to itself and itself to nothing. So far is infancy from being capable of this good that even boyhood cannot hope for it and young manhood is wrong to hope for it; old age can be thankful if it attains it after long study and application. By this definition the good is a matter of intellect. . . .

. . . Only what is perfect in accordance with nature as a whole is truly perfect, and nature as a whole is rational. Other things can be perfect according to their species. A being not capable of the happy life is not capable of the efficient cause of the happy life, and the efficient cause of the happy life is the good. . . .

. . . How can the nature of beings who have had no experience of perfected time be perfect? Time is comprised of three parts—past, present, and future. Animals know only the present, which is the weightiest factor in their limited orbit. There is an occasional recollection of the past, but only at the instance of a present encounter. The good of perfected nature cannot therefore exist in imperfect nature, or if imperfect nature possesses the good so also does plant life. . . .

Good can therefore exist only where reason exists.

What, then, is your peculiar good? Perfect reason. Will you exploit this to its fullest limits, to its maximum potentiality? Pronounce yourself happy only when all your satisfactions are begotten of reason, and when, having surveyed what men struggle for, pray for, watch over, you find nothing to desire let alone prefer. I give you a rule of thumb to assess yourself and ascertain your perfection: You will come into possession when you understand that the "successful" are least successful. Farewell. . . .

MARCUS AURELIUS

The Meditation of Marcus Antoninus

Nowhere either with more quiet or more freedom from trouble does a man retire than into his own soul, particularly when he has within him such thoughts that by looking into them he is immediately in perfect tranquillity; and I affirm that tranquillity is nothing else than the good ordering of the mind. Constantly, then, give to thyself this retreat, and renew thyself; and let thy principles be brief and fundamental, which, as soon as thou shalt recur to them, will be sufficient to cleanse the soul completely, and to send thee back free from all discontent with the things to which thou returnest. For with what art thou discontented? With the badness of men? Recall to thy mind this conclusion, that rational animals exist for one another, and that to endure is a part of justice, and that men do wrong involuntarily.

. . . What is that which is able to conduct a man? One thing and only one, philosophy. But this consists in keeping the daemon within a man free from violence and unharmed, superior to pains and pleasures, doing nothing without a purpose, nor yet falsely and with hypocrisy, not feeling the need of another man's doing or not doing anything; and besides, accepting all that happens, and all that is allotted, as coming from thence, wherever it is, from whence he himself came; and finally, waiting for death with a cheerful mind, as being nothing else than a dissolution of the elements of which every living being is compounded. But if there is no harm to the elements themselves in each continually changing into another, why should a man have any apprehension about the change and dissolution of all the elements? For it is according to nature, and nothing is evil which is according to nature. . . .

—But perhaps the desire of the thing called fame will torment thee.—See how soon everything is forgotten, and look at the chaos of infinite time on each side of the present, and the emptiness of applause, and the changeableness and want of judgment in those who pretend to give praise, and the narrowness of the space within which it is circumscribed, and be quiet at last. . . . Remember to retire into this little territory of thy own, and above all do not distract or strain thyself, but be free, and look at things as a man, as a human being, as a citizen, as a mortal. But among the things readiest to thy hand to which thou shalt turn, let there be these, which are two. One is that things do not touch the soul, for they are external and remain immovable; but our perturbations come only from the opinion which is within. The other is that all these things which thou seest change immediately and will no longer be; and constantly bear in mind how many of these changes thou hast already witnessed. The universe is transformation: life is opinion.

If our intellectual part is common, the reason also, in respect of which we are rational beings, is common: if this is so, common also is the reason which commands us what to do, and what not to do; if this is so, there is a common law also; if this is so, we are fellow-citizens; if this is so, we are members of some political community; if this is so, the world is in a manner a state. For of what other common political community will any one say that the whole human race are members? And from thence, from this common political community comes also our very intellectual faculty and reasoning faculty and our capacity for law; or whence do they come . . . ?

. . . For two reasons it is right to be content with that which happens to thee; the one, because it was done for thee and prescribed for thee, and in a manner had reference to thee, originally from the most ancient causes spun with thy destiny; and the other, because even that which comes severally to every man is to the power which administers the universe a cause of felicity and perfection, nay even of its very continuance. . . .

. . . Reverence that which is best in the universe; and this is that which makes use of all things and directs all things. And in like manner also reverence that which is best in thyself; and this is of the same kind as that. For in thyself also, that which makes use of everything else, is this, and thy life is directed by this.

That which does no harm to the state, does no harm to the citizen. In the case of every appearance of harm apply this rule: if the state is not harmed by this, neither am I harmed. But if the state is harmed, thou must not be angry with him who does harm to the state. Show him where his error is. . . .

Think of the universal substance, of which thou hast a very small portion; and of universal time, of which a short and indivisible interval has been assigned to thee; and of that which is fixed by destiny, and how small a part of it thou art. . . .

. . . Soon, very soon, thou wilt be ashes, or a skeleton, and either a name or not even a name; but name is sound and echo. And the things which are much valued in life are empty and rotten and trifling, and like little dogs biting one another, and little children quarrelling, laughing, and then straightway weeping.

But to have good repute amidst such a world as this is an empty thing. Why then dost thou not wait in tranquillity for thy end, whether it is extinction or removal to another state? And until that time comes, what is sufficient? Why, what else than to venerate the gods and bless them, and to do good to men, and to practise tolerance and self-restraint; but as to everything which is beyond the limits of the poor flesh and breath, to remember that this is neither thine nor in thy power.

Thou canst pass thy life in an equable flow of happiness, if thou canst go by the right way, and think and act in the right way. These two things are common both to the soul of God and to the soul of man, and to the soul of every rational being, not to be hindered by another; and to hold good to consist in the disposition to justice and the practice of it, and in this to let thy desire find its termination. . . .

Of necessity thou must be envious, jealous, and suspicious of those who can take away those things, and plot against those who have that which is valued by thee. Of necessity a man must be altogether in a state of perturbation who wants any of these things; and besides, he must often find fault with the gods. But to reverence and honour thy own mind will make thee content with thyself, and in harmony with society, and in agreement with the gods, that is, praising all that they give and have ordered. . . .

How strangely men act. They will not praise those who are living at the same time and living with themselves; but to be themselves praised by posterity, by those whom they have never seen or ever will see, this they set much value on. But this is very much the same as if thou shouldst be grieved because those who have lived before thee did not praise thee. . . .

. . . Frequently consider the connexion of all things in the universe and their relation to one another. For in a manner all things are implicated with one another, and all in their ways are friendly to one another; for one thing comes in order after another, and this is by virtue of the active movement and mutual conspiration and the unity of the substance.

Adapt thyself to the things with which thy lot has been cast: and the men among whom thou hast received thy portion, love them, but do it truly, sincerely. . . .

Whatever happens to every man, this is for the interest of the universal: this might be sufficient. But further thou wilt observe this also as a general truth, if thou dost observe, that whatever is profitable to any man is profitable also to other men. But let the word profitable be taken here in the common sense as said of things of the middle kind, neither good nor bad.

All things are implicated with one another, and the bond is holy; and there is hardly anything unconnected with any other thing. For things have been coordinated, and they combine to form the same universe (order). For there is one universe made up of all things, and one God who pervades all things, and one substance, and one law, one common reason in all intelligent animals, and one truth; if indeed there is also one perfection for all animals which are of the same stock and participate in the same reason.

Everything material soon disappears in the substance of the whole; and everything formal (causal) is very soon taken back into the universal reason; and the memory of everything is very soon overwhelmed in time.

To the rational animal the same act is according to nature and according to reason. . . .

. . . A rational nature goes on its way well, when in its thoughts it assents to nothing false or uncertain, and when it directs its movements to social acts only, and when it confines its desires and aversions to the things which are in its power, and when it is satisfied with everything that is assigned to it by

he common nature. For of this common nature every particular nature is a part, as the nature of the leaf is a part of the
nature of the plant; except that in the plant the nature of the
leaf is part of a nature which has not perception or reason,
and is subject to be impeded; but the nature of man is part of
a nature which is not subject to impediments, and is intelligent and just, since it gives to everything in equal portions and
according to its worth, times, substance, cause (form), activ-
ty, and incident. But examine, not to discover that any one
thing compared with any other single thing is equal in all
espects, but by taking all the parts together of one thing and
comparing them with all the parts together of another. . . .

. . . In every pain let this thought be present, that there is
no dishonour in it, nor does it make the governing intelligence
worse, for it does not damage the intelligence either so far as
he intelligence is rational or so far as it is social. Indeed, in
he case of most pains let this remark of Epicurus aid thee,
hat pain is neither intolerable nor everlasting, if thou bearest
in mind that it has its limits, and if thou addest nothing to it
n imagination: and remember this too, that we do not perceive that many things which are disagreeable to us are the
same as pain, such as excessive drowsiness, and the being
scorched by heat, and the having no appetite. When then thou
art discontented about any of these things, say to thyself that
thou art yielding to pain. . . .

He who acts unjustly acts impiously. For since the universal nature has made rational animals for the sake of one
another to help one another according to their deserts, but in
no way to injure one another, he who transgresses her will, is
clearly guilty of impiety towards the highest divinity. And he
too who lies is guilty of impiety to the same divinity; for the
universal nature is the nature of things that are; and things
that are have a relation to all things that come into existence.
And further, this universal nature is named truth, and is the
prime cause of all things that are true. He then who lies in-
tentionally is guilty of impiety inasmuch as he acts unjustly by
deceiving; and he also who lies unintentionally, inasmuch as he
is at variance with the universal nature, and inasmuch as he
disturbs the order by fighting against the nature of the world;
for he fights against it, who is moved of himself to that which
is contrary to truth, for he had received powers from nature
through the neglect of which he is not able now to distinguish
falsehood from truth. And indeed he who pursues pleasure as
good, and avoids pain as evil, is guilty of impiety. For of
necessity such a man must often find fault with the universal
nature, alleging that it assigns things to the bad and the good

contrary to their deserts, because frequently the bad are in the enjoyment of pleasure and possess the things which procure pleasure, but the good have pain for their share and the things which cause pain. And further, he who is afraid of pain will sometimes also be afraid of some of the things which will happen in the world, and even this is impiety. And he who pursues pleasure will not abstain from injustice, and this is plainly impiety. Now with respect to the things towards which the universal nature is equally affected—for it would not have made both, unless it was equally affected towards both— towards these they who wish to follow nature should be of the same mind with it, and equally affected. With respect to pain, then, and pleasure, or death and life, or honour and dishonour, which the universal nature employs equally, whoever is not equally affected is manifestly acting impiously. And I say that the universal nature employs them equally, instead of saying that they happen alike to those who are produced in continuous series and to those who come after them by virtue of a certain original movement of Providence, according to which it moved from a certain beginning to this ordering of things, having conceived certain principles of the things which were to be, and having determined powers productive of beings and of changes and of such like successions. . . .

. . . Observe what thy nature requires, so far as thou art governed by nature only: then do it and accept it, if thy nature, so far as thou art a living being, shall not be made worse by it. And next thou must observe what thy nature requires so far as thou art a living being. And all this thou mayest allow thyself, if thy nature, so far as thou art a rational animal, shall not be made worse by it. But the rational animal is consequently also a political (social) animal. Use these rules, then, and trouble thyself about nothing else. . . .

. . . Whether the universe is a concourse of atoms, or nature is a system, let this first be established, that I am a part of the whole which is governed by nature; next, I am in a manner intimately related to the parts which are of the same kind with myself. For remembering this, inasmuch as I am a part, I shall be discontented with none of the things which are assigned to me out of the whole; for nothing is injurious to the part if it is for the advantage of the whole. For the whole contains nothing which is not for its advantage; and all natures indeed have this common principle, but the nature of the universe has this principle besides, that it cannot be compelled even by any external cause to generate anything harmful to itself. By remembering, then, that I am a part of such a whole, I shall be content with everything that happens. And inasmuch as I am in a manner intimately related to the parts which are of the same kind with myself, I shall do nothing unsocial, but I shall rather direct myself to the things which are of the same kind with myself, and I shall turn all my efforts to the common interest, and divert them from the contrary. . . .

. . . Short is the little time which remains to thee of life. Live as on a mountain. For it makes no difference whether a man lives there or here, if he lives everywhere in the world as in a state (political community). Let men see, let them know a real man who lives according to nature. If they cannot endure him, let them kill him. For that is better than to live thus as men do.

No longer talk at all about the kind of man that a good man ought to be, but be such. . . .

A branch cut off from the adjacent branch must of necessity, be cut off from the whole tree also. So too a man when he is separated from another man has fallen off from the whole social community. Now as to a branch, another cuts it off, but a man by his own act separates himself from his neighbour when he hates him and turns away from him, and he does not know that he has at the same time cut himself off from the whole social system. It is in our power to grow again to that which is near to us, and again to become a part which helps to make up the whole. However, if it often happens, this kind of separation, it makes it difficult for that which detaches itself to be brought to unity and to be restored to its former condition. Finally, the branch, which from the first grew together with the tree, and has continued to have one life with it, is not like that which after being cut off is then ingrafted, for this is something like what the gardeners mean when they say it grows with the rest of the tree, but that it has not the same mind with it. . . .

Man, thou hast been a citizen in this great state (the world): what difference does it make to thee whether for five years (or three)? For that which is comfortable to the laws is just for all. Where is the hardship then, if no tyrant nor yet an unjust judge sends thee away from the state, but nature who brought thee into it? The same as if a praetor who has employed an actor dismisses him from the stage.—"But I have not finished the five acts, but only three of them."—Thou sayest well, but in life the three acts are the whole drama; for what shall be a complete drama is determined by him who was once the cause of its composition, and now of its dissolution: but thou art the cause of neither. Depart then satisfied, for he also who releases thee is satisfied.

SECTION III

ROME

The British Empire, it used to be said, was acquired in a fit of absent-mindedness. To some extent the same paradox is true of Rome. A small state, aware of its destiny, yet continually beset with political and constitutional problems, a nation readily accepting the philosophy of the Hellenists, an aristocratic republic that had not yet fully relinquished its tribal nature changing into a great empire, Rome for a six-hundred-year period dominated the world. Rome is not associated with profundity of political thought, but it produced a number of political writers and ideas that have had lasting significance.

In the Roman Republic, political organization was complex and experimental. Essentially, it was based on the conflict between the patrician and the plebeian, the former possessing political privilege based on birth and tradition. It is true that the assembly of *curiae*, the earliest unit of the Roman community, had been virtually replaced by the assembly of the Centuries, which became the most responsible assembly of the whole people. Also, the plebeians elected from among their own members the Tribunes, concerned with protection of the group against the patricians.

But leadership was really in the hands of the patricians, and in the Senate, which was the institutional reflection of the group. They virtually chose the chief executive, and influenced the decisions made by the assembly. The resolutions passed by the plebeians meeting in council (*Concilium*) needed the approval of the *patres* (the heads of aristocratic families), as well as of the assembly of the Centuries.

A complicated political balance of power had been established. The patricians chose the executive, and constituted the large majority of the Senate. The plebeians had their assemblies and were protected by a group they had chosen. This protection became broader with the formulation of a code of law, the Twelve Tables, in 451 B.C.

The internal struggle continued, producing a number of compromises. Resolutions passed in the *Concilium* were to be binding on all, and were not subject to revision by the *patres*. There were to be two consuls, one of whom had to be a plebeian. The choice of the people could be limited discreetly, since election was from a list of names submitted by a presiding officer. Yet, this initial concession having been made to them, plebeians were gradually allowed to occupy the other magisterial positions (dictator, censor, praetor, etc.).

There was little of a democratic nature in this increase of power among the plebeians. Voting was still by groups, not by individuals. In the *Concilium*, voting by tribes was considerably more effective than the complicated method of voting in the assembly of Centuries, even though it meant overrepresentation of the rural element. The possibility even existed that the *Concilium* might become the means by which popular leaders could assert their will, and thereby end the aristocratic domination of Roman politics.

But the Senate reasserted itself when the defeats of the Punic Wars led to a reaction against the popular generals in favor of the old aristocratic families. The Senate, including many men having experience as magistrates, emerged as the dominant body in diplomatic and military policy, and increased its authority (*auctoritas*). It was largely responsible for the formulation of policy, even if magistrates executed it, and generals had some freedom of opinion in conducting military operations. It was often able to dominate the decisions of the Tribunes. Moreover, even if some plebeians entered the Senate, they would quickly become absorbed into the patrician group.

Polybius

This was the intricate political structure that existed when Polybius wrote his *Universal History*. Polybius, born about 200 B.C. in Arcadia, the son of a prominent statesman and an important statesman and soldier in his own right, had been taken as a prisoner from Greece to Rome, where he became a friend of Scipio. Polybius, the Greek-born practical politician, demonstrated the virtues of the Roman system, and explained its success.

This success was the result of a mixed constitution, drawing on aspects of the monarchical, aristocratic and democratic systems. Governmental structures could take more forms than Aristotle had suggested. Polybius explained not only the nature of these structures, but also the inevitability of their degeneration, unless precautions were taken. His theory of constitutional change and of the cyclical recurrence, progress and fall of all governmental systems, was the basis for his advocacy of a mixed constitution, which would produce stability.

The Roman system was one in which several groups possessed power, each connected with and limited by the power of the others. The consuls, the executive monarchical element, depended on the Senate and the whole people for support. The powerful Senate, the aristocratic element, had to take the masses into account. The Tribunes, the democratic element, carried out the decisions of the people. Each group could be checked by the others. But all combined against the common enemy, both internal and external; all co-operated to obtain execution of policy.

Polybius' theory may not be an exact representation of the true state of Roman politics. To speak of a democratic element was to use an inappropriate term. It underestimated both the formal and informal control by the Senate, and the essential aristocratic nature of the Roman system. But the theory of a mixed constitution, and of checks and balances in it, has had its measure of success. It is not surprising that the Founding Fathers of the United States should have been so familiar with this work of Polybius.

Cicero

The idea of a balanced, composite constitution reappeared in Cicero (106–43 B.C.), living during the final crisis of the Republic. He attacked the Gracchi, those two members of the senatorial class who had betrayed it to gain popular support, caused civil war, and disturbed senatorial authority founded on wise statesmanship. Cicero discussed the disadvantages of the three familiar constitutional systems. Monarchy meant that all but one lacked rights; aristocracy limited power to a few; democracy led to incompetent rule. He argued the desirability of a balanced system which would preserve stability and ensure fairness. At the same time, there were vague hints that a leader, perhaps Cicero himself, perhaps Pompey, capable of inspiring all, would be necessary.

Many of his writings have been lost, but in three works Cicero amplified the Stoic inheritance: *De Republica* (on the

Commonwealth), of which only a part remains, written in 51 B.C. and modeled on Plato's *Republic; De Legibus* (On Laws), of which only three books remain and in which Cicero himself appeared as "M," the leading speaker; and *De Officiis* (On Duties), dealing with moral duties.

Cicero was no original theorist, but he expressed clearly and concisely—as one would expect of a great lawyer and orator—the main Stoic thesis. He argued cogently the ideas of law as supreme reason, the existence of reason in both man and God, the possession of right reason in common, the equality of men, since all were capable of possessing virtue. He developed the idea of natural law to which all conformed and all understood through their reason, and which governed the universe. He emphasized the bonds that linked men together and distinguished them from animals, and defined a people as a group, associated by consent and a natural gregariousness. For him, government was a trust dedicated to the welfare of citizens.

If Cicero's analysis of and prescription for the Roman state was out of date, much of his political theory sounds refreshingly modern. If his life did not measure up to his philosophy, if he was sycophantic and ambitious, if he refused to condemn slavery outright, this was the limitation of the man, not of the philosophy.

Roman Law

The specific contributions of Rome to civilization were a magnificent system of roads, a competent administrative structure and bureaucracy, the arch, and law.

The Stoic ideal of a universal society was put into practice almost by accident: the political need of the Roman Empire for a uniform system of law. A remarkable group of lawyers devised textbooks, case books, and codes of law for both the practical use of officials and theoretical elegance. They founded the study of jurisprudence as a system of general rules by which actions could be classified clearly and with definitiveness. Their treatises—written by Gaius, Paulus, Ulpian—are systematic presentations of constitutional and political institutions.

The civil law (*jus civile*) of Rome was inappropriate for its empire. A system of law was needed to unify the disparate peoples and colonies it had conquered, to deal with the numerous aliens in its midst, to promote a common citizenship and, above all, as its commerce expanded, to help settle commercial cases in which foreign traders were involved.

The answer was found by the formulation of a law of nations (*jus gentium*), alongside the Stoic law of nature (*jus naturale*), the law common to all nations and the law common to all men. At first there seemed coincidence between the two, since the common practice of all nations was likely to be *the* natural law. But a more critical view was taken later. Even if every state might agree on a common practice, it might still be wrong, as the case of slavery showed, whereas the law of nature, an ideal, was intrinsically right.

Besides this attempt to formulate a universal law, the Roman lawyers were primarily interested in the distinction between public law—in essence constitutional law—and private law—that which concerned individuals—especially the laws of property relationships. Conservative in its disinclination to abolish any valid law, insular in its reluctance to adopt any foreign law, cautious in its delineation of *libertas*, the liberty of the citizen, traditional in the unwillingness of lawyers to digress very far from the path of their predecessors, Roman law is still a monumental achievement in its clarity and practicality. The Roman concept of a scientific jurisprudence has influenced the whole of Western thought.

There are three ideas in particular in the Roman system that are of interest: *auctoritas, imperium,* leading to sovereignty, and representation.

Auctoritas meant possession of some personal quality or social or family position—prestige or experience—that elicited obedience even where there was no legal compulsion or coercion. Where a group of such distinguished people was gathered, as in the Senate, their collective advice was invariably accepted—*auctoritas senatus*—by the magistrate. This was a realistic confession of Roman inequality, already admitted in another way: some citizens, who had exercised political power or military command, were endowed with *dignitas*. Those who had not, possessed only *libertas,* the power of doing what law allowed.

Imperium was originally the unlimited power possessed by the divinely approved early kings, who fulfilled a number of roles: lawgiver, priest, military commander, judge. Carried over into the Roman Republic, this power was limited in tenure, the community being able to delegate it. In times of crisis, the power was given to a dictator or *magister populi.* Later, the community was supposed to have transferred its right to command to the emperor, who was responsible to no one for his rule.

Here is essentially the conception of sovereignty, the right to make laws and demand obedience. Yet the very conservatism of Roman tradition led to a duality, the combination of absolutism and constitutionalism in one concept. The emperor was "a living law on earth," yet he was "bound by the laws." The community could transfer the sovereign power to those it had chosen to act on its behalf, in the same way as property rights could be transferred to others. In theory there might be limitations to governmental action in this idea of representation, since the community was the ultimate sovereign. But in fact, the whole of power had been transferred, and there was no sense of limitation by contract. This was to come later in political thought.

POLYBIUS
Universal History

The Mixed Constitution

. . . Most of those whose object it has been to instruct us methodically concerning such matters, distinguish three kinds of constitutions, which they call kingship, aristocracy, and democracy. Now we should, I think, be quite justified in asking them to enlighten us as to whether they represent these three to be the sole varieties or rather to be the best; for in either case my opinion is that they are wrong. For it is evident that we must regard as the best constitution a combination of all these three varieties, since we have had proof of this not only theoretically but by actual experience, Lycurgus having been the first to draw up a constitution—that of Sparta—on this principle. Nor on the other hand can we admit that these are the only three varieties; for we have witnessed monarchical and tyrannical governments, which while they differ very widely from kingship, yet bear a certain resemblance to it, this being the reason why monarchs in general falsely assume and use, as far as they can, the regal title. There have also been several oligarchical constitutions which seem to bear some likeness to aristocratic ones, though the divergence is, generally, as wide as possible. The same holds good about democracies. The truth of what I say is evident from the following considerations.

It is by no means every monarchy which we can call straight off a kingship, but only that which is voluntarily accepted by the subjects and where they are governed rather by an appeal to their reason than by fear and force. Nor again can we style every oligarchy an aristocracy, but only that where the government is in the hands of a selected body of the justest and wisest men. Similarly that is no true democracy in which the whole crowd of citizens is free to do whatever they wish or purpose, but when, in a community where it is traditional and customary to reverence the gods, to honour our parents, to respect our elders, and to obey the laws, the will of the greater number prevails, this is to be called a democracy. We should therefore assert that there are six kinds of governments, the three above mentioned which are in everyone's mouth and the three which are naturally allied to them, I mean monarchy, oligarchy, and mob-rule. . . .

Every variety of constitution which is simple and formed on one principle is precarious, as it is soon perverted into the corrupt form which is proper to it and naturally follows on it. . . . Each constitution has a vice engendered in it and inseparable from it. In kingship it is despotism, in aristocracy oligarchy, and in democracy the savage rule of violence; and it is impossible, as I said above, that each of these should not in course of time change into this vicious form. Lycurgus, then, foreseeing this, did not make his constitution simple and uniform, but united in it all the good and distinctive features of the best governments, so that none of the principles should grow unduly and be perverted into its allied evil, but that, the force of each being neutralized by that of the others, neither of them should prevail and outbalance another, but that the constitution should remain for long in a state of equilibrium like a well-trimmed boat, kingship being guarded from arrogance by the fear of the commons, who were given a sufficient share in the government, and the commons on the other hand not venturing to treat the kings with contempt from fear of the elders, who being selected from the best citizens would be sure all of them to be always on the side of justice; so that that part of the state which was weakest owing to its subservience to traditional custom, acquired power and weight by the support and influence of the elders. The consequence was that by drawing up his constitution thus he preserved liberty at Sparta for a longer period than is recorded elsewhere.

Lycurgus then, foreseeing, by a process of reasoning, whence and how events naturally happen, constructed his constitution untaught by adversity, but the Romans while they have arrived at the same final result as regards their form of government, have not reached it by any process of reasoning, but by the discipline of many struggles and troubles, and always choosing the best by the light of the experience gained in disaster have thus reached the same result as Lycurgus, that is to say, the best of all existing constitutions. . . .

. . . The three kinds of government that I spoke of above all shared in the control of the Roman state. And such fairness and propriety in all respects was shown in the use of these three elements for drawing up the constitution and in its subsequent administration that it was impossible even for a native to pronounce with certainty whether the whole system was aristocratic, democratic, or monarchical. This was indeed only natural. For if one fixed one's eyes on the power of the consuls, the constitution seemed completely monarchical and royal; if on that of the senate it seemed again to be aristocratic; and when one looked at the power of the masses, it seemed clearly to be a democracy. The parts of the state falling under the control of each element were and with a few modifications still are as follows.

The consuls, previous to leading out their legions, exercise authority in Rome over all public affairs, since all the other magistrates except the tribunes are under them and bound to obey them, and it is they who introduce embassies to the senate. Besides this it is they who consult the senate on matters of urgency, they who carry out in detail the provisions of its decrees. Again as concerns all affairs of state administered by the people it is their duty to take these under their charge, to summon assemblies, to introduce measures, and to preside over the execution of the popular decrees. As for preparation for war and the general conduct of operations in the field, here their power is almost uncontrolled; for they are empowered to make what demands they choose on the allies, to appoint military tribunes, to levy soldiers and select those who are fittest for service. They also have the right of inflicting, when on active service, punishment on anyone under their command; and they are authorized to spend any sum they decide upon from the public funds, being accompanied by a quaestor who faithfully executes their instructions. So that if one looks at this part of the administration alone, one may reasonably pronounce the constitution to be a pure monarchy or kingship. I may remark that any changes in these matters or in others of which I am about to speak that may be made in present or future times do not in any way affect the truth of the views I here state.

To pass to the senate. In the first place it has the control of the treasury, all revenue and expenditure being regulated by it. For with the exception of payments made to the consuls, the quaestors are not allowed to disburse for any particular object without a decree of the senate. And even the item of expenditure which is far heavier and more important than any other —the outlay every five years by the censors on public works, whether constructions or repairs—is under the control of the senate, which makes a grant to the censors for the purpose. Similarly crimes committed in Italy which require a public investigation, such as treason, conspiracy, poisoning, and assassination, are under the jurisdiction of the senate. Also if any private person or community in Italy is in need of arbitration or indeed claims damages or requires succour or protection, the senate attends to all such matters. Is also occupies itself with the dispatch of all embassies sent to countries outside of Italy for the purpose either of settling differences, or of offering friendly advice, or indeed of imposing demands, or of receiving submission, or of declaring war; and in like manner with respect to embassies arriving in Rome it decides what reception and what answer should be given to them. All these matters are in the hands of the senate, nor have the people anything whatever to do with them. So that again to one residing in Rome during the absence of the consuls the constitution appears to be entirely aristocratic; and this is the conviction of many Greek states and many of the kings, as the senate manages all business connected with them.

After this we are naturally inclined to ask what part in the constitution is left for the people, considering that the senate controls all the particular matters I mentioned, and, what is most important, manages all matters of revenue and expenditure, and considering that the consuls again have uncontrolled authority as regards armaments and operations in the field. But nevertheless there is a part and a very important part left for the people. For it is the people which alone has the right to confer honours and inflict punishment, the only bonds by which kingdoms and in a word human society in general are held together. For where the distinction between these is overlooked or is observed but ill applied, no affairs can be properly administered. How indeed is this possible when good and evil men are held in equal estimation? It is by the people, then, in many cases that offences punishable by a fine are tried when the accused have held the highest office; and they are the only court which may try on capital charges. As regards the latter they have a practice which is praiseworthy and should be mentioned. Their usage allows those on trial for their lives, when found guilty, liberty to depart openly, thus inflicting voluntary exile on themselves, if even only one of the tribes that pronounce the verdict has not yet voted. . . . Again it is the people who bestow office on the deserving, the noblest reward of virtue in a state; the people have the power of approving or rejecting laws, and what is most important of all, they deliberate on the question of war and peace. Further in the case of alliances, terms of peace, and treaties, it is the people who ratify all these or the reverse. Thus here again one might plausibly say that the people's share in the government is the greatest, and that the constitution is a democratic one.

Having stated how political power is distributed among the different parts of the state, I will now explain how each of the three parts is enabled, if they wish, to counteract or co-operate with the others. The consul, when he leaves with his army invested with the powers I mentioned, appears indeed to have absolute authority in all matters necessary for carrying out his purpose; but in fact he requires the support of the people and the senate, and is not able to bring his operations to a conclusion without them. For it is obvious that the legions require constant supplies, and without the consent of the senate, neither corn, clothing, nor pay can be provided; so that the commander's plans come to nothing, if the senate chooses to be deliberately negligent and obstructive. It also depends on the senate whether or not a general can carry out completely his conceptions and designs, since it has the right of either superseding him when his year's term of office has expired or of retaining him in command. Again it is in its power to celebrate with pomp and to magnify the successes of a general or on the other hand to obscure and belittle them. For the processions they call triumphs, in which the generals bring the actual spectacle of their achievements before the eyes of their fellow-citizens, cannot be properly organized and sometimes even cannot be held at all, unless the senate consents and provides the requisite funds. As for the people it is most indispensable for the consuls to conciliate them, however far away from home they may be; for, as I said, it is the people which ratifies or annuls terms of peace and treaties, and what is most important, on laying down office the consuls are obliged to account for their actions to the people. So that in no respect is it safe for the consuls to neglect keeping in favour with both the senate and the people.

The senate again, which possesses such great powers, is obliged in the first place to pay attention to the commons in public affairs and respect the wishes of the people, and it cannot carry out inquiries into the most grave and important offences against the state, punishable with death, and their correction, unless the *senatus consultum* is confirmed by the people. The same is the case in matters which directly affect the senate itself. For if anyone introduces a law meant to deprive the senate of some of its traditional authority, or to abolish the precedence and other distinctions of the senators or even to curtail them of their private fortunes, it is the people alone which has the power of passing or rejecting any such measure. And what is most important is that if a single one of the tribunes interposes, the senate is unable to decide finally about any matter, and cannot even meet and hold sittings; and there it is to be observed that the tribunes are always obliged to act as the people decree and to pay every attention to their wishes. Therefore for all these reasons the senate is afraid of the masses and must pay due attention to the popular will.

Similarly, again, the people must be submissive to the senate and respect its members both in public and in private. Through the whole of Italy a vast number of contracts, which it would not be easy to enumerate, are given out by the censors for the construction and repair of public buildings, and besides this there are many things which are farmed, such as navigable rivers, harbours, gardens, mines, lands, in fact everything that forms part of the Roman dominion. Now all these matters are undertaken by the people, and one may almost say that everyone is interested in these contracts and the work they involve. For certain people are the actual purchasers from the censors of the contracts, others are the partners of these first, others stand surety for them, others pledge their own fortunes to the state for this purpose. Now in all these matters the senate is supreme. It can grant extension of time; it can relieve the contractor if any accident occurs; and if the work proves to be absolutely impossible to carry out it can liberate him from his contract. There are, in fact, many ways in which the senate can either benefit or injure those who manage public property, as all these matters are referred to it. What is even more important is that the judges in most civil trials, whether public or private, are appointed from its members, where the action involves large interests. So that all citizens being at the mercy of the senate, and looking forward with alarm to the uncertainty of litigation, are very shy of obstructing or resisting its decisions. Similarly everyone is reluctant to oppose the projects of the consuls as all are generally and individually under their authority when in the field.

Such being the power that each part has of hampering the others or co-operating with them, their union is adequate to all emergencies, so that it is impossible to find a better political system than this. For whenever the menace of some common danger from abroad compels them to act in concord and support each other, so great does the strength of the state become, that nothing which is requisite can be neglected, as all are zealously competing in devising means of meeting the need of the hour, nor can any decision arrived at fail to be executed promptly, as all are co-operating both in public and in private to the accomplishment of the task they have set themselves; and consequently this peculiar form of constitution possesses an irresistible power of attaining every object upon which it is resolved. When again they are freed from external menace, and reap the harvest of good fortune and affluence which is the result of their success, and in the enjoyment of this prosperity are corrupted by flattery and idleness and wax insolent and overbearing, as indeed happens often enough, it is then especially that we see the state providing itself a remedy for the evil from which it suffers. For when one part having grown out of proportion to the others aims at supremacy and tends to become too predominant, it is evident that, as for the reasons above given none of the three is absolute, but the purpose of the one can be counterworked and thwarted by the others, none of them will excessively outgrow the others or treat them with contempt. All in fact remains *in statu quo,* on the one hand, because any aggressive impulse is sure to be checked and from the outset each estate stands in dread of being interfered with by the others. . . .

(Extracts have been taken from Book VI of the *Universal History.*)

CICERO

(Extracts have been taken from *On the Commonwealth,* the *Laws,* and *On Duties.*)

The Mixed State

PHILUS: . . . for all those who have the power of life and death over a people are tyrants, but they prefer to take the name which belongs to Jupiter the Most High and to call themselves kings. And when a group of men controls the commonwealth by virtue of their wealth, their birth, or any advantages they happen to possess, they form an oligarchy, but they call themselves leading citizens. And again, if the people have the supreme power and if all public business is carried on at their pleasure, we have what is called Liberty, but what in fact is license. Now when the citizens fear each other, when man fears man and class fears class, no one feels secure; and as a result, a contract, as we may call it, is made by the commons and those who have power. From this agreement there arises the composite form of state which Scipio was praising. Thus, neither nature nor deliberate choice but weakness is the mother of justice. For since a man must choose one of three possibilities—either to act unjustly without suffering injustice, or both to act unjustly and to suffer injustice, or neither to act unjustly nor to suffer injustice—the best choice is to act unjustly without suffering the consequences, if you can. The second choice is neither to act unjustly nor to suffer injustice. But the most wretched condition of all is an incessant warfare in which men both do and suffer injustice . . . monarchy is, in my judgment, far the best of the three simple types of state. But even monarchy will be excelled by the kind of state that is formed by an equal balancing and blending of the three unmixed types. For I hold it desirable, first, that there should be a dominant and royal element in the commonwealth; second, that some powers should be granted and assigned to the influence of the aristocracy; and third, that certain matters should be reserved to the people for decision and judgment. Such a government insures at once an element of equality, without which the people can hardly be free, and an element of strength. For, whereas the three forms of simple state readily lapse into the perverted forms opposed to their respective virtues—tyranny arising from monarchy, oligarchy from aristocracy, and turbulent ochlocracy from democracy—and whereas the types themselves are often discarded for new ones, this instability can hardly occur in the mixed and judiciously blended form of state, unless its leaders fall into exceptional degradation. There is, indeed, no cause for change when each individual is firmly set in his proper place, and when there is no inferior position into which he may rapidly decline. . . .

SCIPIO: I hold that the best constituted state is one which is formed by the due combination of the three simple types, monarchy, aristocracy, and democracy, and which does not arouse a wild and untamed spirit [in its citizens] by punishing. . . .

SCIPIO: Accordingly, the even balance of governmental elements in the composite form of state which we have been discussing appears to me to have been common to the Roman constitution and to these other governments. It will be found to consist in a quality the like of which can be discovered in no other state. The elements which I have been hitherto explaining were blended in the Roman monarchy, at Sparta, and at Carthage, but so blended that the balance between them was not maintained. For in a state in which one man holds perpetual power—and especially if his power be royal—his authority predominates; and such a commonwealth cannot fail to be a monarchy both in fact and name, even if there is also a senate, as was the case at Rome under the kings or at

Sparta under the laws of Lycurgus, or if the people themselves possess a certain degree of authority, as was the case in the Roman monarchy. Moreover, the monarchical form of government is particularly unstable because failure on the part of a single individual easily sweeps it headlong to utter ruin. In itself monarchy is not only unobjectionable but, if I were to give my approval to any simple type of state, is probably far preferable to either of the other two simple types, as long as it preserves its own proper nature. Still, it is inherent in the nature of monarchy that the permanent authority, the sense of justice, and the wisdom of a single individual control the safety, the political equality, and the peace of the citizens. A people who live under a monarchy are wholly deprived of many blessings. The first of these is liberty, which consists not in being subject to a lawful master but in being subject to no master at all. . . .

. . . In the very nature of things, it was inevitable that the people, once they were freed from the kings, should demand for themselves a greater degree of authority. This enlargement of their power they attained, after a brief interval of about sixteen years, in the consulate of Postumus Cominius and Spurius Cassius. There was perhaps no element of design in this change, but there is a principle of growth inherent in public affairs which often overrides design. Unless there is in the state such an equal distribution of legal rights, functions, and duties that the magistrates possess an adequate power, the council of the chief men an adequate influence, and the people an adequate measure of liberty, the balance of the commonwealth cannot be preserved unchanged. . . .

(The above extracts are from Book I and Book II of *On the Commonwealth*.)

Nature of Law

M. Law is the highest reason, implanted in Nature, which commands what ought to be done and forbids the opposite. This reason, when firmly fixed and fully developed in the human mind, is Law. And so the most learned men believe that Law is intelligence, whose natural function it is to command right conduct and forbid wrongdoing. They think that this quality has derived its name in Greek from the idea of granting to every man his own, and in our language. I believe it has been named from the idea of choosing. For as they have attributed the idea of fairness to the word law, so we have given it that of selection, though both ideas properly belong to Law. Now if this is correct, as I think it to be in general, then the origin of Justice is to be found in Law, for Law is a natural force; it is the mind and reason of the intelligent man, the standard by which Justice and Injustice are measured.

. . . Law is not a product of human thought, nor is it any enactment of peoples, but something eternal which rules the whole universe by its wisdom in command and prohibition. Law is the primal and ultimate mind of God, whose reason directs all things either by compulsion or restraint. Wherefore that Law which the gods have given to the human race has been justly praised; for it is the reason and mind of a wise lawgiver applied to command and prohibition. . . .

M. . . . those rules which, in varying forms and for the need of the moment, have been formulated for the guidance of nations, bear the title of laws rather by favour than because they are really such. For every law which really deserves that name is truly praiseworthy, as they prove by approximately the following arguments. It is agreed, of course, that laws were invented for the safety of citizens, the preservation of States, and the tranquillity and happiness of human life, and that those who first put statutes of this kind in force convinced their people that it was their intention to write down and put into effect such rules as, once accepted and adopted, would make possible for them an honourable and happy life; and when such rules were drawn up and put in force, it is clear that men called them "laws." From this point of view it can be readily understood that those who formulated wicked and unjust statutes for nations, thereby breaking their promises and agreements, put into effect anything but "laws." It may thus be clear that in the very definition of the term "law" there inheres the idea and principle of choosing what is just and true.

What of the many deadly, the many pestilential statutes which nations put in force? These no more deserve to be called laws than the rules a band of robbers might pass in their assembly. For if ignorant and unskilful men have prescribed deadly poisons instead of healing drugs, these cannot possibly be called physicians' prescriptions; neither in a nation can a statute of any sort be called a law, even though the nation, in spite of its being a ruinous regulation, has accepted it. Therefore Law is the distinction between things just and unjust, made in agreement with that primal and most ancient of all things, Nature; and in conformity to Nature's standard are framed human laws punishing the wicked and defending the good.

(The above extracts are from the *Laws*, Book I, v and vi, and II, iv and v.)

Right Reason and Nature

. . . We ought to follow Nature as our guide, to contribute to the general good by an interchange of acts of kindness, by giving and receiving, and thus by our skill, our industry and our talents to cement human society more closely together, man to man.

. . . Reason and speech constitute the most comprehensive bond that unites together men as men and all to all; and under it the common right to all things that Nature has produced for the common use of man is to be maintained.

And it is no mean manifestation of Nature and Reason that man is the only animal that has a feeling for order, for propriety, for moderation in word and deed. And so no other animal has a sense of beauty, loveliness, harmony in the visible world; and Nature and Reason, extending the analogy of this from the world of sense to the world of spirit, find that beauty, consistency, order are far more to be maintained in thought and deed.

(These extracts are taken from *On Duties*, I, iv, vii, and xvi.)

. . . That animal which we call man, endowed with foresight and quick intelligence, complex, keen, possessing memory, full of reason and prudence, has been given a certain distinguished status by the supreme God who created him; for he is the only one among so many different kinds and varieties of living beings who has a share in reason and thought, while all the rest are deprived of it. But what is more divine, I will not say in man only, but in all heaven and earth, than reason? And reason, when it is full grown and perfected, is rightly called wisdom. Therefore, since there is nothing better than reason, and since it exists both in man and God, the first common possession of man and God is reason. But those who have reason in common must also have right reason in common. And since right reason is Law, we must believe that men have Law also in common with the gods. Further, those who share Law must also share Justice; and so are to be regarded as members of the same commonwealth, a commonwealth of which both gods and men are members.

(This extract is from *Laws*, Book I, vii.)

. . . There is in fact a true law—namely, right reason—which is in accordance with nature, applies to all men, and is unchangeable and eternal. By its commands this law summons men to the performance of their duties; by its prohibitions it restrains them from doing wrong. Its commands and prohibitions always influence good men, but are without effect upon the bad. To invalidate this law by human legislation is never morally right, nor is it permissible ever to restrict its operation, and to annul it wholly is impossible. Neither the senate nor the people can absolve us from our obligation to obey this law, and it requires no Sextus Aelius to expound and interpret it. It will not lay down one rule at Rome and another at Athens, nor will it be one rule today and another tomorrow. But there will be one law, eternal and unchangeable, binding at all times upon all peoples; and there will be, as it were, the common master and ruler of men, namely God, who is the author of this law, its interpreter, and its sponsor. The man who will not obey it will abandon his better self, and, in denying the true nature of a man, will thereby suffer the severest of penalties, though he has escaped all the other consequences which men call punishment.

(This extract is from *On the Commonwealth*, Book III, xxii.)

Justice

. . . If justice were natural, then nature would have laid down our laws; all people would be subject to the same laws; and the same people would not be subject to different laws at different times. Now I put the question to you: If it be the duty of a just man and a good citizen to obey the laws, what laws should he obey? Shall he obey any laws that happen to prevail? But surely rectitude does not admit of inconsistency, and nature does not permit different standards of conduct. Laws, therefore, are obeyed because of the penalties they may inflict and not because of our sense of justice. Consequently, the law has no sanction in nature. It follows, then, that men are not just by nature. Or do they mean that, while there is diversity in human legislation, good men follow true justice rather than that which is merely thought to be just? For rendering unto everything its deserts is said to be the mark of a good and just man.

. . . *If a man wishes to act in accordance with justice, and yet is ignorant of the divine law, he will honor the enactments of his own people as if they were the true law, although they are in general the product, not of justice, but of self-interest. Why indeed have diverse and unlike codes of law been estab-*

*lished among all peoples? Is it not because each people has
enacted for itself such provisions as it thought to be useful in
its own conditions of life? But how wide is the divergence
between justice and utility may be learned from the case of
the Roman people itself. By using the Fetial College in their
declarations of war, they gave acts of aggression the color of
law. Thus, they constantly coveted and seized the possessions
of others and so made themselves the masters of the whole
world.*

Lactantius: *inst.* 6. 9. 2–4.

*Therefore, since the arguments of the philosophers were
weak, Carneades made bold to refute them because he knew
that they could be refuted. The heads of his discourse were as
follows. Men have established laws to serve their own advantages. These laws, of course, were different to suit the different
characters of peoples, and even in the same people they were
often modified to accord with changing conditions. On the
other hand, there is no natural law. All human beings as well
as all other living creatures are led by nature to consult their
own self-interest. Hence, either there is no such thing as justice, or, if there is, it is the height of folly, since a person
would do injury to himself by consulting the interests of others. And Carneades brought forward the following proof. All
peoples who built up empires—including the Romans themselves, who became masters of the world—would be obliged
to return to huts and live in wretched poverty if they wished
to be just, that is, if they should restore all that is not their
own.*

Lactantius: *inst.* 5. 16. 2–4.

(These extracts are from *On the Commonwealth*, Book III,
xi and xii.)

Inasmuch as the whole human race is bound together in
unity, it follows that knowledge of the principles of right
living is what makes men better.

. . . We are so constituted by Nature as to share the sense
of Justice with one another and to pass it on to all men. And
in this whole discussion I want it understood that what I shall
call Nature is [that which is implanted in us by Nature]; that,
however, the corruption caused by bad habits is so great that
the sparks of fire, so to speak, which Nature has kindled in us
are extinguished by this corruption, and the vices which are
their opposites spring up and are established. But if the judgments of men were in agreement with Nature, so that, as
Terence says, they considered "nothing alien to them which
concerns mankind," then Justice would be equally observed

by all. For those creatures who have received the gift of reason from Nature have also received right reason, and therefore they have also received the gift of Law, which is right reason applied to command and prohibition. And if they have received Law, they have received Justice also. Now all men have received reason; therefore all men have received Justice. . . . For Justice is one; it binds all human society, and is based on one Law, which is right reason applied to command the prohibition. Whoever knows not this Law, whether it has been recorded in writing anywhere or not, is without Justice.

But if Justice is conformity to written laws and national customs, and if, as the same persons claim, everything is to be tested by the standard of utility, then anyone who thinks it will be profitable to him will, if he is able, disregard and violate the laws. It follows that Justice does not exist at all, if it does not exist in Nature, and if that form of it which is based on utility can be overthrown by that very utility itself. And if Nature is not to be considered the foundation of Justice, that will mean the destruction [of the virtues on which human society depends]. For where then will there be a place for generosity, or love of country, or loyalty, or the inclination to be of service to others or to show gratitude for favours received? For these virtues originate in our natural inclination to love our fellowmen, and this is the foundation of Justice. Otherwise not merely consideration for men but also rites and pious observances in honour of the gods are done away with; for I think that these ought to be maintained, not through fear, but on account of the close relationship which exists between man and God. But if the principles of Justice were founded on the decrees of peoples, the edicts of princes, or the decisions of judges, then Justice would sanction robbery and adultery and forgery of wills, in case these acts were approved by the votes or decrees of the populace. But if so great a power belongs to the decisions and decrees of fools that the laws of Nature can be changed by their votes, then why do they not ordain that what is bad and baneful shall be considered good and salutary? Or, if a law can make Justice out of Injustice, can it not also make good out of bad? But in fact we can perceive the difference between good laws and bad by referring them to no other standard than Nature; indeed, it is not merely Justice and Injustice which are distinguished by Nature, but also and without exception things which are honourable and dishonourable. For since an intelligence common to us all makes things known to us and formulates them in our minds, honourable actions are ascribed by us to virtue, and dishonourable actions to vice; and only a madman would conclude that these judgments are matters of opinion, and not fixed by Nature.

(These extracts are from *Laws*, I, xii, xv and xvi.)

SECTION IV

EARLY CHRISTIANITY

The civilization of the Western world rests on its Greco-Roman-Judeo-Christian inheritance. From the Greeks and Romans came political and legal concepts, from the latter two, religious and ethical values.

The Jewish legacy is monotheism, universal in its application. The religion brought, largely through the teachings of its prophets, the formulation of the Law—of divine origin and binding on the people—and of the Talmud, the analysis by learned rabbis of the laws and customs of the tribes, the revelation of God to the people and a covenant made with them. The universalism of the creed implied the possibility of universal brotherhood.

The prophets were the conscience of the people, thundering against injustice and advocating a rudimentary social welfare system for the less fortunate. Wealth, though not necessarily limited, was to be devoted to public welfare. There was concern in this Hebraic tradition for business regulation, health and dietary laws, and the observance of the Sabbath, but there was little specifically on political problems.

Christianity adopted the concepts of monotheism, ethics and moral law; it was no more interested in political problems. It implied a separation that had not existed in the Greek world between religious and political values. The aim of life had been altered: instead of self-development, it was now dedication to religious principle, a concern with the importance of the other world, with salvation, with the soul.

Though it employed political terminology, early Christianity was, from the political point of view, negative in its rejection or renunciation of temporal happiness and basically pessimistic in its emphasis on the corrupt nature of man. It stressed humility, self-denial, and the relative unimportance of earthly life. Emphasizing the desirability of the simple life, it minimized the importance of social position or economic wealth.

In early Christianity there was no sustained discussion of political questions, only a relatively few number of references. From these it is not easy to draw precise conclusions on a desirable course of political action in any set of concrete circumstances. But the general emphasis on obedience to political authority, and refusal to countenance resistance to it, is clear.

Yet if early Christianity was conservative, even reactionary, in its political quietism, and in its acceptance of social and economic inequality, its ethical message was radical. All individuals were important, no matter what their economic status or national origin. There was spiritual equality and the brotherhood of all, united in God. If there was no concern with social reform, there was emphasis on the need for all to prepare for the Kingdom of God.

Paul, the founder of the Church, recognized the essential equality of all men in the sight of God. But he still defended or refused to attack the system of slavery, arguing that each was to remain in the occupation to which he had been born. He tended to regard the state and political institutions as ordained by God, the state preserving order so that the Christian life might be realized. Legal obligations had to be met; indirectly, this was obedience to God, for the ruler was the servant of God.

A community developed, emphasizing the role of Jesus as the Messiah, and the sacraments, baptism and communion, as the way to enter into the fellowship. Yet even the idea of spiritual equality had already been tempered by the belief that all were not suitable for redemption. Grace was bestowed by divine love. Whether man was thus predestined remained for fuller development later.

St. Augustine

The introduction of Christianity as a foreign, minority religion into Rome inevitably brought persecution of the Church. Christianity could not ally itself with the state in the role of dependent in a period of Roman emperor-worship. But when Rome needed a world-religion to sustain itself, Christianity was prepared to underwrite it. After Constantine recognized Christianity in 313 as one of the public worships, the religion spread throughout the empire. The latent tension between political and spiritual leaders, however, was to prevent any complete control by either group, and ultimately to lead to both political and religious freedom.

Doctrinal disputes were common and fierce, especially in North Africa, from the fiery Carthaginian Tertullian, of the 2nd and 3rd centuries, the dogmatic, schismatic, the militant attacker of paganism and of Rome, to the Donatists, African nationalists protesting against the clergy who had allied themselves with secular rulers against the best interests of the Church.

Out of these African polemical disputations came St. Augustine (354–430). Converted to Christianity in his twenties, Augustine became the most important spokesman for orthodoxy, and the most influential writer of Christianity until Aquinas. Augustine, in a series of tracts, fought a war on two fronts, one against the pagans who argued that Christianity was responsible for the decline of Rome, and an even fiercer one against the sectarians, especially the Donatists and the Pelagians.

The City of God, written between 413 and 427, is not a systematic treatise, but really a vast polemic defending Christianity, and discussing problems of creation, time and history, miracles, sacrifices and nature, as well as the relations of political institutions to Christian principles. Augustine propounded the first great theory of time and of the historical process, rejecting the Greek concept of cyclical recurrence or inevitable degeneration. He argued, "Christ is the straight way . . . turn away from the unreal and futile cycles of the godless." History was moving to the gradual realization of the City of God.

Augustine's contribution to political theory was his analysis of the two cities, the counterpart of the biblical Jerusalem and Babylon. The city of God was concerned with belief, with obedience, with love of God to the point of contempt of self. The earthly city was a manifestation of pride, sin and lust, of self-love to the point of contempt of God. Self-love was the source of evil in man; man's original sin had disrupted the correct order of love.

All men sought happiness, but this was found by subordination to the divine order and by seeking eternal peace, not in earthly society. "All men, so long as they are mortal, must of necessity be miserable." The city of the world was not rooted in justice, as Cicero had argued, but was bound together by common love or collective interest. It had its place in the universal order. The evils of the world could be explained in

God's larger scheme of things. Man therefore accepted a double allegiance to both cities.

Civil society and government had the purpose of preserving order, protecting property and preventing social strife. Social institutions, slavery, coercion, were both a punishment for man's sin and a remedy for it. Augustine, therefore, approved of temporal rule. It was not wrong in itself, but valuable as a preparation for the true end of man. But he differed from previous Christian theorists in his specific exclusion of justice as essential to the existence of a state. God chose the rulers that man deserved; even Nero could be justified.

The peace established on earth was a good, even if it was not the highest good. Obedience was necessary unless the state tried to enforce a false religion. But it was with the heavenly city that Augustine was really concerned. It is not clear exactly what the *Civitas Dei* is. It may be a real institution, or the spiritual unity of the elect, but certainly it was represented on earth by the Church. The City of God was the most perfect society the world would know, but meanwhile the Church, as the body preparing for the eternal life, could wield strong powers. The extent of these powers was the problem that preoccupied the Church for the next thousand years.

The New Testament

Equality and Freedom

For as many as are of the works of the law, are under the curse: for it is written, Cursed is every one that continueth not in all things which are written in the book of the law to do them.

But that no man is justified by the law in the sight of God, it is evident: for, The just shall live by faith.

And the law is not of faith: but, The man that doeth them shall live in them.

Christ hath redeemed us from the curse of the law, being made a curse for us: for it is written, Cursed is every one that hangeth on a tree:

There is neither Jew nor Greek, there is neither bond nor free, there is neither male nor female: for ye are all one in Christ Jesus.

Galatians, 3

For, brethren, ye have been called unto liberty; only use not liberty for an occasion to the flesh, but by love serve one another.

For all the law is fulfilled in one word, even in this, Thou shalt love thy neighbour as thyself.

Galatians, 5

Art thou called being a servant? care not for it: but if thou mayest be made free, use it rather.

I *Corinthians*, 7

Duties and Obligations

Let every soul be subject unto the highest powers. For there is no power but of God: the powers that be are ordained of God.

Whosoever therefore resisteth the power, resisteth the ordinance of God: and they that resist shall receive to themselves damnation.

For rulers are not a terror to good works, but to the evil. Wilt thou then not be afraid of the power? do that which is good, and thou shalt have praise of the same:

For he is the minister of God to thee for good. But if thou do that which is evil, be afraid; for he beareth not the sword in vain: for he is the minister of God, a revenger to execute wrath upon him that doeth evil.

Wherefore ye must needs be subject, not only for wrath, but also for conscience sake.

For, for this cause pay ye tribute also: for they are God's ministers attending continually upon this very thing.

Render therefore to all their dues: tribute to whom tribute is due, custom to whom custom; fear to whom fear; honour to whom honour.

Romans, 13

I exhort therefore, that, first of all, supplications, prayers, intercessions, and giving thanks, be made for all men;

For kings, and for all that are in authority; that we may lead a quiet and peaceful life in all godliness and honesty.

For this is good and acceptable in the sight of God our Saviour;

I *Timothy*, 2

Dearly beloved, I beseech you as strangers and pilgrims, abstain from fleshly lusts, which war against the soul;

Having your conversation honest among the Gentiles: that, whereas they speak against you as evil doers, they may by your good works, which they shall behold, glorify God in the day of visitation.

Submit yourselves to every ordinance of man for the Lord's sake: whether it be to the king, as supreme;

Or unto governors, as unto them that are sent by him for

the punishment of evil doers, and for the praise of them that do well.

For so is the will of God, that with well doing ye may put to silence the ignorance of foolish men:

As free, and not using your liberty for a cloke of maliciousness, but as the servants of God.

Honour all men. Love the brotherhood. Fear God. Honour the king.

Servants, be subject to your masters with all fear; not only to the good and gentle, but also to the froward.

I Peter, 2

Ye have heard that it hath been said, An eye for an eye, and a tooth for a tooth:

But I say unto you, That ye resist not evil: but whosoever shall smite thee on the right cheek, turn to him the other also.

And if any man will sue thee at the law, and take away thy coat, let him have thy cloke also.

And whosoever shall compel thee to go a mile, go with him twain.

Matthew, 5

Shew me the tribute money. And they brought unto him a penny.

And he saith unto them, Whose is this image and superscription?

They say unto him, Caesar's. Then saith he unto them, Render therefore unto Caesar the things which are Caesar's, and unto God the things that are God's.

Matthew, 22

Let as many servants as are under the yoke count their own masters worthy of all honour, that the name of God and his doctrine be not blasphemed.

And they that have believing masters, let them not despise them, because they are brethren; but rather do them service, because they are faithful and beloved, partakers of the benefit. These things teach and exort.

If any man teach otherwise, and consent not to wholesome words, even the words of our Lord Jesus Christ, and to the doctrine which is according to godliness,

He is proud, knowing nothing, but doting about questions and strifes and words, whereof cometh envy, strife railings, evil surmisings,

Perverse disputings of men of corrupt minds, and destitute of the truth, supposing that gain is godliness: from such withdraw thyself.

But godliness with contentment is great gain.

For we brought nothing into this world, and it is certain we can carry nothing out.

And having food and raiment, let us be therewith content.

But they that will be rich, fall into temptation, and a snare, and into many foolish and hurtful lusts, which drown men in destruction and perdition.

For the love of money is the root of all evil; which while some coveted after, they have erred from the faith, and pierced themselves through with many sorrows.

But thou, O man of God, flee these things; and follow after righteousness, godliness, faith, love, patience, meekness.

Fight the good fight of faith, lay hold on eternal life, whereunto thou art also called, and hast professed a good profession before many witnesses.

I give thee charge in the sight of God, who quickeneth all things, and before Christ Jesus, who before Pontius Pilate witnessed a good confession;

That thou keep this commandment without spot, unrebukeable, until the appearing of our Lord Jesus Christ:

Which in his time he shall shew, who is the blessed and only Potentate, the King of kings, and Lord of lords;

Who only hath immortality, dwelling in the light which no man hath seen, nor can see: to whom be honour and power everlasting. Amen.

Charge them that are rich in this world, that they be not highminded, nor trust in uncertain riches, but in the living God, who giveth us richly all things to enjoy;

I Timothy, 6

SAINT AUGUSTINE
The City of God

The Ordered Universe

Therefore God supreme and true, with His Word and Holy Spirit (which three are one), one God omnipotent, creator and maker of every soul and of every body; by whose gift all are happy who are happy through verity and not through vanity; who made man a rational animal consisting of soul and body, who, when he sinned, neither permitted him to go unpunished, nor left him without mercy; who has given to the good and to the evil, being in common with stones, vegetable life in common with trees, sensuous life in common with brutes, intellectual life in common with angels alone; from whom is every mode, every species, every order; from whom are measure, number, weight; from whom is everything which has an existence in nature, of whatever kind it be, and of whatever value; from whom are the seeds of forms and the forms of seeds, and the motion of seeds and of forms; who gave also to flesh its origin, beauty, health, reproductive fecundity, disposition of members, and the salutary concord of its parts; who also to the irrational soul has given memory, sense, appetite, but to the rational soul, in addition to these, has given intelligence and will; who has not left, not to speak of heaven and earth, angels and men, but not even the entrails of the smallest and most contemptible animal, or the feather of a bird, or the little flower of a plant, or the leaf of a tree, without an harmony, and, as it were, a mutual peace among all its parts;—that God can never be believed to have left the kingdoms of men, their dominations and servitudes, outside of the laws of His providence.

The peace of the body then consists in the duly proportioned arrangement of its parts. The peace of the irrational soul is the harmonious repose of the appetites, and that of the rational soul the harmony of knowledge and action. The peace of body and soul is the well-ordered and harmonious life and health of the living creature. Peace between man and God is the well-ordered obedience of faith to eternal law. Peace between man and man is well-ordered concord. Domestic peace is the well-ordered concord between those of the family who rule and those who obey. Civil peace is a similar concord among the citizens. The peace of the celestial city is the perfectly ordered and harmonious enjoyment of God, and of one another in God. The peace of all things is the tranquillity of order. Order is the distribution which allots things equal and unequal, each to its own place. And hence, though the miserable, in so far as they are such, do certainly not enjoy peace, but are severed from that tranquillity of order in which there is no disturbance, nevertheless, inasmuch as they are deservedly and justly miserable, they are by their very misery connected with order. They are not, indeed conjoined with the blessed, but they are disjoined from them by the law of order. And though they are disquieted, their circumstances are notwithstanding adjusted to them, and consequently they have some tranquillity of order, and therefore some peace. They would, however, be more wretched if they had not that peace which arises from being in harmony with the natural order of things.

(These extracts are from Book v, 11, and Book xix, 13.)

The Love of Self and the Love of God

Pride, too, is not the fault of him who delegates power, not of power itself, but of the soul that is inordinately enamoured of its own power, and despises the more just dominion of a higher authority. Consequently he who inordinately loves the good which any nature possesses, even though he obtain it, himself becomes evil in the good, and wretched because deprived of a greater good.

. . . For if we were beasts, we should love the fleshly and sensual life, and this would be our sufficient good; and when it was well with us in respect of it, we should seek nothing beyond. But we are men, created in the image of our Creator, whose eternity is true, and whose truth is eternal, whose love is eternal and true, and who Himself is the eternal, true, and adorable Trinity, without confusion, without separation; and, therefore, while, as we run over all the works which He has established, we may detect, as it were, His footprints, now more and now less distinct even in those things that are beneath us, since they could not so much as exist, or be bodied forth in any shape, or follow and observe any law, had they not been made by Him who supremely is, and is supremely good and supremely wise; yet in ourselves beholding His image, let us, like that younger son of the gospel, come to ourselves, and arise and return to Him from whom by our sin we had departed. There our being will have no death, our knowledge no error, our love no mishap.

. . . When, therefore, man lives according to man, not according to God, he is like the devil. Because not even an angel might live according to an angel, but only according to God, if he was to abide in the truth, and speak God's truth and not his own lie. When, then, a man lives according to the truth, he lives not according to himself, but according to God; for He was God who said, "I am the truth." When, therefore, man lives according to himself—that is, according to man, not according to God—assuredly he lives according to a lie; not that man himself is a lie, for God is his author and creator, who is certainly not the author and creator of a lie, but because man was made upright, that he might not live according to himself, but according to Him that made him—in other words, that he might do His will and not his own; and not to live as he was made to live, that is a lie. . . . All sin is a lie. For no sin is committed save by that desire or will by which we desire that it be well with us, and shrink from it being ill with us. That, therefore, is a lie which we do in order that it may be well with us, but which makes us more miser-ble than we were. And why is this, but because the source of man's happiness lies only in God, whom he abandons when he sins, and not in himself, by living according to whom he sins?

In enunciating this proposition of ours, then, that because some live according to the flesh and others according to the spirit there have arisen two diverse and conflicting cities, we might equally well have said, "because some live according to man, others according to God." For Paul says very plainly to the Corinthians, "For whereas there is among you envying and strife, are ye not carnal, and walk according to man?" So that to walk according to man and to be carnal are the same; or by *flesh,* that is, by a part of man, man is meant. . . .

(These extracts are from Book XII, 8, Book IX, 28, Book XIV, 4.)

The Two Cities

. . . And thus it has come to pass, that though there are very many and great nations all over the earth, whose rites and customs, speech, arms, and dress, are distinguished by marked differences, yet there are no more than two kinds of human society, which we may justly call two cities, according to the language of our Scriptures. The one consists of those who wish to live after the flesh, the other of those who wish to live after the spirit; and when they severally achieve what they wish, they live in peace, each after their kind.

. . . The city of God has in her communion, and bound to her by the sacraments, some who shall not eternally dwell in the lot of the saints. Of these, some are not now recognised; others declare themselves, and do not hesitate to make common cause with our enemies in murmuring against God, whose sacramental badge they wear. These men you may to-day see thronging the churches with us, to-morrow crowding the theatres with the godless. But we have the less reason to despair of the reclamation even of such persons, if among our most declared enemies there are now some, unknown to themselves, who are destined to become our friends. In truth, these two cities are entangled together in this world, and intermixed until the last judgment effect their separation.

. . . The two cities, the heavenly and the earthly, which are mingled together from the beginning down to the end. Of these, the earthly one has made to herself of whom she would, either from any other quarter, or even from among men, false gods whom she might serve by sacrifice; but she which is heavenly, and is a pilgrim on the earth, does not make false

gods, but is herself made by the true God, of whom she
herself must be the true sacrifice. Yet both alike either enjoy
temporal good things, or are afflicted with temporal evils, but
with diverse faiths, diverse hope, and diverse love, until they
must be separated by the last judgment, and each must receive
her own end, of which there is no end.

. . . Two cities have been formed by two loves: the earthly
by the love of self, even to the contempt of God; the heavenly
by the love of God, even to the contempt of self. The former,
in a word, glories in itself, the latter in the Lord. For the one
seeks glory from men; but the greatest glory of the other is
God, the witness of conscience. The one lifts up its head in its
own glory; the other says to its God, "Thou art my glory, and
the lifter up of mine head." In the one, the princes and the
nations it subdues are ruled by the love of ruling; in the other
the princes and the subjects serve one another in love, the
latter obeying, while the former take thought for all. The one
delights in its own strength, represented in the persons of its
rulers; the other says to its God, "I will love Thee, O Lord,
my strength." And therefore the wise men of the one city,
living according to man, have sought for profit to their own
bodies or souls, or both, and those who have known God
"glorified Him not as God, neither were thankful, but became
vain in their imaginations, and their foolish heart was dark-
ened; professing themselves to be wise"—that is, glorying in
their own wisdom, and being possessed by pride—"they became fools, and changed the glory of the incorruptible God
into an image made like to corruptible man, and to birds, and
four-footed beasts, and creeping things." For they were either
leaders or followers of the people in adoring images, "and
worshipped and served the creature more than the Creator,
who is blessed for ever." But in the other city there is no
human wisdom, but only godliness, which offers due worship
to the true God, and looks for its reward in the society of the
saints, of holy angels as well as holy men, "that God may be
all in all."

. . . But who can enumerate all the great grievances with
which human society abounds in the misery of this mortal
state? If home, the natural refuge from the ills of life, is
itself not safe, what shall we say of the city, which, as it is
larger, is so much the more filled with lawsuits civil and
criminal, and is never free from the fear, if sometimes from
the actual outbreak, of disturbing and bloody insurrections
and civil wars? . . .

. . . But the earthly city, which shall not be everlasting (for
it will no longer be a city when it has been committed to the

extreme penalty), has its good in this world, and rejoices in it with such joy as such things can afford. But as this is not a good which can discharge its devotees of all distresses, this city is often divided against itself by litigations, wars, quarrels, and such victories as are either life-destroying or short-lived. For each part of it that arms against another part of it seeks to triumph over the nations though itself in bondage to vice. If when it has conquered, it is inflated with pride, its victory is life-destroying; but if it turns its thoughts upon the common casualties of our mortal condition, and is rather anxious concerning the disasters that may befall it than elated with the successes already achieved, this victory, though of a higher kind, is still only short-lived; for it cannot abidingly rule over those whom it has victoriously subjugated. But the things which this city desires cannot justly be said to be evil, for it is itself, in its own kind, better than all other human good. For it desires earthly peace for the sake of enjoying earthly goods, and it makes war in order to attain to this peace; since, if it has conquered, and there remains no one to resist it, it enjoys a peace which it had not while there were opposing parties who contested for the enjoyment of those things which were too small to satisfy both. This peace is purchased by toilsome wars; it is obtained by what they style a glorious victory. Now, when victory remains with the party which had the juster cause, who hesitates to congratulate the victor, and style it a desirable peace? These things, then, are good things, and without doubt the gifts of God. But if they neglect the better things of the heavenly city, which are secured by eternal victory and peace never-ending, and so inordinately covet these present good things that they believe them to be the only desirable things, or love them better than those things which are believed to be better—if this be so, then it is necessary that misery follow and ever increase.

. . . The imperial city has endeavoured to impose on subject nations not only her yoke, but her language, as a bond of peace, so that interpreters, far from being scarce, are numberless. This is true; but how many great wars, how much slaughter and bloodshed, have provided this unity! And though these are past, the end of these miseries has not yet come. For though there have never been wanting, nor are yet wanting, hostile nations beyond the empire, against whom wars have been and are waged, yet, supposing there were no such nations, the very extent of the empire itself has produced wars of a more obnoxious description—social and civil wars —and with these the whole race has been agitated, either by the actual conflict or the fear of a renewed outbreak. . . .

. . . But as the word peace is employed in connection with things in this world in which certainly life eternal has no place, we have preferred to call the end or supreme good of this city life eternal rather than peace. But, on the other hand, as those who are not familiar with Scripture may suppose that the life of the wicked is eternal life, either because of the immortality of the soul, which some of the philosophers even have recognised, or because of the endless punishment of the wicked, which forms a part of our faith, and which seems impossible unless the wicked live for ever, it may therefore be advisable, in order that every one may readily understand what we mean, to say that the end or supreme good of this city is either peace in eternal life, or eternal life in peace. For peace is a good so great, that even in this earthly and mortal life there is no word we hear with such pleasure, nothing we desire with such zest, or find to be more thoroughly gratifying. . . .

The whole use, then, of things temporal has a reference to this result of earthly peace in the earthly community, while in the city of God it is connected with eternal peace. And therefore, if we were irrational animals, we should desire nothing beyond the proper arrangement of the parts of the body and the satisfaction of the appetites—nothing, therefore, but bodily comfort and abundance of pleasures, that the peace of the body might contribute to the peace of the soul. For if bodily peace be awanting, a bar is put to the peace even of the irrational soul, since it cannot obtain the gratification of its appetites. And these two together help out the mutual peace of soul and body, the peace of harmonious life and health. . . .

. . . But, as man has a rational soul, he subordinates all this which he has in common with the beasts to the peace of his rational soul, that his intellect may have free play and may regulate his actions, and that he may thus enjoy the well-ordered harmony of knowledge and action which constitutes, as we have said, the peace of the rational soul. And for this purpose he must desire to be neither molested by pain, nor disturbed by desire, nor extinguished by death, that he may arrive at some useful knowledge by which he may regulate his life and manners. But, owing to the liability of the human mind to fall into mistakes, this very pursuit of knowledge may be a snare to him unless he has a divine Master, whom he may obey without misgiving, and who may at the same time give him such help as to preserve his own freedom. And because, so long as he is in this mortal body, he is a stranger to God, he walks by faith, not by sight; and he therefore refers all peace, bodily or spiritual or both, to that peace which mortal man has with the immortal God, so that he exhibits the well-ordered obedience of faith to eternal law. But as this divine Master inculcates two precepts—the love of God and the love of our neighbour—and as in these precepts a man finds three things he has to love—God, himself, and his neighbour—and that he who loves God loves himself thereby, it follows that he must endeavour to get his neighbour to love God, since he is ordered to love his neighbour as himself. . . .

. . . For they who care for the rest rule—the husband the wife, the parents the children, the masters the servants; and they who are cared for obey—the women their husbands, the children their parents, the servants their masters. But in the family of the just man who lives by faith and is as yet a pilgrim journeying on to the celestial city, even those who rule serve those whom they seem to command; for they rule not from a love of power, but from a sense of the duty they owe to others—not because they are proud of authority, but because they love mercy. . . .

But the families which do not live by faith seek their peace in the earthly advantages of this life; while the families which live by faith look for those eternal blessings which are promised, and use as pilgrims such advantages of time and of earth as do not fascinate and divert them from God, but rather aid them to endure with greater ease, and to keep down the number of those burdens of the corruptible body which weigh upon the soul. Thus the things necessary for this mortal life are used by both kinds of men and families alike, but each has its own peculiar and widely different aim in using them. The earthly city, which does not live by faith, seeks an earthly peace, and the end it proposes, in the well-ordered concord of civic obedience and rule, is the combination of men's wills to attain the things which are helpful to this life. The heavenly city, or rather the part of it which sojourns on earth and lives by faith, makes use of this peace only because it must, until this mortal condition which necessitates it shall pass away. Consequently, so long as it lives like a captive and a stranger in the earthly city, though it has already received the promise of redemption, and the gift of the Spirit as the earnest of it, it makes no scruple to obey the laws of the earthly city, whereby the things necessary for the maintenance of this mortal life are administered; and thus, as this life is common to both cities, so there is a harmony between them in regard to what belongs to it. But the earthly city supposed that many gods must be invited to take an interest in human affairs, and assigned to each a separate function and a separate department. . . . The celestial city, on the other hand, knew that one

God only was to be worshipped. It has come to pass that the two cities could not have common laws of religion, and that the heavenly city has been compelled in this matter to dissent, and to become obnoxious to those who think differently.

. . . This heavenly city, then, while it sojourns on earth, calls citizens out of all nations, and gathers together a society of pilgrims of all languages, not scrupling about diversities in the manners, laws, and institutions whereby earthly peace is secured and maintained, but recognising that, however various these are, they all tend to one and the same end of earthly peace. It therefore is so far from rescinding and abolishing these diversities, that it even preserves and adapts them, so long only as no hindrance to the worship of the one supreme and true God is thus introduced. Even the heavenly city, therefore, while in its state of pilgrimage, avails itself of the peace of earth, and, so far as it can without injuring faith and godliness, desires and maintains a common agreement among men regarding the acquisition of the necessaries of life, and makes this earthly peace bear upon the peace of heaven; for this alone can be truly called and esteemed the peace of the reasonable creatures, consisting as it does in the perfectly ordered and harmonious enjoyment of God and of one another in God. When we shall have reached that peace, this mortal life shall give place to one that is eternal, and our body shall be no more this animal body which by its corruption weighs down the soul, but a spiritual body feeling no want, and in all its members subjected to the will. In its pilgrim state the heavenly city possesses this peace by faith; and by this faith it lives righteously when it refers to the attainment of that peace every good action towards God and man; for the life of the city is a social life.

. . . But the peace which we enjoy in this life, whether common to all or peculiar to ourselves, is rather the solace of our misery than the positive enjoyment of felicity. Our very righteousness, too, though true in so far as it has respect to the true good, is yet in this life of such a kind that it consists rather in the remission of sins than in the perfecting of virtues.

The righteousness of a man consists in submitting himself to God, his body to his soul, and his vices, even when they rebel, to his reason, which either defeats or at least resists them. But, in that final peace to which all our righteousness has reference, and for the sake of which it is maintained, as our nature shall enjoy a sound immortality and incorruption, and shall have no more vices, and as we shall experience no resistance either from ourselves or from others, it will not be necessary that reason should rule vices which no longer exist, but God shall rule the man, and the soul shall rule the body, with a sweetness and facility suitable to the felicity of a life which is done with bondage. And this condition shall there be eternal, and we shall be assured of its eternity; and thus the peace of this blessedness and the blessedness of this peace shall be the supreme good.

But, on the other hand, they who do not belong to this city of God shall inherit eternal misery, which is also called the second death, because the soul shall then be separated from God its life, and therefore cannot be said to live, and the body shall be subjected to eternal pains. . . .

(Extracts are from Books XIV 1, I 35, XVIII 54, XIV 28, XIX 5, XV 4, XIX 7, 11, 14, 17, 27, 28.)

The Commonwealth and Justice

. . . True justice has no existence save in that republic whose founder and ruler is Christ, if at least any choose to call this a republic; and indeed we cannot deny that it is the people's weal. But if perchance this name, which has become familiar in other connections, be considered alien to our common parlance, we may at all events say that in this city is true justice; the city of which Holy Scripture says, "Glorious things are said of thee, O city of God."

Justice being taken away, then, what are kingdoms but great robberies? For what are robberies themselves, but little kingdoms? The band itself is made up of men; it is ruled by the authority of a prince, it is knit together by the pact of the confederacy; the booty is divided by the law agreed on. If, by the admittance of abandoned men, this evil increases to such a degree that it holds places, fixes abodes, takes possession of cities, and subdues peoples, it assumes the more plainly the name of a kingdom, because the reality is now manifestly conferred on it, not by the removal of covetousness, but by the addition of impunity. Indeed, that was an apt and true reply which was given to Alexander the Great by a pirate who had been seized. For when that king had asked the man what he meant by keeping hostile possessions of the sea, he answered with bold pride, "What thou meanest by seizing the whole earth; but because I do it with a petty ship, I am called a robber, whilst thou who doest it with a great fleet are styled emperor." . . .

. . . Cicero's *De Republica* briefly defines a republic as the weal of the people. And if this definition be true, there never was a Roman republic, for the people's weal was never attained among the Romans. For the people, according to his definition, is an assemblage associated by a common acknowledgment of right and by a community of interests. And what he means by a common acknowledgment of right he explains at large, showing that a republic cannot be administered without justice. Where, therefore, there is no true justice there can be no right. For that which is done by right is justly done, and what is unjustly done cannot be done by right. . . . Consequently, if the republic is the weal of the people, and there is no people if it be not associated by a common acknowledgment of right, and if there is no right where there is no justice, then most certainly it follows that there is no republic where there is no justice. Further, justice is that virtue which gives every one his due. Where, then, is the justice of man, when he deserts the true God and yields himself to impure demons?

. . . But if we discard this definition of a people, and, assuming another, say that a people is an assemblage of reasonable beings bound together by a common agreement as to the objects of their love, then, in order to discover the character of any people, we have only to observe what they love. Yet whatever it loves, if only it is an assemblage of reasonable beings and not of beasts, and is bound together by an agreement as to the objects of love, it is reasonably called a people; and it will be a superior people in proportion as it is bound together by higher interests, inferior in proportion as as it is bound together by lower. . . .

(Extracts are from Books II 21, IV 4, XIX 21, 24.)

SECTION V

MEDIEVAL LIFE AND THOUGHT

Historians generally date the beginning of the Middle Ages from the downfall of Rome in 476 A.D. With the fall of the universal empire, a series of unstable independent kingdoms appeared. Each was characterized by territorial residence, tribal grouping, common blood relationships, a common law, largely custom, and a leader (*Dux*) who was essentially a warrior. Government control, as direct central government, was weak; local government was the norm, the local lord the important administrative figure. Towns declined with the decrease of trade. Self-supporting villages became the foundation of an agricultural economy based on the manorial system.

Feudal System

In this barbarian tribal system with its weak central institutions and absence of paid armies, the social system was feudalism. Feudalism was essentially a series of defined relationships between landlords and tenants. In a situation with no universal public laws, each social group had legal relationships to others, pledging services to its superiors and obtaining protection from them.

The chief features of this system, which was common to all Western Europe, were vassalage and the fief. Vassalage, whether entered into by formal act or not, meant that the vassal owed the lord fidelity, gave him certain financial aid, and rendered military service. The lord, in return, undertook to protect and defend the vassal. The fief was the land allowed the individual on condition that certain services were performed. Possession of land was conditional, subject to use.

The king, too, possessed land in this way; his possession depended on his care of his people. He gave protection as he received service. Vassals owed a duty to the king, to give service in both men and materials, to attend the King's Court (*Curia Regis*), to provide taxes and make contributions. But the services and duties were customary—they were not to be determined by the king. There was no legal partnership between the king and the people, but he depended on them for advice and consultation. Though these were private rather than public relationships, the series of obligations that all were bound to perform was an anticipation of the later idea of a political contract which bound the parties to it.

In the feudal system, law was not "made" by anyone, so much as recovered. The king therefore "promulgated" it, rather than made it. He was subject to the laws, as was everyone else. Yet, there was substantial difference between this theoretical concept and actual conditions. It was difficult to ensure that the king was actually under the law, the rights possessed by vassals were not always clear, and the right to ownership developed in spite of the theory.

Change took place in this uniform, isolated, self-sufficient system for a variety of reasons. Friction between the king and the nobles led on one side to a claim for more centralized control, and on the other to disobedience and refusal. Diseases and plagues, especially the Black Death, reduced the amount of manpower, and brought a demand for higher wages in the towns. The towns and cities developed as training centers and received charters from the king; the townsmen needed no protection from a lord. The Roman idea of indivisible ownership and private rights became more pronounced with the influence of Roman law. Increasing trade and commerce led to greater use of money, which could be substituted for the rendering of services. With growing centralization and the rise of the territorial state, the system declined.

Regnum and Sacerdotium

In this unified but localized social structure, the Church pressed the idea of a universal Christian Commonwealth. In a period of barbarian kingdoms, the argument was put forward of a single society with two governments, each with separate powers. Pope Gelasius I (492–496) outlined the theory of the two swords. God wanted to separate spiritual and temporal power. The Pope was superior to the secular rule in the ecclesiastical realm; the ruler was superior to the Pope in temporal affairs. But ecclesiastic authority was more important than lay. While the former relied on the coercive power of the ruler in temporal matters, the Christian emperor needed the Church to attain eternal life.

Church and State would become *sacerdotium* and *regnum*, two governments in a single Christian society. With the victories of Charlemagne, the Western Empire was restored, and power transferred from the empire at Constantinople. Charlemagne, King of the Franks, crowned Emperor of the Holy Roman Empire on Christmas Day 800, was to protect the Pope and support his spiritual supremacy as well as restore secular universalism.

But the claim to papal supremacy was increasingly made in this period of dual authority. It was stated most strongly by Gregory VII, Pope (1073–1085), and emphasized both ecclesiastical and papal power. The Pope was supreme head of the Church and could not only control bishops, but also depose the Emperor. The analogy of the sun and moon was developed: the Pope's light shone on the inferior satellite, the Emperor. The ecclesiastical organization could control the secular not only in spiritual, but also in ethical matters. Some, like Manegold of Lautenbach, argued that the king might be deposed if he ruled unjustly. In his analogy of the king to the shepherd responsible for his flock, he expressed an early theory of popular sovereignty, and a contract made between the king and his people.

This ecclesiastical argument was a rationalization of a situation in which the Church, basing its action on its knowledge of divine or natural law, was attempting to act in all spheres, political, social, economic, scholastic. It was in a favorable position, compared with the feudal communities, to influence or control human affairs by canon law and its penal code. The ultimate source of all authority was divine; political participation depended on religious allegiance and orthodoxy.

Those who upheld secular power used the same argument to reach a different conclusion. Since authority was of divine origin, secular rulers were responsible to God alone, unhindered by ecclesiastical interference. Even if the right of excommunication by the Pope were granted, he still had no authority to remove the ruler or absolve subjects of their oaths. The only limitation on secular power was the observance of custom and natural law.

The original premise of dual authority in a unified commonwealth, in which all belonged to a Christian community —a realization of the Stoic universal society—foundered because of the continual disputes. The recurring problems were the appointment or investiture of bishops and their powers, taxation of Church property, the secular powers possessed by ecclesiastical personnel holding fiefs, depositions and excommunications. The intellectual duel between the two powers was largely fought on legal grounds. In general, the canonists upheld the Papal authority, and the lawyers of the University of Bologna based their arguments supporting the Emperor on Roman law, the power of the Caesars, and their sovereignty. The Diet of Worms, in 1122, established a compromise in which the papal power over investiture was differentiated in different countries. But at the end of the 12th century, Innocent III again expressed the theory of papal supremacy. In England, the conflict between the two realms led to the murder of the Archbishop of Canterbury, Becket, by knights of Henry II, in 1170.

John of Salisbury

This was the setting in which John of Salisbury (1110–1180), friend of kings and scholars, and secretary to Becket, wrote his *Policraticus,* the first important medieval political work. John, an eloquent ecclesiastical spokesman, was concerned with the limitation of the ruler by higher or divine law. Under such law, an individual fulfilled his duties, but also could resist the prince if he did not conform to law.

It is a theory of a stable society, understood through an organic analogy. The Commonwealth was "a body endowed with life by the benefit of divine favor." The prince was its head, the priesthood its soul, the Senate its heart, judges and governors its eyes, ears and tongue, officials and soldiers its hands, financial officers its stomach, and husbandmen its feet. All co-operated for the good of the whole interrelated, co-ordinated society.

No one conclusion can be drawn from the book. The prince was "minister of the common interest" and served his fellow servants. Yet also the prince obtained his power from God and performed "those sacred duties which seem unworthy of the hands of the priesthood." Tyranny, the abuse of power by a prince, was part of God's ordering of the universe, yet at times it might be right and just, even a public duty, to kill a tyrant. The higher law, to which all were subject, seemed to put no controls on the prince, for the normal restraints were internal: "The prince puts a bridle on himself." The *Policraticus* shows the nature and complexity of 12th century issues.

The Origin and Significance of Feudalism

(from *Mediaeval Institutions* by Carl Stephenson)

What precisely do we mean when we talk of "feudalism"? The concept, it would seem, is a wholly modern one; neither the English word nor its equivalent in any other language was apparently invented much before the nineteenth century. Although men in the Middle Ages were quite familiar with vassals and fiefs and with vassalage and feudal tenure, they apparently did not think in terms of a broad feudal theory—a set of feudal principles by which to construct a social and political framework. To have any validity, therefore, whatever generalization we make must be squarely based on our knowledge of actual institutions. And those institutions must be of the region where the custom properly called feudal was first developed—that is to say, mediaeval Gaul. A sociology of feudalism there may be, but only comparison with the original feudalism can rightly determine the feudal character of some other custom, wherever it may have existed.

Turning then to the native land of feudalism, we have no trouble in finding the central institution from which our word is derived. It was the *feudum* or fief. Yet this is not the primary element to be examined. Feudalism presupposes vassalage; for a fief could not exist apart from a vassal to hold it. . . . The status of vassal, we know from countless documents of the eleventh and twelfth centuries, could always be acquired, with or without the prospect of a fief, merely by performing homage and swearing fealty. And solely in this way could one become a vassal. Although fiefs might be declared hereditary, vassalage was never inherited. When a vassal died, his fief legally reverted to the lord, in whose hands it remained until such time as the heir performed homage and so qualified himself to receive investiture. Only a vassal could properly be a fief holder, and there can be no doubt that, in the feudal age proper, vassalage was restricted to mature men. The reason is clear: a vassal was supposed to be a warrior. Clergymen, it is true, often held fiefs while debarred from bloodshed by canon law. But the qualifications that came to be put on their homage and fealty were plainly the result of compromise. . . . Feudal tenure, whatever its minor adaptations, was essentially military because the original vassalage was a military relationship. . . .

. . . The basis of the new system, assuredly, was military

need. The king gave fiefs to his vassals and encouraged sub-infeudation on the part of the latter for the primary purpose of securing a better army; and there was an increasing demand for mounted troops. The rapid introduction of heavy-armed cavalry was of profound social significance. The profession of arms came to be governed by an aristocratic code of chivalry —a set of rules that had meaning only for the highborn. Thus in the later Middle Ages knight and noble were virtually synonymous terms. Land held for agrarian rent or service, whatever the nature of the original contract, was no fief; the tenant, however free in law, was no vassal.

The vassal's obligation, being military, was *ipso facto* polit-ical; so, according to Carolingian standards, it was proper for him to receive political privilege in return. The personal rela-tionship of lord to vassal carried with it no power of jurisdic-tion, feudal justice could not be separated from the territorial immunity which every fief was construed to imply. And inso-far as the feudal lord had the right to hold courts, to levy tolls and other imposts, to requisition labor and materials, to raise fortifications, and to muster the population for local defense, he was obviously a public official. It is, indeed, no mere form of words to assert that every fief was an office; for the rule of primogeniture evidently came to be incorporated in feudal law through recognition of this principle. Another phase of the same development may be seen in the fact that by the end of the ninth century the more important agents of the state had been brought within the category of royal vassals. The transi-tion was an informal one, of which the capitularies tell us little, but that the result was quite in accord with Carolingian policy seems clear. If every feudal tenant was to some degree a count within his own territory, when a count became a vassal, would not the county be his fief?

The conclusion thus seems inevitable that to talk of "politi-cal feudalism," as distinguished from "economic feudalism," is misleading. All feudalism was political; and if we wish to refer to the agrarian economy presupposed by feudal tenure, we have the accurate and familiar expression, "manorial sys-tem." The original feudalism was a phase of government de-veloped by the Frankish kings on the basis of a pre-existing barbarian custom of vassalage. It was not, therefore, an in-evitable stage in economic evolution. Although it involved a system of rewarding soldiers with grants of land, it was by no means that alone. Nor was it the mere equivalent of provin-cial autonomy under a failing empire.

. . . As long ago as 1818 Henry Hallam expressed the opinion that the feudal system had much to be said in its favor. Despite its shortcomings it must be valued, he says, as "a school of moral discipline," which nourished a spirit of honorable obligation, a noble sentiment of personal loyalty. Although under that system private war and its attendant disorders flourished everywhere, the "inefficiency of the feudal militia" tended to save Europe from the "danger of universal monarchy." "To the feudal law it is owing that the very names of right and privilege were not swept away, as in Asia, by the desolating hand of power." These sentiments, most of us will agree, are a trifle exuberant. But Hallam makes a good point when he adds:

"It is the previous state of society under the grandchildren of Charlemagne we must always keep in mind if we would appreciate the effects of the feudal system upon the welfare of mankind. The institutions of the eleventh century must be compared with those of the ninth, not with the advanced civilization of modern times. If the view that I have taken of those dark ages is correct, the state of anarchy which we term feudal was the natural result of a vast and barbarous empire feebly administered, and the cause rather than the result of the general establishment of feudal tenures."

Too few historians have followed the lead offered by the eloquent Hallam. Too many have repeated vague generalizations to the effect that feudalism was virtually synonymous with political disintegration. The meaning of such remarks depends altogether on what state they refer to. Will they hold good, in the first place, for the Carolingian Empire? The capitularies of the eighth and ninth centuries reveal on the part of the kings a definite policy of using traditional vassalage to buttress the monarchical authority. Royal vassals, serving as heavy-armed cavalry and leading similar contingents of their own men, formed the principal strength of the army. They were increasingly employed in routine administration as well as for special missions. They came to be placed in many prominent offices of church and state. To enable them to meet their costly obligations, they were commonly endowed with rich benefices that included rights of immunity. But this glorification of vassalage for governmental purposes often tended to weaken and discredit the primitive bond. Vassals living on distant fiefs lost respect for a lord with whom they had little contact. Disloyal officials, in spite of enforced homage, continued to be disloyal. No amount of legal enactment could prevent usurpation or deter men from supporting the immediate lord who gave them sustenance and protection. And the establishment of hereditary tenure, though encouraged by the emperors, perpetuated more abuses than benefits.

In other words, the feudalizing policy of the Carolingians failed, not because it was in itself evil, but because it sought to accomplish the impossible.

The empire of Charlemagne was indeed too "vast and barbarous" and too "feebly administered" to be held together in the troubled period that ensued upon his death. The entire political experience of western Europe for the next three hundred years, down to the new age of economic recovery, demonstrated at least one fact: that a state, in order to survive, had to be relatively small. . . .

If we examine these principalities, the true states of the eleventh century, what do we learn of feudalism and its political significance? A cursory glance shows that feudal custom was generally prevalent in those where the central authority was strong as well as in those where it was weak. The difference between typical members of the two groups is found to lie not in any theoretical powers of the ruler but in his ability to enforce them. The feudal contract allowed each party to denounce the other for stated cause, primarily default of aid or protection; it was the absence of a common superior to render effective justice that resulted in the chronic warfare called private. Within any well-organized state whose military and civil administration depended largely on feudal relationships, the regulation of the latter was imperative—was, in fact, an essential part of the system under which they were supposed to exist. And it is a mistake to consider feudal decentralization an unmitigated evil. The construction of every fief as a restricted sphere of seignorial government may well be compared with the modern establishment of partial autonomy in cities, townships, and other local units. Feudal anarchy there was in many regions of mediaeval Europe, but feudalism was not of necessity anarchical. . . .

The Beginnings of Representation

In the course of the twelfth century, local juries came to be used more and more frequently for a great variety of governmental business: to secure information concerning the privileges of individuals or communities; to assess persons and estates for maintenance of arms or payment of taxes; to bring charges against dishonest officials; to present the names of suspected criminals; to settle disputed titles to land or other property; to answer all sorts of questions put by the royal justices on eyre. Not uncommonly the desired results could best be obtained when the juries were popularly elected, and occasionally it was found convenient to call together a number of juries to consult with the king or his ministers. In the later thirteenth century such assemblies came to be associated with meetings of the great council; and so, we are told, the house of commons ultimately emerged.

At this point, however, I should like to interpose another distinction: that between a jury system and a system of representative government. The one does not inevitably imply the other. The essence of a jury was not that certain men were elected to represent others, but merely that certain men were put on oath to give true answers to questions. Two hundred years after the Norman Conquest the jury remained primarily a fact-finding institution. What was still demanded of the juror was particular knowledge, rather than authority to act on behalf of a community. So long as the king merely wanted information, a system of appointed juries, consulted either singly or in groups, would be entirely adequate. This may be representative government of a sort, but it is not what we recognize by that name in later England. . . .

The origins of parliament are not to be found by tracing into earlier times any political practice that did not involve the actual election of deputies with a delegation of binding authority from the communities of England. The assembling of such communal representatives apparently began in 1254 and developed into a regular custom by the end of the century. Why a king like Edward I should have insisted on these assemblies merely to facilitate the presentation of petitions I cannot understand. But I can understand how the bringing of petitions in parliament would be encouraged by the constant election of burgesses and knights of the shires for other purposes. The principal purpose, I am convinced, was to obtain money—a conclusion that agrees with the known character of the king and the social and economic changes of the age.

The euphemistic language of the royal writs should not mislead us. In 1241 Henry III called at Worcester an assembly of the wealthier Jews from all his boroughs *"ad tractandum nobiscum tam de nostra quam sua utilitate."* But the matter of mutual advantage of which they were to treat was actually a tallage of 20,000 marks. When Edward I notified his good men of various towns that he had commissioned John of Kirkby to explain to them and expedite through them "certain arduous and especial concerns" of his, no one could have been surprised to discover that he was negotiating for a subsidy. And contemporaries were as little mystified when parliamentary representatives were summoned to consider those other "difficult and momentous affairs" to which the writs constantly refer. They knew that they would be fortunate to escape further demands for taxes. . . .

The core of the English representative system has not been
a vague sympathy on the part of self-appointed spokesmen, a
primitive custom of deeming dooms in the name of the people, or even the selection of jurors for a sort of national
inquest. Rather it has been a matter of sheer political necessity, occasioned on the one hand by the king's lack of money
and on the other by the growing strength of the social groups
who could supply it. Although the king might use communal
delegates in a variety of ways, the compelling motive behind
their incorporation as an estate of parliament was economic.
Without the recurring need for general taxation, there would,
I believe, have been no House of Commons.

In concluding, it may also be remarked that some of the
constitutional features praised by Burke as "the ancient tried
usages" of England were by no means so fundamental as he
imagined. It was not the original practice for members of the
commons to be representatives of the nation at large. Actually, the burgesses and knights of the shires were procurators
of the local communities, chosen and instructed by them,
responsible to them, and legally bound to be resident within
them. Contemporary political thought, of course, embraced
no theory of democracy founded on universal suffrage. But it
did recognize the interdependence of representation and popular election, and to it the principle of the mandate was not
wholly foreign—all good Tories to the contrary notwithstanding.

JOHN OF SALISBURY
The Statesman's Book (Policraticus)

*The Difference Between a Prince and a Tyrant and
What Is Meant by a Prince*

Between a tyrant and a prince there is this single or chief
difference, that the latter obeys the law and rules the people
by its dictates, accounting himself as but their servant. It is by
virtue of the law that he makes good his claim to the foremost
and chief place in the management of the affairs of the commonwealth and in the bearing of its burdens; and his elevation
over others consists in this, that whereas private men are held
responsible only for their private affairs, on the prince fall the
burdens of the whole community. Wherefore deservedly there
is conferred on him, and gathered together in his hands, the

power of all his subjects, to the end that he may be sufficient unto himself in seeking and bringing about the advantage of each individually, and of all; and to the end that the state of the human commonwealth may be ordered in the best possible manner, seeing that each and all are members one of another. Wherein we indeed but follow nature, the best guide of life; for nature has gathered together all the senses of her microcosm or little world, which is man, into the head, and has subjected all the members in obedience to it in such wise that they will all function properly so long as they follow the guidance of the head, and the head remains sane. Therefore the prince stands on a pinnacle which is exalted and made splendid with all the great and high privileges which he deems necessary for himself. And rightly so, because nothing is more advantageous to the people than that the needs of the prince should be fully satisfied; since it is impossible that his will should be found opposed to justice. Therefore, the prince is the public power, and a kind of likeness on earth of the divine majesty. . . . The power which the prince has is therefore from God, for the power of God is never lost, nor severed from Him, but He merely exercises it through a subordinate hand, making all things teach His mercy or justice. . . .

(These extracts are from Book IV, chapters 1 and 2.)

Who should not venerate that power which is instituted by God for the punishment of evil-doers and for the reward of good men, and which is promptest in devotion and obedience to the laws? To quote the words of the Emperor, "it is indeed a saying worthy of the majesty of royalty that the prince acknowledges himself bound by the Laws." For the authority of the prince depends upon the authority of justice and law; and truly it is a greater thing than imperial power for the prince to place his government under the laws, so as to deem himself entitled to do nought which is at variance with the equity of justice. . . .

Princes should not deem that it detracts from their princely dignity to believe that the enactments of their own justice are not to be preferred to the justice of God, whose justice is an everlasting justice, and His law is equity. Now equity, as the learned jurists define it, is a certain fitness of things which compares all things rationally, and seeks to apply like rules of right and wrong to like cases, being impartially disposed toward all persons, and allotting to each that which belongs to him. Of this equity the interpreter is the law, to which the will and intention of equity and justice are known. . . .

All law is, as it were, a discovery, and a gift from God, a precept of wise men, the corrector of excesses of the will, the bond which knits together the fabric of the state, and the banisher of crime; and it is therefore fitting that all men should live according to it who lead their lives in a corporate political body. All are accordingly bound by the necessity of keeping the law, unless perchance there is any who can be thought to have been given the license of wrong-doing. However, it is said that the prince is absolved from the obligations of the law; but this is not true in the sense that it is lawful for him to do unjust acts, but only in the sense that his character should be such as to cause him to practice equity not through fear of the penalties of the law but through love of justice; and should also be such as to cause him from the same motive to promote the advantage of the commonwealth, and in all things to prefer the good of others before his own private will. . . . The prince accordingly is the minister of the common interest and the bond-servant of equity, and he bears the public person in the sense that he punishes the wrongs and injuries of all, and all crimes, with even-handed equity. . . .

Those who derive the greatest advantage from his performance of the duties of his office are those who can do least for themselves, and his power is chiefly exercised against those who desire to do harm. Therefore not without reason he bears a sword, wherewith he sheds blood blamelessly, without becoming thereby a man of blood, and frequently puts men to death without incurring the name or guilt of homicide. . . . Truly the sword of princely power is as the sword of a dove, which contends without gall, smites without wrath, and when it fights, yet conceives no bitterness at all. For as the law pursues guilt without any hatred of persons, so the prince most justly punishes offenders from no motive of wrath but at the behest, and in accordance with the decision, of the passionless law. . . .

That the Prince Is the Minister of the Priests and Inferior to Them; and of What Amounts to Faithful Performance of the Prince's Ministry.

This sword, then, the prince receives from the hand of the Church, although she herself has no sword of blood at all. Nevertheless she has this sword, but she uses it by the hand of the prince, upon whom she confers the power of bodily coercion, retaining to herself authority over spiritual things in the person of the pontiffs. The prince is, then, as it were, a minister of the priestly power, and one who exercises that side of the sacred offices which seems unworthy of the hands of the priesthood. For every office existing under, and concerned with the execution of, the sacred laws is really a religious office, but that is inferior which consists in punishing crimes, and which therefore seems to be typified in the person of the hangman. . . .

Again, according to the testimony of the teacher of the gentiles, greater is he who blesses man than he who is blessed; and so he in whose hands is the authority to confer a dignity excels in honor and the privileges of honor him upon whom the dignity itself is conferred. Further, by the reasoning of the law it is his right to refuse who has the power to grant, and he who can lawfully bestow can lawfully take away. . . . But if one who has been appointed prince has performed duly and faithfully the ministry which he has undertaken, as great honor and reverence are to be shown to him as the head excels in honor all the members of the body. Now he performs his ministry faithfully when he is mindful of his true status, and remembers that he bears the person of the *universitas* of those subject to him; and when he is fully conscious that he owes his life not to himself and his own private ends, but to others, and allots it to them accordingly, with duly ordered charity and affection. Therefore he owes the whole of himself to God, most of himself to his country, much to his relatives and friends, very little to foreigners, but still somewhat . . .

And so let him be both father and husband to his subjects, or, if he has known some affection more tender still, let him employ that; let him desire to be loved rather than feared, and show himself to them as such a man that they will out of devotion prefer his life to their own, and regard his preservation and safety as a kind of public life. . . .

What a Commonwealth Is

(This extract is from Book IV, chapter 3.)

A commonwealth, according to Plutarch, is a certain body which is endowed with life by the benefit of divine favor, which acts at the prompting of the highest equity, and is ruled by what may be called the moderating power of reason. Those things which establish and implant in us the practice of religion, and transmit to us the worship of God fill the place of the soul in the body of the commonwealth. And therefore those who preside over the practice of religion should be looked up to and venerated as the soul of the body. For who doubts that the ministers of God's holiness are His representatives? Furthermore, since the soul is, as it were, the prince of the body, and has rulership over the whole thereof, so those whom our author calls the prefects of religion preside over the entire body. . . .

The place of the head in the body of the commonwealth is filled by the prince, who is subject only to God and to those who exercise His office and represent Him on earth, even as in the human body the head is quickened and governed by the soul. The place of the heart is filled by the Senate, from which proceeds the initiation of good works and ill. The duties of eyes, ears, and tongue are claimed by the judges and the governors of provinces. Officials and soldiers correspond to the hands. Those who always attend upon the prince are likened to the sides. Financial officers may be compared with the stomach and intestines, which, if they become congested through excessive avidity, and retain too tenaciously their accumulations, generate innumerable and incurable diseases, so that through their ailment the whole body is threatened with destruction. The husbandmen correspond to the feet, which always cleave to the soil, and need the more especially the care and foresight of the head, since while they walk upon the earth doing service with their bodies, they meet the more often with stones of stumbling, and therefore deserve aid and protection all the more justly since it is they who raise, sustain, and move forward the weight of the entire body. Take away the support of the feet from the strongest body, and it cannot move forward by its own power, but must creep painfully and shamefully on its hands, or else be moved by means of brute animals. . . .

It has been said that the prince holds the place of the head, and is guided solely by the judgment of his own mind. And so, as has been said, he is placed by the divine governance at the apex of the commonwealth, and preferred above all others, sometimes through the secret ministry of God's providence, sometimes by the decision of His priests, and again it is the votes of the whole people which concur to place the ruler in authority. . . .

We read in the Book of Kings that Saul, when about to be made king, appeared before the face of the people, and was lifted up on their shoulders, above the whole people. Why so, I ask, if not because he that is to be over others ought in heart and countenance to show that he has strength sufficient to embrace as it were the breadth of the whole people in the arms of his good works. . . .

Those are called the feet who discharge the humbler offices, and by whose services the members of the whole commonwealth walk upon solid earth. Among these are to be counted the husbandmen, who always cleave to the soil, busied about their plough-lands or vineyards or pastures or flower-gardens. To these must be added the many species of cloth-making, and the mechanic arts, which work in wood, iron, bronze and the different metals; also the menial occupations, and the manifold forms of getting a lifelihood and sustaining life, or increasing household property, all of which, while they do not pertain to the authority of the governing power, are yet in the highest degree useful and profitable to the corporate whole of the commonwealth. All these different occupations are so numerous that the commonwealth in the number of its feet exceeds not only the eight-footed crab but even the centipede, and because of their very multitude they cannot be enumerated: for while they are not infinite by nature, they are yet of so many different varieties that no writer on the subject of offices or duties has ever laid down particular precepts for each special variety. But it applies generally to each and all of them that in their exercise they should not transgress the limits of the law, and should in all things observe constant reference to the public utility. For inferiors owe it to their superiors to provide them with service, just as the superiors in their turn owe it to their inferiors to provide them with all things needful for their protection and succor. Therefore Plutarch says that that course is to be pursued in all things which is of advantage to the humbler classes, that is to say to the multitude; for small numbers always yield to great. Indeed the reason for the institution of magistrates was to the end that subjects might be protected from wrongs, and that the commonwealth itself might be "shod," so to speak, by means of their services. . . . Then and then only will the health of the commonwealth be sound and flourishing when the higher members shield the lower, and the lower respond faithfully and fully in like measure to the just demands of their superiors, so that each and all are as it were members one of another by a sort of reciprocity, and each regards his own interest at best served by that which he knows to be most advantageous for the others. . . .

. . . So long as the duties of each individual are performed with an eye to the welfare of the whole, so long, that is, as justice is practised, the sweetness of honey pervades the allotted sphere of all.

But the happiness of no body politic will be lasting unless the head is preserved in safety and vigor and looks out for the whole body. . . . The pontiff laughed and congratulated me upon having spoken with such frankness, he finally put before me an apology after this kind: Once upon a time all the members of the body conspired together against the stomach, as against that which by its greediness devoured utterly the labors of all the rest. The eye is never sated with seeing, the ear with hearing, the hands go on laboring, the feet become callous from walking, and the tongue itself alternates advantageously between speech and silence. In fine, all the members provide watchfully for the common advantage of all; and in the midst of such care and toil on the part of all, only the stomach is idle, yet it alone devours and consumes all the fruits of their manifold labors. What remains to be said? They swore to abstain from work and to starve that idle public enemy. Thus passed one day: that which followed was more irksome. The third was so fatal that almost all commenced to be faint. Then, under the pressure of necessity, the brothers again gathered together to take action concerning their own welfare and the state of the public enemy. When all were present, the eyes were found to be dim, the foot failed to sustain the weight of the body, the arms were numb, and the tongue itself, cleaving to the feeble palate, did not make bold to state the common cause. Accordingly all took refuge in the counsel of the heart and after deliberation there, it became plain that these ills were all due to that which had before been denounced as the public enemy. Because the tribute which they paid it was cut off, like a public rationer it withdrew the sustenance of all. . . .

. . . Far more beneficial would it be that he should be supplied with somewhat to distribute than that through his starvation all the other members should go hungry. And so it was done; persuaded by reason, they filled the stomach, the members were revived, and the peace of all was restored. And so the stomach was acquitted, which, although it is voracious and greedy of that which does not belong to it, yet seeks not for itself but for the others, who cannot be nourished if it is empty. "In the body of the commonwealth, wherein, though the magistrates are most grasping, yet they accumulate not so much for themselves as for others. For if they are starved, there is nought to be distributed among the members. For the stomach in the body and the prince in the commonwealth perform the same office. . . . Do not therefore seek to measure our oppressiveness or that of temporal princes, but attend rather to the common utility of all."

. . . I am satisfied and persuaded that loyal shoulders should uphold the power of the ruler; and not only do I submit to his power patiently, but with pleasure, so long as it is exercised in subjection to God and follows His ordinances. But on the other hand if it resists and opposes the divine commandments, and wishes to make me share in its war against God; then with unrestrained voice I answer back that God must be preferred before any man on earth. Therefore inferiors should cleave and cohere to their superiors, and all the limbs should be in subjection to the head; but always and only on condition that religion is kept inviolate. . . . An injury to the head is brought home to all the members, and that a wound unjustly inflicted on any member tends to the injury of the head. Furthermore whatsoever is attempted foully and with malice against the head, or corporate community, of the members, is a crime of the greatest gravity and nearest to sacrilege; for as the latter is an attempt against God, so the former is an attack upon the prince, who is admitted to be as it were the likeness of deity upon earth. And therefore it is called the crime of lèse majesté, for the reason that is aimed against the likeness of Him who alone wears the truth of true and native majesty. . . .

For no one doubts that the members ought to be healed. . . . Furthermore that they should be removed is clear from the fact that it is written, "If thine eye or thy foot offend, pluck it out and cast it from thee." This precept I think should be followed by the prince in the case of all the members, so that not only should they be plucked out, cut off, and cast away if they become an offence to the faith or to the public safety, but should be utterly consumed and destroyed to the end that by the extermination of one, the soundness of all may be procured. Surely neither ear, nor tongue, nor any other thing which exists in the body of the commonwealth is immune if it rises up against the soul for whose sake even the eyes themselves are plucked out.

Thus a king is sometimes called by the name of tyrant, and conversely a tyrant is at times called by the name of prince, according to the saying: "Thy princes are faithless and the companions of thieves." For in the priesthood as well as elsewhere are to be found many who strive with all their ambition and all the arts thereof to use the duties of their office as but a pretext under cover whereof to practise tyranny. For the commonwealth of the ungodly has also its head and members, and strives to correspond, as it were, to the civil institutions of a legitimate commonwealth. The tyrant who is its head is the likeness of the devil; its soul consists of heretical, schismatic, and sacrilegious priests, and, to use the language of Plutarch, prefects of religion who wage war on the law of the Lord; its heart of unrighteous counsellors is like a senate of iniquity; its eyes, ears, tongue, and unarmed hand are unjust judges, laws and officials; its armed hand consists of soldiers of violence whom Cicero calls brigands; its feet are those who in the humbler walks of life go against the precepts of the Lord and His lawful institutions. All these can easily be restrained by their superiors. But surely priests ought not to become indignant with me if I must confess that among them too can be found tyrants. . . .

(Extracts are from Book v, Chapters 2, 6; Book vi Chapters 20, 22, 24, 25, 26; Book viii, Chapter 17.)

SECTION VI

THE TWO REALMS: THE LAST PHASE

The struggle for supremacy in secular affairs, accompanied by internal disputes in both realms of government, continued in the 13th and 14th centuries. Innocent IV, Pope (1243–54), in his struggle against Frederick II, claimed supreme power as Pope, as Vicar of Christ having power over infidels as well as Christians. He supported his argument with the forged Donation of Constantine that had given the whole of the Western Empire to the Pope, claiming that this merely recognized the existing situation.

The bitter fight between Boniface VIII, Pope (1294–1303), and Philip IV of France, over church property and taxation as well as ultimate authority, led in 1302 to the papal bull *Unam Sanctam*, arguing that "for every human creature it is absolutely necessary for salvation to be subject to the Roman Pontiff." Similar conclusions, based on different arguments, were stated by Egidius Romanus, Giles of Rome and James of Viterbo. Yet Boniface lost the fight; the Papacy left Rome for the "Babylonish captivity" at Avignon in 1305. The position of the ecclesiastical realm in the struggle had been immeasurably weakened.

Among the writers advocating the claim of the state to independence, and sometimes even control over the Church, were Dante, Marsiglio of Padua, and William of Ockham.

The great Florentine poet Dante (1265–1321) argued in his *De Monarchia* against the Papal claim to control secular authority in the Empire. He admitted that man had two separate ends, earthly and eternal, that the Emperor and the Pope were guides to these ends, and that both received their authority from God. Emphasizing the importance of secular life, he stressed the supremacy of the Emperor in everything relating to the secular world. The need for universal peace and the life of reason meant a universal ruler, the Emperor, who would be independent both of the Pope and the Church.

The most significant political treatise of this group of writers was the *Defensor Pacis* of Marsiglio of Padua (1280–1343). His starting point was the individuality and aggressiveness of man, and therefore the need to maintain peace and order in the community. Civil society was dependent on all carrying out their function and contributing to the common good. Secular rule was quite different from religion, and could be discussed as a separate function. Man's religion, or his inner life, was private; external acts were subject to control.

Marsiglio of Padua was primarily interested in the "ruling section," the executive, directing organ of the "human legislator" (the whole political community). But he stressed the need for law to obtain community approval, by the people or "its weightier part." This part did not necessarily need to be a majority, for quality was to be taken into account as well as quantity. It was this community approval that made law valid and gave it effective coercive power. The prince was controlled by the legislative power of which he was the servant.

In a similar fashion, Marsiglio proposed that the ultimate ecclesiastical authority should be "the whole body of the faithful including both clerics and laymen," again exercised through the ruling part. The role of the Pope, therefore, was a subordinate one. It was the General Council, elected by the faithful and convoked by the secular authority, which was the governing body of the Church, having power over the Pope and ultimate decision over all spiritual questions.

It is incorrect to see all this as modern democratic theory. Yet the arguments of Marsiglio that the people is the source of law and the ruler is agent, that all power, ecclesiastical or temporal, is vested in the community, and that the state is omnipotent in temporal matters, point the way to theories of secular liberalism, representation and constitutionalism.

A similar, if more polemical, attitude toward the relationship of community and Papacy was taken by William of Ockham (1290?–1349). The whole community would participate, through a hierarchy of elected organizations, in the choice of a Council. Because of the careful and fair way in which Ockham stated opposing views without concluding with a statement of his own position, it is not clear whether such a Council would have had ultimate authority. But as a partisan of Lewis of Bavaria in his struggle against Pope John XXII, he asserted the independence of the temporal power.

Aquinas

In the 13th century, the works of Aristotle, which had been forgotten by all except Arabic scholars, reappeared in Western Europe, giving impetus to the idea of a secular community. At first the Church was opposed to Aristotelianism, especially in its Averroistic form—from the influence of the Arab, Averroes. The reconciliation of Greek philosophy with Christianity was the great contribution to political philosophy made by Thomas Aquinas (1224–1274). Born of an influential, ambitious family, kinsman of the Emperor, member of the Dominican order, friend of the Pope, Aquinas is the most systematic political philosopher of medieval Catholicism, even though his political writings are secondary to his theological discussions.

Augustine and the Church Fathers had held that governmental institutions were the result of sin and necessary to mitigate its consequences. Aristotle's starting point was that man was a social animal, and that the state was a natural phenomenon. The compromise of Aquinas was to admit the element of sin, but to agree that political organization was natural to man, and necessary for his proper development. Ultimately, all political authority came from God, but there were many possible intermediaries between God and political regimes, and purposes, such as the securing of justice, that government should seek to fulfill.

Aquinas accepted the Aristotelian thesis of happiness as the end of man and the importance of the temporal world. But the principal end of man was still the supernatural, the salvation of his soul and future eternal blessedness. Future life was more significant than earthly existence; the Church as the organization concerned with this future life was superior to, and the directing guide of, secular power, as the body was subject to the soul. Yet, the state was still important. Not only did it preserve order, but it also performed a positive, educational function.

Aquinas' discussion of law revolved around four different types. Eternal law governed the entire universe, including animate and inanimate objects as well as man. Natural law enabled those possessing reason to understand and conform to eternal law. Human law entailed the making of concrete, detailed variable rules in accordance with natural law. Divine law was the ultimate will of God. Law was rational and binding.

In all this, there is an implicit restriction on the extent of power: political authority was binding only if it was in conformity with natural law, divine law and the common good of

the whole community. If it did not comform, governmental
power was tyrannical, and might be resisted. If the tyranny
was excessive, disobedience was permissible, and then only if
it was organized by public authority. It was this cautious
approval of resistance by an aristocratic group that led Lord
Acton to call Aquinas "the first Whig."

Though the primacy of the ecclesiastical power was always
emphasized, and the supremacy of the Pope acknowledged,
Aquinas admitted the autonomy of the state, and the natural-
ness and value of political institutions. His emphasis on the
importance of the good life and the common good as the
object of human law and the end of the state, meant greater
stress on secular values. His discussion of law meant support
for the power of the whole community or its representatives.
This discussion was another illustration of the rapidly increasing revival of Roman law which was challenging the acceptance of custom as the basis for rules.

Ideas of Representation

Not only were there disputes and a struggle for supremacy
between *regnum* and *sacerdotium;* there were also divisions
and struggles within each realm. In the latter, the Pope had
long emerged from mere pre-eminence in the Church to the
dominant authority. In the former, royal power expanded as
distinct nations began to develop out of the original tribal
groupings. This expansion and move toward stronger centralized authority was accompanied by the development of an
embryonic civil service. In England, Henry II had used an
administrative system and judges to issue a series of commands which became accepted as common law. Edward I
introduced Roman law into the country at the end of the 13th
century. In France, lawyers for Philip the Fair had advocated
those strong powers which led him to victory over Pope Boniface VIII. But in both realms the argument had been put
forward that governmental power was derived from the community, which might limit the ruler.

The secular ruler increasingly had to take account of subjects not bound by feudal ties, by townsmen, guilds and corporations. The first steps toward a representative system were
taken in the 13th century. The extracts in this section of
summons and writs issued by the English kings illustrate the
gradual move in the course of the century from mere consultation of individuals to their delegation with "full and sufficient power," *plena potestas*. In England, France and Spain,

historic constitutional principles were in the formative stage of development. By this process, the king grew more powerful, gained assent for his policies, which could be effectively carried out, and got access to money. But those consulted were able to present petitions to him—soon he would have to hear and settle grievances before taxation would be approved.

In the ecclesiastical realm, a similar double process was occurring. On one hand, increased papal power was advocated by the theory of fullness of power, *plenitudo potestatis,* making the Pope an absolute monarch. On the other hand, papal supremacy was challenged by the claims of the bishops, and increasingly by the College of Cardinals. The bishops, exercising canon law, objected to the attempts of the Papacy to establish uniform ecclesiastical law, and sometimes might support the Emperor in his fight against the Pope. In the College of Cardinals there were frequent complaints from the 11th century on that the Cardinals were being bypassed in ecclesiastical affairs. Canon lawyers increasingly put forward the view that the Pope was limited by existing canon law.

This general position was supported by all 14th century antipapalists and developed by the 15th century Conciliar writers. The disputed papal election of 1378, beginning the Great Schism which lasted until 1417, weakened the position of the Papacy. The Church Councils, in 1409 at Pisa and in 1415 at Constance, attempted a reorganization of the Church. The argument at Constance that "the General Council has authority immediately from Christ" has been called "probably the most revolutionary official document in the history of the world."

The group of Conciliar writers included two important thinkers, Gerson (1363–1429), Chancellor of the University of Paris, and Nicholas of Cusa. They argued that the Church rather than the Pope was the ultimate ecclesiastical authority, and that the Pope was only the minister, not the monarch. A council was the only authority that could validly interpret the needs of the Church. For Gerson, the Council, "the assembling together and unified structure" of the Church had unfailing possession of the truth. For Nicholas, the emphasis was on consent: "Since all men are by nature free, every government . . . is derived solely from the common agreement and consent of the subjects." The group had gone considerably further than the anti-papalists of the previous century in claiming Conciliar supremacy over the Pope. Although the Papacy fought back and won at the Council of Basle, its powers had been reduced.

DANTE

On World Government (De Monarchia)

The Need for Unity and Peace

First we must ascertain what temporal monarchy is, both in essence and purpose. Temporal monarchy, or empire, is a single government extending over all people in time, that is, over all things that are measured by time. Three main questions concerning it require discussion. First, we may ask whether it is necessary for the well-being of the world; second, whether the Roman people were right in taking it upon themselves and third, whether its authority derives directly from God or from some minister or vicar of God.

. . . If there exists a purpose for human society, then this purpose will be the basic principle by which to test the validity of the arguments that follow. For it would be irrational to believe that one society has one purpose and another society another and that there is no single purpose common to all.

. . . We must now determine what is the purpose of human society as a whole. Having determined this, more than half our task is done, as the Philosopher (Aristotle) tells us in his *Nichomachean Ethics*. In order to see the point more clearly we must observe that just as Nature fashions the thumb for one purpose, the whole hand for another, the arm for yet another, and the entire man for one different from all these, so she creates for one purpose the individual, for another the family, for another the village, for another the city, for another the kingdom, and finally, for an ultimate purpose, by means of His art, which is Nature, the Eternal God brings into being the human race in its totality.

. . . There is, then, some distinct function for which humanity as a whole is ordained, a function which neither an individual nor a family, neither a village nor a city, nor a particular kingdom has power to perform. . . . So the specific characteristic of man is not simple existence, for that is shared by the elements; nor existence in combination, for that is met with in minerals; nor animate existence, for that is found in plants; nor intelligent existence, for that is participated in by brute animals; it is rather the possible intellect, or capacity for intellectual growth. Although angelic beings possess intellect, it is not intellect distinguished by potentiality, as in man's. Such beings are intelligent in a limited sense, and their existence is no other than the uninterrupted act of understanding;

hey would otherwise not be eternal. It is evident, therefore,
hat the specific characteristic of humanity is a distinctive
:apacity or power of intellect.

And since this capacity as a whole cannot be transformed
.nto action at one time through one man, or through any one
of the groups described above, there must be a multiplicity of
mankind to exercise the power of primal matter. Were it not
so, we should be granting the existence of unactualized po-
.entiality, which is impossible.

. . . The proper function of the human race, taken in the
aggregate, is to actualize continually the entire capacity of the
possible intellect, primarily in speculation, then, through its
extension and for its sake, in action. And since it is true that
whatever modifies a part modifies the whole, and that the individual man seated in quiet grows perfect in knowledge and
wisdom, it is plain that amid the calm and tranquillity of peace
the human race accomplishes most freely and easily its given
work. How nearly divine is this function is revealed in the
words: "Thou hast made him a little lower than the angels."
Whence it is manifest that universal peace is the best of those
things which are ordained for happiness.

. . . Our first question was whether a single, temporal government was necessary for the well-being of the world. Its
necessity can be gainsaid with no force of reason or authority,
and can be proved by the most powerful and patent arguments, of which the first is taken on the testimony of the
Philosopher in his *Politics*. There this venerable authority asserts that when several things are ordained for one end, one of
them must regulate or rule, and the others submit to regulation or rule. . . . We are now agreed that the whole human
race is ordered for one end, as already shown. It is meet,
therefore, that the leader and lord be one, and that he be
called Monarch, or Emperor. Thus it becomes obvious that
for the well-being of the world there is needed a Monarchy or
Empire. . . . And so all parts which we have designated as
included in kingdoms themselves, should be ordered with reference to one ruler or rule, that is to one Monarch or Monarchy.

Further, mankind is a whole with relation to certain parts,
and it is a part with relation to a certain whole. It is a whole,
of course, with relation to particular kingdoms and nations, as
was shown above, and it is a part with relation to the whole
universe. Therefore, in the manner in which the constituent
parts of collective humanity correspond to humanity as a
whole, so, we say, collective humanity corresponds as a part
to its larger whole. That the constituent parts of collective

humanity correspond to humanity as a whole through the one only principle of submission to a single Prince, can be easily gathered from what goes before. And therefore humanity corresponds to the universe itself, or to its Prince, who is God and Monarch, simply through one only principle, namely, the submission to a single Prince. We conclude from this that Monarchy is necessary to the world for its well-being.

. . . The human race, therefore, is ordered well, nay, is ordered best, when according to the utmost of its power it becomes like unto God. But the human race is most like God when it is most one, for the principle of unity dwells in Him alone. Wherefore it is written: "Hear, O Israel, the Lord our God is one Lord."

But the human race is most one when all are united together, a state which is manifestly impossible unless humanity as a whole becomes subject to one Prince, and consequently comes most into accordance with that divine intention which we showed is the good, nay, the best disposition of mankind.

. . . It is self-evident that between any two princes, neither of whom owes allegiance to the other, controversy may arise either by their own fault or by the fault of their subjects. For such, judgment is necessary. And inasmuch as one owing no allegiance to the other can recognize no authority in him (for an equal cannot control an equal), there must be a third prince with more ample jurisdiction, who may govern both within the circle of his right . . . A primal and highest judge must be reached, by whose judgments all disputes are settled mediately or immediately. And this judge will be Monarch or Emperor.

. . . Justice is preeminent only under a Monarch; therefore, that the world may be disposed for the best, there is needed a Monarchy or Empire. To make the assumption plain, it must be understood that Justice, considered in itself and in its distinctive nature, is a certain directness or rule of action avoiding the oblique on either side, and refusing the comparison of more or less in degree. . . .

Man's disposition to Justice may meet opposition in the will; for when will is not wholly unstained by cupidity, even if Justice be present, she may not appear in the perfect splendor of her purity, having encountered a quality which resists her to some degree, be it never so little. So it is right to repulse those who attempt to impassion a judge. In its operation, Man's justice may meet opposition through want of power; for since Justice is a virtue involving other persons, how can one act according to its dictates without the power of allotting to each man what belongs to him? It is obvious from this that in proportion to the just man's power will be the extent of his exercise of Justice.

From our exposition we may proceed to argue thus: Justice is most effective in the world when present in the most willing and powerful man; only a Monarch is such a man; therefore Justice subsisting in a sole Monarch is the most effective in the world.

. . . The former statement is apparent from the forerunning explanation; the latter, first, in regard to the will, second, in regard to the power, is unfolded thus. In regard to the will, it must first be noted that the worst enemy of Justice is cupidity, as Aristotle signifies in the fifth book of his *Nicomachean Ethics*. When cupidity is removed altogether, nothing remains inimical to Justice . . . Cupidity is impossible when there is nothing to be desired, for passions cease to exist with the destruction of their objects. Since his jurisdiction is bounded only by the ocean, there is nothing for a Monarch to desire. This is not true of other princes, whose realms terminate in those of others . . . So we conclude that among mortals the purest subject for the indwelling of Justice is the Monarch.

Moreover, to the extent however small that cupidity clouds the mental attitude toward Justice, charity or right love clarifies and brightens it. In whomever, therefore, right love can be present to the highest degree, in him can Justice find the most effective place. Such is the Monarch, in whose person Justice is or may be most effective. . . .

That right love should indwell in the Monarch more than in all men beside reveals itself thus: Everything loved is the more loved the nearer it is to him who loves; men are nearer to the Monarch than to other princes; therefore they are or ought to be most loved by him . . . Then among mortals he is the most universal cause of man's well-being, and the good of man is loved by him above all others.

Who doubts now that a Monarch is most powerfully equipped for the exercise of Justice? None save he who understands not the significance of the word, for a Monarch can have no enemies. The assumed proposition being therefore sufficiently explained, the conclusion is certain that Monarchy is indispensable for the best ordering of the world.

If the principle of freedom is explained, it will be apparent that the human race is ordered for the best when it is most free. Observe, in the minds of few, that the basic principle of our freedom is freedom of the will. Men come even to the point of saying that free will is free judgment in matters of will . . . So if judgment entirely controls desire, and is hindered by it in no way, judgment is free; but if desire influences judgment by hindering it in some manner, judgment cannot be free, for it acts not of itself, but is dragged captive by another.

. . . With this in mind we may understand that this freedom, or basic principle of our freedom is, as I said, the greatest gift bestowed by God upon human nature, for through it we attain to joy here as men, and to blessedness there as gods. If this is so, who will not admit that mankind is best ordered when able to use this principle most effectively? But the race is most free under a Monarch. Wherefore let us know . . . that whatever exists for its own sake and not for the sake of another is free . . .

Only if a Monarch rules can the human race exist for its own sake; only if a Monarch rules can the crooked policies be straightened, namely democracies, oligarchies and tyrannies which force mankind into slavery, as he sees who goes among them, and under which kings, aristocrats, called the best men, and zealots of popular liberty play at politics. For since a Monarch loves men greatly, a point already touched upon, he desires all men to do good, which cannot be among players at crooked policies.

. . . Wherefore it is also evident that although consul or king may be lord of others with respect to means of governing, they are servants with respect to the means of governing; and without doubt the Monarch must be held the chief servant of all. Now it becomes clear that a Monarch is conditioned in the matter of laws by his previously determined end. Therefore the human race existing under a Monarch is best ordered, and from this it follows that a Monarchy is essential to the well-being of the world.

. . . The Monarch is capable of the highest degree of judgment and Justice, and is therefore perfectly qualified, or especially well qualified, to rule. These two qualities are most befitting a maker and executor of the law, as that holiest of kings testifies by his petition to God for the attributes meet for a king and the son of a king, praying: "Give the king Thy judgments, O God, and Thy righteousness unto the king's son."

It was rightly assumed, then, that the Monarch alone is capable of supreme qualification to rule. Hence the Monarch is best able to direct others. Therefore it follows that for the best ordering of the world, Monarchy is necessary.

. . . But rather let it be understood that the human race will be governed by him in general matters pertaining to all peoples, and through him will be guided to peace by a government common to all. And this rule, or law, individual princes should receive from him, just as for any operative conclusion the practical intellect receives the major premise from the speculative intellect.

. . . Likewise I affirm that being and unity and goodness exist *seriatim* according to the fifth mode of priority. Being is naturally antecedent to unity, and unity to goodness; that which has completest being has completest unity and completest goodness. And as far as anything is from completest being, just so far is it from unity and also from goodness. In every class of objects the best is the most unified . . . We can thus see that to sin is naught else than to despise unity, and to depart therefrom to multiplicity.

. . . All concord depends upon unity in wills; mankind at its best is a concord of a certain kind. For just as one man at his best in body and spirit is a concord of a certain kind, and as a household, a city, and a kingdom is likewise a concord, so it is with mankind in its totality. Therefore the human race for its best disposition is dependent on unity in wills. But this state of concord is impossible unless one will dominates and guides all others into unity . . . Nor is this directing will a possibility unless there is one common Prince whose will may dominate and guide the wills of all others.

The Autonomy of the State

Besides, if the Church has power to confer authority on the Roman Prince, she would have it either from God, or from herself, or from some Emperor, or from the unanimous consent of mankind, or at least from the consent of the most influential. There is no other least crevice through which the power could have diffused itself into the Church. But from none of these has it come to her, and therefore the aforesaid power is not hers at all.

Here is the proof that it has come from none of these sources. If she had received it from God, it would have been by divine or natural law . . . But this ecclesiastical right came not by natural law, for nature imposes no law save her own effects, and inadequacy is not possible to God where He brings something into being without secondary agents . . . It is indisputable that nature gave not this law to the Church.

Neither did this power come by divine law; for in the bosom of the two Testaments, wherein is embodied every divine law, I am unable to discover any command for the early or later priesthood to have care or solicitude in temporal things.

. . . Also, that this power came not from the Church is easily seen. Nothing can give what it does not possess.

. . . And who doubts that it came not from the unanimous consent of men, or from the most influential? Not only all the people of Asia and Africa, but even the greater part of those inhabiting Europe would deny such consent.

. . . Although by the method of reduction to absurdity it has been shown that the authority of Empire has not its source in the Chief Pontiff, yet it has not been fully proved, save by an inference, that its immediate source is God, seeing that if the authority does not depend on the Vicar of God, we conclude that it depends on God Himself. For a perfect demonstration of the proposition we must prove directly that the Emperor, or Monarch, of the world has an immediate relationship to the Prince of the universe, who is God.

. . . Man may be considered with regard to either of his essential parts, body or soul. If considered in regard to the body alone, he is perishable; if in regard to the soul alone, he is imperishable.

. . . And inasmuch as every nature is ordained for a certain ultimate end, it follows that there exists for man a twofold end, in order that as he alone of all beings partakes of the perishable and the imperishable, so he alone of all beings should be ordained for two ultimate ends. One end is for that in him which is perishable, the other for that which is imperishable.

Ineffable Providence has thus designed two ends to be contemplated of man: first, the happiness of this life, which consists in the activity of his natural powers, and is prefigured by the terrestrial Paradise; and then the blessedness of life everlasting, which consists of the enjoyment of the countenance of God, to which man's natural powers may not attain unless aided by divine light, and which may be symbolized by the celestial Paradise.

. . . Wherefore a twofold directive agent was necessary to man, in accordance with the twofold end: the Supreme Pontiff to lead the human race to life eternal by means of revelation, and the Emperor to guide it to temporal felicity by means of philosophic instruction. And since none or few— and these with exceeding difficulty—could attain this port, were not the waves of seductive desire calmed, and mankind made free to rest in the tranquillity of peace, therefore this is the goal which he whom we call the guardian of the earth and Roman Prince should most urgently seek; then would it be possible for life on this mortal threshing floor to pass in freedom and peace. The order of the world follows the order inherent in the revolution of the heavens. To attain this order it is necessary that instruction productive of liberality and peace should be applied by the guardian of the realm, in due place and time, as dispensed by him who is the ever present Watcher of the whole order of the heavens. And He alone foreordained this order, that by it in His providence He might link together all things, each in its own place.

If this is so, and there is none higher than He, only God elects and only God confirms. Whence we may further conclude that neither those who are now, nor those who in any way whatsoever have been called Electors have the right to be so called; rather should they be entitled heralds of divine providence. Whence it is that those in whom is vested the dignity of proclamation suffer dissension among themselves at times, when, all or part of them being shadowed by the clouds of passion, they discern not the face of God's dispensation.

It is established, then, that the authority of temporal Monarchy descends, without mediation, from the fountain of universal authority. And this fountain, one in its purity of source, flows into multifarious channels out of the abundance of its excellence.

Methinks I have now approached close enough to the goal I had set myself, for I have taken the kernels of truth from the husks of falsehood, in that question which asked whether the office of Monarchy was essential to the welfare of the world, and in the next which made inquiry whether the Roman people rightly appropriated the Empire, and in the last which sought whether the authority of the Monarch derived from God immediately, or from some other. But the truth of this final question must not be restricted to mean that the Roman Prince shall not be subject in some degree to the Roman Pontiff, for felicity that is mortal is ordered in a measure after felicity that is immortal. Wherefore let Caesar honor Peter as a first-born son should honor his father, so that, refulgent with the light of paternal grace, he may illumine with greater radiance the earthly sphere over which he has been set by Him who alone is Ruler of all things spiritual and temporal.

MARSIGLIO OF PADUA
Defensor Pacis

The Validity of Law

Let us say in accordance with Aristotle in III *Politics*, ch. II, that the legislator, or prime and proper effective cause of law, is the people or body of citizens, or its more weighty part, through its choice or will orally expressed in the general assembly of citizens, commanding or determining, in regard to the civil actions of men, that something be done or not done, under penalty of temporal punishment. The more weighty part, I say, taking into consideration the number and the quality of persons in that community for which the law is enacted. The whole corporation of citizens, or its weightier part, either makes law itself, directly, or entrusts this task to some person or persons, who are not and cannot be the legislator in the absolute sense, but only for specific matters, and temporarily, and by virtue of the authority of the prime legislator. And I say in consequence that laws and anything whatever that is established by choice ought to receive the necessary approval by none other than that same prime legislator, with whatever solemnities may be appropriate. . . . By that same authority laws, and other things that are established by choice, ought to undergo addition or diminution or total change, interpretation, and suspension, in accordance with the exigency of times or places or other circumstances which make such change expedient for the sake of the common welfare. . . .

Moreover, following Aristotle, I mean by citizen any man who participates in the civil community, in the principate or the council or the jury, according to his rank. And the weightier part should be discovered in accordance with the opinion of Aristotle in VI *Politics*, ch. 3.

. . . Let us return to our announced purpose: namely, to demonstrate that the human authority of legislation belongs only to the corporation of citizens or to its more weighty part. . . . The primary human authority, in an absolute sense, to make or institute laws, belongs only to him from whom alone the best laws can proceed. Now this is the corporation of citizens, or its more weighty part, which represents the whole corporation, because it is not easy or possible to bring all persons to one opinion on account of the deficient nature of some, who through individual perversity or ignorance dissent from the common opinion but whose irrational protestations or contradictions ought not to impede or frustrate the common benefit. Therefore the authority to make or institute laws belongs only to the corporation of citizens, or to its more weighty part.

. . . The best law is that which is made for the common benefit of the citizens . . . the truth of anything is more certainly judged and its common utility more diligently stud-

ied, when the whole corporation of citizens directs upon it its
intellect and desire. For a greater number can give more attention to a defect in a proposed law than can any part of that
number, since the whole of any body is at least greater in
mass and in virtues than is any of its parts separately. Also,
the common utility of a law is given more attention by a
whole multitude, since no one knowingly harms himself . . .
the approval, interpretation, and suspension of laws, and the
other things belong to the authority of the legislator alone.

. . . It is suitable and very useful that the search for, or the
discovery and examination of the rules of just and beneficial
civil actions . . . which are to be made laws or statutes should
be entrusted by the corporation of citizens to prudent and
expert men: either each of the primary parts of the state . . .
should elect some of these prudent and expert men, in accordance with the proportion of each, or all the citizens assembled together should elect them all. And this will be a
suitable and useful way of coming together for the discovery
of laws without injury to the rest of the multitude, namely, of
the less learned, who would be of little help in seeking out
rules of this sort and would be disturbed from their other
work and other necessary things, which would be harmful
both to them as individuals and to the community.

But when these rules . . . have been discovered and diligently examined, they ought to be submitted for approval or
rejection to the assembled corporation of citizens, in order
that, if it seems to any of the citizens that something ought to
be added to them, or subtracted, or if something should be
altered or totally rejected, he may say so; because in this way
the law can be more usefully ordained. For, as we have already said, the less learned citizens can sometimes notice
something to be corrected in regard to the proposed law,
although they would not have known how to discover the law.
Also, because laws thus passed by the hearing and consent of
the whole multitude will be better observed, and no one will
have an occasion of protest against them.

Now when the said rules . . . have been made public and
those citizens who wish to say anything rationally against
them have been heard, such men as we have described ought
again to be chosen in the way described, or the aforesaid
confirmed, who, representing the name and authority of the
corporation of citizens, will approve or reject the aforesaid
rules in whole or in part; or, if it so wishes, the whole corporation of citizens or its weightier part may do this. And

after this approval, and not before, the aforesaid rules are laws. . . .

. . . Let us say, following the opinion of Aristotle in III *Politics,* ch. 6, that the efficient power of instituting the principate, or of choosing the ruler, belongs to the legislator or corporation of citizens. . . . The method varies from one country to another. But in every case this election or institution must always be made by the authority of the legislator which, as we have often said, is the corporation of citizens, or its more weighty part . . . an elected ruler, without hereditary succession, is greatly preferable for a polity to those who are not elected or those who are established with dynastic succession.

. . . The primary cause which effects, institutes, and determines the other offices or parts of the state is the legislator, and we say that the secondary and, as it were, instrumental or executive cause is the ruler, through the authority conferred upon him by the legislator and in accordance with the form which it has established for him: namely, the law, in accordance with which he should always, so far as possible, conduct and administer civil acts. . . . For although the legislator, as the first and proper cause, ought to determine who should fittingly fill these offices in the state, yet the ruling part, as in the case of any law, prescribes the execution or, if necessary, restrains it.

(Extracts from Book I, chapters 12, 13, 15.)

Restraint of the ruler

Because the ruler, being a man, . . . is capable of false judgments or perverse desires, or both, which result in his doing things which are contrary to the determinations of the law, therefore the ruler is made accountable for such actions to someone who has authority to judge and regulate him in accordance with the law . . . ; otherwise his principate would become despotic, and the life of the citizens would become servile and insufficient. . . .

Moreover, the judgment, decision, and execution of any correction of the ruler in accordance with his deserts or his transgression ought to be made by the legislator or by some person or persons appointed to this office by the authority of the legislator. . . . Also, the office of the prince who is to be corrected ought to be temporarily suspended, particularly in relation to the person or persons who are to judge of his transgressions, lest a schism and disturbance and conflict occur in the community because of the plurality of ruling authority, and because the ruler is not corrected as such but as a subject who has transgressed the law.

(Extract from Book I, chapter 18.)

Unity and order

. . . The state is like a kind of animate or animal nature. . . . Therefore, what health is to an animal and its parts, tranquillity, it seems, is to the city or kingdom and its parts instituted in accordance with reason. Now health is that good disposition of an animal by which each of its parts can perfectly perform the function appropriate to its nature; and according to this analogy tranquillity will be that good disposition of a city or kingdom by which each of its parts can perfectly perform the functions suitable to it, in accordance with reason and its institution.

Moreover, I say that the supreme government will necessarily be one in number, not plural, if the kingdom or city is to be rightly disposed. And I say the same concerning the ruler of the principate: not, indeed, that the ruler must be a single human being, but that the office of the ruler must be one. For there is a kind of principate, numerically one, supreme and well tempered, in which several men rule as one: as in the case of the aristocracy and the polity. . . . Yet these several men are numerically one principate in regard to their office because of the numerical unity of every action that proceeds from them, whether judgment, decision, or command; for such actions cannot proceed from any one of them by himself, but from the common decision and consent of them all, or of their more weighty part, in accordance with the laws established for these matters. . . .

. . . If there were more than one principate in a city or kingdom, and if these were not reduced or subordinated under some one supreme principate, the judgment, command, and execution of just and beneficial things would be defective; and thence, on account of the unpunished injustices of men, there would ultimately arise strife and the dissolution and destruction of the city or kingdom.

. . . The numerical unity of a city or kingdom is a unity of order: not unity in the strict sense, but a plurality of persons which is called one, or who are called one, not because they are one in number formally, through some form, but because they are ordained to something which is numerically one, namely, the principate, to which and by which they are ordained and governed. For a city or kingdom is not one through any unitary natural form, as the form of a composite or mixture, because its parts or offices, and the subjects or parts of these parts, are many entities, formally distinct from one another, separated both in place and in subject. Thus they are not a unity either through any one form inherent in them, or through any one thing permeating them or containing them like a wall, but as they are all ordained, through their will, to a single supreme principate.

(Extracts from Book I, chapters 2 and 17.)

Regnum and sacerdotium

. . . Now there is a difficult question to be considered. For we said . . . that the human legislator itself, either directly or through its ruling part, is the active cause of the institution of all the offices or parts of the state. But we also recall that we said . . . that the priesthood or sacerdotal office of the New Law was first instituted by Christ alone; and, as we have shown . . . , He renounced all secular rule and temporal lordship and was not the human legislator. . . . Consequently, someone may well wonder to whom, especially in what are now perfect communities of believers, the authority to institute the priesthood really belongs; for the things we have said on this point seem to be inconsistent with each other.

Let us, therefore, try to solve the apparent contradiction. . . . In so far as it involves the personal qualification which the teachers of the Holy Scripture call the priestly "character," the efficient cause of the priesthood, immediately and as its maker, is God. . . .

. . . But after the time of the apostles, when the number of priests had grown considerably, in order to avoid scandal and schism the priests chose one of themselves to direct and ordain the others in regard to the performance of the ecclesiastical office and service, and the distribution of the offerings made to the church, and the disposition of other matters in the more suitable way, lest the affairs and service of the temples be confused by a diversity of wishes, as they would be if everyone were acting at his own pleasure and whenever it suited him. And he who, according to this later custom, was chosen to rule the other priests kept for himself alone the name of bishop, or overseer, since he was overseer not only of the faithful people (for which reason all priests in the primitive church were called bishops) but also of the rest of his fellow priests. . . .

But this human election or institution conferred on the priest so chosen has no more of essential merit, or sacerdotal authority, or the power first described above, but only a certain power of managerial rule in the house or temple of God, of ordaining others to be priests, deacons, and the rest of the officers, and of regulating the terms on which power was given to the monks of those times. It involved, I assert, no coercive authority whatever, except in so far as such power might have been granted by the human legislator, . . . nor any other intrinsic dignity or power. . . . It follows that the bishop of Rome has no more of essential sacerdotal authority than any other priest, even as the blessed Peter had no more than the other apostles. For all received this authority from Christ equally and immediately. . . .

I wish further to draw the necessary inference that in already perfect communities of Christians it belongs only to the human legislator, or the multitude of Christians of the place over which the minister is to be established, to elect, determine, and present persons to be promoted to ecclesiastical order; and that no priest or bishop singly, nor any single college thereof, is permitted to confer such orders without the permission of the human legislator or of the ruler who bears its authority.

By the authority of Scripture this is evident from Acts 6: [1–6]. For the holy apostles, needing deacons to minister for themselves and for the people, summoned the multitude of Christians as that body whose it was to choose and determine such persons. But if, in the presence of the apostles, such an election was entrusted to a less perfect multitude, that the best qualified should be more certainly chosen (since a whole multitude may know something, especially of the morals and life of a man, of which a very learned man is often ignorant), how much more ought the election of priests, who have more need of virtue and wisdom than deacons, in the absence of such prelates as the apostles, and in a perfect community of Christians, to be entrusted to the whole body, that fuller and more certain knowledge of the candidate may be secured. . . .

Now, moreover, I wish to show by probable reason—if the necessary can be called probable—that the election and approval of a candidate for holy orders, in already perfect communities of Christians, belongs to . . . the decision of the human legislator; as does his secondary institution, by which he is made bishop or parish priest over some Christian people in a specific place . . . ; also his removal from or deprivation of his office; and, if necessary, compelling him to perform his office. Then I shall show to whom belongs the allotment of ecclesiastical temporals, called benefices.

. . . Legislation and the institution of rulers belong to the body of citizens substituting for the term "law" or "ruler" the election or approval of a candidate for holy orders, and his institution or appointment to the charge of a certain people or province, and his deprivation of or removal from the same on account of delinquency or some other rational cause.

Moreover, in these arguments the necessity of doing these things through the legislator or body of citizens is more evident in proportion as error in regard to a candidate for the priesthood or some other ecclesiastical rank and for the pastoral office is more perilous than an error in regard to human law or a ruler instituted in accordance therewith. For if a man who is morally perverse or ignorant or otherwise deficient is promoted to the priesthood and is thus given the care and direction of a Christian people, the peril of eternal death and of many civil disadvantages thereby threatens the people. . . . And the Christian people has, and reasonably ought to have, the power of discretion or caution, for otherwise it could not avoid this evil. . . .

(Extracts from Book II, chapters 6 and 7.)

EGIDIUS ROMANUS
De Ecclesiastica Potestate

The Plenitude of Power of the Pope

. . . Plenitude of power is in some agent when that agent can do without a second cause anything that he can do with a second cause. For if an agent does not have such power, it follows that he does not have full power, since he does not have the power in which all power is contained. Therefore, in so far as the Supreme Pontiff has the power in which all power is contained, we say that he has full power. Now in God Himself there is plenitude of power, since He can do without a second cause anything that He can do with a second cause. Therefore the power of all agents is contained in the first agent: namely, in God.

. . . So the Supreme Pontiff also, to the extent of the power which is in the church, has plenitude of power and can without a second cause do anything that he can do with a second cause: for instance, in the case of the election of a bishop, how the election of a bishop ought to be held and how the electors should be weighed in regard to zeal and merit and number—that is, how many and what sort of electors there ought to be so that the candidate may be deemed rightly elected—depends on the institution of the Supreme Pontiff; therefore such an election depends on the Supreme Pontiff's decreeing and ordaining the method of election, even as the production of natural things depends on God as a primary cause, Who lays down His laws for natural things, how they shall act and how they shall produce their effects. The election of a prelate depends also on the agreement of the canons as on a second cause, even as the production of natural things depends on natural things themselves under one first agent: namely, under God. Truly, therefore, to the extent of the power which is in the church, there resides a plenitude of power in the Supreme Pontiff, since he can do without a second cause what he can do with a second cause. For he could provide for any church without election by the chapter; and in so doing he would not act in accordance with the common laws which he has imposed but in accordance with his own plenitude of power. For, as we have said, the election of a prelate is made by a primary cause, the Supreme Pontiff, who decrees how the election shall be made, and by a second cause, namely, by the election carried out by the electors according to the form given them. Yet the Supreme Pontiff could, without a second cause of this sort (that is, without election by the electors) provide any church with a prelate. And what has been said about the election of a prelate holds true for other ecclesiastical matters, because the Supreme Pontiff can act without other agents as the one who has plenitude of power, in whom all the power of the church is recognized to reside.

(This extract is from Book III, Chapter 9.)

WILLIAM OF OCKHAM
Dialogus

The Right to Choose Rulers

. . . It is inferred by evident reason that, unless the contrary is ordained by the person or persons whose interests are involved, those who are to be ruled have the right to choose their ruler and set him over themselves, whence no ruler ought to be given them against their will. This can be proved by many examples and arguments, but I shall adduce a few. And the first is that no one should be set over a body of mortals except by their choice and consent. Further, what touches all should be done by all; now, the setting of someone over others touches all; therefore, it ought to be done by all. Again, those who can make law for themselves can, if they wish, elect their head; but any people or state can make law for themselves, which is called civil law; therefore, the people or state can make their own law and choose their head. And thus the election of a ruler always belongs to those who are to be ruled, unless the contrary is ordained by the person or persons whose interest is involved.

And this qualification is made for the following reason: that, in many cases at least, they can yield their right and transfer it to some other person or persons; and thus, although by natural law in the third sense the people has the right to establish laws, it has transferred that power to the emperor; and thus it was in the power of the emperor to transfer the right of election to some other person or persons. . . .

It seems that it would be better to say that, according to that opinion, the Romans have the right to elect their bishop from the law of peoples, since the principle that all those over whom someone is to be made ruler have the right to choose that ruler, unless they yield their right or a superior ordains the contrary, belongs to the law of peoples.

Although many things that belong to the law of peoples are natural rights in the third sense of natural law, yet, according to that opinion, it is more proper to say that the Romans have the right to elect their bishop from natural law in the third sense than from the law of peoples, for this reason: that to have a Catholic bishop does not belong to the law of peoples but to divine law, although the principle that he who is to be set over others ought to be elected by those over whom he is to be set belongs to the law of peoples. It belongs no less to divine law, for this reason: that it can be inferred from those things which are in the Scriptures, putting one with another; and thus the two suppositions from which it is inferred that the Romans have the right to elect their bishop belong, though in different ways, to divine law, whereas only one of the two belongs to the law of peoples. And for this reason it is more proper to say that the Romans have the right to elect their bishop from divine law, or from natural law in the third sense, than from the law of peoples.

(Extract from part 3, tr. 2, Book 3, chapter 6.)

AQUINAS

Summa Theologica

The Essence of Law

. . . Law is a rule and measure of acts whereby man is induced to act or is restrained from acting; for *lex* (law) is derived from *ligare* (to bind), because it binds one to act. Now the rule and measure of human acts is the reason, which is the first principle of human acts, as is evident from what has been stated above, since it belongs to the reason to direct to the end, which is the first principle in all matters of action, according to the Philosopher. Now that which is the principle in any genus is the rule and measure of that genus: for instance, unity in the genus of numbers, and the first movement in the genus of movements. Consequently it follows that law is something pertaining to reason.

Reason has its power of moving from the will . . . for it is due to the fact that one wills the end that the reason issues its commands as regards things ordained to the end. But in order that the volition of what is commanded may have the nature of law, it needs to be in accord with some rule of reason. And in this sense is to be understood the saying that the will of the sovereign has the force of law; otherwise the sovereign's will would savor of lawlessness rather than of law.

. . . The first principle in practical matters, which are the object of the practical reason, is the last end; and the last end of human life is bliss or happiness. . . . Consequently the law must needs regard principally the relationship to happiness. Moreover, since every part is ordained to the whole, as imperfect to perfect; and since one man is a part of the perfect community, the law must needs regard properly the relationship to universal happiness. Wherefore the Philosopher, in the above definition of legal matters, mentions both happiness and the body politic, for he says that we call those legal matters *just*, "which are adapted to produce and preserve happiness and its parts for the body politic," since the state is a perfect community, as he says in *Politics* i.i.

. . . A law, properly speaking, regards first and foremost the order to the common good. Now to order anything to the common good belongs either to the whole people or to someone who is the vicegerent of the whole people. And therefore the making of a law belongs either to the whole people or to a public personage who has care of the whole people, since in all other matters the directing of anything to the end concerns him to whom the end belongs.

A private person cannot lead another to virtue efficaciously, for he can only advise, and if his advice be not taken, it has no coercive power, such as the law should have in order to prove an efficacious inducement to virtue, as the Philosopher says. But this coercive power is vested in the whole people or in some public personage to whom it belongs to inflict penalties. . . . Wherefore the framing of laws belongs to him alone.

As one man is a part of the household, so a household is part of the state; and the state is a perfect community, according to *Politics* i.i. And therefore, as the good of one man is not the last end, but is ordained to the common good, so, too, the good of one household is ordained to the good of a single state, which is a perfect community. Consequently he that governs a family can indeed make certain commands or ordinances, but not such as to have properly the force of law.

Thus from the four preceding articles the definition of law may be gathered; and it is nothing else than an ordinance of reason for the common good, made by him who has care of the community, and promulgated.

The natural law is promulgated by the fact that God instilled it into man's mind so as to be known by him naturally.

Those who are not present when a law is promulgated are bound to observe the law, in so far as it is notified or can be notified to them by others, after it has been promulgated.

(Extract from I-II, 90.)

The Various Kinds of Law

. . . A law is nothing else but a dictate of practical reason emanating from the ruler who governs a perfect community. Now it is evident, granted that the world is ruled by divine providence that the whole community of the universe is governed by divine reason. Wherefore the very Idea of the government of things in God the Ruler of the universe has the nature of a law. . . . This kind of law must be called eternal.

. . . Since all things subject to divine providence are ruled and measured by the eternal law . . . It is evident that all things partake somewhat of the eternal law, in so far as, namely, from its being imprinted on them, they derive their respective inclinations to their proper acts and ends. Now among all others the rational creature is subject to divine providence in the most excellent way, in so far as it partakes of a share of providence, by being provident both for itself and for others. Wherefore it has a share of the eternal reason, whereby it has a natural inclination to its proper act and end: and this participation of the eternal law in the rational creature is called the natural law. . . . It is therefore evident that the natural law is nothing else than the rational creature's participation of the eternal law.

Every act of reason and will in us is based on that which is according to nature . . . for every act of reasoning is based on principles that are known naturally, and every act of appetite in respect of the means is derived from the natural appetite in respect of the last end. Accordingly the first direction of our acts to their end must needs be in virtue of the natural law.

Even irrational animals partake in their own way of the eternal reason, just as the rational creature does. But because the rational creature partakes thereof in an intellectual and rational manner, therefore the participation of the eternal law in the rational creature is properly called a law, since a law is something pertaining to reason. Irrational creatures, however, do not partake thereof in a rational manner, wherefore there is no participation of the eternal law in them, except by way of similitude.

. . . A law is a dictate of the practical reason. . . . Just as, in the speculative reason, from naturally known indemonstrable principles we draw the conclusions of the various sciences, the knowledge of which is not imparted to us by nature, but acquired by the efforts of reason; so, too, it is from the precepts of the natural law, as from general and indemonstrable principles, that the human reason needs to proceed to the more particular determination of certain matters. These particular determinations, devised by human reason, are called human laws.

The practical reason is concerned with practical matters, which are singular and contingent, but not with necessary things, with which the speculative reason is concerned. Wherefore human laws cannot have that inerrancy that belongs to the demonstrated conclusions of sciences. Nor is it necessary for every measure to be altogether unerring and certain, but according as it is possible in its own particular genus.

. . . Besides the natural and the human law it was necessary for the directing of human conduct to have a divine law. And this for four reasons. First, because it is by law that man is directed how to perform his proper acts in view of his last end . . . since man is ordained to an end of eternal happiness which is inproportionate to man's natural faculty, as stated above, therefore it was necessary that, besides the natural law and the human law, man should be directed to his end by a law given by God.

Secondly, because, on account of the uncertainty of human judgment, especially on contingent and particular matters, different people form different judgments on human acts; whence also different and contrary laws result. In order, therefore, that man may know without any doubt what he ought to do and what he ought to avoid, it was necessary for man to be directed in his proper acts by a law given by God, for it is certain that such a law cannot err.

Thirdly, because man can make laws in those matters of which he is competent to judge. But man is not competent to judge of interior movements that are hidden, but only of exterior acts which appear; and yet for the perfection of virtue it is necessary for man to conduct himself aright in both kinds of acts. Consequently human law could not sufficiently curb and direct interior acts, and it was necessary for this purpose that a divine law should supervene.

Fourthly, because, as Augustine says, human law cannot punish or forbid all evil deeds; since while aiming at doing away with all evils, it would do away with many good things, and would hinder the advance of the common good, which is necessary for human intercourse. In order, therefore, that no evil might remain unforbidden and unpunished, it was necessary for the divine law to supervene, whereby all sins are forbidden.

A law is nothing else than a dictate of reason in the ruler by [which] his subjects are governed. Now the virtue of any subordinate thing consists in its being well subordinated to that by which it is regulated. . . . But every law aims at being obeyed by those who are subject to it. Consequently it is evident that the proper effect of law is to lead its subjects to their proper virtue; and since virtue is "that which makes its subject good," it follows that the proper effect of law is to make those whom it is given good, either simply or in some particular respect.

. . . And since law is given for the purpose of directing human acts as far as human acts conduce to virtue, so far does law make men good.

. . . A tyrannical law, through not being according to reason, is not a law, absolutely speaking, but rather a perversion of law; and yet in so far as it is something in the nature of a law, it aims at the citizens being good. For all it has in the nature of law consists in its being an ordinance made by a superior to his subjects, and aims at being obeyed by them, which is to make them good, not simply, but with respect to that particular government.

(Extracts from I-II, 91 and 92.)

The Eternal Law

God, by His wisdom, is the creator of all things, in relation to which He stands as the artificer to the products of his art. . . . Moreover, He governs all the acts and movements that are to be found in each single creature. . . . Wherefore as the type of the divine wisdom, inasmuch as by it all things are created, has the character of art, exemplar or idea, so the type of divine wisdom, as moving all things to their due end, bears the character of law. Accordingly, the eternal law is nothing else than the type of divine wisdom, as directing all actions and movements.

. . . Law denotes a kind of plan directing acts toward an end. Now wherever there are movers ordained to one another, the power of the second mover must needs be derived from the power of the first mover, since the second mover does not move except in so far as it is moved by the first. Wherefore we observe the same in all those who govern, so that the plan of government is derived by secondary governors from the governor-in-chief: thus the plan of what is to be done in a state flows from the king's command to his inferior administrators; and again in things of art the plan of whatever is to be done by art flows from the chief craftsman to the under-craftsmen who work with their hands. Since then the eternal law is the plan of government in the chief Governor, all the plans of government in the inferior governors must be derived from the eternal law. But the plans of inferior governors are all other laws besides the eternal law. Therefore all laws, in so far as they partake of right reason, are derived from the eternal law. Hence Augustine says that "in temporal law there is nothing just and lawful but what man has drawn from the eternal law."

Human law has the nature of law in so far as it partakes of right reason; and it is clear that, in this respect, it is derived from the eternal law. But in so far as it deviates from reason, it is called an unjust law and has the nature, not of law, but of violence. Nevertheless even an unjust law, in so far as it retains some appearance of law, through being framed by one who is in power, is derived from the eternal law, since all power is from the Lord God.

(Extract from I-II, 93.)

Natural Law

. . . The first principle in the practical reason is one founded on the notion of good, viz., that *good is that which all things seek after.* Hence this is the first precept of law, that *good is to be done and ensued, and evil is to be avoided.* All other precepts of the natural law are based upon this, so that whatever the practical reason naturally apprehends as man's good (or evil) belongs to the precepts of the natural law as something to be done or avoided.

Since, however, good has the nature of an end, and evil the

nature of a contrary, hence it is that all those things to which man has a natural inclination are naturally apprehended by reason as being good and, consequently, as objects of pursuit, and their contraries as evil and objects of avoidance. Wherefore the order of the precepts of the natural law is according to the order of natural inclinations. Because in man there is first of all an inclination to good in accordance with the nature which he has in common with all substances, inasmuch as every substance seeks the preservation of its own being, according to. its nature; and by reason of this inclination, whatever is a means of preserving human life and of warding off its obstacles belongs to the natural law. Secondly, there is in man an inclination to things that pertain to him more specially, according to that nature which he has in common with other animals; and in virtue of this inclination, those things are said to belong to the natural law "which nature has taught to all animals," such as sexual intercourse, education of offspring, and so forth. Thirdly, there is in man an inclination to good, according to the nature of his reason, which nature is proper to him: thus man has a natural inclination to know the truth about God and to live in society; and in this respect, whatever pertains to this inclination belongs to the natural law, for instance, to shun ignorance, to avoid offending those among whom one has to live, and other such things regarding the above inclination.

. . . to the natural law belong those things to which a man is inclined naturally; and among these it is a special property of man to be inclined to act according to reason. Now reason proceeds from what is common, or general, to what is proper, or special. But there is a difference in this regard between the speculative reason and practical reason. The speculative reason is concerned primarily with what is necessary, that is, with those things which cannot be other than they are; and therefore, in the case of speculative reason, both the common principles and the special conclusions are necessarily true. In the case of the practical reason, on the other hand, which is concerned with contingent matters, such as human actions, even though there be some necessary truth in the common principles, yet the more we descend to what is proper and peculiar, the more deviations we find. . . . But in the case of the proper or peculiar conclusions of the practical reason there is neither the same truth and rectitude among all men, nor, where it does exist, is it equally known to all.

. . . Natural law in its first common principles is the same among all men, both as to validity and recognition (something is right for all and is so by all recognized). But as to certain proper or derived norms, which are, as it were, conclusions of these common principles, they are valid and are so recognized by all men only in the majority of cases. For in special cases they may prove defective both as to validity because of certain particular impediments (just as things of nature in the sphere of generation and corruption prove to be defective because of impediments) and also as to recognition. And this because some men have a reason that has been distorted by passion, or by evil habits, or by bad natural relations.

A thing is said to belong to the natural law in two ways. First, because nature inclines thereto: e.g., that one should not do harm to another. Secondly, because nature did not bring in the contrary: thus we might say that for man to be naked is of the natural law because nature did not give him clothes, but art invented them. In this sense, "the possession of all things in common and universal freedom" are said to be of the natural law because, to wit, the distinction of possessions and slavery were not brought in by nature, but devised by human reason for the benefit of human life. Accordingly the law of nature was not changed in this respect, except by addition.

(Extract from I-II, 94)

Human Law

Man has a natural aptitude for virtue, but the perfection of virtue must be acquired by man by means of some kind of training. . . . But since some are found to be depraved and prone to vice, and not easily amenable to words, it was necessary for such to be restrained from evil by force and fear, in order that, at least, they might desist from evil-doing and leave others in peace, and that they themselves, by being habituated in this way, might be brought to do willingly what hitherto they did from fear, and thus become virtuous. Now this kind of training which compels through fear of punishment is the discipline of laws. Therefore, in order that man might have peace and virtue, it was necessary for laws to be framed, for, as the Philosopher says, "as man is the most noble of animals if he be perfect in virtue, so is he the lowest of all if he be severed from law and righteousness"; because man can use his reason to devise means of satisfying his lusts and evil passions, which other animals are unable to do.

Men who are well disposed are led willingly to virtue by being admonished better than by coercion, but men who are evilly disposed are not led to virtue unless they are compelled.

As Augustine said, "that which is not just seems to be no law at all"; wherefore the force of a law depends on the extent of its justice. Now in human affairs a thing is said to be just from being right according to the rule of reason. But the first rule of reason is the law of nature. . . . Consequently, every human law has just so much of the nature of law as it is derived from the law of nature. But if in any point it deflects from the law of nature, it is no longer a law but a perversion of law.

But it must be noted that something may be derived from the natural law in two ways: first, as a conclusion from premises; secondly, by way of determination of certain generalities. The first way is like to that by which, in the sciences, demonstrated conclusions are drawn from the principles, while the second mode is likened to that whereby, in the arts, general forms are particularized as to details: thus the craftsman needs to determine the general form of a house to some particular shape. . . .

Accordingly, both modes of derivation are found in the human law. But those things which are derived in the first way are contained in human law, not as emanating therefrom exclusively, but having some force from the natural law also. But those things which are derived in the second way have no other force than that of human law.

. . . Now, in the notion of human law, many things are contained in respect of any of which human law can be divided properly and of itself. For in the first place it belongs to the notion of human law to be derived from the law of nature. In this respect positive law is divided into the "law of nations" and "civil law," according to the two ways in which something may be derived from the law of nature. Because to the law of nations belong those things which are derived from the law of nature as conclusions from premises, e.g., just buyings and sellings, and the like, without which men cannot live together, which is a point of the law of nature, since man is by nature a social animal, as is proved in *Politics* i.2. But those things which are derived from the law of nature by way of particular determination belong to the civil law, according as each state decides on what is best for itself.

Secondly, it belongs to the notion of human law to be ordained to the common good of the state. In this respect human law may be divided according to the different kinds of men who work in a special way for the common good: e.g., priests, by praying to God for the people; princes, by governing the people; soldiers, by fighting for the safety of the people. Wherefore certain special kinds of law are adapted to these men.

Thirdly, it belongs to the notion of human law to be framed by that one who governs the community of the state. In this respect there are various human laws according to the various forms of government.

Fourthly, it belongs to the notion of human law to direct human actions. In this respect, according to the various matters of which the law treats, there are various kinds of laws differentiated, not on account of the authors, but on account of the matters to which they refer.

. . . Whatever is for an end should be proportionate to that end. Now the end of law is the common good; because, as Isidore says, "law should be framed, not for any private benefit, but for the common good of all the citizens." Hence human laws should be proportionate to the common good. Now the common good comprises many things. Wherefore law should take account of many things, as to persons, as to [activities], and as to times; because the community of the state is composed of many persons and its good is procured by many actions; nor is it established to endure for only a short time, but to last for all time by the citizens succeeding one another, as Augustine says.

On the Power of Human Law

Now human law is framed for a number of human beings, the majority of whom are not perfect in virtue. Wherefore human laws do not forbid all vices from which the virtuous abstain, but only the more grievous vices from which it is possible for the majority to abstain; and chiefly those that are to the hurt of others, without the prohibition of which human society could not be maintained: thus human law prohibits murder, theft, and suchlike.

The purpose of human law is to lead men to virtue, not suddenly, but gradually. Wherefore it does not lay upon the multitude of imperfect men the burdens of those who are already virtuous, viz., that they should abstain from all evil. Otherwise these imperfect ones, being unable to bear such precepts, would break out into yet greater evils.

The natural law is a participation in us of the eternal law, while human law falls short of the eternal law. Now Augustine says: "The law which is framed for the government of states allows and leaves unpunished many things that are punished by divine providence. Nor, if this law does not attempt to do everything, is this a reason why it should be blamed for what it does." Wherefore, too, human law does not prohibit everything that is forbidden by the natural law.

Now all the objects of virtues can be referred either to the private good of an individual or to the common good of the multitude: thus matters of fortitude may be achieved either for the safety of the state or for upholding the rights of a friend, and in like manner with the other virtues. But law is ordained to the common good. Wherefore there is no virtue whose acts cannot be prescribed by the law. Nevertheless human law does not prescribe concerning all the acts of every virtue, but only in regard to those that are ordainable to the common good—either immediately, as when certain things are done directly for the common good, or mediately, as when a lawgiver prescribes certain things pertaining to [proper instruction] whereby the citizens are directed in the upholding of the common good of justice and peace.

Now laws are said to be just—from the end, when, to wit, they are ordained to the common good—and from their author, that is to say, when the law that is made does not exceed the power of the lawgiver—and from their form, when, to wit, burdens are laid on the subjects, according to an equality of proportion and with a view to the common good.

On the other hand, laws may be unjust in two ways: first, by being contrary to human good, through being opposed to the things mentioned above—either in respect of the end, as when an authority imposes on his subjects burdensome laws, conducive, not to the common good, but rather to his own cupidity or vainglory; or in respect of the author, as when a man makes a law that goes beyond the power committed to him; or in respect of the form, as when burdens are imposed unequally on the community, although with a view to the common good. The like are acts of violence rather than laws. . . .

Secondly, laws may be unjust through being opposed to the divine good: such are the laws of tyrants inducing to idolatry or to anything else contrary to the divine law; and laws of this kind must nowise be observed because, as stated in Acts v. 29, "we ought to obey God rather than men."

The sovereign is said to be "exempt from the law," as to its coercive power, since, properly speaking, no man is coerced by himself, and law has no coercive power save from the authority of the sovereign. Thus then is the sovereign said to be exempt from the law, because none is competent to pass sentence on him if he acts against the law.—But as to the directive force of law, the sovereign is subject to the law by his own will, according to the statement that "whatever law a man makes for another, he should keep himself." And a wise authority says: "Obey the law that thou makest thyself." Hence, in the judgment of God, the sovereign is not exempt from the law as to its directive force, but he should fulfill it of his own free will and not of constraint.—Again the sovereign is above the law in so far as, when it is expedient, he can change the law and dispense with it according to time and place.

Every law is directed to the common weal of men and derives the force and nature of law accordingly. Now it happens often that the observance of some point of law conduces to the common weal in the majority of instances, and yet, in some cases, is very hurtful. Since, then, the lawgiver cannot have in view every single case, he shapes the law according to what happens most frequently, by directing his attention to the common good. Wherefore, if a case arise wherein the observance of that law would be hurtful to the general welfare, it should not be observed.

(Extracts from I-II, 96 and 97)

On Kingship
(De Regimine Principum)

The Need for Political Authority

In all things which are ordered toward an end wherein this or that course may be adopted, some directive principle is needed through which the due end may be reached by the most direct route. . . . Now, man has an end to which his whole life and all his actions are ordered; for man is an intelligent agent, and it is clearly the part of an intelligent agent to act in view of an end. Men also adopt different methods in proceeding toward their proposed end, as the diversity of men's pursuits and actions clearly indicates. Consequently man needs some directive principle to guide him toward his end.

To be sure, the light of reason is placed by nature in every man, to guide him in his acts toward his end. Yet it is natural for man, more than for any other animal, to be a social and political animal, to live in a group.

This is clearly a necessity of man's nature.

It is therefore necessary for man to live in a multitude so that each one may assist his fellows, and different men may be occupied in seeking, by their reason, to make different discoveries—one, for example, in medicine, one in this pursuit and another in that.

If, then, it is natural for man to live in the society of many, it is necessary that there exist among men some means by which the group may be governed. For where there are many men together and each one is looking after his own interest, the multitude would be broken up and scattered unless there were also an agency to take care of what appertains to the common weal.

Therefore in every multitude there must be some governing power.

In the government of a multitude there is a distinction between right and wrong. A thing is rightly directed when it is led toward a befitting end, wrongly when it is led toward an unbefitting end. If, therefore, a multitude of free men is ordered by the ruler toward the common good of the multitude, that rulership will be right and just, as is suitable to free men. If, on the other hand, a rulership aims, not at the common good of the multitude, but at the private good of the ruler, it will be an unjust and perverted rulership.

The aim of any ruler should be directed toward securing the welfare of that which he undertakes to rule. The duty of the pilot, for instance, is to preserve his ship amidst the perils of the sea and to bring it unharmed to the port of safety. Now the welfare and safety of a multitude formed into a society lies in the preservation of its unity, which is called peace. If this is removed, the benefit of social life is lost and, moreover, the multitude in its disagreement becomes a burden to itself. The chief concern of the ruler of a multitude, therefore, is to procure the unity of peace. Now it is manifest that what is itself one can more efficaciously bring about unity than several—just as the most efficacious cause of heat is that which is by its nature hot. Therefore the rule of one man is more useful than the rule of many.

Several are said to be united according as they come closer to being one. So one man rules better than several who come near being one.

Again, whatever is in accord with nature is best, for in all things nature does what is best. Now every natural governance is governance by one. In the multitude of bodily members there is one which is the principal mover, namely, the heart; and among the powers of the soul one power presides as chief, namely, the reason. Among bees there is one king bee, and in the whole universe there is one God, Maker and Ruler of all things. And there is a reason for this. Every multitude is derived from unity. Wherefore, if artificial things are an imitation of natural things and a work of art is better according as it attains a closer likeness to what is in nature, it follows that it is best for a human multitude to be ruled by one person.

(Extracts from chs. 1 and 2)

The Dangers of Tyranny

Now, as has been shown above, monarchy is the best government. If, therefore, "it is the contrary of the best that is worst," it follows that tyranny is the worst kind of government.

Further, a united force is more efficacious in producing its effect than a force which is scattered or divided. Many persons together can pull a load which could not be pulled by each one taking his part separately and acting individually. Therefore, just as it is more useful for a force operating for a good to be more united, in order that it may work good more effectively, so a force operating for evil is more harmful when it is one than when it is divided. Now, the power of one who rules unjustly works to the detriment of the multitude, in that he diverts the common good of the multitude to his own benefit. Therefore, for the same reason that, in a just government, the government is better in proportion as the ruling power is one—thus monarchy is better than aristocracy, and aristocracy better than polity—so the contrary will be true of an unjust government, namely, that the ruling power will be more harmful in proportion as it is more unitary. Consequently, tyranny is more harmful than oligarchy and oligarchy more harmful than democracy.

Moreover, a government becomes unjust by the fact that the ruler, paying no heed to the common good, seeks his own private good. Wherefore the further he departs from the common good the more unjust will his government be.

Therefore, since the rule of one man, which is the best, is to be preferred, and since it may happen that it be changed into a tyranny, which is the worst (all this is clear from what has been said), a scheme should be carefully worked out which would prevent the multitude ruled by a king from falling into the hands of a tyrant.

First, it is necessary that the man who is raised up to be king by those whom it concerns should be of such condition that it is improbable that he should become a tyrant. Then, once the king is established, the government of the kingdom must be so arranged that opportunity to tyrannize is removed. At the same time his power should be so tempered that he cannot easily fall into tyranny. How these things may be done we must consider in what follows.

Finally, provision must be made for facing the situation should the king stray into tyranny.

Indeed, if there be not an excess of tyranny it is more expedient to tolerate the milder tyranny for a while than, by acting against the tyrant, to become involved in many perils more grievous than the tyranny itself. For it may happen that those who act against the tyrant are unable to prevail and the tyrant then will rage the more.

If the excess of tyranny is unbearable, some have been of the opinion that it would be an act of virtue for strong men to slay the tyrant and to expose themselves to the danger of death in order to set the multitude free.

Should private persons attempt on their own private presumption to kill the rulers, even though tyrants, this would be dangerous for the multitude as well as for their rulers. This is because the wicked usually expose themselves to dangers of this kind more than the good, for the rule of a king, no less than that of a tyrant, is burdensome to them. Consequently, by presumption of this kind, danger to the people from the loss of a good king would be more probable than relief through the removal of a tyrant.

Furthermore, it seems that to proceed against the cruelty of tyrants is an action to be undertaken, not through the private presumption of a few, but rather by public authority.

If to provide itself with a king belongs to the right of a given multitude, it is not unjust that the king be deposed or have his power restricted by that same multitude if, becoming a tyrant, he abuses the royal power. It must not be thought that such a multitude is acting unfaithfully in deposing the tyrant, even though it had previously subjected itself to him in perpetuity, because he himself has deserved that the covenant with his subjects should not be kept, since, in ruling the multitude, he did not act faithfully as the office of a king demands.

If, on the other hand, it pertains to the right of a higher authority to provide a king for a certain multitude, a remedy against the wickedness of a tyrant is to be looked for from him.

Should no human aid whatsoever against a tyrant be forthcoming, recourse must be had to God, the King of all, Who is a helper in due time in tribulation. For it lies in his power to turn the cruel heart of the tyrant to mildness.

(Extracts from chs. 3 and 6)

NICHOLAS OF CUSA
De Concordantia Catholica

The Need for Consent in the Church

. . . Thus even as a republic is a common thing of the people, and a common thing is a thing of the state, and the state is a multitude of men brought to a kind of bond of concord . . . , so he who presides in the pastoral court corresponds to him to whom a republic is entrusted. Whence all who are under the court are understood to be united in him who presides as if he were one soul and they the body which the soul has to animate. Whence such a people, thus united with their pastor, constitute a church. . . . Whence even as the universal church is the mystic body of Christ, so particular churches are the mystic bodies of those who preside over them as delegates of Christ. . . . And this is one premise of our proposition: that the church is in the bishop through union, and thus the bishop symbolizes and represents them, since he is a public person with regard to that group; and this is a premise of all that will be said hereafter. . . .

. . . it clearly appears that the law and the canon is the rule of every judge, and that every law and canon is superior to any judging judge. Further, if canons are approved by agreement, use, and acceptance, then the validity of any statute rests on its acceptance. Wherefore the ecclesiastical canons are rightly declared by the common council, for the church is a congregation. One man cannot rightly produce the ecclesiastical canons. From this it follows that we see canons produced in the council by concordant acceptance, consent, and subscription; moreover, the decretals or judicial decisions of the Roman pontiffs, or decisions on dubious points as they arise, have derived their vigour, validity, and justice not from an intrinsically authoritative will, but from the fact that the canons established it as fitting that decisions be so made. . . .

Now, from the foregoing it is certain that the binding force of all statutes consists in agreement and consent, tacit or explicit, either by acceptance in use or by the pronouncement of those who potentially represent others by a certain embassy or presidency. For even as a bishop and his chapter are said to compose a diocesan church, because that group potentially represents all the other members of that church, in the same way the metropolitan and his suffragans constitute a provincial church, and a patriarch and the metropolitans constitute a patriarchal church. Whence the authority of each group extends potentially through all the members of the representative group.

Thus the priesthood receives from the inferior people the motive, vegetative, and sensitive power of a presidency, which power comes from the potency of the matter of the subjects, through voluntary subjection; but through the sacraments it receives from God the power of a rational soul, which comes from above; that thus in sweet concordance, by supernal power mediated through extracted and surrendered power, it may flow into the body of the subjects, who are perfected to salutary union with Christ the Head. . . . And this is a beautiful thought; that all powers, spiritual as well as temporal and corporal, are latent in the people in potency, although, in order that the presidential power may be actually constituted, the concurrence of the formative ray from above is necessary to constitute it in being; and I speak concerning ordained power. . . .

. . . Superiors ought to be obeyed, so long as they do not overstep the bounds within which the power of each one is enclosed. And first we must consider the power of the Roman pontiff, because, as Gregory says (*Decretum*, c. 45, C. 2, q. 7), a reforming council should begin with the head. . . . Whence, if it is done in such a way that every power uses in its government the rules laid down by the universal council, necessarily the best reform follows. . . . All members of the one church and mystic body of Christ have their individual offices, in which they cannot be impeded by others without a disturbance of order. Moreover, a disturbance of order is a disturbance of the whole bond of union of the church, with a resulting diffusion of deformity and sickness into the whole body of the church (*Decretum*, c. 39, C. 11, q. 1). See also the words of Gregory (*Decretum*, c. 1, di. 89), saying that it is noxious and most shameful that one member should usurp the office of another and not distribute ministries to separate individuals. Therefore, neither the head nor any member whatever has the power to usurp the office of any other member, if the one whose office is usurped is healthy and alive and innocent of negligence; such usurpation results in an injurious disturbance of the whole body. Thus, if we discover what things befit each member of the ancient rules, we shall see how it has come about that the body of the church is deformed. For it would not be deformed if it were not for the intervention of excess and abuse. And because when the head is sick the other members suffer, the health of those who preside is the health of the subject. Wherefore, no greater deformity can be caused by anyone than is caused by one who through contemplation of his own great power comes to believe that all things are permitted to him and infringes upon the rights of his subjects.

. . . . Although all the apostles were rectors, pastors, and vicars of Christ, . . . yet the holy doctors affirm that in that pastorate, rectorate, and vicarage Peter had the primacy by more abundant grace, through this fact: that the keys were promised and given to him and, by the words 'Feed My sheep,' the pastorate was assigned to him as representing the whole church. . . . Moreover, that principate of Peter does not consist in superiority in the power of binding and loosing in the penitential court or in the confection of the sacraments; no one has any doubt concerning the latter, nor ought there to be doubt concerning the former . . . because the spiritual judicial power of all bishops is the same, as was that of the apostles, since this flows from Christ by way of the priesthood. . . . Nor was Peter through that primacy superior to the church, since he was named for the church and for its sake. . . . Therefore the superiority of Peter was not superiority over the church, but within it. Whence, although he was the mouth and head of the apostles of the church, and made proposals in its name yet nevertheless he was under it as a member . . . the good ordained government of the church was committed by Christ to Peter that, even as he was the first of individual members, so he would be servant and minister of all; because, if Peter derived his name from *petra* on behalf of the church, and if the church is nothing other than a union of the faithful, there rightly exists a presidency in order to abolish schism on behalf of the union of the faithful. Wherefore the union of the faithful is that for whose preservation and maintenance a presidency over individuals exists. And for this reason the union of the faithful which we call the church, or the universal council of the catholic church representing the church, is over its minister and over him who presides over individual members; and thus I understand the saying of the Saviour, that he who was greater among the apostles distributively ought to be minister of all collectively; because thus they form a church. . . . Wherefore all spiritual power is properly founded in liberty, not in coercion, as regards that root by which it is from Christ. But, because the principal presidency itself, ordained to that unity for the sake of preventing schism, is from God, then that unity cannot rightly be conserved unless there is some coercion in the ecclesiastical prince himself, but without that dominion by which the princes of the Gentiles domi-

nate. For it is necessary that putrid limbs and feet be cut off
and the eye that scandalizes be torn out from the church, i
the body of the church is to be kept healthy. Wherefore tha
coercion will not be as the princes of the Gentiles dominate
because that kind of domination is through force over bodies
and things; but it will be coercion initiated through the free
subjection of all or of a majority, and without any punish
ment that does not tend to salvation. Christ constituted Pete
with the concurrent consent of the apostles, and thus this
special kind of coercive power of a superior against his sub
jects is rooted in their election and consent. For they who
were at first most free submit themselves to a president by
electing him over themselves. . . .

. . . (but) all ecclesiastical and spiritual presidency is constituted by Christ through the mediation of human assent . .
(Extracts are from Book I, chapter 6; Book II, chapters 14
15, 19, 27, 34.)

SECTION VII

THE RENAISSANCE

The concept of a unified Christian society had broken down for a variety of reasons. Economic development had led to the growth of commerce, the expansion of towns, international trade, trade fairs and exhibitions, the increasing use of money and the start of a banking system. The geographical voyages of discovery had opened up a whole world to trade as well as to religion. Centralized national states were emerging, with national languages and cultures. A secular tone of life was developing with a growing population, a wealthy laity, scientific methodology, and humanistic philosophy. The clerical monopoly of education ended with the invention of printing, the increasing degree of literacy, lay education and patronage, the founding of universities and libraries.

The Renaissance—the rebirth of the human spirit—dawned in the 15th century when, as Vasari wrote of the great artists of the age, "the glorious minds that sprang from the soil of Tuscany did what their predecessors could not do, turn the ruins of ancient Rome to their advantage." Botticelli, Brunelleschi, Donatello, Ghiberti, Raphael, Leonardo and Michelangelo, were among the glorious. Burckhardt, in his classic, *The Civilization of the Renaissance in Italy,* suggested that the core of the Renaissance was the new man, the individual concerned with glory and fame, with self-realization and joy rather than religious faith or asceticism.

Machiavelli

The political development of the Renaissance was a secular concept of the state, "the state as a work of art," in which

decisions were determined by political, not religious or chival-
ric criteria. The most powerful, indeed notorious, advocate of
this new art of politics was Machiavelli. Born in Florence in
1469, Machiavelli had been a diplomatic emissary and political adviser. On one of his foreign missions he had met and
studied the bellicose Cesare Borgia. When the Republic fell to
the Medicis in 1512, Machiavelli was exiled. In his exile he
wrote a number of works, of which *The Prince,* a short book
addressed to the ruler Lorenzo himself, and the *Discourses*
have been the most influential.

The Prince, not officially published until 1532, achieved
immediate success. Within twenty years of Machiavelli's
death, it had run into 25 editions. He was bitterly attacked,
his very name taken up as an epithet of opprobrium; the
writing of anti-Machiavells became a steady occupation. The
achievement of Machiavelli was "opening up a new route,"
eliminating theological and moral argument, taking the secular state for granted, and inquiring scientifically into its behavior. Politics had to be understood from the viewpoint of
purely political criteria. Political activities were to be examined and praised as they achieved the purpose for which they
were intended. This was political realism, accompanied by a
neutral attitude toward political objectives. This was a study
of power: "Men do not rule states with paternosters in their
hands."

Machiavelli advocated the use of history as example—the
Discourses are ostensibly a large commentary on the *Histories*
of Livy. Since human nature remained unchanged throughout
history, historical situations repeated themselves, and therefore general laws of political behavior could be deduced from
the past. Political activity, to be successful, had to take account of these laws and base itself on imitation of great men.
"Read and consider the lives and fortunes of great men." For
this instruction Machiavelli went back to the classical world,
but to Rome, not Greece, for his storehouse of example. "The
conduct of Rome must be imitated in every particular."

Machiavelli's name has become synonymous with the devil
largely because of his argument that evil means were sometimes necessary to achieve desired ends, that cruelty, deceit,
terrorism, ruthless use of force and treachery were all permissible, and desirable, on occasion. Machiavelli was the first
writer to use *raison d'etat* as an explanation and defense of
political action. Yet this is amorality, not immorality. Machiavelli nowhere denied the idea of goodness or disguised the
nature of evil. The consideration of goodness and evil was
simply irrelevant to political success. *Virtu* was the possession

of qualities necessary for success, and for taking advantage of Fortune and Necessity, which limited and conditioned the actions of men. It is evident in the *Discourses,* as well as from his own career, that he preferred republics to princedoms as political regimes. But this personal preference, he thought, was irrelevant to the need of preserving order and stability in 16th century conditions in Italy.

Machiavelli had little interest in spiritual matters, none in theological. His was a public, not a private philosophy. His interest in religion was solely political. A prince did not have to be religious, but it was important for him to appear so. Religion was necessary or helpful in keeping order, controlling the people, strengthening the will of soldiers. Savonarola, the ascetic monk, was unsuccessful not because he was a false prophet, but because he was an unarmed one.

To the Church, Machiavelli was more hostile. Christianity was the chief reason for the failure to imitate ancient Rome. It had led to resignation and humility. The Church, causing weakness, was the greatest opponent of the well-being of Italy. Much of Machiavelli's writing is concerned with the need for a strong army, for a national militia, and the bringing to an end of the mercenary system. His ideas on the future of Italy were somewhat vague, and it is easy to make too much of the last chapter of *The Prince,* with its patriotic and even nationalistic appeal. But this chapter, appealing for the liberation of Italy, is the only one in his work which is passionate and urgent. To see him as a 19th-century liberal nationalist would be misleading, but he was certainly an indication of the new Italianness, the pride in "the ancient worth."

Parliament in the Nation-State

The era of the nation-state had dawned. National boundaries were more clearly defined, national languages replaced the universal Latin, a consciousness of unity developed. Centralized government expanded its control in England under the Tudors, in France under Louis XI, and in Spain under Ferdinand and Charles V. Monarchy was strengthened by civil wars in which the nobles were destroying themselves. The English Wars of the Roses settled little, but they disposed of a substantial part of the aristocracy. A series of civil disturbances and assassinations in France brought Henry IV to the throne in 1589, and toleration with the Edict of Nantes nine years later. Councils, administrative organizations, a series of capable ministers—Sully, Mazarin, Richelieu, Wolsey, Thomas Cromwell, Cecil—helped execute efficient government and tackle the new financial responsibility of trade and currency.

An awareness of and pride in the secular institutions of one's native country developed. In the mid-15th century, this pride was shown by Sir John Fortescue (1394?–1476?), a judge for 19 years and chief justice of the King's Bench. He had defended the Lancastrian party in the Wars of the Roses because it adhered to the precept of natural law forbidding succession through the female line, and was exiled by the opposing, winning group. In exile in France, Fortescue between 1468 and 1470 wrote his *De Laudibus Legum Anglie*. Together with his *The Governance of England,* the first book on political institutions to be written in English, it explained the working of the British system. In its contrast of the desirable British with the unsatisfactory French system, it was inaugurating the study of comparative politics.

The British system, a limited monarchy, fulfilled obligations of justice and natural law, while the French "regal government" was arbitrary government based on force. In Britain, the ruler was controlled by the law, which he could not alter without the consent of his people. Limitations on him were imposed not only by natural law, but also by common law, resting on historical foundations, custom, the ethics of the legal profession and the Inns of Court conscious of legal tradition, and by the need to get the assent of parliament in matters of taxation and legislation. This last limitation demonstrates the rise in importance of Parliament during the 15th century.

Fortescue's argument used both medieval and modern concepts. It wedded an analysis of existing institutions to a defense of a parliamentary, monarchial system, and a eulogy of the often pernicious jury system. His thesis about the interaction of the constitution and the law, and his attempts at comparative jurisprudence, were to be developed by Sir Thomas Smith, Selden, Hale and later by Maine. His argument that national differences in legal and constitutional institutions may be due to economic and social differences, was a shrewd anticipation of Bodin and Montesquieu.

A century later, Sir Thomas Smith (1513–1577), followed the example of Fortescue, producing both an institutional analysis and a panegyric of the British system. Smith, professor of Greek and of civil law at Cambridge, provost of Eton, dean of Carlisle, one of two chief secretaries of state, wrote his *De Republica Anglorum* while ambassador to France in 1562. It is a totally secular work, with nothing on divine right, the law of God or even natural law. He was primarily concerned with the different kinds of law and the system of courts, of which Parliament itself was "the highest and most authentic." Even though he was more concerned with its position relative to other courts than with its sovereignty, Smith's assertion of the power of Parliament was a skillful evaluation of a changing constitutional scene.

MACHIAVELLI

The Prince and *The Discourses*

The Art of Politics

Those who by the exercise of abilities become princes, obtain their dominions with difficulty but retain them easily, and the difficulties which they have in acquiring their dominions arise in part from the new rules and regulations that they have to introduce in order to establish their position securely. It must be considered that there is nothing more difficult to carry out, nor more doubtful of success, nor more dangerous to handle, than to initiate a new order of things. For the reformer has enemies in all those who profit by the old order, and only lukewarm defenders in all those who would profit by the new order, this lukewarmness arising partly from fear of their adversaries, who have the laws in their favour; and partly from the incredulity of mankind, who do not truly believe in anything new until they have had actual experience of it. Thus it arises that on every opportunity for attacking the reformer, his opponents do so with the zeal of partisans, the others only defend him half-heartedly, so that between them he runs great danger. It is necessary, however, in order to investigate thoroughly this question, to examine whether these innovators are independent, or whether they depend upon others, that is to say, whether in order to carry out their designs they have to entreat or are able to compel. In the first case they invariably succeed ill, and accomplish nothing; but when they can depend on their own strength and are able to use force, they rarely fail. Thus it comes about that all armed prophets have conquered and unarmed ones failed; for besides what has been already said, the character of peoples varies, and it is easy to persuade them of a thing, but difficult to keep them in that persuasion. And so it is necessary to order things so that when they no longer believe, they can be made to believe by force. Moses, Cyrus, Theseus, and Romulus would not have been able to keep their constitutions observed for so long had they been disarmed, as happened in our own time with Fra Girolamo Savonarola, who failed entirely in his new rules when the multitutde began to disbelieve in him, and he had no means of holding fast those who had believed nor of compelling the unbelievers to believe. Therefore such men as these have great difficulty in making their way, and all their dangers are met on the road and must be overcome by their own abilities; but when once they have overcome them and have begun to be held in veneration, and have suppressed those who envied them, they remain powerful and secure, honoured and happy.

Reviewing thus all the actions of the duke Cesare Borgia, I find nothing to blame, on the contrary, I feel bound, as I have done, to hold him up as an example to be imitated by all who by fortune and with the arms of others have risen to power. For with his great courage and high ambition he could not have acted otherwise, and his designs were only frustrated by the short life of Alexander and his own illness. Whoever, therefore, deems it necessary in his new principality to secure himself against enemies, to gain friends, to conquer by force or fraud, to make himself beloved and feared by the people, followed and reverenced by the soldiers, to destroy those who can and may injure him, introduce innovations into old customs, to be severe and kind, magnanimous and liberal, suppress the old militia, create a new one, maintain the friendship of kings and princes in such a way that they are glad to benefit him and fear to injure him, such a one can find no better example than the actions of this man.

In taking a state the conqueror must arrange to commit all his cruelties at once, so as not to have to recur to them every day, and so as to be able, by not making fresh changes, to reassure people and win them over by benefiting them. Whoever acts otherwise, either through timidity or bad counsels, is always obliged to stand with knife in hand, and can never depend on his subjects, because they, owing to continually fresh injuries are unable to depend upon him. For injuries should be done all together, so that being less tasted, they will give less offence. Benefits should be granted little by little, so that they may be better enjoyed. And above all, a prince must live with his subjects in such a way that no accident of good or evil fortune can deflect him from his course; for necessity arising in adverse times, you are not in time with severity, and the good that you do does not profit, as it is judged to be forced upon you, and you will derive no benefit whatever from it.

He who becomes prince by help of the nobility has greater difficulty in maintaining his power than he who is raised by the populace, for he is surrounded by those who think themselves his equals, and is thus unable to direct or command as he pleases. But one who is raised to leadership by popular favour finds himself alone, and has no one, or very few, who are not ready to obey him. Besides which, it is impossible to satisfy the nobility by fair dealing and without inflicting injury on others, whereas it is very easy to satisfy the mass of the people in this way. For the aim of the people is more honest than that of the nobility, the latter desiring to oppress, and the former merely to avoid oppression. It must also be added that the prince can never insure himself against a hostile populace on account of their number, but he can against the hostility of the great, as they are but few. The worst that a prince has to expect from a hostile people is to be abandoned, but from hostile nobles he has to fear not only desertion but their active opposition, and as they are more far-seeing and more cunning, they are always in time to save themselves and take sides with the one whom they expect will conquer.

. . . And many have imagined republics and principalities which have never been seen or known to exist in reality; for how we live is so far removed from how we ought to live, that he who abandons what is done for what ought to be done, will rather learn to bring about his own ruin than his preservation. A man who wishes to make a profession of goodness in everything must necessarily come to grief among so many who are not good. Therefore it is necessary for a prince, who wishes to maintain himself, to learn how not to be good, and to use this knowledge and not use it, according to the necessity of the case.

. . . I know that every one will admit that it would be highly praiseworthy in a prince to possess all the qualities that are reputed good, but as they cannot all be possessed or observed, human conditions not permitting of it, it is necessary that he should be prudent enough to avoid the scandal of those vices which would lose him the state, and guard himself if possible against those which will not lose it him, but if not able to, he can indulge them with less scruple. And yet he must not mind incurring the scandal of those vices, without which it would be difficult to save the state, for if one considers well, it will be found that some things that seem virtues would, if followed, lead to one's ruin, and some others which appear vices result in one's greater security and well-being.

. . . And of all things that a prince must guard against, the most important are being despicable or hated, and liberality will lead you to one or other of these conditions. It is, therefore, wiser to have the name of a miser, which produces disgrace without hatred, than to incur of necessity the name of being rapacious, which produces both disgrace and hatred.

From this arises the question whether it is better to be loved more than feared, or feared more than loved. The reply is that one ought to be both feared and loved, but as it is difficult for the two to go together, it is much safer to be feared than loved, if one of the two has to be wanting. For it may be said of men in general that they are ungrateful, voluble, dissemblers, anxious to avoid danger, and covetous of gain; as long as you benefit them, they are entirely yours; they offer you their blood, their goods, their life, and their children, as I have before said, when the necessity is remote; but when it approaches, they revolt. And the prince who has relied solely on their words, without making other preparations, is ruined; for the friendship which is gained by purchase and not through grandeur and nobility of spirit is bought but not secured, and at a pinch is not to be expended in your service. And men have less scruple in offending one who makes himself loved than one who makes himself feared; for love is held by a chain of obligation which, men being selfish, is broken whenever it serves their purpose; but fear is maintained by a dread of punishment which never fails.

Still, a prince should make himself feared in such a way that if he does not gain love, he at any rate avoids hatred; for fear and the absence of hatred may well go together, and will be always attained by one who abstains from interfering with the property of his citizens and subjects or with their women. And when he is obliged to take the life of any one, let him do so where there is a proper justification and manifest reason for it; but above all he must abstain from taking the property of others, for men forget more easily the death of their father than the loss of their patrimony. Then also pretexts for seizing property are never wanting, and one who begins to live by rapine will always find some reason for taking the goods of others, whereas causes for taking life are rarer and more fleeting.

How laudable it is for a prince to keep good faith and live with integrity, and not with astuteness, every one knows. Still the experience of our times shows those princes to have done great things who have had little regard for good faith, and have been able by astuteness to confuse men's brains, and who have ultimately overcome those who have made loyalty their foundation.

There are two methods of fighting, the one by law, the other by force: the first method is that of men, the second of beasts; but as the first method is often insufficient, one must have recourse to the second. It is therefore necessary for a prince to know well how to use both the beast and the man. This was covertly taught to rulers by ancient writers, who relate how Achilles and many others of those ancient princes were given to Chiron the centaur to be brought up and educated under his discipline. The parable of this semi-animal, semi-human teacher is meant to indicate that a prince must know how to use both natures, and that the one without the other is not durable.

A prince being thus obliged to know well how to act as a beast must imitate the fox and the lion, for the lion cannot protect himself from traps, and the fox cannot defend himself from wolves. One must therefore be a fox to recognise traps, and a lion to frighten wolves. Those that wish to be only lions do not understand this. Therefore, a prudent ruler ought not to keep faith when by so doing it would be against his interest, and when the reasons which made him bind himself no longer exist. If men were all good, this precept would not be a good one; but as they are bad, and would not observe their faith with you, so you are not bound to keep faith with them. Nor have legitimate grounds ever failed a prince who wished to show colourable excuse for the non-fulfillment of his promise. Of this one could furnish an infinite number of modern examples, and show how many times peace has been broken, and how many promises rendered worthless, by the faithlessness of princes, and those that have been best able to imitate the fox have succeeded best. But it is necessary to be able to disguise this character well, and to be a great feigner and dissembler; and men are so simple and so ready to obey present necessities, that one who deceives will always find those who allow themselves to be deceived.

I will only mention one modern instance. Alexander VI did nothing else but deceive men, he thought of nothing else, and found the occasion for it; no man was ever more able to give assurances, or affirmed things with stronger oaths, and no man observed them less; however, he always succeeded in his deceptions, as he well knew this aspect of things.

It is not, therefore, necessary for a prince to have all the above-named qualities, but it is very necessary to seem to have them. I would even be bold to say that to possess them and always to observe them is dangerous, but to appear to possess them is useful. Thus it is well to seem merciful, faithful, humane, sincere, religious, and also to be so; but you must have the mind so disposed that when it is needful to be otherwise you may be able to change to the opposite qualities. And it must be understood that a prince, and especially a new prince, cannot observe all those things which are considered good in men, being often obliged, in order to maintain the state, to act against faith, against charity, against humanity, and against religion. And, therefore, he must have a mind disposed to adapt itself according to the wind, and as the variations of fortune dictate, and, as I said before, not deviate from what is good, if possible, but be able to do evil if constrained.

A prince must take great care that nothing goes out of his mouth which is not full of the above-named five qualities, and, to see and hear him, he should seem to be all mercy, faith, integrity, humanity, and religion. And nothing is more necessary than to seem to have this last quality, for men in general judge more by the eyes than by the hands, for every one can see, but very few have to feel. Everybody sees what you appear to be, few feel what you are, and those few will not dare to oppose themselves to the many, who have the majesty of the state to defend them; and in the actions of men, and especially of princes, from which there is no appeal, the end justifies the means. Let a prince therefore aim at conquering and maintaining the state, and the means will always be judged honourable and praised by every one, for the vulgar is always taken by appearances and the issue of the event; and the world consists only of the vulgar, and the few who are not vulgar are isolated when the many have a rallying point in the prince.

(Extracts from *The Prince*, Chapters 6, 7, 8, 9, 15, 16, 17, 18.)

The Political Value of Religion

Of all men who have been eulogized, those deserve it most who have been the authors and founders of religions; next come such as have established republics or kingdoms.

. . . Numa, finding a very savage people, and wishing to reduce them to civil obedience by the arts of peace, had recourse to religion as the most necessary and assured support of any civil society; and he established it upon such foundations that for many centuries there was nowhere more fear of the gods than in that republic, which greatly facilitated all the enterprises which the Senate or its great men attempted. Whoever will examine the actions of the people of Rome as a body, or of many individual Romans, will see that these citizens feared much more to break an oath than the laws; like men who esteem the power of the gods more than that of men. . . .

. . . And whoever reads Roman history attentively will see in how great a degree religion served in the command of the armies, in uniting the people and keeping them well conducted, and in covering the wicked with shame. . . . In truth, there never was any remarkable lawgiver amongst any people who did not resort to divine authority, as otherwise his laws would not have been accepted by the people; for there are many good laws, the importance of which is known to the sagacious lawgiver, but the reasons for which are not sufficiently evident to enable him to persuade others to submit to them; and therefore do wise men, for the purpose of removing this difficulty, resort to divine authority. . . .

. . . I conclude that the religion introduced by Numa into Rome was one of the chief causes of the prosperity of that city; for this religion gave rise to good laws, and good laws bring good fortune, and from good fortune results happy success in all enterprises. And as the observance of divine institutions is the cause of the greatness of republics, so the disregard of them produces their ruin; for where the fear of God is wanting, there the country will come to ruin, unless it be sustained by the fear of the prince, which may temporarily supply the want of religion.

Princes and republics who wish to maintain themselves free from corruption must above all things preserve the purity of all religious observances, and treat them with proper reverence; for there is no greater indication of the ruin of a country than to see religion contemned. And this is easily understood, when we know upon what the religion of a country is founded; for the essence of every religion is based upon some one main principle. . . . It is therefore the duty of princes and heads of republics to uphold the foundations of the religion of their countries, for then it is easy to keep their people religious, and consequently well conducted and united. And therefore everything that tends to favor religion (even though it were believed to be false) should be received and availed of to strengthen it; and this should be done the more, the wiser the rulers are, and the better they understand the natural course of things. Such was, in fact, the practice observed by sagacious men; which has given rise to the belief in the miracles that are celebrated in religions, however false they may be.

The system of auguries was not only the principal basis of the ancient religion of the Gentiles, but was also the cause of the prosperity of the Roman republic. Whence the Romans esteemed it more than any other institution, and resorted to it in their Consular Comitti, in commencing any important enterprise, in sending armies into the field, in ordering their battles, and in every other important civil or military action. Nor would they ever have ventured upon any expedition unless the augurs had first persuaded the soldiers that the gods promised them victory. Amongst other auspices the armies were always accompanied by a certain class of soothsayers, termed Pollari (guardians of the sacred fowls), and every time before giving battle to the enemy, they required these Pollari to ascertain the auspices; and if the fowls ate freely, then it was deemed a favorable augury, and the soldiers fought confidently, but if the fowls refused to eat, then they abstained from battle. Nevertheless, when they saw a good reason why certain things should be done, they did them anyhow, whether the auspices were favorable or not; but then they turned and interpreted the auguries so artfully, and in such manner, that seemingly no disrespect was shown to their religious belief.

(Extracts from the *Discourses*, I 10, 11, 12, 14.)

Anti-Clericalism

. . . And certainly, if the Christian religion had from the beginning been maintained according to the principles of its founder, the Christian states and republics would have been much more united and happy than what they are. Nor can there be a greater proof of its decadence than to witness the fact that the nearer people are to the Church of Rome, which is the head of our religion, the less religious are they. And whoever examines the principles upon which that religion is founded, and sees how widely different from those principles its present practice and application are, will judge that her ruin or chastisement is near at hand. But as there are some of the opinion that the well-being of Italian affairs depends upon the Church of Rome, I will present such arguments against that opinion as occur to me; two of which are most important, and cannot according to my judgment be controverted. The first is, that the evil example of the court of Rome has destroyed all piety and religion in Italy, which brings in its train infinite improprieties and disorders; for as we may presuppose all good where religions prevails, so where it is wanting we have the right to suppose the very opposite. We Italians then owe to the Church of Rome and to her priests our having become irreligious and bad; but we owe her a still greater debt, and one that will be the cause of our ruin, namely, that the Church has kept and still keeps our country divided. And certainly a country can never be united and happy, except when it obeys wholly one government, whether a republic or a monarchy, as is the case in France and in Spain; and the sole cause why Italy is not in the same condition, and is not governed by either one republic or one sovereign, is the Church; for having acquired and holding a temporal dominion, yet she has never had sufficient power or courage to enable her to seize the rest of the country and make herself sole sovereign of all Italy. And on the other hand she has not been so feeble that the fear of losing her temporal power prevented her from calling in the aid of a foreign power to defend her against such others as had become too powerful in Italy. . . . The Church, then, not having been powerful enough to be able to master all Italy, nor having permitted any other power to do so, has been the cause why Italy has never been able to unite under one head, but has always remained under a number of princes and lords, which occasioned her so many dissensions and so much weakness that she became a prey not only to the powerful barbarians, but of whoever chose to assail her. This we other Italians owe to the Church of Rome, and to none other.

Reflecting now as to whence it came that in ancient times the people were more devoted to liberty than in the present, I believe that it resulted from this, that men were stronger in those days, which I believe to be attributable to the difference of education, founded upon the difference of their religion and ours. For, as our religion teaches us the truth and the true way of life, it causes us to attach less value to the honors and possessions of this world; whilst the Pagans, esteeming those things as the highest good, were more energetic and ferocious in their actions. We may observe this also in most of their institutions, beginning with the magnificence of their sacrifices as compared with the humility of ours, which are gentle solemnities rather than magnificent ones, and have nothing of energy or ferocity in them. . . . Besides this, the Pagan religion deified only men who had achieved great glory, such as commanders of armies and chiefs of republics, whilst ours glorifies more the humble and contemplative men than the men of action. Our religion, moreover, places the supreme happiness in humility, lowliness, and a contempt for worldly objects, whilst the other, on the contrary, places the supreme good in grandeur of soul, strength of body, and all such other qualities as render men formidable; and if our religion claims of us fortitude of soul, it is more to enable us to suffer than to achieve great deeds.

These principles seem to me to have made men feeble, and caused them to become an easy prey to evil-minded men, who can control them more securely, seeing that the great body of men, for the sake of gaining Paradise, are more disposed to endure injuries than to avenge them. And although it would seem that the world has become effeminate and Heaven disarmed, yet this arises unquestionably from the baseness of men, who have interpreted our religion according to the promptings of indolence rather than those of virtue. For if we were to reflect that our religion permits us to exalt and defend our country, we should see that according to it we ought also to love and honor our country, and prepare ourselves so as to be capable of defending her. It is this education, then, and this false interpretation of our religion, that is the cause of there not being so many republics nowadays as there were anciently; and that there is no longer the same love of liberty amongst the people now as there was then. . . .

(Extracts from the *Discourses*, I 14; II 2.)

The Liberation of Italy

And although before now a gleam of hope has appeared which gave hope that some individual might be appointed by God for her redemption, yet at the highest summit of his career he was thrown aside by fortune, so that now, almost lifeless, she (Italy) awaits one who may heal her wounds and put a stop to the pillaging of Lombardy, to the rapacity and extortion in the Kingdom of Naples and in Tuscany, and cure her of those sores which have long been festering. Behold how she prays God to send some one to redeem her from this barbarous cruelty and insolence. Behold her ready and willing to follow any standard if only there be some one to raise it. There is nothing now she can hope for but that your illustrious house may place itself at the head of this redemption, being by its power and fortune so exalted, and being favoured by God and the Church, of which it is now the ruler. . . . Here is a just cause. . . . Here is the greatest willingness, nor can there be great difficulty where there is great willingness, provided that the measures are adopted of those whom I have set before you as examples. Besides this, unexampled wonders have been seen here performed by God, the sea has been opened, a cloud has shown you the road, the rock has given forth water, manna has rained, and everything has contributed to your greatness, the remainder must be done by you. God will not do everything, in order not to deprive us of freewill and the portion of the glory that falls to our lot. . . .

If your illustrious house, therefore, wishes to follow those great men who redeemed their countries, it is before all things necessary, as the true foundation of every undertaking, to provide yourself with your own forces, for you cannot have more faithful, or truer and better soldiers. And although each one of them may be good, they will united become even better when they see themselves commanded by their prince, and honoured and favoured by him. It is therefore necessary to prepare such forces in order to be able with Italian Prowess to defend the country from foreigners. . . .

This opportunity must not, therefore, be allowed to pass, so that Italy may at length find her liberator. I cannot express the love with which he would be received in all those provinces which have suffered under these foreign invasions, with what thirst for vengeance, with what steadfast faith, with what love, with what grateful tears. What doors would be closed against him? What people would refuse him obedience? What envy could oppose him? What Italian would withhold allegiance? This barbarous domination stinks in the nostrils of every one. May your illustrious house therefore assume this task with that courage and those hopes which are inspired by a just cause, so that under its banner our fatherland may be raised up, and under its auspices be verified that saying of Petrarch:

Valour against fell wrath
Will take up arms; and be the combat quickly sped!
For, sure, the ancient worth,
That in Italians stirs the heart, is not yet dead.

(Extract from *The Prince*, chapter 26.)

FORTESCUE

A learned Commendation of the Political Laws of England

(De Laudibus Legum Anglie)

A Limited Monarchy

. . . The king of England is not able to change the laws of his kingdom at pleasure, for he rules his people with a government not only regal but also political. If he were to preside over them with a power entirely regal, he would be able to change the laws of his realm, and also impose on them tallages and other burdens without consulting them; this is the sort of dominion which the civil laws indicate when they state that *What pleased the prince has the force of law*. But the case is far otherwise with the king ruling his people politically, because he is not able himself to change the laws without the assent of his subjects nor to burden an unwilling people with strange imposts, so that, ruled by laws that they themselves desire, they freely enjoy their properties, and are despoiled neither by their own king nor any other. The people, forsooth, rejoice in the same way under a king ruling entirely regally, provided he does not degenerate into a tyrant. . . .

Just as in natural bodies, what is left over after decapitation is not a body, but is what we call a trunk, so in bodies politic a community without a head is not by any means a body. So a people wishing to erect itself into a kingdom or any other body politic must always set up one man for the government of all that body, usually called a king. As in this way the physical body grows out of the embryo, regulated by one head, so the kingdom issues from the people, and exists as a body mystical, governed by one man as head. And just as in the body natural, as Aristotle said, the heart is the source of life, having in itself the blood which it transmits to all the members thereof, whereby they are quickened and live, so in the body politic the will of the people is the source of life, having it in the blood, namely, political forethought for the interest of the people, which it transmits to the head and all the members of the body, by which the body is maintained and quickened.

The law, indeed, by which a group of men is made into a people, resembles the nerves of the body physical, for, just as the body is held together by the nerves, so this body mystical is bound together and united into one by the law, which is derived from the word "ligando," and the members and bones of this body, which signify the solid basis of truth by which the community is sustained, preserve their rights through the law, as the body natural does through the nerves. And just as the head of the body physical is unable to change its nerves, or to deny its members proper strength and due nourishment of blood, so a king who is head of the body politic is unable to change the laws of that body, or to deprive that same people of their own substance uninvited or against their wills. A king of this sort is obliged to protect the law, the subjects, and their bodies and goods, and he has power to this end issuing from the people, so that it is not permissible for him to rule his people with any other power. I briefly answer the question: how came it that the power of kings should differ so widely?

This difference is due solely to diversity in the institution of those dignities which I have mentioned, as you can understand by the light of reason from what has been said. For thus the kingdom of England blossomed forth into a dominion regal and political out of Brutus's band of Trojans, whom he led out of the territories of Italy and of the Greeks. And thus Scotland, which at one time was obedient thereto as a duchy, grew into a kingdom political and regal. Many other realms also have been destined by such an origin as this to be ruled not only regally, but also politically. . . .

It only remains, then, to examine whether or not the statutes of the English are good. These, indeed, do not emanate from the will of the prince alone, as do the laws in kingdoms which are governed entirely regally, there so often statutes secure the advantage of their maker only, thereby redounding to the loss and undoing of the subjects. Sometimes, also, by the negligence of such princes and the inertia of their counsellors, those statutes are made so ill-advisedly that they deserve the name of corruptions rather than laws. But the statutes of England cannot so arise, since they are made not only by the Prince's will, but also by the assent of the whole realm, so they cannot be injurious to the people nor fail to secure their advantage. Furthermore, it must be supposed that they are necessarily replete with prudence and wisdom, since they are promulgated by the prudence not of one counsellor nor of a hundred only, but of more than three hundred chosen men as those who know the form of the summons, the order, and the procedure of parliament can more clearly describe. And if statutes ordained with such solemnity and care happen not to give full effect to the intention of the makers, they can speedily be revised, and yet not without the assent of the commons and nobles of the realm, in the manner in which they first originated. . . . In the realm of England, no one billets himself in another's house against its master's will, unless in public hostelries, nor does anyone take with impunity the goods of another without the permission of the proprietor of them; nor, in that realm, is anyone hindered from providing himself with salt or any goods whatever, at his own pleasure and of any vendor. The king, indeed, may, by his officers, take necessaries for his household, at a reasonable price to be assessed at the discretion of the constables of the villages, without the owners' permission. But none the less he is obliged by his own laws to pay this price out of hand or at a day fixed by the greater officers of his household, because by those laws he cannot despoil any of his subjects of their goods without due satisfaction for them. Nor can the king there, by himself or by his ministers, impose tallages, subsidies, or any other burdens whatever on his subjects, nor change their laws, nor make new ones, without the concession or assent of his whole realm expressed in his parliament. . . .

The inhabitants are not brought to trial except before the

ordinary judges, where they are treated justly according to the law of the land. Nor are they examined or impleaded in respect of their chattels, or possessions, nor arrested for crime of whatever magnitude and enormity, except according to the laws of that land and before the aforesaid judges. These are the fruits which the political and regal government yields. . . .

. . . Hence, all the power of a king ought to be applied to the good of his realm, which in effect consists in the defense of it against invasions by foreigners, and in the protection of the inhabitants of the realm and their goods from injuries and rapine by natives. Therefore, a king who cannot achieve these things is necessarily to be adjudged impotent. . . .

(Extracts from chapters 9, 13, 18, 36.)

SIR THOMAS SMITH
De Republica Anglorum

The Powers of Parliament

The most high and absolute power of the realme of Englande, consisteth in the Parliament. For as in warre where the king himselfe in person, the nobilitie, the rest of the gentilitie, and the yeomanrie are, is the force and power of Englande: so in peace and consultation where the Prince is to give life, and the last and highest commaundement, the Baronie for the nobilitie and higher, the knightes, esquiers, gentlemen and commons for the lower part of the common wealth, the bishoppes for the clergie bee present to advertise, consult and shew what is good and necessarie for the common wealth, and to consult together, and upon mature deliberation everie bill or lawe being thrise reade and disputed uppon in either house, the other two partes first each a part, and after the Prince himselfe in presence of both the parties doeth consent unto and alloweth. That is the Princes and whole realmes deede: whereupon justlie no man can complaine, but must accommodate himselfe to finde it good and obey it.

That which is doone by this consent is called firme, stable, and *sanctum,* and is taken for lawe. The Parliament abrogateth olde lawes, maketh newe, giveth orders for thinges past, and for thinges hereafter to be followed, changeth rightes, and possessions of private men, legittimateth bastards, establisheth formes of religion, altereth weightes and measures, giveth formes of succession to the crowne, defineth of doubtful rightes, whereof is no lawe alreadie made, appointeth subsidies, tailes, taxes, and impositions, giveth most free pardons and absolutions, restoreth in bloud and name as the highest court, condemneth or absolveth them whom the Prince will put to that triall: And to be short, all that ever the people of Rome might do either in *Centuriatis comitis* or *tributis,* the same may be dooned by the parliament of Englande, which representeth and hath the power of the whole realme both the head and the bodie. For everie Englishman is entended to bee there present, either in person or by procuration and attornies, of what preheminence, state, dignitie, or qualitie soever he be, from the Prince (be he King or Queene) to the lowest person of Englande. And the consent of the Parliament is taken to be everie mans consent.

(Extract from Book 2, Chapter 1.)

SECTION VIII

THE REFORMATION

Political and social change was accompanied by religious. Indeed, the 16th century Reformation was not produced by doctrinal disputes only. Political problems and opposition between the new states and the Church—on taxation, investiture, powers of the clerical courts, control over education, church property, ecclesiastical exactions of tithes, and indulgences—also played their part. The Reformation was a complex phenomenon in which the theological doctrines of return to the simplicity of the Scriptures, justification by faith, the need for grace and personal piety, were only part of the wider intellectual dissatisfaction with clerical control, the moral protest against a corrupt ecclesiastical hierarchy, and the new economic aggressiveness which refused to be bound by theological restrictions. The Reformation was marked not only by doctrinal treatises, but also by war, civil war, persecution and property transfer. Whether a country would remain in the old Church, as did France, or turn to the new, as did England and Scotland, was largely determined by political and military, not theological, considerations. The idea of a universal Christendom, with the Pope as its responsible leader, disappeared with the rise of national churches, as well as nation-states.

For political theory, there are two important trends of thought emerging from the Reformation. One comes from the Protestant supporters of their national monarchs, Luther and Melanchthon. The other results from the extremists on both sides, the Calvinists and the Jesuits, who, adopting similar political positions from opposing theological views, argued in favor of resistance to rulers who were persecuting their religions.

Both the two great religious reformers, Luther and Calvin, asserted the right of individual conscience and the possibility of direct relationship between the individual and God, against Papal supremacy. But politically, for Luther this meant a claim for secular independence, and for obedience to those princes in Germany who had adopted the new religion. For Calvin, it led to ecclesiastical association with the secular power, and even theocracy, if that power was Protestant, and, for his supporters, to resistance if persecuted. Protestantism gives no single answer to the political problems of authority and obedience. A variety of answers are forthcoming, from the Anabaptists, arguing that all secular power was harmful, to Luther, arguing that the prince ought to reform the Church in his territory.

There was a crossing of theological lines. Church and state were unified for English Protestants and French Catholics. Scottish and French Protestants and Spanish Catholics would argue the possibility, and sometimes the necessity, of resistance. All drew on the common stock of religious knowledge to reach their differing political conclusions.

Luther

Luther (1483–1546), not a powerful political thinker, maintained a respect for civil authority, rejecting the view that it was fundamentally evil. He had always argued that the Church had no coercive authority, and that the clergy were subject to secular power as were all other individuals. The function of civil authority was to promote those conditions suitable for the true Christian life; the state assisted the kingdom of God by protecting its members. With the civil disturbances of the Peasants War of 1525, Luther's insistence on the need for secular coercion became stronger. Rebellion was a breach of God's commandment. To have faith in God "is a simple obedience of the Spirit."

Originally, he thought Church reform would be undertaken by local authorities in the parish. But his idea of secular control coincided happily with the political ambition of the German princes wanting to assert their independence from Rome. Luther supported the appointment and approval of ecclesiastical personnel by the sovereign, who was responsible for making rules and governing the Church.

Yet, if secular authority could undertake the reform of the

Church, it could not control Christian belief and conscience, which depended on man's individual examination of the Scriptures. All men were priests; there was no need for mediation through ecclesiastical hierarchy or sacraments. Spiritual and true liberty was more important than all other liberty, which was external. But in practice the Word had to be interpreted and uniformity reached. Luther's later work emphasized, partly because of mass illiteracy, the need for the sovereign to maintain the true religion by force, and even to exterminate dissenters and heretics. Whereas at one point he argued, "Heretics must be conquered with the pen and not with fire," later he stressed the disturbances of Christian society that heresies created.

His ideas of political economy were somewhat primitive. The prince was father of his country, the lord was father of his estate, the employer father of his workers. Luther could understand an agricultural system, but not a business one. He denounced trading companies and monopolies, usury, foreign trade, profit-taking on business transactions, and dishonest activity. As with the medieval Church, he argued for the maintenance of a just price. Inequality was natural; it was wrong to advocate the abolition of serfdom with the argument that Christ had freed everyone. Private property was inevitable and work a remedy for sin, but the community as a whole had an obligation to look after the weak.

Luther advocated obedience to secular power. There was no possibility of resistance to authority, or of reconstruction of society. But the state was responsible for its charges. It had positive functions to fulfill, such as the encouragement of education, culture and physical welfare. The state was responsible for the over-all guidance of its citizens. The intellectual legacy of Luther in secular matters was a patriarchal social organization, a traditional agricultural economy and a powerful political state.

Calvin

Calvin (1509–1564), French-born, was educated in theology and law, and destined for the Church. Converted to Protestantism, he wrote his *Institutes of the Christian Religion,* and left for Geneva in 1536, where he spent the rest of his life, apart from a period of exile at Strasbourg.

For Calvin, civil power was "as necessary as bread and water, light and air, and more excellent." It was necessary to control the inevitable sin and wickedness of man, to establish order, to prepare men for the right kind of life, and to preserve the true religion and defend the church. It could use its powers of coercion to enforce discipline, and preserve social peace and harmony.

The state was divinely instituted—"God maintains principalities." Christ reigned in the state as he did in the church. The whole of life, therefore, should be subject to Christian regulations and purposes. The task of control was one in which church and state were united, each retaining its distinct character. Both church and state acknowledged God as the ultimate sovereign, bestowing His grace by an act of will on the elect; Divine Will itself was responsible for existing inequality. Religion became the glorification of God, and the means to salvation.

Because the church was necessary as an intermediary to salvation, princes, the lieutenants of God, were subordinate to it. Both temporal and ecclesiastic discipline were necessary. The church could not use the sword, because it had no power to coerce, but it could censure, admonish and excommunicate. Calvinism in Geneva was based on discipline and obedience, with a Ministry and a Consistory to control social, political and individual behavior. Though not a theocracy, in the strict sense of clerical government, the Geneva regime closely resembled it, for civil officials enforced the decisions on morality made by the Consistory. Its control was severe and thorough. Its intolerance was demonstrated by the burning of Servetus for theological differences on the Trinity. Where Calvinists constituted a majority, an autocratic system of this kind was instituted. But what if Calvinists, as a minority religion, were persecuted? Calvin's advice to move or devote oneself to prayer was not heartening to the persecuted.

But Calvinism had its politically progressive side also. It demanded an educated, literate people who could read and understand their Bible and ministers. A system of education open to all was started. In economics, Calvin's attitude was more progressive than Luther's. He might object to some kinds of business, but clearly recognized the value of production and trade, and introduced the manufacture of cloth and of watches in Geneva. The injunction to work hard, to limit spending, meant accumulation of capital, the foundation of modern industry. Profit-making was legitimate, although profits were to be devoted to public works. "Calvin," said R. H. Tawney, "did for the 16th-century bourgeoisie what Marx did for the 19th-century proletariat." Good works were not a way of obtaining salvation, but a proof that salvation had been gained.

LUTHER

Secular Authority: To What Extent It Should Be Obeyed, 1523, and An Open Letter Concerning the Hard Book Against the Peasants, 1525

The Divine Nature of Secular Authority

We must firmly establish secular law and the sword, that no one may doubt that it is in the world by God's will and ordinance. The passages which establish this are the following: Romans xiii, "Let every soul be subject to power and authority, for there is no power but from God. The power that is everywhere is ordained of God. He then who resists the power resists God's ordinance. But he who resists God's ordinance shall bring himself under condemnation." Likewise, I Peter ii, "Be subject to every kind of human ordinance, whether to the king as supreme, or to the governors, as to those sent of Him for the punishing of the evil and for the reward of the good."

This penal law existed from the beginning of the world.

We must divide all the children of Adam into two classes; the first belong to the kingdom of God, the second to the kingdom of the world. Those belonging to the kingdom of God are all true believers in Christ and are subject to Christ. For Christ is the King and Lord in the kingdom of God, as the second Psalm and all the Scriptures say. For this reason He came into the world, that He might begin God's kingdom and establish it in the world. Therefore He says before Pilate, "My kingdom is not of the world, but whoever is of the truth hears My voice"; and continually in the Gospel He refers to the kingdom of God and says, "Amend your ways, the kingdom of God is at hand." Likewise, "Seek first the kingdom of God and His righteousness." He also calls the Gospel, a Gospel of the kingdom, for the reason that it teaches, governs, and contains God's kingdom.

Now observe, these people need no secular sword or law. And if all the world were composed of real Christians, that is, true believers, no prince, king, lord, sword, or law would be needed. For what were the use of them, since Christians have in their hearts the Holy Spirit, who instructs them and causes them to wrong no one, to love every one, willingly and cheerfully to suffer injustice and even death from every one. Where every wrong is suffered and every right is done, no quarrel, strife, trial, judge, penalty, law or sword is needed. Therefore, it is not possible for the secular sword and law to find any work to do among Christians, since of themselves they do much more than its laws and doctrines can demand. Just as Paul says in I Timothy i, "The law is not given for the righteous, but for the unrighteous."

Why is this? Because the righteous does of himself all and more than all that all the laws demand. But the unrighteous do nothing that the law demands, therefore they need the law to instruct, constrain, and compel them to do what is good. A good tree does not need any teaching or law to bear good fruit, its nature causes it to bear according to its kind without any law and teaching. A man would be a fool to make a book of laws and statutes telling an apple tree how to bear apples and not thorns, when it is able by its own nature to do this better than man with all his books can define and direct. Just so, by the Spirit and by faith all Christians are throughout inclined to do well and keep the law, much more than any one can teach them with all the laws, and need so far as they are concerned no commandments nor law.

You ask, Why then did God give to all men so many commandments, and why did Christ teach in the Gospel so many things to be done? . . . Paul says that the law is given for the sake of the unrighteous, that is, that those who are not Christians may through the law be externally restrained from evil deeds, as we shall hear later. Since, however, no one is by nature Christian or pious, but every one sinful and evil, God places the restraints of the law upon them all, so that they may not dare give rein to their desires and commit outward, wicked deeds. In addition, St. Paul gives the law another function in Romans vii and Galatians iii. It is to teach men to recognize sin, that they may be made humble unto grace and unto faith in Christ. Christ also does this here, when He teaches in Matthew v that we should not resist evil, and thereby glorifies the law and teaches how a real Christian ought to be and must be disposed, as we shall hear further on.

All who are not Christians belong to the kingdom of the world and are under the law. Since few believe and still fewer live a Christian life, do not resist the evil, and themselves do no evil, God has provided for non-Christians a different government outside the Christian estate and God's kingdom, and has subjected them to the sword, so that, even though they would do so, they cannot practice their wickedness, and that, if they do, they may not do it without fear nor in peace and prosperity. . . . If it were not so, seeing that the whole world is evil and that among thousands there is scarcely one true Christian, men would devour one another, and no one could preserve wife and child, support himself and serve God; and thus the world would be reduced to chaos. For this reason God has ordained the two governments; the spiritual, which by the Holy Spirit under Christ makes Christians and pious people, and the secular, which restrains the unchristian and wicked so that they must needs keep the peace outwardly, even against their will. So Paul interprets the secular sword, Romans xiii, and says it is not a terror to good works, but to the evil. And Peter says it is for the punishment of evil doers.

If any one attempted to rule the world by the Gospel, and put aside all secular law and the secular sword, on the plea that all are baptised and Christian, and that according to the Gospel, there is to be among them neither law nor sword, nor necessity for either, pray, what would happen? He would lose the bands and chains of the wild and savage beasts, and let them tear and mangle every one, and at the same time say they were quite tame and gentle creatures; but I would have the proof in my wounds. Just so would the wicked under the name of Christian abuse this freedom of the Gospel, carry on their knavery, and say that they were Christians subject neither to law nor sword. . . .

It is indeed true that Christians, so far as they themselves are concerned, are subject to neither law nor sword and need neither; but first take heed and fill the world with real Christians before ruling it in a Christian and evangelical manner. This you will never accomplish; for the world and the masses are and always will be unchristian, although they are all baptised and are nominally Christian. Christians, however, are few and far between, as the saying is. Therefore it is out of the question that there should be a common Christian government over the whole world, nay even over one land or company of people, since the wicked always outnumber the good. Hence a man who would venture to govern an entire country or the world with the Gospel would be like a shepherd who should place in one fold wolves, lions, eagles, and sheep together and let them freely mingle with one another and say, Help yourselves, and be good and peaceful among yourselves; the fold is open, there is plenty of food; have no fear of dogs and clubs. The sheep, forsooth, would keep the peace and would allow themselves to be fed and governed in peace, but they would not live long; nor would any beast keep from molesting another.

For this reason these two kingdoms must be sharply distinguished, and both be permitted to remain; the one to produce piety, the other to bring about external peace and prevent evil deeds; neither is sufficient in the world without the other. For no one can become pious before God by means of the secular government, without Christ's spiritual rule. Hence Christ's rule does not extend over all, but Christians are always in the minority and are in the midst of non-Christians. Where there is only secular rule or law, there, of necessity, is sheer hypocrisy, though the commandments be God's very own. Where . . . the spiritual government rules alone over land and people, there evil is given free rein and the door is opened for every kind of knavery; for the natural world cannot receive or comprehend spiritual things.

But perhaps you will say, since Christians do not need the secular sword and the law, why does Paul say to all Christians, in Romans xiii, "Let all souls be subject to power and authority?" And St. Peter says, "Be subject to every human ordinance," etc., as quoted above. I answer, as I have said, that Christians, among themselves and by and for themselves, need no law or sword, since it is neither necessary nor profitable for them. Since, however, a true Christian lives and labors on earth not for himself, but for his neighbor, therefore the whole spirit of his life impels him to do even that which he need not do, but which is profitable and necessary for his neighbor. Because the sword is a very great benefit and necessary to the whole world, to preserve peace, to punish sin and to prevent evil, he submits most willingly to the rule of the sword, pays tax, honors those in authority, serves, helps, and does all he can to further the government, that it may be sustained and held in honor and fear. Although he needs none of these things for himself and it is not necessary for him to do them, yet he considers what is for the good and profit of others, as Paul teaches in Ephesians v.

He serves the State as he performs all other works of love, which he himself does not need. He visits the sick, not that he may be made well; feeds no one because he himself needs food: so he also serves the State not because he needs it, but because others need it,—that they may be protected and that the wicked may not become worse. He loses nothing by this, and such service in no way harms him, and yet it is of great profit to the world. If he did not do it, he would be acting not as a Christian but contrary even to love, and would also be setting a bad example to others, who like him would not submit to authority, though they were no Christians. In this way the Gospel would be brought into disrepute, as though it taught rebellion and made self-willed people, unwilling to benefit or serve any one, when in reality it makes a Christian the servant of every one. Thus in Matthew xvii, Christ gave the tribute money that He might not offend them, although He did not need to do it.

Thus you observe in the words of Christ quoted above from Matthew v that He indeed teaches that Christians among themselves should have no secular sword nor law. He does not, however, forbid one to serve and obey those who have the secular sword and the law; much rather, since you have no need of them and are not to have them, are you to serve those who have not progressed so far as you and still need them. Although you do not need to have your enemy punished, your weak neighbor does. You should help him, that he may have peace and that his enemy may be curbed; which is not possible unless power and authority are honored and feared. Christ does not say, "Thou shalt not serve the State or be subject to it," but "Thou shalt not resist evil." As though He said, "Take heed that you bear everything, so that you may not need the State to help and serve you and be of profit to you, but that you may on the other hand, help, serve, and be of profit and use to it. I would have you to be far too exalted and noble to have any need of it, but it should have need of you."

You ask whether a Christian, also, may bear the secular sword and punish the wicked, since Christ's words, "Thou shalt not resist the evil," are so clear and definite that the sophists have had to make a counsel of them. I answer, You have now heard two propositions. The one is that the sword can have no place among Christians, therefore you cannot bear it among and against Christians, who do not need it. The question, therefore, must be directed to the other side, to the non-Christians, whether as a Christian you may there bear it. Here the other proposition applies, that you are under obligation to serve and further the sword by whatever means you can, with body, soul, honor or goods. For it is nothing that you need, but something quite useful and profitable for the whole world and for your neighbor. Therefore, should you see that there is a lack of hangmen, beadles, judges, lords, or princes, and find that you are qualified, you should offer your services and seek the place, that necessary government may by no means be despised and become inefficient or perish. For the world cannot and dare not dispense with it.

The reason you should do this is, that in this case you would enter entirely into the service and work of others, which benefited neither yourself nor your property nor your character, but only your neighbor and others; and you would

o it not to avenge yourself or to recompense evil for evil, but
or the good of your neighbor and for the maintenance of the
afety and peace of others. As concerns yourself, you would
bide by the Gospel and govern yourself according to Christ's
vord, gladly turning the other cheek and letting the mantle go
vith the coat, when the matter concerned you and your cause.
n this way, then things are well balanced, and you satisfy at
he same time God's kingdom inwardly and the kingdom of
he world outwardly. . . .

(Extracts from *Secular Authority,* Part I, sections 1, 3, 4,
, 6.)

The Extent of Secular Authority

Every kingdom must have its own laws and regulations,
nd without law no kingdom or government can exist, as daily
xperience sufficiently proves. Wordly government has laws
vhich extend no farther than to life and property and what is
external upon earth. For over the soul God can and will let no
one rule but Himself. Therefore, where temporal power pre-
umes to prescribe laws for the soul, it encroaches upon God's
government and only misleads and destroys the souls. We
desire to make this so clear that every one shall grasp it, and
hat our junkers, the princes and bishops, may see what fools
hey are when they seek to coerce the people with *their* laws
nd commandments into believing one thing or another.

When a man-made law is imposed upon the soul, in order
o make it believe this or that, as that man prescribes, there is
certainly no word of God for it. If there is no word of God
or it, it is uncertain whether God will have it so, for we
cannot be certain that what He does not command pleases
Him. Nay, we are sure that it does not please Him, for He
desires that our faith be grounded simply and entirely on His
divine word, as He says in Matthew xvi, "On this rock will I
build my church"; and in John x, "My sheep hear my voice
and know me; but the voice of strangers they hear not, but
flee from them." It follows from this that the secular power
forces souls to eternal death with such an outrageous law, for
it compels them to believe as right and certainly pleasing to
God what is nevertheless uncertain, nay, what is certainly
displeasing to Him, since there is no clear word of God for it.
For whoever believes that to be right which is wrong or uncer-
ain denies the truth, which is God Himself, and believes in
ies and errors and counts that right which is wrong.

Hence it is the height of folly when they command that one
shall believe the Church, the fathers, the councils, though

there be no word of God for it. The devil's apostles command
such things, not the Church: for the Church commands nothing unless it is sure it is God's Word, as St. Peter says, "If any
man speak let him speak as the oracles of God." It will be a
very long time, however, before they prove that the statements
of the councils are God's Word. Still more foolish is it when
they assert that kings and princes and the mass of men believe
thus and so. If you please, we are not baptised unto kings,
princes, or even unto the mass of men, but unto Christ and
unto God himself; neither are we called kings, princes or
common folk, but Christians. No one shall can command
the soul, unless he can show it the way to heaven; but this no
man can do, only God. Therefore in matters which concern
the salvation of souls nothing but God's Word shall be taught
and accepted.

Again, consummate fools though they are, they must confess that they have no power over souls. For no human being
can kill a soul or make it alive, conduct it to heaven or hell.
And if they will not believe us in this, Christ indeed will
certify strongly enough to it, since He says in Matthew x,
"Fear not them which kill the body and after that have power
to do naught; but rather fear Him Who after He has killed the
body has power to condemn to hell." I consider that here it is
sufficiently clear that the soul is taken out of all human hands
and is placed under the power of God alone. Now tell me
how much wit is there in the head of him who imposes commandments where he has no power at all? Who would not
regard one as insane if he commanded the moon to shine
when he desired it? . . . Nevertheless, our emperors and wise
princes continue to permit pope, bishops and sophists to lead
them on, one blind man leading the other, to command their
subjects to believe, without God's Word, whatever they please
and still would be known as Christian princes. . . .

. . . You say Temporal power does not force men to believe, but simply prevents them from being misled by false
doctrines; otherwise how could heretics be prevented from
preaching? I answer, This the bishops should do, to whom
and not to the princes, such duty is entrusted. Heresy can
never be prevented by force. That must be taken hold of in a
different way, and must be opposed and dealt with otherwise
than with the sword. Here God's Word must strive; if that
does not accomplish the end it will remain unaccomplished
through secular power, though it fill the world with blood.
Heresy is a spiritual matter, which no iron can strike, no fire
burn, no water drown. God's Word alone avails here, as Paul
says, II Corinthians x, "Our weapons are not carnal, but

mighty through God to destroy every counsel and high thing that exalteth itself against the knowledge of God, and to bring into captivity every thought to the obedience of Christ."

Moreover, faith and heresy are never so strong as when men oppose them by sheer force, without God's Word. For men count it certain that such force is for a wrong cause and is directed against the right, since it proceeds without God's Word, and does not know how to further its cause except by force, just as the brute beasts do. For even in secular affairs force can be used only after the wrong has been legally condemned. How much less possible is it to act with force, without justice and God's Word, in these high, spiritual matters. See, therefore, what fine, shrewd nobles they are. They would drive out heresy, and set about it in such a way that they only strengthen the opposition, make themselves suspected, and justify the heretics. Friend, would you drive out heresy, then you must find a plan to tear it first of all from the heart and altogether to turn men's wills away from it; force will not accomplish this, but only strengthen the heresy. What avails it to strengthen heresy in the heart and to weaken only its outward expression, and to force the tongue to lie? God's Word, however, enlightens the hearts; and so all heresies and errors perish of themselves from the heart.

(Extract from *Secular Authority*, Part II.)

. . . There are two kingdoms, one the kingdom of God, the other the kingdom of the world. . . . God's kingdom is a kingdom of grace and mercy, not of wrath and punishment. In it there is only forgiveness, consideration for one another, love, service, the doing of good, peace, joy, etc. But the kingdom of the world is a kingdom of wrath and severity. In it there is only punishment, repression, judgment, and condemnation, for the suppressing of the wicked and the protection of the good. For this reason it has the sword, and a prince or lord is called in Scripture God's wrath, or God's rod (Isaiah xiv).

The words of Scripture that speak of mercy apply to the kingdom of God and to Christians, not to the kingdom of the world, for it is a Christian's duty not only to be merciful, but to endure every kind of suffering—robbery, arson, murder, devil and hell. It goes without saying that he is to smite, slay and recompense no one. But the kingdom of the world is nothing else than the servant of God's wrath upon the wicked, and is a real precursor of hell and everlasting death. It should not be merciful, but strict, severe and wrathful in the fulfilment of its work and duty. Its tool is not a wreath of roses or a flower of love, but a naked sword; and a sword is a symbol of wrath, severity and punishment. It is turned only against the wicked, to hold them in check and keep them at peace, and to protect and save the righteous. Therefore God decrees, in the law of Moses and in Exodus xxii, where He institutes the sword, "Thou shalt take the murderer even from mine altar, and shalt not have mercy on him," and the Epistle to the Hebrews confesses that he who acts against the law shall die without mercy. This shows that in the exercise of their office, worldly rulers cannot and ought not be merciful, though out of grace, they may give their office a holiday.

Now he who would confuse these two kingdoms—as our false fanatics do—would put wrath into God's kingdom and mercy into the world's kingdom; and that is the same as putting the devil in heaven and God in hell. Both of these things these sympathizers with the peasants would like to do. First they wanted to go to work with the sword, fight for the Gospel as "Christian brethren," and kill other people, when it was these others' duty to be merciful and patient. Now that the kingdom of the world has overcome them, they want to have mercy in it; that is to say, they would endure no worldly kingdom, but would not grant God's kingdom to anyone. Can you imagine anything more perverse? Not so, dear friends! If one has deserved wrath in the kingdom of the world, let him submit, and either take his punishment, or humbly sue for pardon. . . .

(Extract from *An Open Letter Concerning the Hard Book Against the Peasants*, 1525.)

The Duty of Princes

Christ Himself describes the nature of temporal princes in Luke xxii, when he says, "The wordly princes exercise lordship, and they that are chief exercise authority." For if they are born princes or chosen to office, they think only that it is their right to be served and to rule with power. He who would be a Christian prince certainly must lay aside the intention to rule and to use force. For cursed and condemned is every kind of life lived and sought for selfish profit and good; cursed are all works not done in love. But they are done in love when they are directed with all one's heart, not toward selfish pleasure, profit, honor, ease and salvation, but toward the profit, honor and salvation of others.

. . . If a prince himself is not wiser than his jurists, and does not know more than is in the law-books, he will surely rule according to the saying in Proverbs xxviii, "A prince that wanteth understanding will oppress many with injustice." No matter how good and equitable the laws are, they all make exceptions of cases of necessity, in which they cannot be enforced. Therefore a prince must have the law in hand as firmly as the sword, and decide in his own mind when and where the law must be applied strictly or with moderation, so that reason may always control all law and be the highest law and rule over all laws. A housefather who, although he appoints a definite time and amount of work and food for his servants and children, must yet reserve the power to change or omit such regulations if his servants happen to be sick, imprisoned, detained, deceived, or otherwise hindered, and not deal as severely with the sick as with the well. I say this in order that men may not think it sufficient and an excellent thing if they follow the written law or the legal advisers; more than that is required.

What should a prince do, if he is not sufficiently wise, and must follow the directions of jurists and law books? I answer, for this reason I said that the position of a prince is a perilous one, and if he is not wise enough to master both the law and his advisers, the saying of Solomon is fulfilled, "Woe to the land whose king is a child." Solomon recognized this; therefore he despaired of all law, even of that which Moses, through God, had prescribed for him and of all his princes and counselors, and turned to God Himself and prayed to Him for a wise heart to rule the people. A prince must follow this example and proceed with fear; he must depend neither upon dead books nor upon living heads, but cling solely to God, pray without ceasing to Him, and ask for a right understanding, above all books and masters, wisely to rule his subjects. Therefore I know of no law to prescribe for a prince, but will simply instruct him what the attitude of his heart and mind ought to be with respect to all laws, counsels, decisions and actions, so that if he govern himself thereby God will surely grant him the power to carry out all laws, counsels, and actions in a proper and godly way.

He must consider his subjects and rightly dispose his heart toward them in this matter. He does this if he applies his whole mind to making himself useful and serviceable to them, and does not think, "Land and people are mine; I will do as I please"; but thus, "I belong to land and people; I must do what is profitable and good for them. My concern must be, not how I may rule and be haughty, but how they may be protected and defended by a good peace". . . he should interest himself in the need of his subjects . . . a prince's duty is fourfold: First, that toward God consists in true confidence and in sincere prayer; second, that toward his subjects consists in love and Christian service, third, that toward his counselors and rulers consists in an open mind and unfettered judgment; fourth, that toward evil doers consists in proper zeal and firmness. Then his state is right, outwardly and inwardly, pleasing to God and to the people. But he must expect much envy and sorrow,—the cross will soon rest on the shoulders of such a ruler.

Finally, in addition, I must make answer to those who dispute about restitution, that is, about the returning of goods unlawfully acquired. . . . No more definite law can be found on this subject than the law of love. In the first place, when such a case is brought before you, in which one is to make restitution to another, the matter is soon settled if they are both Christians; for neither will withhold what belongs to the other, nor will either of them demand that it be returned. If only one is a Christian, namely, the one to whom restitution is to be made, it is again easy to settle, for he does not care whether it never be returned. The same is true if the one who is to make restitution is a Christian; he will do so. But whether one is a Christian or not a Christian, you must decide the restitution as follows. If the debtor is poor and unable to make restitution, and the other party is not poor, then you should let the law of love prevail and acquit the debtor. For, according to the law of love, the other party, too, owes it to him to relinquish the debt, and if necessary to give him something besides. But if the debtor is not poor, then let him restore as much as he can, all, half, a third, or a fourth of it, provided that you leave him enough to assure a house, food and clothing for himself, his wife and children; for this you would owe him if you could give it, much less ought you to take it away now, since you do not need it and he cannot do without it.

But if neither is a Christian, or if either is unwilling to be judged by the law of love, you may ask them to call in another judge, and announce to them that they are acting against God and the law of nature, even though they may obtain absolute justice through human law. For nature, like love, teaches that I should do as I would be done by. Therefore I cannot strip any one else, even if I have the very best right to do so, if I myself am not willing to be stripped of my goods, but as I would that another should relinquish his right to me in such an instance, even so should I also relinquish my rights. Thus one should deal with all property unlawfully held, whether in public or private, that love and the law of nature may always prevail. For when you judge according to love, you will easily decide and adjust matters without any law-books. But when you ignore love and natural law, you will never succeed in pleasing God, though you have devoured all the law-books and jurists; they will only cause you to err, the more you depend on them. A good and just decision must not and cannot be given out of books, but must come from a free mind, as though there were not a single book. Such a free decision, however, is given by love and by the law of nature, of which the reason is full. . . .

(Extract from *Secular Authority*, Part III.)

CALVIN

Institutes of the Christian Religion

The Ruler as Minister of God

This consideration constitutes true royalty: to acknowledge yourself in the government of your kingdom to be the minister of God. For where the glory of God is not made the end of the government, it is not a legitimate sovereignty, but a usurpation. And he is deceived who expects lasting prosperity in that kingdom which is not ruled by the scepter of God, that is, his holy word; for that heavenly oracle cannot fail which declares that "where there is no vision, the people perish." Nor should you be seduced from this pursuit by a contempt of our meanness. We are fully conscious to ourselves how very mean and abject we are, being miserable sinners before God, and accounted most despicable by men; being (if you please) the refuse of the world, deserving of the vilest appellations that can be found; so that nothing remains for us to glory in before God but his mercy alone, by which, without any merit of ours, we have been admitted to the hope of eternal salvation, and before men nothing but our weakness, the slightest confession of which is esteemed by them as the greatest disgrace. But our doctrine must stand, exalted above all the glory, and invincible by all the power of the world; because it is not ours but the doctrine of the living God, and of His Christ, whom the Father hath constituted King, that he may have dominion from sea to sea, and from the river even to the ends of the earth, and that he may rule in such a manner that the whole earth, with its strength of iron and with its splendor of gold and silver smitten by the rod of his mouth, may be broken to pieces like a potter's vessel; for thus do the prophets foretell the magnificence of his kingdom.

The Idea of Christian Liberty

Christian liberty, according to my judgment, consists of three parts. The first part is that the consciences of believers, when seeking an assurance of their justification before God, should raise themselves above the law and forget all the righteousness of the law. For since the law leaves no man righteous, either we must be excluded from all hope of justification or it is necessary for us to be delivered from it, and that so completely as not to have any dependence on works. For he who imagines that in order to obtain righteousness he must produce any works, however small, can fix no limit or boundary, but renders himself a debtor to the whole law. Avoiding, therefore, all mention of the law and dismissing all thought of our own works, in reference to justification, we must embrace the Divine mercy alone, and turning our eyes from ourselves, fix them solely on Christ. For the question is not how we can be righteous, but how, though unrighteous and unworthy, we can be considered as righteous. And the conscience that desires to attain any certainty respecting this must give no admission to the law. Nor will this authorize anyone to conclude that the law is of no use to believers, whom it still continues to instruct and exhort and stimulate to duty, although it has no place in their consciences before the tribunal of God. For these two things, being very different, require to be properly and carefully distinguished by us. The whole life of Christians ought to be an exercise of piety, since they are called to sanctification. It is the office of the law to remind them of their duty and thereby to excite them to the pursuit of holiness and integrity. But when their consciences are solicitous how God may be propitiated, what answer they shall make, and on what they shall rest their confidence, if called to his tribunal, there must then be no consideration of the requisitions of the law, but Christ alone must be proposed for righteousness, who exceeds all the perfection of the law.

The second part of Christian liberty, which is dependent on the first, is that their consciences do not observe the law, as being under any legal obligation; but that, being liberated from the yoke of the law, they yield a voluntary obedience to the will of God. For being possessed with perpetual terrors, as long as they remain under the dominion of the law, they will never engage with alacrity and promptitude in the service of God unless they have previously received this liberty. . . . If they advert to the law, they see that every work they attempt or meditate is accursed. Nor is there the least reason for any person to deceive himself by concluding that an action is not necessarily altogether evil because it is imperfect, and that therefore the good part of it is accepted by God. For the law, requiring perfect love, condemns all imperfection unless its rigor be mitigated. Let him consider his work, therefore, which he wished to be thought partly good, and he will find that very work to be a transgression of the law because it is imperfect.

See how all our works, if estimated according to the rigor of the law, are subject to its curse. How, then, could unhappy souls apply themselves with alacrity to any work for which they could expect to receive nothing but a curse? On the contrary, if they are liberated from the severe exaction of the law or rather from the whole of its rigor, and hear God calling them with paternal gentleness, then with cheerfulness and prompt alacrity they will answer to his call and follow his guidance. In short, they who are bound by the yoke of the law are like slaves who have certain daily tasks appointed by their masters.

The third part of Christian liberty teaches us that we are bound by no obligation before God respecting external things, which in themselves are indifferent, but that we may indifferently sometimes use them and at other times omit them. And the knowledge of this liberty also is very necessary for us; for without it we shall have no tranquility of conscience, nor will there be any end of superstitions.

"I know," says Paul, "that there is nothing unclean of itself; but to him that esteemeth anything to be unclean, to him it is unclean." In these words he makes all external things subject to our liberty, provided that our minds have regard to this liberty before God. But if any superstitious notion cause us to scruple, those things which were naturally pure become contaminated to us.

. . . We see, in short, the tendency of this liberty, which is that, without any scruple of conscience or perturbation of mind, we should devote the gifts of God to that use for which he has given them; by which confidence our souls may have peace with him and acknowledge his liberality toward us. For this comprehends all ceremonies, the observation of which is left free, that the conscience may not be bound by any obligation to observe them, but may remember that by the goodness of God it may use them or abstain from them, as shall be most conducive to edification.

Now it must be carefully observed that Christian liberty is in all its branches a spiritual thing; all the virtue of which consists in appeasing terrified consciences before God, whether they are disquieted and solicitous concerning the remission of their sins or are anxious to know if their works, which are imperfect and contaminated by the defilements of the flesh, be acceptable to God; or are tormented concerning the use of things that are indifferent. Wherefore they are guilty of perverting its meaning who either make it the pretext of their irregular appetites, that they may abuse the Divine blessings to the purposes of sensuality, or who suppose that there is no liberty but what is used before men, and therefore in the exercise of it totally disregard their weak brethren. The former of these sins is the more common in the present age. There is scarcely anyone whom his wealth permits to be sumptuous, who is not delighted with luxurious splendor in his entertainments, in his dress, and in his buildings; who does not desire a pre-eminence in every species of luxury; who does not strangely flatter himself on his elegance. And all these things are defended under the pretext of Christian liberty. They allege that they are things indifferent; this I admit provided they be indifferently used. . . .

But amidst an abundance of all things, to be immersed in sensual delights, to inebriate the heart and mind with present pleasures, and perpetually to grasp at new ones—these things are very remote from a legitimate use of the Divine blessings. Let them banish, therefore, immoderate cupidity, excessive profusion, vanity, and arrogance; that with a pure conscience they may make a proper use of the gifts of God. When their hearts shall be formed to this sobriety, they will have a rule for the legitimate enjoyment of them. On the contrary, without this moderation even common and ordinary pleasures are chargeable with excess. . . . Let all men, in their respective stations, whether of poverty, of competence, or of splendor, live in the remembrance of this truth that God confers his blessings on them for the support of life, not for luxury. . . .

Many persons err likewise in this respect that, as if their liberty would not be perfectly secure unless witnessed by men, they make an indiscriminate and imprudent use of it—a disorderly practice which occasions frequent offense to their weak brethren. There are some to be found, in the present day, who imagine their liberty would be abridged if they were not to enter on the enjoyment of it by eating animal food on Friday. Their eating is not the subject of my reprehension; but their minds require to be divested of this false notion; for they ought to consider that they obtain no advantage from their liberty before men, but with God; and that it consists in abstinence as well as in use. . . . But they fall into a very pernicious error in disregarding the infirmity of their brethren, which it becomes us to bear, so as not rashly to do anything which would give them the least offense. But it will be said that it is sometimes right to assert our liberty before men. This I confess; yet the greatest caution and moderation must be observed lest we cast off all concern for the weak, whom God has so strongly recommended to our regards . . . our liberty is not given us to be used in opposition to our weak neighbors, to whom charity obliges us to do every possible service, but rather in order that, having peace with God in our minds, we may also live peaceably among men. . . .

. . . Nothing can be plainer than this rule that our liberty should be used if it conduces to our neighbor's edification; but that if it be not beneficial to our neighbor, it should be abridged. There are some who pretend to imitate the prudence of Paul in refraining from the exercise of liberty, while they are doing anything but exercising the duties of charity. For to promote their own tranquility, they wish all mention of liberty to be buried; whereas it is no less advantageous to our neighbors sometimes to use our liberty to their benefit and edification, than at other times to moderate it for their accommodation. But a pious man considers this liberty in external things as granted him in order that he may be the better prepared for all the duties of charity.

. . . It becomes us, indeed, to have regard to charity, but we must not offend God for the love of our neighbor. We cannot approve the intemperance of those who do nothing but in a tumultuous manner, and who prefer violent measures to lenient ones. Nor must we listen to those who, while they show themselves the leaders in a thousand species of impiety, pretend that they are obliged to act in such a manner that they may give no offense to their neighbors; as though they are not at the same time fortifying the consciences of their neighbors in sin, especially since they are always sticking in the same mire without any hope of deliverance.

. . . Now, since the consciences of believers, being privileged with the liberty which we have described, have been delivered by the favor of Christ from all necessary obligation to the observance of those things in which the Lord has been pleased they should be left free, we conclude that they are exempt from all human authority. For it is not right that Christ should lose the acknowledgments due to such kindness, or our consciences the benefit of it. . . .

Man is under two kinds of government—one spiritual, by which the conscience is formed to piety and the service of God; the other political, by which a man is instructed in the duties of humanity and civility, which are to be observed in an intercourse with mankind. They are generally, and not improperly, denominated the spiritual and the temporal jurisdiction, indicating that the former species of government pertains to the life of the soul, and that the latter relates to the concerns of the present state, not only to the provision of food and clothing, but to the enactment of laws to regulate a man's life among his neighbors by the rules of holiness, integrity, and sobriety. For the former has its seat in the interior of the mind, whilst the latter only directs the external conduct: one may be termed a spiritual kingdom, and the other a political one. But these two, as we have distinguished them, always require to be considered separately; and while the one is under discussion, the mind must be abstracted from all consideration of the other. For man contains, as it were, two worlds, capable of being governed by various rulers and various laws. This distinction will prevent what the Gospel inculcates concerning spiritual liberty from being misapplied to political regulations, as though Christians were less subject to the external government of human laws because their consciences have been set at liberty before God, as though their freedom of spirit necessarily exempted them from all carnal servitude. Again, because even in those constitutions which seem to pertain to the spiritual kingdom, there may possibly be some deception, it is necessary to discriminate between these also—which are to be accounted legitimate, as according with the Divine word, and which, on the contrary, ought not to be received among believers.

Therefore, as works respect men, so conscience regards God, so that a good conscience is no other than inward integrity of heart. In which sense Paul says that "the end of the commandment is charity, out of a pure heart, and of a good conscience, and of faith unfeigned." Afterwards also, in the same chapter, he shows how widely it differs from understanding, saying that "some, having put away a good conscience, concerning faith have made shipwreck." For these words indicate that it is a lively inclination to the service of God and a sincere pursuit of piety and holiness of life. Sometimes, indeed, it is likewise extended to me; as when the same apostle declares, "Herein do I exercise myself, to have always a conscience void of offense toward God and toward men." But the reason of this assertion is that the fruits of a good conscience reach even to men. But in strict propriety of speech it has to do with God alone, as I have already observed. Hence it is that a law which simply binds a man without relation to other men, or any consideration of them, is said to bind the conscience.

The Need for Government

. . . Some men, when they hear that the Gospel promises a liberty which acknowledges no king or magistrate among them, but submits to Christ alone, think they can enjoy no advantage of their liberty while they see any power exalted above them. They imagine, therefore, that nothing will prosper unless the whole world be modeled in a new form, without any tribunals or laws, or magistrates, or anything of a similar kind which they consider injurious to their liberty. But he who knows how to distinguish between the body and the soul, between this present transitory life and the future eternal one, will find no difficulty in understanding that the spiritual kingdom of Christ and civil government are things very different and remote from each other. . . .

. . . Yet this distinction does not lead us to consider the whole system of civil government as a polluted thing which has nothing to do with Christian men. Some fanatics who are pleased with nothing but liberty, or rather licentiousness without any restraint, do indeed boast and vociferate, That since we are dead with Christ to the elements of this world and, being translated into the kingdom of God, sit among the celestials, it is a degradation to us and far beneath our dignity to be occupied with those secular and impure cares which relate to things altogether uninteresting to a Christian man. Of what use, they ask, are laws without judgments and tribunals? But what have judgments to do with a Christian man? And if it be unlawful to kill, of what use are laws and judgments to us? But as we have just suggested that this kind of government is distinct from that spiritual and internal reign of Christ, so it ought to be known that they are in no respect at variance with each other. For that spiritual reign, even now upon earth, commences within us some preludes of the heavenly kingdom, and in this mortal and transitory life affords us some prelibations of immortal and incorruptible blessedness; but this civil government is designed, as long as we live in this world, to cherish and support the external worship of God, to preserve the pure doctrine of religion, to defend the constitution of the Church, to regulate our lives in a manner requisite for the society of men, to form our manners to civil justice, to promote our concord with each other, and to establish general peace and tranquility—all of which I confess to be superfluous if the kingdom of God, as it now exists in us, extinguishes the present life. But if it is the will of God that while we are aspiring toward our true country, we be pilgrims on the earth, and if such aids are necessary to our pilgrimage, they who take them from man deprive him of his human nature. They plead that there should be so much perfection in the Church of God that its order would suffice to supply the place of all laws; but they foolishly imagine a perfection which can never be found in any community of men. For since the insolence of the wicked is so great, and their iniquity so obstinate, that it can scarcely be restrained by all the severity of the laws, what may we expect they would do if they found themselves at liberty to perpetuate crimes with impunity whose outrages even the arm of power cannot altogether prevent?

But for speaking of the exercise of civil polity, there will be another place more suitable. At present we only wish it to be understood that to entertain a thought of its extermination is inhuman barbarism; it is equally as necessary to mankind as bread and water, light and air, and far more excellent. For it not only tends to secure the accommodations arising from all these things, that men may breathe, eat, drink, and be sustained in life, though it comprehends all these things while it causes them to live together, yet I say this is not its only tendency; its objects also are that idolatry, sacrileges against the name of God, blasphemies against his truth, and other offenses against religion may not openly appear and be disseminated among the people; that the public tranquility may not be disturbed; that every person may enjoy his property without molestation; that men may transact their business together without fraud or injustice; that integrity and modesty may be cultivated among them; in short, that there may be a public form of religion among Christians, and that humanity may be maintained among men. Nor let anyone think it strange that I now refer to human polity the charge of the due maintenance of religion, which I may appear to have placed beyond the jurisdiction of men. For I do not allow men to make laws respecting religion and the worship of God now any more than I did before, though I approve of civil government which provides that the true religion contained in the law of God be not violated and polluted by public blasphemies with impunity.

. . . The Lord has not only testified that the function of magistrates has his approbation and acceptance, but has eminently commended it to us, by dignifying it with the most honorable titles. . . .

The authority possessed by kings and other governors over all things upon earth is not a consequence of the perverseness of men but of the providence and holy ordinance of God, who has been pleased to regulate human affairs in this manner; for as much as he is present, and also presides among them, in making laws and in executing equitable judgments. This is clearly taught by Paul, when he enumerates governments among the gifts of God, which, being variously distributed according to the diversity of grace, ought to be employed by the servants of Christ to the edification of the Church. . . .

. . . . Wherefore no doubt ought now to be entertained by any person that civil magistracy is a calling not only holy and legitimate, but far the most sacred and honorable in human life.

Those who would wish to introduce anarchy reply that though, in ancient times, kings and judges presided over a rude people, that servile kind of government is now quite incompatible with the perfection which accompanies the Gospel of Christ. Here they betray not only their ignorance but their diabolical pride, in boasting of perfection of which not the smallest particle can be discovered in them. . . .

If magistrates remember that they are the vicegerents of God, it behooves them to watch with all care, earnestness, and diligence, that in their administration they may exhibit to men an image, as it were, of the providence, care, goodness, benevolence, and justice of God. And they must constantly bear this in mind that if in all cases "he be cursed that doeth the work of the Lord deceitfully," a far heavier curse awaits those who act fraudulently in a righteous calling.

I shall by no means deny that either aristocracy or a mixture of aristocracy and democracy far excels all others; and that indeed not of itself, but because it very rarely happens that kings regulate themselves so that their will is never at variance with justice and rectitude; or, in the next place, that they are endued with such penetration and prudence as in all cases to discover what is best. The vice or imperfection of men therefore renders it safer and more tolerable for the government to be in the hands of many, that they may afford each other mutual assistance and admonition, and that if any one arrogate to himself more than is right, the many may act as censors and masters to restrain his ambition. And as I readily acknowledge that no kind of government is more happy than this where liberty is regulated with becoming moderation and properly established on a durable basis, so also I consider those as the most happy people who are permitted to enjoy such a condition; and if they exert their strenuous and constant efforts for its preservation and retention, I admit that they act in perfect consistence with their duty. And to this object the magistrates likewise ought to apply their greatest diligence, that they suffer not the liberty, of which they are constituted guardians, to be in any respect diminished, much less to be violated; if they are inactive and unconcerned about this, they are perfidious to their office, and traitors to their country. But if those to whom the will of God has assigned another form of government transfer this to themselves so as to be tempted to desire a revolution, the very thought will be not only foolish and useless, but altogether criminal. . . .

For if it be his pleasure to appoint kings over kingdoms, and senators or other magistrates over free cities, it is our duty to be obedient to any governors whom God has established over the places in which we reside.

Here it is necessary to state in a brief manner the nature of the office of magistracy, as described in the word of God, and wherein it consists. If the Scripture did not teach that this office extends to both tables of the law, we might learn it from heathen writers; for not one of them has treated of the office of magistrates, of legislation, and civil government, without beginning with religion and Divine worship. And thus they have all confessed that no government can be happily constituted unless its first object be the promotion of piety, and that all laws are preposterous which neglect the claims of God and merely provide for the interests of men. Therefore, as religion holds the first place among all the philosophers, and as this has always been regarded by the universal consent of all nations, Christian princes and magistrates ought to be ashamed of their indolence if they do not make it the object of their most serious care. We have already shown that this duty is particularly enjoined upon them by God; for it is reasonable that they should employ their utmost efforts in asserting and defending the honor of Him whose vicegerents they are and by whose favor they govern. And the principal commendations given in the Scripture to the good kings are for having restored the worship of God when it had been corrupted or abolished, or for having devoted their attention to religion, that it might flourish in purity and safety under their reigns. . . .

We see, therefore, that they are constituted the protectors and vindicators of the public innocence, modesty, probity, and tranquility, whose sole object it ought to be to promote the common peace and security of all. But as they cannot do this unless they defend good men from the injuries of the wicked and aid the oppressed by their relief and protection, they are likewise armed with power for the suppression of crimes, and the severe punishment of malefactors whose wickedness disturbs the public peace. For experience fully verifies the observation of Solon: "That all states are supported by reward and punishment; and that when these two things are removed, all the discipline of human societies is broken and destroyed." For the minds of many lose their regard for equity and justice unless virtue be rewarded with due honor; nor can the violence of the wicked be restrained unless crimes are followed by severe punishments. And these two parts are included in the injunction of the prophet to kings and other governors to "execute judgment and righteousness." "Righteousness" means the care, patronage, defense, vindication, and liberation of the innocent; "judgment" imports the repression of the audacity, the coercion of the violence, and the punishment of the crime of the impious.

The Duty of Obedience

The first duty of subjects toward their magistrates is to entertain the most honorable sentiments of their function, which they know to be a jurisdiction delegated to them from God, and on that account to esteem and reverence them as God's ministers and vicegerents. For there are some persons to be found who show themselves very obedient to their magistrates and have not the least wish that there were no magistrates for them to obey, because they know them to be so necessary to the public good, but who, nevertheless, consider the magistrates themselves as no other than necessary evils. But something more than this is required of us by Peter when he commands us to "honor the king"; and by Solomon, when he says, "Fear thou the Lord and the king"; for Peter, under the term "honor," comprehends a sincere and candid esteem; and Solomon, by connecting the king with the Lord, attributes to him a kind of sacred veneration and dignity. It is also a remarkable commendation of magistrates which is given by Paul, when he says that we "must needs be subject, not only for wrath, but also for conscience' sake"; by which he means that subjects ought to be induced to submit to princes and governors, not merely from a dread of their power, as persons are accustomed to yield to an armed enemy, who they know will immediately take vengeance upon them if they resist; but because the obedience which is rendered to princes and magistrates is rendered to God, from whom they have received their authority. I am not speaking of the persons as if the mask of dignity ought to palliate or excuse folly, ignorance, or cruelty, and conduct the most nefarious and flagitious, and so to acquire for vices the praise due to virtues; but I affirm that the station itself is worthy of honor and reverence, so that, whoever our governors are, they ought to possess our esteem and veneration on account of the office which they fill.

Hence follows another duty—that, with minds disposed to honor and reverence magistrates, subjects approve their obedience to them in submitting to their edicts, in paying taxes, in discharging public duties, and bearing burdens which relate to the common defense, and in fulfilling all their other commands. Paul says to the Romans, "Let every soul be subject unto the higher powers. Whosoever resisteth the power, resisteth the ordinance of God." Under this obedience I also include the moderation which private persons ought to prescribe to themselves in relation to public affairs, that they do not without being called upon, intermeddle with affairs of state or rashly intrude themselves into the office of magistrates, or undertake anything of a public nature. If there be anything in the public administration which requires to be corrected, let them not raise any tumults or take the business into their own hands, which ought to be all bound in this respect, but let them refer it to the cognizance of the magistrate, who is also authorized to regulate the concerns of the public. I mean that they ought to attempt nothing without being commanded; for when they have the command of a governor, then they also are invested with public authority. For, as we are accustomed to call the counsellors of a prince "his eyes and ears," so they may not unaptly be called "his hands" whom he has commissioned to execute his commands.

. . . Certainly the minds of men have always been naturally disposed to hate and execrate tyrants as much as to love and reverence legitimate kings.

But, if we direct out attention to the word of God, it will carry us much farther: even to submit to the government, not only of those princes who discharge their duty to us with becoming integrity and fidelity, but of all who possess the sovereignty, even though they perform none of the duties of their function. For, though the Lord testifies that the magistrate is an eminent gift of his liberality to preserve the safety of men, and prescribes to magistrates themselves the extent of their duty, yet he at the same time declares that whatever be their characters, they have their government only from him; that those who govern for the public good are true specimens and mirrors of his beneficence; and that those who rule in an unjust and tyrannical manner are raised up by him to punish the iniquity of the people; that all equally possess that sacred majesty with which he has invested legitimate authority.

If we have this constantly present to our eyes and impressed upon our hearts, that the most iniquitous kings are placed on their thrones by the same decree by which the authority of all kings is established, those seditious thoughts will never enter our minds that a king is to be treated according to his merits, and that it is not reasonable for us to be subject to a king who does not on his part perform toward us those duties which his office requires.

If we are inhumanly harassed by a cruel prince; if we are rapaciously plundered by an avaricious or luxurious one; if we are neglected by an indolent one; or if we are persecuted, on account of piety, by an impious and sacrilegious one—let us first call to mind our transgressions against God, which he undoubtedly chastises by these scourges. Thus our impatience will be restrained by humility. Let us, in the next place, consider that it is not our province to remedy these evils, and that nothing remains for us but to implore the aid of the Lord, in whose hand are the hearts of kings and the revolutions of kingdoms. It is "God" who "standeth in the congregation of the mighty," and "judgeth among the gods"; whose presence shall confound and crush all kings and judges of the earth who shall not have kissed his Son; "that decree unrighteous decrees, to turn aside the needy from judgment, and to take away the right from the poor, that widows may be their prey, and that they may rob the fatherless." . . .

But whatever opinion be formed by the acts of men, yet the Lord equally executed his work by them when he broke the sanguinary scepters of insolent kings and overturned tyrannical governments. Let princes hear and fear. But, in the meanwhile, it behooves us to use the greatest caution, that we do not despise or violate that authority of magistrates which is entitled to the greatest veneration, which God has established by the most solemn commands, even though it reside in those who are most unworthy of it, and who, as far as in them lies, pollute it by their iniquity. For though the correction of tyrannical domination is the vengeance of God, we are not, therefore, to conclude that it is committed to us who have received no other command than to obey and suffer. This observation I always apply to private persons. For if there be, in the present day, any magistrates appointed for the protection of the people and the moderation of the power of kings, such as were, in ancient times, the Ephori, who were a check upon the kings among the Lacedaemonians, or the popular tribunes upon the consuls among the Romans, or the Demarchi upon the senate among the Athenians; or with power such as perhaps is now possessed by the three estates in every kingdom when they are assembled; I am so far from prohibiting them, in the discharge of their duty, to oppose the violence or cruelty of kings that I affirm that if they connive at kings in their oppression of their people, such forbearance involves the most nefarious perfidy because they fraudulently betray the liberty of the people, of which they know that they have been appointed protectors by the ordination of God.

But in the obedience which we have shown to be due to the authority of governors, it is always necessary to make one exception, and that is entitled to our first attention—that it do not seduce us from obedience to him to whose will the desires of all kings ought to be subject, to whose decrees all their commands ought to yield, to whose majesty all their scepters ought to submit. And, indeed, how preposterous it would be for us, with a view to satisfy men, to incur the displeasure of him on whose account we yield obedience to men! The Lord, therefore, is the King of kings; who, when he has opened his sacred mouth, is to be heard alone, above all, for all, and before all; in the next place, we are subject to those men who preside over us, but no otherwise than in him. If they command anything against him, it ought not to have the least attention, nor, in this case, ought we to pay any regard to all that dignity attached to magistrates, to which no injury is done when it is subjected to the unrivaled and supreme power of God.

SECTION IX

THE RIGHT
OF RESISTANCE

Protestant

The struggle between the different religious groups led to the conviction that resistance to authority was not inevitably wicked. In France, the Protestant Huguenots elaborated the medieval view that kingship was held in trust and that its authority was limited by that of the community as a whole. It was a thesis that went back to Aquinas, and led forward to modern constitutionalism.

The most powerful and influential of the works of this group was the *Vindiciae contra Tyrannos (A Defense of Liberty against Tyrants)*, written pseudonymously by Stephen Junius Brutus in 1579, seven years after the St. Bartholomew's Day Massacre, when perhaps 30,000 people were killed by religious fanaticism. The *Vindiciae* discussed the problem of whether an individual must obey or could resist a ruler violating the law of God or oppressing the state. Two contracts had been made, between the ruler and his people, and among the ruler, people and God. If the ruler broke these contracts, he could be resisted and deposed, if necessary to maintain the worship of God or of just rule. However, the resistance must be offered not by private citizens, but by magistrates on their behalf.

The *Vindiciae* brought to the forefront of political theory the ideas of contract, the trusteeship powers of rulers, ultimate sovereignty of the people, a law higher than that of the state, a public right of resistance. Similar conclusions were reached by Hotman, Althusius, and by Scottish Protestants. Francois Hotman (1524–1590) in his *Francogallia* of 1573 relied on French historical experience and ancient constitutional arrangements to justify the Huguenot case for resistance. In his analysis of French history Hotman, a professor of law, held that French political problems were the result of monarchical power which limited the traditional power of the public council. France needed the revival of those traditional constitutional arrangements by which parliaments had a legal right to meet and to check the King.

The kingdom was superior to the individual king whose powers were based on popular consent. The crown was bestowed by the people's representatives on the king who must be checked by various means such as law, custom, the courts as well as by the representatives of the estates. These representatives not only had elected kings but could also depose them if they violated their duties of office.

Hotman's writings influenced both those Huguenots wanting to justify resistance to the king and who claimed the right of the people to control the king, and also those who held the nation was superior to the individual ruler.

Althusius, chief magistrate of Emden, in his *Systematic Politics* of 1610, developed theories both of sovereignty and of a social contract. For him, the guardians of the rights of the community would be the "euphors." In Britain, the extreme Protestants became the leading monarchomachs, (a term coined by Barclay for those advocating resistance). John Knox, in his *An Admonition to England and Scotland to call them to Repentance,* thundered in favor of deposing and punishing a ruler "who fought against God." Buchanan in 1600, in his *De Jure Regni apud Scotos*—a work, paradoxically enough, written for the future James I—argued that the authority of the king must be limited by representatives of the people. Not only was resistance justifiable; a tyrant could be killed at any time. Calvinism, in contradiction to the views of its founder, was pleading the cause of disobedience, and ushering in political freedom.

Catholic

The religious wars and persecutions in the Netherlands, France, Germany and England, and the growing strength of Protestant monarchies, led Catholic theologians to re-examine the problem of obedience. A group of Spanish Jesuits, the order founded in 1534 to combat heresy, took the lead in advocating the possibility of resistance to secular authority.

Mariana (1536–1624), learned and distinguished teacher, returned to his native Toledo in 1574 to begin writing. In his *De Rege et Regis Institutione* (*On Kingship and the Education of a King*) in 1599, he argued that civil authority was created by the community for its own earthly welfare. It was exercised by the Cortes, which had delegated the executive functions to a ruler, who had promised to provide good government. The assembly was therefore a check on the ruler, who was under the law. If the ruler disregarded the law, on financial matters or on religious, he could be deposed or assassinated. Both Buchanan and Rossaeus suggested tyrannicide, but it was with Mariana, advocating assassination either by the assembly or by an individual, if it was not in session, and specifically approving the killing of Henry III of France, that the concept became identified. Assassination was a prescription that had already been followed in practice. Attempts on the lives of Protestant rulers, Elizabeth of England, William of Orange and the convert Henry IV of France, had resulted in the deaths of the latter two monarchs.

Suárez (1548–1617), an equally distinguished Jesuit theologian, argued in his *De legibus, ac Deo legislatore* (*On Law and God the Lawgiver*) in 1603, that power was of divine origin and was given not to any one person, but to mankind as a whole. The Church was an authority with its own code of law directing people to attain their supernatural ends. Its code was not subordinate to the civil law of the political realm. Government was exercised with the consent of the community and the power of the ruler depended on the pact he had made with his people. If the ruler did not govern for the public welfare, he could be deposed—though this was not a power to be used lightly—and even killed. It is hardly surprising that James I had one of the books of Suárez burned on the steps of St. Paul's, a fate it also suffered in France.

The Jesuits, in their successful leadership of the Counter-Reformation, had surrendered the papal claim to secular supremacy. They limited secular power and wanted tyranny checked by the power of the community. At the same time, they acknowledged papal authority over the Church. Without paradox, they could argue for an absolute Pope and a non-absolute ruler.

The most gifted polemicist of the Church was Bellarmine (1542–1621). Nephew of one Pope, learned theologian and spokesman for other Popes, the Jesuit who had received the submission of Galileo and only mildly rebuked him, Bellarmine advocated the indirect power of the Pope.

Many of the major writings of Bellarmine were directed at answering William Barclay, Scottish lawyer living in France, who, arguing largely from canon law, had advocated the exclusive power of the king in civil affairs. Bellarmine held that the secular power of the prince was not a gift from God, but had been transferred by the community. But the king ruled under God, since the end of the community was spiritual. The Pope alone possessed spiritual authority. Though his power in secular affairs was limited, his religious power ultimately affected secular power. Though the Pope had no direct authority, in the sense of making laws, he could declare that subjects were no longer bound to obedience by an heretical prince.

Vindiciae Contra Tyrannos
(A Defence of Liberty Against Tyrants)

The Legitimacy of Resistance

. . . in so much as it is the duty of a good magistrate rather to endeavour to hinder and prevent a mischief than to chastise the delinquents after the offence is committed, as good physicians who prescribe a diet to allay and prevent diseases, as well as medicines to cure them, in like manner a people truly affected to true religion, will not simply consent themselves to reprove and repress a prince who would abolish the law of God, but also will have special regard, that through malice and wickedness he innovate nothing that may hurt the same, or that in tract of time may corrupt the pure service of God; and instead of supporting public offences committed against the Divine Majesty, they will take away all occasions wherewith the offenders might cover their faults.

If their assaults be verbal, their defence must be likewise verbal; if the sword be drawn against them, they may also take arms, and fight either with tongue or hand, as occasion is . . . provided always that they carefully distinguish between advantageous stratagems, and perfidious treason, which is always unlawful.

But I see well, here will be an objection made. What will you say? That a whole people, that beast of many heads, must they run in a mutinous disorder, to order the business of the commonwealth? What address or direction is there in an unruly and unbridled multitude? What counsel or wisdom, to manage the affairs of state?

When we speak of all the people, we understand by that, only those who hold their authority from the people, to wit, the magistrates, who are inferior to the king, and whom the people have substituted, or established, as it were, consorts in the empire, and with a kind of tribunitial authority, to restrain the encroachments of sovereignty, and to represent the whole body of the people. We understand also, the assembly of the estates, which is nothing else but an epitome, or brief collection of the kingdom, to whom all public affairs have special and absolute reference; such were the seventy ancients in the kingdom of Israel, amongst whom the high priest was as it were president, and they judged all matters of greatest importance, those seventy being first chosen by six out of each tribe, which came out of the land of Egypt, then the heads or governors of provinces. In like manner the judges and provosts of towns, the captains of thousands, the centurions and others who commanded over families, the most valiant, noble, and otherwise notable personages, of whom was composed the body of the states, assembled divers times as it plainly appears by the word of the holy scripture. . . . Now, it is no way probable, that all the people, one by one, met together there. Of this rank there are in every well governed kingdom, the princes, the officers of the crown, the peers, the greatest and most notable lords, the deputies of provinces, of whom the ordinary body of the estate is composed, or the parliament or the diet, or other assembly, according to the different names used in divers countries of the world; in which assemblies, the principal care is had both for the preventing and reforming either of disorder or detriment in church or commonwealth.

. . . Let us conclude . . . that all the people by the authority of those, into whose hands they have committed their power, or divers of them, may, and ought to reprove and repress a prince who commands things against God. In like manner, that all, or at the least, the principals of provinces or towns, under the authority of the chief magistrates, established first by God, and secondly by the prince, may according to law and reason, hinder the entrance of idolatry within the enclosure of their walls, and maintain their true religion: yea, further, they may extend the confines of the church, which is but one, and in failing hereof, if they have means to do it, they justly incur the penalty of high treason against the Divine Majesty.

Whether Private Men May Resist by Arms

It remains now that we speak of particulars who are private persons. First, particulars or private persons are not bound to take up arms against the prince who would compel them to become idolaters. The covenant between God and all the people who promise to be the people of God, does not in any sort bind them to that; for as that which belongs to the whole universal body is in no sort proper to particulars, so, in like manner, that which the body owes and is bound to perform cannot by any sensible reason be required of particular persons: neither does their duty anything oblige them to it; for every one is bound to serve God in that proper vocation to which he is called. Now private persons, they have no power; they have no public command, nor any calling to unsheathe the sword of authority; and therefore as God has not put the sword into the hands of private men, so does He not require in any sort that they should strike with it. On the contrary the apostles say of magistrates, they carry not the sword in vain. If particular men draw it forth they make themselves delinquents. If magistrates be slow and negligent to use it when just occasion is offered, they are likewise justly blameable of negligence in performing their duties, and equally guilty with the former.

But you will say unto me, has not God made a covenant, as well with particular persons as with the generality, with the least as well as the highest? For as all the subjects of a good and faithful prince, of what degree soever they be, are bound to obey him; but some of them, notwithstanding, have their particular duty, as magistrates must hold others in obedience; in like manner all men are bound to serve God; but some are placed in a higher rank, have received greater authority, in so much as they are accountable for the offences of others, if they attend not the charges of the commonalty carefully.

The kings, the commonalties of the people, the magistrates into whose hands the whole body of the commonwealth has committed the sword of authority, must and ought to take care that the church be maintained and preserved; particulars ought only to look that they render themselves members of this church. Kings and popular estates are bound to hinder the pollution or ruin of the temple of God, and ought to free and defend it from all corruption within, and all injury from without. Private men must take order, that their bodies, the temples of God, be pure, that they may be fit receptacles for the Holy Ghost to dwell in them. What shall then private men do, if the king will constrain them to serve idols? If the magistrates into whose hands the people have consigned their authority do oppose these proceedings of the king, let them in God's name obey their leaders, and employ all their means (as in the service of God) to aid the holy and commendable enterprises of those who oppose themselves lawfully against his wicked intention. But if the princes and magistrates approve the course of an outrageous and irreligious prince, or if they do not resist him, we must lend our ears to the counsel of

Jesus Christ, to wit, retire ourselves into some other place. Let us rather forsake our livelihoods and lives, than God, let us rather be crucified ourselves, than crucify the Lord of Life: fear not them (saith the Lord) who can only kill the body.

. . . To what purpose should the magistrates bear the sword, if it be not to serve God, who has committed it to them, to defend the good and punish the bad? Can they do better service than to preserve the church from the violence of the wicked, and to deliver the flock of Christ from the swords of murderers?

Now, if to bear arms and to make war be a thing lawful, can there possibly be found any war more just than that which is taken in hand by the command of the superior, for the defence of the church, and the preservation of the faithful? Is there any greater tyranny than that which is exercised over the soul? Can there be imagined a war more commendable than that which suppresses such a tyranny?

Kings are Made by the People

We have shewed before that it is God that does appoint kings, who chooses them, who gives the kingdom to them: now we say that the people establish kings, put the sceptre into their hands, and who with their suffrages, approve the election. God would have it done in this manner, to the end that the kings should acknowledge, that after God they hold their power and sovereignty from the people, and that it might the rather induce them, to apply and address the utmost of their care and thoughts for the profit of the people, without being puffed with any vain imagination, that they were formed of any matter more excellent than other men, for which they were raised so high above others. . . . But let them remember and know, that they are of the same mould and condition as others, raised from the earth by the voice and acclamations, now as it were upon the shoulders of the people unto their thrones, that they might afterwards bear on their own shoulders the greatest burdens of the commonwealth.

. . . And that to the end that kings may always remember that it is from God, but by the people, and for the people's sake that they do reign, and that in their glory they say not (as is their custom) they hold their kingdom only of God and their sword, but withal add that it was the people who first girt them with that sword. . . .

. . . Kings were at the first constituted by the people; and although the sons and dependants of such kings, inheriting their fathers' virtues, may in a sort seem to have rendered their kingdoms hereditary to their offsprings, and that in some kingdoms and countries, the right of free election seems in a sort buried; yet, notwithstanding, in all well-ordered kingdoms, this custom is yet remaining. The sons do not succeed the fathers, before the people have first, as it were, anew established them by their new approbation: neither were they acknowledged in quality, as inheriting it from the dead; but approved and accounted kings then only, when they were invested with the kingdom, by receiving the sceptre and diadem from the hands of those who represent the majesty of the people. One may see most evident marks of this in Christian kingdoms, which are at this day esteemed hereditary; for the French king, he of Spain and England, and others, are commonly sacred, and, as it were, put into possession of their authority by the peers, lords of the kingdom, and officers of the crown, who represent the body of the people; no more nor less than the emperors of Germany are chosen by the electors, and the kings of Polonia, by the yawodes and palatines of the kingdom, where the right of election is yet in force.

In like manner also, the cities give no royal reception, nor entries unto the king, but after their inauguration, and anciently they used not to count the times of their reign, but from the day of their coronation, the which was strictly observed in France. . . . Nay, which is more by authority of the people in the same kingdom, the crown has been transported (the lawful inheritors living) from one lineage to another, as from that of Merove to that of the Charlemains, and from that of the Charlemains, to that of Capets, the which has also been done in other kingdoms, as the best historians testify.

. . . All kings at the first were altogether elected, and those who at this day seem to have their crowns and royal authority by inheritance, have or should have, first and principally their confirmation from the people. Briefly, although the people of some countries have been accustomed to choose their kings of such a lineage, which for some notable merits have worthily deserved it, yet we must believe that they choose the stock itself, and not every branch that proceeds from it; neither are they so tied to that election, as if the successor degenerate, they may not choose another more worthy, neither those who come and are the next of that stock, are born kings, but created such, nor called kings, but princes of the blood royal.

The Whole Body of the People Is Above the King

Now, seeing that the people choose and establish their kings, it follows that the whole body of the people is above the king; for it is a thing most evident, that he who is established by another, is accounted under him who has established him, and he who receives his authority from another, is less than he from whom he derives his power. . . . The people establish the king as administrator of the commonwealth. Good kings have not disdained this title; yea, the bad ones themselves have affected it. Furthermore, it must necessarily be, that kings were instituted for the people's sake, neither can it be, that for the pleasure of some hundreds of men, and without doubt more foolish and worse than many of the other, all the rest were made, but much rather that these hundred were made for the use and service of all the other, and reason requires that he be preferred above the other, who was made only to and for his occasion: so it is, that for the ship's sail, the owner appoints a pilot over her, who sits at the helm, and looks that she keep her course, nor run not upon any dangerous shelf; the pilot doing his duty, is obeyed by the mariners; yea, and of himself who is owner of the vessel, notwithstanding, the pilot is a servant as well as the least in the ship, from whom he only differs in this, that he serves in a better place than they do.

In a commonwealth, commonly compared to a ship, the king holds the place of pilot, the people in general are owners of the vessel, obeying the pilot, whilst he is careful of the public good; as though this pilot neither is nor ought to be esteemed other than servant to the public; as a judge or general in war differs little from other officers, but that he is bound to bear greater burdens, and expose himself to more dangers. . . .

. . . Furthermore, there is an infinite sort of people who live without a king, but we cannot imagine a king without people. And those who have been raised to the royal dignity were not advanced because they excelled other men in beauty and comeliness, nor some excellency of nature to govern them as shepherds do their flocks, but rather being made out of the same mass with the rest of the people, they should acknowledge that for them, they, as it were, borrow their power and authority. . . .

. . . Let the people forsake the king, he presently falls to the ground, although before, his hearing and sight seemed most excellent, and that he was strong and in the best disposition that might be; yea, that he seemed to triumph in all magnificence, yet in an instant he will become most vile and contemptible . . . the people are above the king? . . .

. . . If it be objected that kings were enthronized, and received their authority from the people who lived five hundred years ago, and not by those now living, I answer that the commonwealth never dies, although kings be taken out of this life one after another: for as the continual running of the water gives the river a perpetual being, so the alternative revolution of birth and death renders the people immortal. . . .

. . . The prince is altogether unsupportable, who, because he succeeds a tyrant, or has kept the people (by whose suffrages he holds the crown) in a long slavery, or has suppressed the officers of the kingdom (who should be protectors of the public liberty), that therefore presumes, that what he affects is lawful for him to effect, and that his will is not to be restrained or corrected by any positive law whatsoever. For prescription in tyranny detracts nothing from the right of the people; nay, it rather much aggravates the prince's outrages. But what if the peers and principal officers of the kingdom make themselves parts with the king? What if betraying the public cause the yoke of tyranny upon the people's neck? . . .

. . . This conspiracy of the great ones combined to ruin the inferiors cannot disannul the right of the people. In the mean season, those great ones incur the punishment that the same allots against prevaricators, and for the people, the same law allows them to choose another advocate and afresh to pursue their cause, as if it were then only to begin. . . .

FRANÇOIS HOTMAN
Francogallia

The Old Constitutional Form

It seems necessary to explain the form in which the kingdom of Francogallia came to be constituted. We have shown earlier that the people in their assemblies reserved all power to themselves in creating and also in deposing a king. Our Gauls possessed that same form of government before they were brought under the power of the Romans, for, as Caesar says, the people had no less power and authority over a king than a king had over the people. It is agreed, nonetheless, that our Franks assumed this form of constituting their commonwealth from the German peoples rather than from the Gauls. In this respect Tacitus writes in his *Customs of the Germans*: 'The power of their kings is neither unlimited nor free.' It is clear that no form of government is more remote from tyranny than this. For, as Aristotle says in his *Politics*: 'The fewer the things over which the authority of the king extends, the longer will the kingdom endure.' It may be observed that not one of the three signs of tyranny defined by the ancient philosophers is to be found in the form in which our kingdom was constituted. First, in so far as the government involved compulsion, that is to say, where a king rules over his subjects against their will, we have already indicated that the highest authority in both electing and deposing kings lay in the people. As to the second mark of tyranny, the existence of a foreign bodyguard, so far were our kings of Francogallia from employing foreigners and alien mercenaries for their guards that they generally did not even make use of citizens or local people as their bodyguard . . .

. . . Now it has been observed that the third mark of tyranny occurs when all matters are judged by the comfort and will of him who governs rather than by the ease and desire of the commonwealth and the subjects. Through many ages no such blemish became established in our commonwealth, and hence it may be seen, that the highest administrative authority in the kingdom of Francogallia lay in the formal public council of the nation, which in later times was called the assembly of the three estates. In the book entitled *The Monarchy of France* Claude de Seyssel considers that this assembly is named after the three orders of citizens. He regards the first of these as the nobility, the second as comprising the lawyers and merchants and the third the artisans and farmers. This is virtually what he writes in the thirteenth chapter: 'In this kingdom there is a certain aspect of the commonwealth which is greatly to be admired and ought to be preserved, because it is of great influence in establishing the harmony of all the orders. For it is indubitable that, so long as the legal right and dignity of each order is preserved, it is difficult for the kingdom to be overthrown. Each order has its fixed prerogative, and, while that is maintained, one order cannot subvert another, and the three cannot conspire together against the prince and the monarchy. There should be but three estates or orders, and the clergy should not be added to them, since they are already a mixture of the existing orders. The first estate is the nobility; the middle estate consists of those among the people who are said to be well-off; and the last is the lowest common people.'

However, this division into three orders is not intended as a description of the basis of ordinary society but rather is related to the public council of the nation (wherefore the council is commonly called the council of the three estates). Let us see, then, whether it would not be more convenient if it could correspond to the three kinds of government embodied in the council—that is to the regal, the aristocratic and the popular types. For such indeed was the form of government which the old philosophers (including Plato and Aristotle, whom Polybius and Cicero imitated) considered the best and most excellent, a form which was mixed and tempered from the three elements of monarchy, aristocracy and democracy. This was the form of commonwealth approved before all others by Cicero in his book of the *Republic*. For, since a kingly and a popular government are by nature at variance with each other, it is necessary to add some third or intermediate element common to both. Such is the rôle of the princes or nobles, who, because of the splendour and antiquity of their stock, approach the status of royalty, and who, because of their position as dependants (or, as it is commonly put, subjects), have less dislike for those of plebeian birth. For, like the common sort, they recognize one and the same person as magistrate of the whole people.

. . . In constituting the kingdom of Francogallia our ancestors accepted Cicero's opinion that the best form of a commonwealth is that which is tempered by the mixture of the three kinds of government. This can be shown by a variety of proofs, especially from the speech of King Louis, known as the Pious, delivered to all the estates of Francogallia, and also from Ansegius' book on Frankish law, where an official report is quoted as follows: 'Yet, however mighty this royal office may seem to be in our person, our office is known by both divine authority and human ordinance to be so divided throughout its parts that each one of you in his own place and rank may be recognized as possessing a piece. Hence it seems that we should be your counsellor, and all of you should be our deputies. And we are aware that it is fitting for each one of you to have a piece of authority vested in you.' Later Ansegius writes to the same effect: 'And as we have said, each one of you is distinguished by having your part among the many segments of our office.' Again, he says: 'We urge your loyalty so that you may recall both your desire for the trust placed in us and the office which in part has been entrusted to you.'

For this reason our ancestors accepted this mixed and tempered commonwealth embodying the three kinds of government, and very wisely laid it down that every year there should be a public council of the whole kingdom on the first of May, and that at this council the greatest affairs of the commonwealth should be dealt with through the general advice of all the estates. In this manner that ancient and golden law prevailed: 'LET THE WELFARE OF THE PEOPLE BE THE SUPREME LAW.' The wisdom and utility of this practice is very apparent in three respects. First, the large number of men of prudence ensured that there would be an amplitude of advice, and advice of a kind to procure the welfare of the people, such as might satisfy Solomon (Proverbs 11 and 15) and other wise men. Next, because it is an attribute of liberty that those at whose peril a thing is done should have some say and authority in arranging it, or, as it is customarily and commonly said, what touches all should be approved by all. Lastly, those who have great influence with the king, and are foremost in great affairs of government, should, in the performance of their office, be held in fear of this council, in which the requests of the provinces are freely heard. When certain kingdoms are governed by the will and pleasure of a single king—as today the Turks are ruled—their government would lack the advice of free men and enlightened opinion and would be like that of cattle and beasts, as Aristotle rightly observes in his *Politics*. For in such circumstances they are like cattle who are not controlled by one of their own kind, or like boys and youths, who are governed by someone of superior status rather than by one of their own age.

In the same way a multitude of men ought not to be ruled and governed by one of their own number, who, peradventure, sees less than others do when taken together, but rather by proven men of excellence, selected with the consent of all, who act by combined advice as if they possessed one mind composed from many. Although kings customarily have an attendant senate, whose advice, they say, is used in governing a commonwealth, the counsellor of a kingdom is something other than the counsellor of a king. The former cares for the whole commonwealth and gives his advice in public, whereas the latter serves the profit and convenience of a single man. Moreover, since senators of the latter kind either attend at one place only or are for ever attached to the court of the prince, they cannot easily see and be acquainted with the condition of remote provinces. Besides, they are seduced by the allurements of life at the royal court, and are easily depraved by a lust to dominate others, by ambition and by avarice. Ultimately they seem not to be counsellors of the kingdom and commonwealth, but rather flatterers of a single king and servants of his and their own appetites.

. . . the ancient Romans provided the king with a senate in the customary way. So that the welfare of the people might be the supreme law, they reserved the highest authority neither for the king nor for his senate, but for the people themselves and their assemblies. For this reason it was an established law under all the kings that the people should appoint the magistrates in their assemblies, that they should enact the laws and determine matters concerning war, the Roman people in early times were divided into thirty sections which were called *curiae*, because the king of the commonwealth paid attention [*cura*] to the opinions expressed by the sections. Hence are derived the terms 'curial laws' and *curiata*, the most ancient of all assemblies.

In his letters Seneca gives an opinion he had himself learnt from the books of Cicero's *Republic*, namely that APPEALS AGAINST THE AUTHORITY OF THE KINGS WERE MADE TO THE PEOPLE. Cicero further supports this in his *Tusculan Disputations* as follows: 'From the origin of the city, when the ordinances of the kings, and in part also the laws, regulated the auguries, rites, assemblies, appeals to the people . . . and the entire military organisation . . .' But in his speech on behalf of hearth and home he said: 'I do not believe that it was possible by any public right for the commonwealth as such to have made use of these laws, although I do say that within the commonwealth a citizen could not be affected by any misfortune of this kind without a judgment being delivered under the law, and this applied even in the time of the kings. Hence nothing could be done against the life and goods of a citizen without the judgment of the senate, or of the people, or of those who had been made judges in a particular case.' From these references it is clear that the Romans, even in the age when they submitted to kings, held this law we have mentioned above as inviolable: 'LET THE WELFARE OF THE PEOPLE BE THE SUPREME LAW.' And I do not think there has ever been any kingdom other than that of the Turks, or those like them, in which the citizens have not retained some concept of liberty based upon the unique right of holding assemblies.

In constituting the commonwealth our ancestors, therefore, reduced these difficulties as if they were avoiding dangerous precipices, and arranged that the commonwealth should be administered by a general council of all the estates. In order to hold this council the king, the nobility and those chosen from individual provinces met at a fixed time of the year. We note that this same practice was also observed by many other nations. We have shown above from the commentaries of Caesar that this was first effected in our free and ancient Gaul by a general council of notables.

But since we are concerned with recounting the constitutional practices of a kingdom it may suffice to say that in Greece in ancient times the council of Amphictyon was instituted by King Amphictyon, the son of Deucalion (as Suidas and others testify), who arranged that at a fixed time of the year delegates from twelve states of Greece should meet at Thermopylae and should there deliberate in a general council about the most important matters in the kingdom and commonwealth. For this reason Cicero calls it the 'common council' of Greece, and Pliny the 'public council' of Greece. Thus Aristotle writes in the third book of his *Ethics* that in the time of Homer, when kings were recognized, it was the custom for them first to refer such matters to a council of the people.

. . . It seems that the Germans exercised a like wisdom in the establishment of the German empire. There the emperor represents monarchy, the princes aristocracy and the deputies of the cities the democratic element. And nothing which has to do with the welfare of the German commonwealth may be constituted, established and made permanent unless it be done in a meeting of those three estates. This was also the purpose of that celebrated law of the Spartans associating the ephors with the kings so that, as Plato records, they acted as restraints on the kings and the latter governed the commonwealth by their advice and authority.

Indeed the same form of government is to be found in the kingdom of England, as Polydore Virgil indicates in his *History of England*, where he states: 'Before these times (he was writing on the life of King Henry I) the kings did not maintain the assembly of the people, which existed to give advice but seldom met. Hence it can be said with certainty that, while that institution was ordered by Henry, it was so fashioned in earlier times and always had such deep roots that it has survived to the present day. This was because whatever had to be considered relating to the welfare and preservation of the commonwealth was submitted to the council, and, if any decree was issued by command either of the king or the people, it was entirely without force unless it were approved in this way by the authority of the council. Lest the council be hindered by the judgment of an inexperienced and vulgar multitude which was incapable of judging anything wisely, it was made clear from the beginning by a specific law who from the convocation of clergy, and who and how many from the rest of the people, should be summoned to this council. They commonly call it parliament according to the French usage. Each king customarily calls it at the beginning of his reign, and thereafter he convokes it by his own decision as often as occasion may demand.' Such are the words of Polydore Virgil. A certain ancient writer [Fortescue] who was chancellor of England offers the same opinion in a work entitled *A Learned Commendation*: 'A king', he says, 'may not himself or through his ministers impose tallages, subsidies or any other burdens whatsoever upon his subjects, nor may he change their laws, nor make new laws without the agreement and consent of his whole kingdom expressed in his parliament.'

The King and the Assembly

To return to the main issue, our commonwealth, as we have shown above, was established on the most praiseworthy foundation by our ancestors as a mixed state incorporating the three forms. Every year, and more often than this if occasion so demanded, a solemn and public council was convened. The assembly was called the parliament of the three estates, since this phrase implies a conference and convention of men, gathered together from many districts in one place in order to deliberate on the general welfare. In this way meetings called to establish a peace or a truce among enemies are always given that ancient name of parliament in our chronicles. Sitting on his golden throne, the king presided at this council. Below him were the princes and magistrates of the kingdom, while beneath them came those representing individual provinces, who were described as deputies in the common speech. On the day appointed for the council the king was escorted to the meeting place, as if it were the most august and holy temple of Gallic justice, with a ceremony which seemed more appropriate to popular moderation than to regal magnificence.

. . . We believe we have said enough to explain both the form of the commonwealth under the Merovingian kings and the extent of the authority of the public council. It follows that we should now explain its nature under the Carolingians. From all our own historians, and the German historians also, it is quite evident that the same authority of the orders or estates was entirely preserved, and that the ultimate judgment and decision on all issues rested not with Pepin or Charles or Louis but with the royal majesty. As we have shown earlier, the true and proper seat of this majesty lay in the solemn council, and this arrangement bore the unvaried consent of many generations.

The first proof of this is contained in Regino's chronicle under the year 806, where the author refers to Charlemagne. 'The emperor', he writes, 'held an assembly of the chief men and nobility of the Franks for the purpose of creating and preserving peace among his sons and of partitioning the kingdom.' A little further on he states: 'He made an addition to his will about this partition, which was confirmed by an oath taken by the Franks.' In that work which we have praised several times already, Einhard explains what happened after the death of Pepin in these terms: 'The Franks solemnly convened their general assembly and appointed both his sons as their kings, on the condition that the whole body of the kingdom should be divided and that Charles should rule that part of it which their father Pepin had held, while Carloman should acquire the part controlled by their uncle Carloman.'

The Limits on the King

We believe, therefore, that it has been sufficiently shown that a boundless and unlimited power was not allowed the kings of Francogallia by their subjects, and they cannot be described as free from all laws. Rather were they restrained by defined laws and compacts, and we have shown the first and foremost of these was that they should preserve the authority of the public council as something holy and inviolate, and should honour that assembly with their presence as often as the need of the commonwealth might demand. There are, indeed, a great many laws established to restrict kings. But we shall set forth only those of our own laws which no one who is not completely mad, or admits himself to be the enemy of his country, his parents and his children, will deny to be worth relating.

The first of these particular laws may be defined as follows: That it is not lawful for the king to determine anything that affects the condition of the commonwealth as a whole without the authority of the public council. In this regard we have put forward irrefutable evidence from earlier times and, equally, there is a very precise and clear remnant of the practice which has lasted right down to our own age, namely, that the parlement of Paris, which in great part has appropriated to itself the authority of the ancient parliament, allows neither the king's laws nor his edicts to be enacted unless they have been examined and given the parlement's consideration, and approved by the opinions of its judges. So it may not be inappropriate to say that the authority of the parlement seems to be similar in kind to the power of the ancient tribunes of the people, who were wont to wait in the vestibule of the senate while its decrees were brought out to them. They examined these decrees on behalf of the council to see if they appeared to be of value to the common people, and signed them with the letter T as a mark and indication of their consent. But, if they did not agree, they signified their prohibition and opposed the measure.

(Extracts from *Francogallia*, chs. 10, 13, 15 and 25.)

MARIANA

The king and the Education of the king
(De Rege et Regis Institutione)

The Right To Destroy a Tyrant

. . . (it is argued that) if it is unlawful to raise hands against a praetor although he is in the act of assaulting someone unjustly and inconsiderately, how much less may one assault Kings, though they have profligate morals? These God and the Commonwealth have placed at the head of things, to be viewed by the subjects as divinities, as more than mortals.

Further, they who try to change princes often bring great misfortune to the state; nor is government overturned without serious disturbance, during which the instigators themselves generally are crushed. . . .

Therefore, people conclude that the unjust prince must be accepted like the just, and that the rule of the former must be alleviated by passive obedience. The mildness of kings and leaders depends not only on their own characters but also on that of their subjects. . . .

Moreover, how will respect for princes (and what is government without this?) remain constant, if the people are persuaded that it is right for the subjects to punish the sins of the rulers? The tranquility of the commonwealth will often be disturbed with pretended as well as real reasons. And when a revolt takes place every sort of calamity strikes, with one section of the populace armed against another part. If anyone does not think these evils must be avoided by every means, he would be heartless, wanting in the universal commonsense of mankind. Thus they argue who protect the interests of the tyrant.

The protectors of the people have no fewer and lesser arguments. Assuredly the republic, whence the regal power has its source, can call a king into court, when circumstances require and, if he persists in senseless conduct, it can strip him of his principate.

For the commonwealth did not transfer the rights to rule into the hands of a prince to such a degree that it has not reserved a greater power to itself; for we see that in the matters of laying taxes and making permanent laws the state has made the reservation that except with its consent no change can be made. But nevertheless, only with the desire of the people are new imposts ordered and new laws made; and, what is more, the rights to rule, though hereditary, are settled by the agreement of the people on a successor.

Besides, we reflect, in all history, that whoever took the lead in killing tyrants was held in great honor. What indeed carried the name of Thrazybulus in glory to the heavens unless it was the fact that he freed his country from the oppressive domination of the Thirty Tyrants? . . .

You may add, that a tyrant is like a beast, wild and monstrous, that throws himself in every possible direction, lays everything waste, seizes, burns, and spreads carnage and grief with tooth, nail and horn.

Would you be of the opinion that anyone who delivered the State safely at the peril of his own life ought to be ignored, or rather would you not honor him? Would you determine that all must make an armed fight against something resembling a cruel monster that is burdening the earth? . . . Would you leave to the tyrant your native land, to which you owe more than to your parents, to be harassed and disturbed at his pleasure? . . .

These are the arguments of both sides; and after we have considered them carefully it will not be difficult to set forth what must be decided about the main point under discussion. Indeed in this I see that both the philosophers and theologians agree, that the Prince who seizes the State with force and arms, and with no legal right, no public, civic approval, may be killed by anyone and deprived of his life and position. Since he is a public enemy and afflicts his fatherland with every evil, since truly and in a proper sense he is clothed with the title and character of tyrant, he may be removed by any means and gotten rid of by as much violence as he used in seizing his power. . . .

It is true that if the prince holds the power with the consent of the people or by hereditary right, his vices and licentiousness must be tolerated up to the point when he goes beyond those laws of honor and decency by which he is bound. Rulers, really, should not be lightly changed, lest we run into greater evils, and serious disturbances arise, as was set forth at the beginning of this discussion.

But if he is destroying the state, considers public and private fortunes as his prey, is holding the laws of the land and our holy religion in contempt, if he makes a virtue out of haughtiness, audacity, and irreverence against Heaven, one must not ignore it.

Nevertheless, careful consideration must be given to what measures should be adopted to get rid of the ruler, lest evil pile on evil, and crime is avenged with crime.

Now, if the opportunity for public meeting exists, a very quick and safe way is to deliberate about the issue in an atmosphere of public harmony, and to confirm and ratify what has developed as the common sentiment.

In this the procedure should be by the following steps: First the prince must be warned and invited to come to his senses. If he complies, if he satisfies the commonwealth, and corrects the error of his way, I think that it must stop there, and sharper remedies must not be attempted. If he refuses to mend his ways, and if no hope of a safe course remains, after the resolution has been announced, it will be permissible for the commonwealth to rescind his first grant of power. And since war will necessarily be stirred up, it will be in order to arrange the plans for driving him out, for providing arms, for imposing levies on the people for the expenses of the war. Also, if circumstances require, and the commonwealth is not able otherwise to protect itself, it is right, by the same law of defense and even by an authority more potent and explicit, to declare the prince a public enemy and put him to the sword.

Let the same means be available to any individual, who, having given up the hope of escaping punishment and with disregard for his personal safety, wishes to make the attempt to aid the commonwealth. . . .

If the sacred fatherland is falling in ruins and its fall is attracting the public enemies into the province, I think that he who bows to the public's prayers and tries to kill the tyrant will have acted in no wise unjustly. And this is strengthened enough by those arguments against the tyrant which are put at a later place in this discussion.

So the question of fact remains, who justly may be held to be a tyrant, for the question of law is plain that it is right to kill one.

Now there is no danger that many, because of this theory, will make mad attempts against the lives of the princes on the pretext that they are tyrants. For we do not leave this to the decision of any individual, or even to the judgment of many, unless the voice of the people publicly takes part, and learned and serious men are associated in the deliberation. . . .

The desire for self-preservation, often not disposed to attempt big things, will hold back very many people. . . .

Nevertheless it is a salutary reflection that the princes have been persuaded that if they oppress the state, if they are unbearable on account of their vices and foulness, their position is such that they can be killed not only justly but with praise and glory. Perhaps this fear will give some pause lest they deliver themselves up to be deeply corrupted by vice and flattery; it will put reins on madness.

This is the main point, that the prince should be persuaded that the authority of the commonwealth as a whole is greater than that of one man alone; and he should not put faith in the very worst men when they affirm the contrary in their desire to please him; which is a great disaster. . . .

We are of the opinion that upheavals in the commonweath must be avoided. Precaution must be taken lest joy run wild briefly on account of the deposition of a tyrant and then turn out sterile. On the other hand, every remedy must be tried to bring the ruler to right views before that extreme and most serious course is reached. But if every hope is gone, if the public safety and the sanctity of religion are put in danger, who will be so unintelligent as not to admit that it is permissible to take arms and kill the tyrant, justly and according to the statutes? . . .

So, it is generally known that it is legal to kill a tyrant openly by force of arms, either by breaking into his palace or by starting a civil disturbance.

But it has been undertaken also by guile and treachery. This Ehud did; by bringing gifts and feigning a message from above he got close enough, and when the witnesses had left he killed Eglon, King of the Moabites.

It is, indeed, more manly and spirited to show your hate openly, to rush upon the enemy of the state in public; but it is not less prudent to seize the opportunity for guileful strategems, which may be carried out without commotion and surely with less public and individual danger. . . .

Yet there is a question whether there is equal virtue in killing a public enemy and tyrant by poison and lethal herbs. . . . By this method the public joy is not less, when the enemy is destroyed, but the author and architect of the public safety and liberty is saved.

However, we regard not what men are likely to do but what is permitted by natural law; and from a rational standpoint, what difference does it make whether you kill by steel or poison, especially since the means of acting by fraud and deceit are conceded? . . .

Truly we think it cruel, and also foreign to Christian principles to drive a man, though covered with infamy, to the point that he commit suicide by plunging a dagger into his abdomen, or by taking deadly poison which has been put into his food or drink. It is equally contrary to the laws of humanity and the natural law; since it is forbidden that anyone take his own life.

We deny therefore that the enemy, whom we admit it is lawful to kill by treachery, may be made away with by poison. . . .

Neither may be deadly draught be given to an enemy nor deadly poison be put into his food and drink for his destruction.

Yet we may in this discussion have this qualification in the use of poison—that the man who is being done away with is not compelled to drink it, by taking which into his very marrow he perishes; but it may be employed externally by another, provided that he who is to die does not cooperate in any way. For the strength of poison is so great that it has the power to kill if even a chair or robe is smeared with it. . . .

. . . Now at the beginning I shall grant freely that the regal authority is supreme in the kingdom for all those matters which in accordance with the custom of the nation, its statute and undoubted law have been committed to the judgment of the Prince, whether it is a question of carrying on war, or dispensing justice to his subjects, or appointing leaders or magistrates. In these matters he will have greater authority not only than the individuals but also than the whole body, so that he stops for nothing and does not give an account of his actions to anyone.

. . . Nevertheless I would believe, in certain other functions, that the authority of the Commonwealth is greater than that of the Prince, provided that the people are wholly united in one resolution. Assuredly, in levying taxes, or abrogating laws, and especially in the matters that concern the succession, if the multitude opposes, the authority of the Prince is not a match for it. And if any other things, according to the customs of the nation, have been reserved to the whole body politic, they are by no means placed within the discretion of the Prince.

Finally, and this is the main point, I prefer that the power of restraining the Prince abide in the Commonwealth, if he is infected with vices and wickedness, and, ignoring the true path of glory, prefers to be feared by the citizens rather than to be loved, and if, become a tyrant, he continues to rule his subjects, who are shaken and quaking with terror, and is set to do them hurt.

Appeal to the Commonwealth has been taken away for a double reason . . . because, I suppose, the power of the King is supreme in deciding private suits; and because a practice had to be devised for punishing crimes and ending suits, lest the latter go on without end. Who indeed would say that the state has been given preference and that the government is in the hands of the people, when no power is left to the people and none to the nobles in the administration of the individual functions of the state?

. . . Who is able to set the King aright, if the Commonwealth's power is completely subordinated?

And since mention is made of the Roman Pontiff, not even his authority, though next to divine (which some use as an argument), can cause maximum authority without limitation to be given to kings as against the Commonwealth as a whole.

Indeed, many wise and serious men . . . make the Roman Pontiffs subject to the Church Universal when, in fact, it is deliberating in general council about religion and morals. . . . But they nevertheless make them subordinate, after the fashion of regal power.

Those who think and act otherwise, in their preference for the pontifical authority over the universal, when their opinion is attacked on the grounds that the regal power is subject to the State, get around it with the following distinction. The regal authority has sprung from the State and is rightly subject to it; while the pontifical is answerable to God, whom the Pope considers his sole source of authority through Christ, because He, while on earth, delegated sacred jurisdiction to Peter and his successors over the whole world, whether the conduct of the people is to be regulated, or a decision is to be taken on matters of faith or divine worship.

From this answer it may be plainly concluded that while they disagree on the Pope's authority they agree on the regal, that it is less than the State's. . . .

Indeed, government is kingly which restrains itself within the bounds of modesty and moderation, while by an excess of power, which the unwise are busy at increasing daily, it is reduced and weakened through and through. We foolishly are deceived with an appearance of greater power and slip off into the opposite error, not giving the matter sufficient consideration, and not realizing that power is finally safe only when it places a limit on its own strength.

It is a difficult matter to keep Princes of great and distinguished power within the bounds of moderation. It is hard to persuade them, if they are corrupted by an abundance of wealth and puffed up by the empty talk of their courtiers, not to be thinking that it is pertinent to their dignified status and to the increase of their grandeur to augment their resources and power, or that they are considered to be subject to the authority of anybody.

However, the fact really is otherwise. Nothing, indeed, strengthens regal power more than moderation, if it is fixed in the minds and impressed on the very innermost consciences of Princes, when they are about to adopt a manner of thought and life, that they should serve first God, whose will governs the countries of the world and at whose nod empires rise and fall; secondly, that they should be modest and honest, for by these good qualities we merit divine protection, and the well-wishing of men is thus won to them in whose hands rests the governance of affairs. Also, the judgment of the citizens should be heeded, and one should often reflect as to what history will indeed say in the far distant future. As a matter of fact, it is characteristic of a noble spirit to aspire, next to heaven, to an immortal name.

Despise fame and you despise virtue. . . .

. . . Lastly, the Prince must be convinced that the sacrosanct laws, by which the public weal is maintained, will at last be stable only if he makes them hallowed by his own example. He therefore so orders his life that he permits neither himself nor anyone else to be mightier than the laws.

. . . The great philosophers say that the Prince is guided by precept and that he is not forced by legal penalty against his will. Although the double force of ordering and coercing the disobedient exists, they subject the Prince to the law only from the first of these, that is, by precept—making it a matter for his conscience, if he forsakes his obligation under the law. They claim that other people are subject to the law under both its aspects. This reasoning is agreeable to me.

I might even grant that the Prince, when there is question of those laws which the State has made, whose power we have said is greater than the Princes, may be, if necessary, coerced by penalties. For it has been conceded that he is to be removed from office and even punished with death under exceptional circumstances. On the other hand, if he obeys of his own accord those laws which he himself has made, I am satisfied; I grant that no one should force him, against his will, or coerce him with sanctions. But above all the mind of the Prince should be trained from an early age to be convinced that he himself is more bound by the laws than the others who obey his rule; that he involves himself seriously in conscience if he resists; that he is the protector and guarantor of the laws; and that he will effect this better by example than by fear, which latter does not teach us lasting lessons of duty.

If he will acknowledge that he is bound by the laws, he will govern the state very easily, he will keep it happy, he will curb the insolence of the nobles, so that they will not think it more in consonance with their dignity to despise their fathers' customs and show that they are free from the laws.

(Extracts from chapters 8 and 9.)

FRANCISCO SUAREZ

On Law and God the Lawgiver and A Defence of the Catholic and Apostolic Faith

Does Man Possess the Power to Make Laws?

1. We are speaking of man's nature and of his legislative power viewed in itself; for we are not considering, at present, the question of whether anything has been added to or taken from that power through divine law, a matter which will be taken up later.

The question under consideration, then, is as follows: is it possible—speaking solely with reference to the nature of the case—for men to command other men, binding the latter by [man's] own laws?

A reason for doubting that they can do so, may lie in the fact that man is by his nature free and subject to no one, save only to the Creator, so that human sovereignty is contrary to the order of nature and involves tyranny.

Secondly, the same doubt is confirmed by the words of Augustine, who discusses the fact that God said (*Genesis*, Chap. i [, v. 26]): 'Let us make man', &c., 'and let him have dominion over the fishes of the sea, and the fowls of the air, and the beasts [and the whole] earth'; whereas He did not say: 'Let him have dominion over men', a distinction which indicates that such domination is not natural to man. 'Therefore,' says [Augustine, *ibid.*], 'the first just men were not kings, but shepherds of flocks, and they were so called.' Thus Gregory the Great, too, indicates that authority of this kind was introduced through sin and acquired through usurpation.

Thirdly, the doubt may be confirmed by the testimony of a number of passages which show that God alone is the king, the lawgiver and the lord of men. 'For the Lord is our judge, the Lord is our king, the Lord is our lawgiver'. And again, 'There is one lawgiver, and judge', &c.

Finally, we have this confirmation, namely: there is no true law save that which is binding in conscience; but one man cannot bind another in conscience, since this power would seem to be exclusively a property of God, Who alone can save and destroy; therefore, . . .

2. At this point, mention might be made of various errors

among the heretics; but it will be better to touch upon those errors later.

Accordingly, leaving them aside, we shall make first the following statement: a civil magistracy accompanied by temporal power for human government is just and in complete harmony with human nature. This conclusion is certainly true, and a matter of faith. It may be sufficiently proved by the example set by God Himself, when He established a government of this kind over the Jewish people, first by means of judges, and later by means of kings, endowed doubtless with the princely office and temporal power, and held in such veneration that they were even called gods, according to the passage in *Psalms* (lxxxi [, v. 1]): 'God hath stood in the congregation of gods: and being in the midst of them he judgeth gods.' Nor is there any validity in the objection which may be made that those judges and kings had their power from God Himself; for that power nevertheless did not in itself exceed the limits set by nature, even though the mode through which it was held was extraordinary and the result of a special providence; and therefore, this [divine derivation of the power in question] does not render it impossible for the power to be held justly in some other way. Furthermore, from that same contention there follows this argument, namely, that power of that kind is in harmony with nature itself, in so far as it is necessary to the proper government of a human community.

Again, this contention derives a fuller confirmation from human custom, since kings existed long before the times of which we were speaking, even kings who were holy and praised in the Scriptures, as was Melchisedech. Abraham, too, is thought to have been a king or sovereign prince. Moreover, a like example is to be found in *Job*, &c.

And finally, we read in *Proverbs* the general statement: 'By me kings reign.'

The point is clearly set forth in the writings of the Holy Fathers, to whom I shall refer in the course of our discussion.

3. The basic reason for this assertion is to be sought in Aristotle's *Politics* (Bk. I [, chap. v =p. 1254 B]). This reason is expounded by St. Thomas and also, very neatly, by St. Chrysostom (*On First Corinthians*, Homily XXXIV [, no. 5]). It is founded, moreover, upon two principles.

The first principle is as follows: man is a social animal, and cherishes a natural and right desire to live in a community. In this connexion, we should recollect the principle already laid down, that human society is twofold: imperfect, or domestic; and perfect, or political. Of these divisions, the former is in the highest degree natural and (so to speak) fundamental, because it arises from the fellowship of man and wife, without which the human race could not be propagated nor preserved; wherefore it has been written, 'It is not good for man to be alone'. From this union there follows as a direct consequence the fellowship of children and parents; for the earlier form of union is ordained for the rearing of the children, and they require union and fellowship with their parents (in early life, at least, and throughout a long period of time) since otherwise they could not live, nor be fittingly reared, nor receive the proper instruction. Furthermore, to these forms of domestic society there is presently added a connexion based on slavery or servitude and lordship, since, practically speaking, men require the aid and service of other men.

Now, from these three forms of connexion there arises the first human community, which is said to be imperfect from a political standpoint. The family is perfect in itself, however, for purposes of domestic or economic government.

But this community—as I have already indicated, above—is not self-sufficing; and therefore, from the very nature of the case, there is a further necessity among human beings for a political community, consisting at least of a city state (*ciuitas*), and formed by the coalition of a number of families. For no family can contain within itself all the offices and arts necessary for human life, and much less can it suffice for attaining knowledge of all things needing [to be known].

Furthermore, if the individual families were divided one from another, peace could scarcely be preserved among men, nor could wrongs be duly averted or avenged; so that Cicero has said: 'Nothing in human affairs is more pleasing to God our Sovereign, than that men should have among themselves an ordered and perfect society, which (continues Cicero) is called a city state (*ciuitas*).' Moreover, this community may be still further augmented, becoming a kingdom or principality by means of the association of many city states; a form of community which is also very appropriate for mankind—appropriate, at least, for its greater welfare—owing to the above-stated reasons, applied in due proportion, although the element of necessity is not entirely equal in the two cases.

4. The second principle is as follows: in a perfect community, there must necessarily exist a power to which the government of that community pertains. This principle, indeed, would seem by its very terms to be a self-evident truth. For as the Wise Man says (*Proverbs*, Chap. xi [, v. 14]): 'Where there is no governor, the people shall fall'; but nature is never wanting in essentials; and therefore, just as a perfect

community is agreeable to reason and natural law, so also is the power to govern such a community, without which power there would be the greatest confusion therein.

This argument is confirmed by analogy with every other form of human society. For the union of man and woman, since it is natural, consequently involves a head, the man, according to this passage from *Genesis* (Chap. iii [, v. 16]): '[. . .] thou shalt be under thy husband's power.' Thus it is that Paul says: 'Let women be subject to their husbands.' To this, Jerome [on *Titus*, Chap. ii, v. 5] adds the words: 'in accordance with the common law of nature.' Similarly, in that second relationship of parents and children, the father has over his child a power derived from nature. And in the third, the relationship of servants and master, it is also clear that a governing power resides in the master, as Paul teaches, saying that servants ought to be obedient to their lords, as to God. For though the relationship of servitude is one derived not entirely from nature, but rather through human volition, nevertheless, given the existence of this relationship, subordination and subjection are obligatory by natural law, on the ground of justice. Filial subjection, too, is supported by this same natural bond and basis, that is to say, natural origin, from which it derives a higher degree of perfection by the title of [filial] piety. This point, moreover, is emphatically brought out in the Fourth Commandment of the Decalogue.

Finally, it follows from all this, that in a domestic community, or family, there exists by the very nature of the case, a suitable power for the government of that community, a power residing principally in the head of the family. Furthermore, the same situation is necessarily found to exist in the case of any community whatsoever that consists of one sole household, even though that community be founded, not upon the bond of matrimony, but upon some other kind of human society; and therefore, it is likewise necessary, in the case of a perfect society, that there shall exist some governing power suitable thereto.

5. There is, in fine, an *a priori* reason in support of this view, a reason touched upon by St. Thomas: that no body can be preserved unless there exists some principle whose function it is to provide for and seek after the common good thereof, such a principle as clearly exists in the natural body, and likewise (so experience teaches) in the political. The reason for this fact, in turn is also clear. For each individual member has a care for its individual advantages, and these are often opposed to the common good, while furthermore, it occasionally happens that many things are needful to the common

good, which are not thus pertinent in the case of individuals and which, even though they may at times be pertinent, are provided for, not as common, but as private needs; and therefore, in a perfect community, there necessarily exists some public power whose official duty it is to seek after and provide for the common good.

The righteousness of and necessity for civil magistracy are clearly to be deduced from the foregoing, since the term 'civil magistracy' signifies nothing more nor less than a man or number of men in whom resides the above-mentioned power of governing a perfect community. For it is manifest that such power must dwell in men, inasmuch as they are not naturally governed in a polity by the angels, nor directly by God Himself, Who acts, by the ordinary law, through appropriate secondary causes; so that, consequently, it is necessary and natural that they should be governed by men.

6. I hold, secondly, that a human magistracy, if it is supreme in its own order, has the power to make laws proper to its sphere; that is to say, civil or human laws which, by the force of natural law, it may validly and justly establish, provided that the other conditions essential to law be observed.

. . . The reason [on which the said conclusion is based,] is as follows: a civil magistracy is a necessity in the state for its government and regulation, a fact which has already been pointed out; but one of the most necessary acts is the establishment of law, therefore, this legislative power does exist in a political magistracy. For he who is invested with a given office, is invested with all the power necessary for the fitting exercise of that office. This is a self-evident principle of law.

[7.] Whence it follows that such power to make human laws is identified with the human magistracy endowed with supreme jurisdiction in the state.

This fact is evident from what has already been said where we showed that the power in question pertains to a perfect jursidiction. That entire discussion should be applied here. Moreover, it holds true in a universal sense. For solely in the prince, or [supreme] magistrate, does that public power reside which is ordained for public action, concerns the community as a whole, and includes an efficacious binding and compelling force; yet this twofold force is essential to law, according to Aristotle (*Ethics*, Bk. X, last chapter), the *Digest* (I. iii. 7), and, also, the proof adduced above; and therefore, only that magistrate who has supreme power in the commonwealth, has also the power to make human, or civil law. Finally, this supreme power is a certain form of dominion, but a form of dominion that calls, not for strict servitude to a despot, but rather for civil obedience; therefore, it is the dominion of jurisdiction, of the sort that resides in the prince, or king.

8. . . . Law, properly speaking, is related to the power of sovereign command, as may easily be seen from what we have already said regarding the essence of law; and therefore, the power which is *per se* necessary to law, is not the power of jurisdiction.

9. St. Thomas makes this clear in the passage where he proves that jurisdiction is necessary in order to pass a sentence for the reason that jurisdiction is necessary to law, because a sentence is a particular law and also has coercive force; and thus, *a fortiori*, any law howsoever particular its character may seem, requires jurisdiction; for no [other] law is ever so particular in character as a sentence, and the latter always has or always should have annexed to it some means of coercion—as is evident from the *Ethics* of Aristotle (as cited above) and from the laws already mentioned—since directive without coercive force is of no value. Indeed, no one has ever doubted that jurisdiction is required for the passing of a sentence. And thus our contention is confirmed; for if jurisdiction is necessary for the declaration of law, it is much more necessary for the making of law.

10. As to the fundamental position of the authors in question, the [basic] assumption which they make may be denied. For statutes are either not true laws or else not made without jurisdiction; points which will be accorded more attention in later pages.

As for the confirmation, in so far as concerns the laws cited in that [confirmatory argument], I shall point out that the term 'jurisdiction', in the full and proper sense, refers to political—that is, governmental—power of dominion, the sense in which we are here using the word. And jurisdiction, thus interpreted, is included as intrinsically a part of political sovereignty, in order to differentiate the latter from tyranny. Such is the argument set forth in the *Decretum* where supreme governmental power over the state is called 'legitimate sovereignty' (*legitimum imperium*); and the degree and mode of sovereignty will be in accordance with the degree and mode of jurisdiction. Sometimes, to be sure, 'jurisdiction' is understood strictly according to the etymology of the term, as signifying the simple power of passing judgment. For law is properly declared, or interpreted, by means of a sentence; and, if one is speaking in this sense, it is not incongruous that the power to judge should reside in a given person apart from the legislative, although such a person is never without some coercive power, such as would seem at times to be denoted by the word 'sovereignty', when the latter, also, is strictly interpreted. Thus it is that, on the other hand, the power given to the magistrate for the punishment of crimes and extending even to the death penalty, is ordinarily spoken of in the civil law simply as sovereignty, and is apparently so treated in the laws above mentioned. . . .

The power in question does not reside in the whole community of mankind, since the whole of mankind does not constitute one single commonwealth or kingdom. Nor does that power reside in any one individual, since such an individual would have to receive it from the hands of men, and this is inconceivable, inasmuch as men have never agreed to confer it [thus], nor to establish one sole head over themselves. Furthermore, not even by title of war, whether justly or unjustly, has there at any time been a prince who made himself temporal sovereign over the whole world. This assertion is clearly borne out by history. And therefore, the ordinary course of human nature points to the conclusion that a human legislative power of universal character and worldwide extent does not exist and has never existed, nor is it morally possible that it should have done so.

Thus the whole world—even though it be governed and bound by civil laws, as is morally certain in the case of all nations enjoying any form of civil government and not entirely barbarous—is nevertheless not ruled throughout by the same laws; on the contrary, each commonwealth or kingdom is governed, in accordance with an appropriate distribution, by means of its own particular laws.

Do Kings Have Supreme Power in Civil Affairs?

. . . We must assert that Christian kings do possess supreme civil power within their own order and that they recognize no other person, within that same temporal or civil order, as a direct superior upon whom they essentially depend in the exercise of their own proper power. Whence it follows that there exists within the Church no one supreme temporal prince over that whole body, that is to say, over all the kingdoms of the Church; but that, on the contrary, there are as many princes as there are kingdoms, or sovereign states.

This is the more widely accepted and approved opinion, among Catholics, and we shall shortly refer to those authorities who support it.

But the proof of the first part thereof depends upon the proof of the latter part. For if there exists no one temporal head, the inference necessarily drawn is that the many kings are all supreme, in accordance with the proposition which we have already laid down; since it is not our intention at this point to examine specifically the question of whether this or that particular king is supreme, nor to compare the various temporal princes one with another, inasmuch as these are matters quite foreign to our present purpose.

7. It is for the same reason that we do not deal here with the question of whether or not the emperor is superior in jurisdiction over all Christian provinces and kingdoms, being consequently the supreme monarch of the whole Church. For though this question might be related to the latter part of our assertion, still, it bears scarcely any relation at all to the explanation of the dogmas of the faith. Therefore, we shall briefly assume that—whatever may be the opinion of Bartolus and certain other jurists—the emperor does not possess such dominion, or supreme temporal jurisdiction, over the whole Church; for he either never has possessed it, or else, having once done so, has lost the greater portion of it.

Indeed, the proposition that he never did possess this power is very probably correct; inasmuch as he did not receive it in a supernatural or an extraordinary manner from Christ the Lord, nor from the Roman Pontiff, as will become evident, *a fortiori*, from what we say below; neither did he acquire it by any human right, since at no time, whether through election or through a just war, has a single emperor subjected to his sway the whole world, or the whole Church.

. . . No just title can be assigned by which the Pope properly possesses direct jurisdictional dominion in temporal matters over all the kingdoms of the Church, so that, consequently, he does not possess such jurisdiction, since it cannot be acquired without a just title.

The assumption that no just title can be assigned may be proved as follows: such a title would be based either upon positive divine law, or else upon human law, since it is evident from what has already been said that this title cannot be based directly upon natural law; for we have demonstrated that only a perfect human community incorporated politically in one unified state, is endowed directly by natural law with supreme temporal jurisdiction over itself; whereas the congregation of the Church—though it is the single spiritual, or mystic body of Christ, and possesses in this spiritual sense a unity in faith, in baptism, and in its head—nevertheless is not unified after the manner of a single political congregation; rather does it contain various kingdoms and commonwealths not possessed of any political unity binding them one with another; therefore, by the force of natural law, there exists within the whole community of the Church no one immediate and supreme jurisdiction of a temporal and universal nature, extending over the Church as a whole; for, on the contrary, there are as many supreme temporal jurisdictions as there are separate political communities which do not form part of one unified political kingdom or commonwealth.

12. Whence we draw the equally evident conclusion that the said power does not exist in any ecclesiastical prince, by any human title through which this natural power might have been transferred to such a prince.

For that title would consist in one of several alternatives. It might be a title by election and by the consent of the people; an alternative which (as is self-evident) cannot be applied to the case under discussion, since it has never come to pass that all Christian peoples have of their own volition and by their own consent, subjected themselves to one man as their supreme temporal prince. Or, it might be a title by just war; and this alternative, too, is clearly inapplicable in the case of an ecclesiastical prince. Again, it might be a title by lawful succession; another hypothesis which is untenable in the present instance, if we take our stand strictly upon human law. For it presupposes the existence of a legitimate title and dominion in the predecessor, so that, tracing it back in this fashion, we must necessarily come to some person who acquired such dominion independently of succession, by some other and earlier human title, one which must consist either in the consent of peoples, or else in a war that was just from the beginning, or was made just by the tacit consent of the subject persons, extending throughout the lawfully required period of time; but none of these suppositions is tenable in the case of any Pope, of whatsoever period or past age. Or finally, the title in question might be founded upon some grant made by human agency; and this hypothesis may be answered with very nearly the same reasoning as that applied to the hypothesis of title by succession. For no one can give that which he does not himself possess; and no prince, even of a temporal sort, has ever possessed supreme temporal jurisdiction directly over all Christian provinces and kingdoms (a point on which I have touched, above); therefore, there is no person who can have made such a grant to the Church, nor to the Pope.

. . . The Pope possesses direct temporal jurisdiction only over the kingdom and the states pertaining to the patrimony of Peter; a patrimony under which we include all temporal dominion now held by the Pope, whether the whole patrimony was granted by Constantine, or whether it originated with him and was subsequently increased by other kings and princes.

The title based upon positive divine law is yet to be mentioned, a title which could have originated only through the gift of Christ the Lord, and which could have persisted only through legitimate succession. But no such gift was ever bestowed by Christ the Lord; consequently, there can be no legitimate succession with regard to such temporal jurisdiction; and therefore, jurisdiction of the kind in question does not pertain to the Pope by this title. . . .

. . . The temporal kingdom was not necessary to Christ for His honour and majesty, while it was expedient, as an example to us and for our redemption, that He should not take that kingdom for himself.

Thus, on the basis of our foregoing remarks, it is easy to prove the truth of our first conclusion, namely, that Christ did not confer upon His vicar, a power which He did not Himself assume.

It will be objected that Christ, although He possessed no temporal kingdom of a perishable and imperfect sort, nevertheless did possess in His humanity, by the grace of [His] union [with the Godhead], a superior dominion, through which He could have used at will all temporal things or kingdoms whatsoever, so that, furthermore, He could have availed Himself of that dominion to bestow temporal kingdoms and a direct temporal jurisdiction upon His vicar.

We reply that we do not deny that He could have done so, even as He also could have assumed [such kingly power and jurisdiction] for Himself; but we infer that He did not bestow [this gift], since He did not assume for Himself this [temporal kingship and] since He left behind Him on earth only His vicar for that kingdom which He did in actual fact assume for Himself; a kingdom which is spiritual, as we have shown, and which, indeed, attains its perfect consummation in glory, yet has its beginning in this world, in the Church militant. Moreover, inasmuch as Christ Himself held perfect spiritual power without direct temporal jurisdiction, it was likewise possible for Him to impart to His vicar a spiritual jurisdiction that was perfect—that is to say, sufficient—unaccompanied by any other jurisdiction of a directly temporal nature. And finally, just as it was expedient that Christ Himself should not assume temporal jurisdiction, so also was it fitting that he should refrain from communicating such jurisdiction to His vicar, lest He should disturb the kings of the earth, or should seem to mingle the spiritual with the secular.

18. Thus we draw our final proof from reasoning, as fol-

lows: temporal dominion with direct jurisdiction of a civil nature over the whole Church was not necessary for the spiritual government of the Church, as is self-evident, nor was it even of use for that same purpose; on the contrary, it might rather have proved to be a grave impediment; and therefore, it is improbable that such jurisdiction was granted by Christ.

The Coercive Power of the Pope

. . . If God has endowed the Pope with directive power, He will have endowed him with coercive power, inasmuch as any different system would be imperfect and ineffectual. Accordingly, the theologians, by reasoning to the contrary, maintain that the Church has not the power to prescribe acts of a strictly internal nature, since it is not possible to pass judgment regarding such acts, nor, consequently, to impose penalties for them, a process which pertains to coercive power. And therefore, conversely, since the Pope is able, by his command, to direct temporal power efficaciously in its own sphere of action, he is also able to coerce and to punish those princes who disobey his just commands.

. . . Our position is confirmed by the power of binding and loosing, which was granted especially to Peter; for the power to bind includes also coercive and punitive power.

. . . The Church has always understood that there resides in her pastors the power to coerce—through the censure of excommunication, at least, which is a spiritual penalty.

. . . This same papal power may extend to the coercion of kings by means of temporal punishments, and deposition from their thrones, if necessity so demands.

. . . For Christ the Lord gave to Peter and his successors the power to correct all Christians, even kings, and, consequently, the power to coerce and punish them when they are disobedient and incorrigible. Nor did He limit this to the authority for imposing ecclesiastical censures. Therefore the said power cannot be limited by us nor by any prince within the Church; rather does it pertain to the Pope of Rome to decide and prescribe the fitting punishment for the occasion or necessity that may arise.

. . . One may draw up the following argument: the Universal Church cannot err in those matters which pertain to faith and morals; she has given her consent to acts of the sort under discussion and has approved them as being in harmony with divine and natural law; and, similarly, she approves canon laws which impose penalties of the kind in question upon temporal princes, because of the gravest crimes and contumacy on their part, and especially in the case of heresy; therefore, it is as certain that the Pope may coerce and punish temporal princes with such penalties, as it is that the Church cannot err in matters of faith and morals.

17. Thirdly, the same truth may be proved by reasoning. For this power was required in the supreme head and pastor of the Church, on two grounds: that is to say, both from the standpoint of the emperors or kings and temporal princes of all kinds, and from the standpoint of the peoples subject to them.

The said power is required, on the first ground, in order that the Pope may correct and reform, or may even fittingly punish, a rebellious prince. For both the corrective and punitive functions are proper to the office of a pastor; and it frequently happens that censures alone do not suffice for these purposes, an inadequacy sufficiently brought out by daily experience; therefore, one must conclude that Christ did bestow the power in question upon His Vicar, since He made that Vicar pastor over Christian princes no less than over the rest of Christendom.

. . . Finally, in view of the foregoing, we may readily establish another ground for the existence of such power over kings, namely, that it exists for the defence of the subjects. For it is the function of a pastor not simply to bring back the wandering sheep to the right way and recall them to the fold, but also to ward off the wolves, defending his charges from enemies, lest they be dragged beyond the fold and perish.

(Extracts from *A Treatise on Laws and God the Lawgiver*, Book 3, chapters 1 and 5, and *A Defense of the Catholic and Apostolic Faith*, Book 3, chapters 1 and 5.)

BELLARMINE
The Power of the Pope in Temporal Affairs

The Indirect Power of the Pope

. . . When we said in consequence of the judgment of the Popes that the power of the earthly kings is of God, we do not mean that it is directly from God in the way that the power of the Pope is from God; but that it is from God because God willed there be political government among mankind; and therefore He gave to men a certain natural instinct to select for themselves magistrates by whom they should be ruled; and besides God wishes that the political government be distinct from the ecclesiastical for if there were direct spiritual and temporal power in the Pope, and the Pope were king of the world, as he is Pontifex of the Church universal, and the other kings were mere executors of the temporal jurisdiction, certainly the Pope could by his own will deprive any kings of their administration and execution of the temporal jurisdiction and in this way he could take away political government and fuse it with the ecclesiastical. And he would be greater than Christ, since he could take away, or fuse the powers, which He desired to be in existence and to be distinct. But if the spiritual power is placed in the Pope only directly and the temporal indirectly, it does not follow that the Pope can take away, or fuse the political government, but it only follows that the Pope can through his spiritual and very overriding Apostolic authority direct and correct the political power, and take it away from one prince, if there be need for the spiritual end, and confer it on another. . . .

God desired that among men there be political government, and this, distinct from the ecclesiastical; so, when the Pope transfers a kingdom from one to another, he is not taking away what God gave, but he is setting it in order and directing; and as God gives kingdoms to men indirectly by the consent and counsel of men, also he can and is wont to change them and transfer them from nation to nation, with the direct consent and counsel of the same men; thus he can with a greater reason change them and transfer them on account of the spiritual end through his own general Vicar, whom He placed over his whole family. . . .

By the very fact that he was made the Pastor of the whole flock and placed over the whole family, and is the head of the whole body of the Church in place of Christ, he is understood to have the mandate to rule, direct, and correct all the sheep of the whole flock, all the servants that are in the family, and all the members that are in the body; nor are emperors and kings excepted, unless they should want to be excepted from the number of the sheep of Christ, and of the servants of Christ, and of the members of the body of Christ. . . .

The Pope by divine law has the power of disposing of the temporal affairs of all Christians in the order to the spiritual end. This indeed is known from the Scriptures; for in the matter of the keys of the kingdom of Heaven, given to Peter the Apostle and his successors, Matthew 16, the keys of the kingdom of the world indeed are not meant, of which no mention is made in the Gospel, because it was not necessary that the supreme Prince of the Church be at the same time the temporal monarch of this world; but the power of disposing of temporal affairs is understood, so far they aid in revealing the kingdom of Heaven to the faithful, or impede or obstruct revealing the kingdom of Heaven to the faithful. . . .

I already have said that the power, of which we speak, is held expressly from the Scriptures, but generally, not in particular . . . and that also from these same divine testimonies is gathered that same accession and association of power to dispose of temporal matters in the order to the spiritual end. For by Christ it was with sufficient clarity signified in the passages cited; and by the Apostle it was also indicated I Cor. 6:3, "Know ye not that ye shall judge angels? how much more things that pertain to this life?"; and by the successors of Peter and Paul, that is, by the Roman Pontiffs in fact it was demonstrated by the deposition of kings and emperors, from the time of the year of Our Lord 700, for before that time either the necessity or the opportunity was lacking. . . .

. . . On the joining and separation of the Ecclesiastical and political powers there can be a double question—one, whether the Ecclesiastical power could exist without the political, to the degree that there would be no political prince in the Church; and the contrary, whether a political power could be found in any nation where there may be no ecclesiastical prelate; and in this we grant that it can be found that these powers are wholly separated; for in the early times of the Church there was on earth a Church without any Christian temporal prince, and at the same time there were and are now some kingdoms of the infidels where there are no Ecclesiastical Prelates. The other question can be: whether the highest Ecclesiastical or spiritual power could be granted which would not have in some manner the annexed power of disposing of temporal matters in the order to the spiritual matters; and because of this restriction we deny that the supreme ecclesiastical or spiritual power can be given that does not have annexed the temporal power in some degree, that is, in the order with respect to spiritual matters. For even in that time in which there were no temporal princes in the Church the Ecclesiastical Prince could command the faithful to support the ministers of the Sacraments with their temporal goods; likewise that the faithful should compose civil suits among themselves and not go to the infidel tribunals for these services. Also the Church could not tolerate an infidel Prince over itself, if he should attempt to turn the faithful from the worship of the true God. Lastly at that time the use of this power was lacking against the princes because there were none, but the power itself was not lacking, for power is one thing and the exercise of it, another. . . .

(Extract from *The Power of the Pope*, chapter 5.)

SECTION X

SOVEREIGNTY AND DIVINE RIGHT

Sovereignty

In the late 16th century, a group of French politicians and lawyers, distressed by the disruption caused by rival religious fanaticisms, were arguing the contrary to the Jesuits and the Calvinist monarchomachs. The group, collectively known as the *Politiques,* was largely Catholic, but had supported the claim of the Huguenot Henry of Navarre to the throne, in order to end the religious civil war. Persecution had led to disorder; a strong secular ruler and a policy of religious toleration were vital to maintain order and preserve unity. The group asserted the concepts of divine right and sovereignty, and denied—as in the case of Barclay, one of its members—the power of the Pope to intervene in French affairs.

The most notable member of the group was Bodin (1530–1596), a member of the States-General and a writer on a variety of topics, including the mystical sciences of economics and sorcery. Writing in a period when the centralized nation-state had emerged under powerful monarchs, who were fighting off both feudal and ecclesiastical claims in their effort to create unified systems, Bodin provided the classic definition of sovereignty in *The Six Books of the Republic* in 1579.

Hotman in France had already argued for the existence of a supreme power that had no superior. Bodin, too, contended that there existed such a supreme power to make the laws—an abstract concept, *majestas,* not an attribute of the prince. Sovereignty was the absolute and perpetual power of commanding in a state. It was absolute because power was given to the prince without any conditions attached. It was perpetual because it could not be revoked. It was the power of giving orders to all, and receiving orders from none. The sovereign was above and could not be bound by his own laws. His authority to demand obedience resulted from the ends for which society existed.

Yet, the sovereign did not possess unlimited power. He was bound by natural law, the eternal law of God (which he himself would define), and by fundamental laws, such as the Salic law, treaties, and the preservation of private property. In this way, Bodin limited or qualified his thesis on the nature of sovereignty.

Divine Right

Paralleling the concept of sovereignty in strengthening the power of the monarch was the idea of divine right of kings, at once a denial of ecclesiastical control, and a declaration of power in the secular realm. The argument was that monarchy was a divinely ordained institution, that kings were accountable to God only, that they ruled by the laws of heredity, and that resistance to them was sinful.

Dante had claimed that the Emperor ruled by divine right, Marsiglio that the ruler's power came from God, Wyclif that the king reflected the Godhood of Christ while the priest represented only His manhood, Belloy and Barclay, members of the *Politiques*, that Divine Providence bestowed the crown on a particular individual and that this action of God could not be disobeyed by anyone, including the Pope.

In England the theory was argued by Sir Robert Filmer and James I. The latter's *The True Law of Free Monarchies*, written in 1598, five years before he succeeded to the English throne, expressed views he held to the end of his life. His belief was that the king, who came to his position by heredity, controlled the whole land, that the coronation oath he took was to God alone, that there were no limits to his powers over his subjects. His absolute prerogative could not be disputed; he was "above the law, both the author and giver of strength to it."

The oath of allegiance—recognizing James as the lawful king, and denying the authority of the Pope to depose him— which all were forced to take, ended any possible threat of Catholic disobedience. In effect, divine right was anti-clerical, directed against both Catholics and Puritans. To James I, Jesuits were "nothing but Puritan-papists." He declared, "No bishop, no King," but his alliance with his church against Catholicism was completely a political one.

Monarchy, obedience, non-resistance went together in this

theory of divine right allied to sovereignty. The theory was disputed by Sir Edward Coke, Lord Chief Justice, who put forward a claim to limitation of royal prerogative, on behalf of the common law. The theory of divine right was to help lead to the Civil War in 1642, as well as the mass emigration of Puritans to America and thus the setting up of a new Anglo-Saxon nation.

External Sovereignty and International Law

Sovereignty had its external aspects also, bringing with it new problems. How could one nation claim the territory of another? How could relations between separate states be regulated without the common bond previously supplied by the Pope or Emperor? What ties united peoples of different states? With the increase in international trade and commerce in the 17th century, the study of international law, stimulated by Grotius, dealt with problems of this kind.

Grotius, (1583–1645), official historian of the Dutch Republic at twenty, chief magistrate of Rotterdam at thirty, was arrested and imprisoned as a leader of the Republican party, for partly political, partly religious reasons. He escaped, legend has it, through the guile of his wife, in a laundry basket. He fled to France, where in 1625 he wrote *De Jure Belli ac Pacis (On the Rights of War and Peace)*.

Grotius' book was to some extent the outcome of his career as a lawyer, in which he had acted for a large commercial company engaged in international trade, and which had stimulated his interest in the relationship between sovereign states. Important contributions to international law were made by Suárez, Victoria, Gentilis and Ayala, three Spaniards and an Italian, but it is the exiled Dutchman whose work has been most influential in this field.

The argument of Grotius was that sovereign states could not live in isolation, any more than could individuals. Compelled to associate for self-preservation, they made contracts among themselves, in the same way as did individuals, based on natural law, itself a product of reason, and the law of nations. This law among states was obligatory for them; it could be executed by appropriate agents. It derived its force from the will of nations. It had to be observed, or the social order could not be maintained. States had to keep their contracts if peace was to be preserved.

Above all, Grotius was concerned with the problem of war. Law between nations held in war as in peace. War ought not to be started except "for the enforcement of rights," and should be waged "only within the bounds of law and good faith." Wars occurred because there was no superior organization in the same relation to individual states as the state was to its citizens, capable of imposing its will on all. Until such an organization was created, there were three methods of avoiding war: conferences, arbitration and lot. It is a fitting tribute to this dedicated advocate of international law that the library of the Permanent Court of Justice at The Hague should have a special section devoted to the works of Grotius.

BODIN

Six Books of the Republic

The Concept of Sovereignty

Sovereignty is that absolute and perpetual power vested in a commonwealth which in Latin is termed *majestas*. . . .

I have described it as *perpetual* because one can give absolute power to a person or group of persons for a period of time, but that time expired they become subjects once more. Therefore even while they enjoy power, they cannot properly be regarded as sovereign rulers, but only as the lieutenants and agents of the sovereign ruler, till the moment comes when it pleases the prince or the people to revoke the gift. The true sovereign remains always seized of his power. Just as a feudal lord who grants land to another retains his eminent domain over them, so the ruler who delegates authority to judge and command, whether it be for a short period, or during pleasure, remains seized of those rights of jurisdiction actually exercised by another in the form of a revocable grant, or precarious tenancy. For this reason the law requires the governor of a province, or the prince's lieutenant, to make a formal surrender of the authority committed to him, at the expiration of his term of office. In this respect there is no difference between the highest officer of state and his humblest subordinate. If it were otherwise, and the absolute authority delegated by the prince to a lieutenant was regarded as itself sovereign power, the latter could use it against his prince who would thereby forfeit his eminence, and the subject could command his lord, the servant his master. This is a manifest absurdity, considering that the sovereign is always excepted personally, as a matter of right, in all delegations of authority, however extensive. However much he gives there always remains a reserve of right in his own person, whereby he may command, or intervene by way of prevention, confirmation, evocation, or any other way he thinks fit, in all matters delegated to a subject, whether in virtue of an office or a commission. Any authority exercised in virtue of an office or a commission can be revoked, or made tenable for as long or short a period as the sovereign wills. . . .

But supposing the king grants absolute power to a lieutenant for the term of his life, is not that a perpetual sovereign power? For if one confines *perpetual* to that which has no termination whatever, then sovereignty cannot subsist save in aristocracies and popular states, which never die. If one is to include monarchy too, sovereignty must be vested not in the king alone, but in the king and the heirs of his body, which supposes a strictly hereditary monarchy. In that case there can be very few sovereign kings, since there are only a very few strictly hereditary monarchies. Those especially who come to the throne by election could not be included.

A perpetual authority therefore must be understood to mean one that lasts for the lifetime of him who exercises it. If a sovereign magistrate is given office for one year, or for any other predetermined period, and continues to exercise the authority bestowed on him after the conclusion of his term, he does so either by consent or by force and violence. If he does so by force, it is manifest tyranny. The tyrant is a true sovereign for all that. The robber's possession by violence is true and natural possession although contrary to the law, for those who were formerly in possession have been disseized. But if the magistrate continues in office by consent, he is not a sovereign prince, seeing that he only exercises power on sufferance. Still less is he a sovereign if the term of his office is not fixed, for in that case he has no more than a precarious commission. . . .

What bearing have these considerations on the case of the man to whom the people has given absolute power for the term of his natural life? One must distinguish. If such absolute power is given him simply and unconditionally, and not in virtue of some office or commission, nor in the form of a revocable grant, the recipient certainly is, and should be acknowledged to be, a sovereign. The people has renounced and alienated its sovereign power in order to invest him with it and put him in possession, and it thereby transfers to him all its powers, authority, and sovereign rights, just as does the man who gives to another possessory and proprietary rights over what he formerly owned. The civil law expresses this in the phrase "all power is conveyed to him and vested in him."

But if the people give such power for the term of his natural life to anyone as its official or lieutenant, or only gives the exercise of such power, in such a case he is not a sovereign, but simply an officer, lieutenant, regent, governor, or agent, and as such has the exercise only of a power inhering in another. When a magistrate institutes a perpetual lieutenant, even if he abandons all his rights of jurisdiction and leaves their exercise entirely to his lieutenant, the authority to command and to judge nevertheless does not reside in the lieutenant, nor the action and force of the law derive from him. If he exceeds his authority his acts have no validity, unless approved and confirmed by him from whom he draws his authority. . . .

Let us now turn to the other term of our definition and consider the force of the word *absolute*. The people or the magnates of a commonwealth can bestow simply and unconditionally upon someone of their choice a sovereign and perpetual power to dispose of their property and persons, to govern the state as he thinks fit, and to order the succession, in the same way that any proprietor, out of his liberality, can freely and unconditionally make a gift of his property to another. Such a form of gift, not being qualified in any way, is the only true gift, being at once unconditional and irrevocable. . . . Similarly sovereign power given to a prince charged with conditions is neither properly sovereign, nor absolute, unless the conditions of appointment are only such as are inherent in the laws of God and of nature. . . .

If we insist however that absolute power means exemption from all law whatsoever, there is no prince in the world who can be regarded as sovereign, since all the princes of the earth are subject to the laws of God and of nature, and even to certain human laws common to all nations. On the other hand, it is possible for a subject who is neither a prince nor a ruler, to be exempted from all the laws, ordinances, and customs of the commonwealth. We have an example in Pompey the Great who was dispensed from the laws for five years, by express enactment of the Roman people, at the instance of the Tribune Gabinius . . . But notwithstanding such exemptions from the operations of the law, the subject remains under the authority of him who exercises sovereign power, and owes him obedience.

On the other hand it is the distinguishing mark of the sovereign that he cannot in any way be subject to the commands of another, for it is he who makes law for the subject, abrogates law already made, and amends obsolete law. No one who is subject either to the law or to some other person can do this. That is why it is laid down in the civil law that the prince is above the law, for the word *law* in Latin implies the command of him who is invested with sovereign power. . . .

If the prince is not bound by the laws of his predecessors, still less can he be bound by his own laws. One may be subject to laws made by another, but it is impossible to bind oneself in any matter which is the subject of one's own free exercise of will. . . . It follows of necessity that the king cannot be subject to his own laws. Just as, according to the canonists, the Pope can never tie his own hands, so the sovereign prince cannot bind himself, even if he wishes.

It is far otherwise with divine and natural laws. All the princes of the earth are subject to them, and cannot contravene them without treason and rebellion against God. His yoke is upon them, and they must bow their heads in fear and reverence before His divine majesty. The absolute power of princes and sovereign lords does not extend to the laws of God and of nature.

But supposing the prince should swear to keep the laws and customs of his country, is he not bound by that oath? One must distinguish. If a prince promises in his own heart to obey his own laws, he is nevertheless not bound to do so, any more than anyone is bound by an oath taken to himself. Even private citizens are not bound by private oaths to keep agreements. The law permits them to cancel them, even if the agreements are in themselves reasonable and good. But if one sovereign prince promises another sovereign prince to keep the agreements entered into by his predecessors, he is bound to do so even if not under oath, if that other prince's interests are involved. If they are not, he is not bound either by a promise, or even by an oath.

The same holds good of promises made by the sovereign to the subject, even if the promises were made prior to his election (for this does not make the difference that many suppose). It is not that the prince is bound either by his own laws or those of his predecessors. But he is bound by the just covenants and promises he has made, whether under oath to do so or not, to exactly the same extent that a private individual is bound in like case. A private individual can be released from a promise that was unjust or unreasonable, or beyond his competence to fulfil, or extracted from him by misrepresentations or fraud, or made in error, or under restraint and by intimidation, because of the injury the keeping of it does him. In the same way a sovereign prince can make good any invasion of his sovereign rights, and for the same reasons. So the principle stands, that the prince is not subject to his own laws, or those of his predecessors, but is bound by the just and reasonable engagements which touch the interests of his subjects individually or collectively. . . .

A law and a covenant must therefore not be confused. A law proceeds from him who has sovereign power, and by it he binds the subject to obedience, but cannot bind himself. A covenant is a mutual undertaking between a prince and his subjects, equally binding on both parties, and neither can contravene it to the prejudice of the other, without his consent. The prince has no greater privilege than the subject in this matter. But in the case of laws, a prince is no longer bound by his promise to keep them when they cease to satisfy the claims of justice. Subjects however must keep their engagements to one another in all circumstances, unless the prince releases them from such obligations. Sovereign princes are not bound by oath to keep the laws of their predecessors. If they are so bound, they are not properly speaking sovereign. . . .

The constitutional laws of the realm, especially those that concern the king's estate being, like the Salic law, annexed and united to the Crown, cannot be infringed by the prince. Should he do so, his successor can always annul any act prejudicial to the traditional form of the monarchy, since on this is founded and sustained his very claim to sovereign majesty. . . .

As for laws relating to the subject, whether general or particular, which do not involve any question of the constitution, it has always been usual only to change them with the concurrence of the three estates, either assembled in the States-General of the whole of France, or in each bailiwick separately. Not that the king is bound to take their advice, or debarred from acting in a way quite contrary to what they wish, if his acts are based on justice and natural reason. . . .

We must agree then that the sovereignty of the king is in no wise qualified or diminished by the existence of Estates. On the contrary his majesty appears more illustrious when formally recognized by his assembled subjects, even though in such assemblies princes, not wishing to fall out with their people, agree to many things which they would not have consented to, unless urged by the petitions, prayers, and just complaints of a people burdened by grievances unknown to the prince. After all, he depends for his information on the eyes and ears and reports of others.

From all this it is clear that the principal mark of sovereign majesty and absolute power is the right to impose laws generally on all subjects regardless of their consent. . . .

But may it not be objected that if the prince forbids a sin, such as homicide, on pain of death, he is in this case bound to keep his own law? The answer is that this is not properly the prince's own law, but a law of God and nature, to which he is more strictly bound than any of his subjects. Neither his council, nor the whole body of the people, can exempt him from his perpetual responsibility before the judgement-seat of God, as Solomon said in unequivocal terms. Marcus Aurelius also observed that the magistrate is the judge of persons, the prince of the magistrates, and God of the prince. Those who say without qualification that the prince is bound neither by any law whatsoever, nor by his own express engagements, insult the majesty of God, unless they intend to except the laws of God and of nature, and all just covenants and solemn agreements.

. . . There is one other point. If the prince is bound by the laws of nature, and the civil law is reasonable and equitable, it would seem to follow that the prince is also bound by the civil law.

. . . (But) just as the prince can choose the most useful among profitable laws, so he can choose the most just among equitable laws, even though while some profit by them others suffer, provided it is the public that profits, and only the private individual that suffers. It is however never proper for the subject to disobey the laws of the prince under the pretext that honour and justice require it. . . .

Edicts and ordinances therefore do not bind the ruler except in so far as they embody the principles of natural justice; that ceasing, the obligation ceases. But subjects are bound till the ruler has expressly abrogated the law, for it is a law both divine and natural that we should obey the edicts and ordinances of him whom God has set in authority over us, providing his edicts are not contrary to God's law . . . From this principle we can deduce that other rule, that the sovereign prince is bound by the covenants he makes either with his subjects, or some other prince. Just because he enforces the covenants and mutual engagements entered into by his subjects among themselves, he must be the mirror of justice in all his own acts . . . He has a double obligation in this case. He is bound in the first place by the principles of natural equity, which require that conventions and solemn promises should be kept, and in the second place in the interests of his own good faith, which he ought to preserve even to his own disadvantage, because he is the formal guarantor to all his subjects of the mutual faith they owe one another. . . .

A distinction must therefore be made between right and

law, for one implies what is equitable and the other what is commanded. Law is nothing else than the command of the sovereign in the exercise of his sovereign power. (But to) take the goods of their subjects at will is contrary to the law of God. They err who assert that in virtue of their sovereign power princes can do this. It is rather the law of the jungle, an act of force and violence. . . . absolute power only implies freedom in relation to positive laws, and not in relation to the law of God. God has declared explicitly in His Law that it is not just to take, or even to covet, the goods of another. Those who defend such opinions are even more dangerous than those who act on them. They show the lion his claws, and arm princes under a cover of just claims. . . .

Since then the prince has no power to exceed the laws of nature which God Himself, whose image he is, has decreed, he cannot take his subjects' property without just and reasonable cause, that is to say by purchase, exchange, legitimate confiscation, or to secure peace with the enemy when it cannot be otherwise achieved. Natural reason instructs us that the public good must be preferred to the particular, and that subjects should give up not only their mutual antagonisms and animosities, but also their possessions, for the safety of the commonwealth. . . .

It remains to be determined whether the prince is bound by the covenants of his predecessors, and whether, if so, it is a derogation of his sovereign power . . . A distinction must be made between the ruler who succeeds because he is the natural heir of his predecessor, and the ruler who succeeds in virtue of the laws and customs of the realm. In the first case the heir is bound by the oaths and promises of his predecessors just as is any ordinary heir. In the second case he is not so bound even if he is sworn, for the oath of the predecessor does not bind the successor. He is bound however in all that tends to the benefit of the kingdom.

There are those who will say that there is no need of such distinctions since the prince is bound in any case by the law of nations, under which covenants are guaranteed. But I consider that these distinctions are necessary nevertheless, since the prince is bound as much by the law of nations, but no more, than by any of his own enactments. If the law of nations is iniquitous in any respect, he can disallow it within his own kingdom, and forbid his subjects to observe it, as was done in France in regard to slavery. He can do the same in relation to any other of its provisions, so long as he does nothing against the law of God. If justice is the end of the law, the law the work of the prince, and the prince the image of God, it follows of necessity that the law of the prince should be modelled on the law of God.

. . . The attributes of sovereignty are peculiar to the sovereign prince, for if communicable to the subject, they cannot be called attributes of sovereignty . . . Just as Almighty God cannot create another God equal with Himself, since He is infinite and two infinities cannot co-exist, so the sovereign prince, who is the image of God, cannot make a subject equal with himself without self-destruction.

If this is so, it follows that rights of jurisdiction are not attributes of sovereignty since they are exercised by subjects as well as the prince. The same is true of the appointment and dismissal of officials, for this power also the prince shares with the subject, not only in regard to the lesser offices of justice, of police, of the armed forces, or of the revenues, but also in regard to responsible commanders in peace and war . . . The infliction of penalties and the bestowing of awards is not an attribute of sovereignty either, for the magistrate has this power, though it is true he derives it from the sovereign. Nor is taking counsel about affairs of state an attribute of sovereignty, for such is the proper function of the privy council or senate in the commonwealth, a body always distinct from that in which sovereignty is vested. Even in the popular state, where sovereignty lies in the assembly of the people, so far from it being the function of the assembly to take counsel, it ought never be permitted to do so, as I shall show later. . . .

. . . The word law signifies the right command of that person, or those persons, who have absolute authority over all the rest without exception, saving only the law-giver himself, whether the command touches all subjects in general or only some in particular. To put it another way, the law is the rightful command of the sovereign touching all his subjects in general, or matters of general application . . . As to the commands of the magistrate, they are not properly speaking laws but only edicts. Such orders are only binding on those subject to his jurisdiction, and are only in force for his term of office.

The first attribute of the sovereign prince therefore is the power to make law binding on all his subjects in general and on each in particular. But to avoid any ambiguity one must add that he does so without the consent of any superior, equal, or inferior being necessary. If the prince can only make law with the consent of a superior he is a subject; if of an equal he shares his sovereignty; if of an inferior, whether it be a council of magnates or the people, it is not he who is sovereign. The names of the magnates that one finds appended to a royal edict are not there to give force to the law, but as witnesses, and to make it more acceptable . . .

It may be objected however that not only have magistrates the power of issuing edicts and ordinances, each according to his competence and within his own sphere of jurisdiction, but private citizens can make law in the form of general or local custom. It is agreed that customary law is as binding as statute law. But if the sovereign prince is author of the law, his subjects are the authors of custom. But there is a difference between law and custom. Custom establishes itself gradually over a long period of years, and by common consent, or at any rate the consent of the greater part. Law is made on the instant and draws its force from him who has the right to bind all the rest. Custom is established imperceptibly and without any exercise of compulsion. Law is promulgated and imposed by authority, and often against the wishes of the subject. For this reason Dion Chrysostom compared custom to the king and law to the tyrant. Moreover law can break custom, but custom cannot derogate from the law, nor can the magistrate, or any other responsible for the administration of law, use his discretion about the enforcement of law as he can about custom. Law, unless it is permissive and relaxes the severity of another law, always carries penalties for its breach. Custom only has binding force by the sufferance and during the good pleasure of the sovereign prince, and so far as he is willing to authorize it. Thus the force of both statutes and customary law derives from the authorization of the prince . . . Included in the power of making and unmaking law is that of promulgating it and amending it when it is obscure, or when the magistrates find contradictions and absurdities. . . .

All the other attributes and rights of sovereignty are included in this power of making and unmaking law, so that strictly speaking this is the unique attribute of sovereign power. It includes all other rights of sovereignty, that is to say of making peace and war, of hearing appeals from the sentences of all courts whatsoever, of appointing and dismissing the great officers of state; of taxing, or granting privileges of exemption to all subjects, of appreciating or depreciating the value and weight of the coinage, of receiving oaths of fidelity from subjects and liege-vassals alike, without exception of any other to whom faith is due. . . .

But because *law* is an unprecise and general term, it is as well to specify the other attributes of sovereignty comprised in it, such as the making of war and peace. This is one of the most important rights of sovereignty, since it brings in its train either the ruin or the salvation of the state. This was a right of sovereignty not only among the ancient Romans, but has always been so among all other peoples . . .

The third attribute of sovereignty is the power to institute the great officers of state. I confine it to high officials, for there is no commonwealth in which these officers, and many guilds and corporate bodies besides, have not some power of appointing their subordinate officials. They do this in virtue of their office, which carries with it the power to delegate. But this power is devolved upon them by the prince . . . It is therefore not the mere appointment of officials that implies sovereign right, but the authorization and confirmation of such appointments. It is true however that in so far as the exercise of this right is delegated, the sovereignty of the prince is to that extent qualified, unless his concurrence and express consent is required.

The fourth attribute of sovereignty, and one which has always been among its principal rights, is that the prince should be the final resort of appeal from all other courts . . . Even though the prince may have published a law, as did Caligula, forbidding any appeal or petition against the sentences of his officers, nevertheless the subject cannot be deprived of the right to make an appeal, or present a petition, to the prince in person. For the prince cannot tie his own hands in this respect, nor take from his subjects the means of redress, supplication, and petition, notwithstanding the fact that all rules governing appeals and jurisdictions are matters of positive law, which we have shown does not bind the prince.

(Extracts from chapters 8 and 10.)

JAMES I
The True Law of Free Monarchies

The Divine Right of Kings

. . . I haue chosen to set downe in this short Treatise, the trew grounds of the mutuall duetie, and alleageance betwixt a free and absolute *Monarche,* and his people . . .

First then, I will set downe the trew grounds, whereupon I am to build, out of the Scriptures, since *Monarchie* is the trew paterne of Diuinitie, next, from the fundamental Lawes of our owne Kingdome, which nearest must concerne vs: thirdly, from the law of Nature, by diuers similitudes drawne out of the same:

The Princes duetie to his Subjects is so clearly set downe in many places of the Scriptures, and so openly confessed by all the good Princes, according to their oath in their Coronation, as not needing to be long therein,

Kings are called Gods by the propheticall King *Dauid*, because they sit vpon GOD his Throne in the earth, and haue the count of their administration to giue vnto him. . . .

And therefore in the Coronation of our owne Kings, as well as of euery Christian *Monarche* they giue their Oath, first to maintaine the Religion presently professed within their countrie, according to their lawes, whereby it is established, and to punish all those that should presse to alter, or disturbe the profession thereof; And next to maintaine all the lowable and good Lawes made by their predecessours: to see them put in execution, and the breakers and violaters thereof, to be punished, according to the tenour of the same: And lastly, to maintaine the whole countrey, and euery state therein, in all their ancient Priuiledges and Liberties, as well against all forreine enemies, as among themselues: And shortly to procure the weale and flourishing of his people, not onely in maintaining and putting to execution the olde lowable lawes of the countrey, and by establishing of new . . . but by all other meanes possible to fore-see and preuent all dangers, and to maintaine concord, wealth, and ciuilitie among them, as a louing Father, and careful watchman, caring for them more then for himselfe, knowing himselfe to be ordained for them, and they not for him; and therefore countable to that great God, who placed him as his lieutenant ouer them, vpon the perill of his soule to procure the weale of both soules and bodies, as farre as in him lieth, of all them that are committed to his charge. And this oath in the Coronation is the clearest, ciuill, and fundamentall Law, whereby the Kings office is properly defined.

By the Law of Nature the King becomes a naturall Father to all his Lieges at his Coronation: And as the Father of his fatherly duty is bound to care for the nourishing, education, and vertuous gouernment of his children; euen so is the king bound to care for all his subiects. . . . As the kindly father ought to foresee all inconuenients and dangers that may arise towards his children, and though with the hazard of his owne person presse to preuent the same; so ought the King towards his people. . . . to take vp in two or three sentences, the duetie, and alleageance of the people to their lawfull king, their obedience, I say, ought to be to him, as to Gods Lieutenant in earth, obeying his commands in all thing, except directly against God, as the commands of Gods Minister, acknowledging him a Iudge set by GOD ouer them, hauing power to iudge them, but to be iudged onely by GOD, whom

to onely hee must giue count of his iudgement; fearing him as
their Iudge, louing him as their father; praying for him as
their protectour; for his continuance, if he be good; for his
amendement, if he be wicked; following and obeying his lawfull commands, eschewing and flying his fury in his vnlawfull,
without resistance, but by sobbes and teares to God, according to that sentence vsed in the primitiue Church in the time
of the persecution.

. . . the king is ouer-lord ouer the whole lands, . . . if a
hoord be found vnder the earth, because it is no more in the
keeping or vse of any person, it of the law pertains to the
king. If a person, inheritour of any lands or goods, dye without any sort of heires, all his landes and goods returne to
the king. . . . so is he Master ouer euery person that inhabiteth
the same, hauing power ouer the life and death of euery one
of them: For although a iust Prince will not take the life of
any of his subiects without a cleare law; yet the same lawes
whereby he taketh them, are made by himselfe, or his predecessours; and so the power flowes alwaies from him selfe; as
by daily experience we see, good and iust Princes will from
time to time make new lawes and statutes. . . . Not that I
deny the old definition of a King, and of a law; which makes
the king to bee a speaking law, and the Law a dumbe king: for
certainely a king that gouernes not by his lawe, can neither be
countable to God for his administration, nor haue a happy
and established raigne: . . . the King is aboue the law, as both
the author and giuer of strength thereto; yet a good king will
not onely delight to rule his subiects by the lawe, but euen will
conforme himselfe in his owne actions thereuneto, alwaies
keeping that ground, that the health of the common-wealth be
his chiefe lawe . . . And therefore generall lawes, made pub-
likely in Parliament, may vpon knowen respects to the King
by his authoritie bee mitigated, and suspended vpon causes
onely knowen to him.

. . . a good king will frame all his actions to be according to
the Law; yet is hee not bound thereto but of his good will,
and for good example-giuing to his subiects . . . And if it be
not lawfull to any particular Lordes tenants or vassals, vpon
whatsoeuer pretext, to controll and displace their Master, and
ouer-lord how much lesse may the subiects and vassals of the
great ouer-lord the KING controll or displace him? And since
in all inferiour iudgements in the land, the people may not
vpon any respects displace their Magistrates, although but
subaltern: If these, I say (whereof some are but inferiour,
subaltern, and temporall Magistrates, and none of them equall
in any sort to the dignitie of a King) cannot be displaced for

any occasion or pretext by them that are ruled by them: how much lesse is it lawfull vpon any pretext to controll or displace the great Prouost, and great Schoolemaster of the whole land: except by inuerting the order of all Law and reason, the commanded may be made to command their commander, the iudged to iudge their Iudge, and they that are gouerned, to gouerne their time about their Lord and gouernour.

And the agreement of the Law of nature in this our ground with the Lawes and constitutions of God, and man, already alledged, will by two similitudes easily appeare. The King towards his people is rightly compared to a father of children, and to a head of a body composed of diuers members: For as fathers, the good Princes, and Magistrates of the people of God acknowledged themselues to their subjects. And for all otherwell ruled Common-wealths, the stile of *Pater patriæ* was euer, and is commonly vsed to Kings. And the proper office of a King towards his Subiects, agrees very wel with the office of the head towards the body, and all members thereof: For from the head, being the seate of Iudgement, proceedeth the care and foresight of guiding, and preuenting all euill that may come to the body or any part thereof. The head cares for the body, so doeth the King for his people. As the discourse and direction flows from the head, and the execution according thereunto belongs to the rest of the members, euery one according to their office: so it is betwixt a wise Prince, and his people.

As to this contract alledged made at the coronation of a King, although I deny any such contract to bee made then . . . yet I confesse, that a king at his coronation, or at the entry to his kingdome, willingly promiseth to his people, to discharge honorably and trewly the office giuen him by God ouer them: But presuming that thereafter he breaks his promise vnto them neuer so inexcusable; the question is, who should bee iudge of the breake . . . of all Law, either ciuil or municipal of any nation, a contract cannot be thought broken by the one partie, and so the other likewise to be freed therefro, except that first a lawfull triall and cognition be had by the ordinary Iudge of the breakers thereof: Or else euery man may be both party and Iudge in his owne cause; which is absurd once to be thought. Now in this contract betwixt the king and his people, God is doubtles the only Iudge, both because to him onely the king must make count of his administration as likewise by the oath in the coronation, God is made iudge and reuenger of the breakers . . . Then since God is the onely Iudge betwixt the two parties contractors, the cognition and reuenge must onely appertaine to him: It followes therefore of necessitie, that God must first giue sentence vpon the King that breaketh, before the people can thinke themselues freed of their oath. What iustice then is it, that the partie shall be both iudge and partie, vsurping vpon himselfe the office of God, may by this argument easily appeare: And shall it lie in the hands of headlesse multitude, when they please to weary of subjection, to cast off the yoake of gouernement that God hath laid vpon them, to iudge and punish him, whom-by they should be iudged and punished, and in that case to vse the office of an vngracious Iudge or Arbiter? Nay, to speak trewly of that case, as it stands betwixt the king and his people, none of them ought to iudge of the others break . . .

. . . the duty and alleageance, which the people sweareth to their prince, is not only bound to themselues, but likewise to their lawfull heires and posterity, the lineall succession of crowns being begun among the people of God, and happily continued in diuers christian common-wealths: So as no obiection either of heresie, or whatsoeuer priuate statute or law may free the people from their oath-giuing to their king, and his succession, established by the old fundamentall lawes of the kingdome: For, as hee is their heritable ouer-lord, and so by birth, not by any right in the coronation, commeth to his crowne; it is a like vnlawful to displace him that succeedeth thereto, as to eiect the former: For at the very moment of the expiring of the king reigning, the nearest and lawful heire entreth in his place . . .

Not that by all this former discourse of mine, and Apologie for kings, I meane that whatsoeuer errors and intollerable abominations a souereigne prince commit, hee ought to escape all punishment, as if thereby the world were only ordained for kings, & they without controlment to turne it vpside down at their pleasure: but by the contrary, by remitting them to God (who is their onely ordinary Iudge) I remit them to the sorest and sharpest schoolemaster that can be deuised for them . . .

Extracts from Two Speeches of James I

a) Speech of 1609

The State of MONARCHIE is the supremest thing vpon earth: For Kings are not onely GODS Lieutenants vpon earth, and sit vpon GODS throne, but euen by GOD himselfe they are called Gods. There bee three principall similitudes that illustrates the state of MONARCHIE: One taken out of the word of GOD; and the two other out of the grounds of Policie and Philosophie. In the Scriptures Kings are called gods, and so their power after a certaine relation compared to the Diuine power. Kings are also compared to Fathers of families: for a King is trewly *Parens patriæ*, the politique father of his people. And lastly, Kings are compared to the head of this Microcosme of the body of man.

Kings are iustly called Gods, for that they exercise a manner or resemblance of Diuine power vpon earth: For if you will consider the Attributes to God, you shall see how they agree in the person of a King. God hath power to create, or destroy, make, or vnmake at his pleasure, to giue life, or send death, to iudge all, and to be iudged nor accomptable to none: To raise low things, and to make high things low at his pleasure, and to God are both soule and body due. And the like power haue Kings: they make and vnmake their subiects: they haue power of raising, and casting downe: of life, and of death: Iudges ouer all their subiects, and in all causes, and yet accomptable to none but God onely. . . . And to the King is due both the affection of the soule, and the seruice of the body of his subiects . . .

As for the Father of a familie, they had of olde vnder the Law of Nature *Patriam potestatem*, which was *Potestatem vitæ & necis*, ouer their children or familie (I meane such Fathers of families as were the lineall heires of those families whereof Kings did originally come:) For Kings had their first originall from them, who planted and spread themselves in *Colonies* through the world. Now a Father may dispose of his Inheritance to his children, at his pleasure . . . make them beggars, or rich at his pleasure; restraine, or banish out of his presence, as hee findes them giue cause of offence, or restore them in fauour againe with the penitent sinner: So may the King deale with his Subiects.

And lastly, as for the head of the naturall body, the head hath the power of directing all the members of the body to that vse which the iudgement in the head thinkes most conuenient. It may apply sharpe cures, or cut off corrupt members, let blood in what proportion it thinkes fit, and as the body may spare, but yet is all this power ordained by God.

b) Speech in Star Chamber, 1616

. . . this I commend vnto your speciall care to blunt the sharpe edge and vaine popular humour of some Lawyers at the Barre, that thinke they are not eloquent and bold spirited enough, except they meddle with the Kings Prerogatiue: But doe not you suffer this; for certainely if this liberty be suffered, the Kings Prerogatiue, the Crowne, and I, shall bee as much wounded by their pleading, as if you resolued what they disputed: That which concernes the mysterie of the Kings power, is not lawfull to be disputed; for that is to wade into the weaknesse of Princes, and to take away the mysticall reuerence, that belongs vnto them that sit in the Throne of God. . . .

Courts ought to keepe their owne limits and boundes of their Commission and Instructions, according to the ancient Presidents: And like as I declare that my pleasure is, that euery of these shall keepe their owne limits and boundes; So the Courts of Common Lawe are not to encroach vpon them, no more then it is my pleasure that they should encroach vpon the Common Law. And this is a thing Regall, and proper to a King, to keep euery Court within his owne bounds. . . .

Keepe you therefore all in your owne bounds, and for my part, I desire you to giue me no more right in my priuate Prerogatiue, then you giue to any Subiect; and therein I will be acquiescent: As for the absolute Prerogatiue of the Crowne, that is no Subiect for the tongue of a Lawyer, nor is lawfull to be disputed.

It is Athiesme and blasphemie to dispute what god can doe: good Christians content themselues with his will reuealed in his word. So, it is presumption and high contempt in a Subiect, to dispute what a King can doe, or say that a King cannot doe this, or that; but rest in that which is the Kings reuealed will in his Law.

GROTIUS

The Rights of War and Peace
(De Jure Belli ac Pacis)

The Need for International Law

The municipal law of Rome and of other states has been treated by many, who have undertaken to elucidate it by means of commentaries or to reduce it to a convenient digest. That body of law, however, which is concerned with the mutual relations among states or rulers of states, whether derived from nature, or established by divine ordinances, or having its origin in custom and tacit agreement, few have touched upon.

Up to the present time no one has treated it in a comprehensive and systematic manner; yet the welfare of mankind demands that this task be accomplished. . . .

Such a work is all the more necessary because in our day, as in former times, there is no lack of men who view this branch of law with contempt as having no reality outside of an empty name. Of like implication is the statement that for those whom fortune favours might makes right, and that the administration of a state cannot be carried on without injustice.

Furthermore, the controversies which arise between peoples or kings generally have Mars as their arbiter. That war is irreconcilable with all law is a view held not alone by the ignorant populace; expressions are often let slip by well-informed and thoughtful men which lend countenance to such a view. Nothing is more common than the assertion of antagonism between law and arms. . . .

Since our discussion concerning law will have been undertaken in vain if there is no law, in order to open the way for a favourable reception of our work and at the same time to fortify it against attacks, this very serious error must be briefly refuted. In order that we may not be obliged to deal with a crowd of opponents, let me assign to them a pleader. And whom should we choose in preference to Carneades? . . .

Carneades, . . . said that, for reasons of expediency, men imposed upon themselves laws, which vary according to customs, and among the same peoples often undergo changes as times change; moreover that there is no law of nature, because all creatures, men as well as animals, are impelled by nature toward ends advantageous to themselves; that, consequently, there is no justice, or, if such there be, it is supreme folly, since one does violence to his own interests if he consults the advantage of others.

What the philosopher here says, and the poet reaffirms in verse,

And just from unjust Nature cannot know,

must not for one moment be admitted. Man is, to be sure, an animal, but an animal of a superior kind, much farther removed from all other animals than the different kinds of animals are from one another; evidence on this point may be found in the many traits peculiar to the human species. But among the traits characteristic of man is an impelling desire for society, that is, for the social life—not of any and every sort, but peaceful, and organized according to the measure of his intelligence, with those who are of his own kind; this social trend the Stoics called "sociableness." Stated as a universal truth, therefore, the assertion that every animal is impelled by nature to seek only its own good cannot be conceded.

Some of the other animals, in fact, do in a way restrain the appetency for that which is good for themselves alone, to the advantage, now of their offspring, now of other animals of the same species. . . . The mature man has knowledge which prompts him to similar actions under similar conditions, together with an impelling desire for society, for the gratification of which he alone among animals possesses a special instrument, speech. He has also been endowed with the faculty of knowing and of acting in accordance with general principles. Whatever accords with that faculty is not common to all animals, but peculiar to the nature of man.

This maintenance of the social order, which is consonant with human intelligence, is the source of law properly so called. To this sphere of law belong the abstaining from that which is another's, the restoration to another of anything of his which we may have, together with any gain which we may have received from it; the obligation to fulfil promises, the making good of a loss incurred through our fault, and the inflicting of penalties upon men according to their deserts.

From this signification of the word law there has flowed another and more extended meaning. Since over other animals man has the advantage of possessing not only a strong bent towards social life, but also a power of discrimination which enables him to decide what things are agreeable or harmful: in such things it is meet for the nature of man, within the limitations of human intelligence, to follow the direction of a well-tempered judgement. . . . Whatever is clearly at variance with such judgement is understood to be contrary also to the law of nature, that is, to the nature of man.

To this exercise of judgement belongs moreover the rational allotment to each man, or to each social group, of those things which are properly theirs, as the conduct of each or the nature of the thing suggests.

Another source of law besides the source in nature is the free will of God, to which beyond all cavil our reason tells us we must render obedience. But the law of nature comprising alike that which relates to the social life of man and that which is so called in a larger sense, proceeding as it does from the essential traits implanted in man, can nevertheless rightly be attributed to God, because of His having willed that such traits exist in us. . . .

There is an additional consideration in that, by means of the laws which He has given, God has made those fundamental traits more manifest, even to those who possess feebler reasoning powers; and He has forbidden us to yield to impulses drawing us in opposite directions—affecting now our own interest, now the interest of others—in an effort to control more effectively our more violent impulses and to restrain them within proper limits. . . .

Since it is a rule of the law of nature to abide by pacts (for it was necessary that among men there be some method of obligating themselves one to another, and no other natural method can be imagined), out of this source the bodies of municipal law have arisen.

The very nature of man, which even if we had no lack of anything would lead us into the mutual relations of society, is the mother of the law of nature. But the mother of municipal law is that obligation which arises from mutual consent; and since this obligation derives its force from the law of nature, nature may be considered, so to say, the great-grandmother of municipal law.

The law of nature nevertheless has the reinforcement of expediency; for the Author of nature willed that as individuals we should be weak, and should lack many things needed in order to live properly, to the end that we might be the more constrained to cultivate the social life. But expediency afforded an opportunity also for municipal law, since that kind of association of which we have spoken, and subjection to authority, have their roots in expediency. Those who prescribe laws for others in so doing are accustomed to have, or ought to have, some advantage in view.

But just as the laws of each state have in view the advantage of that state, so by mutual consent it has become possible that certain laws should originate as between all states, or a great many states; and it is apparent that the laws thus originating had in view the advantage, not of particular states, but of the great society of states. And this is what is called the law of nations, whenever we distinguish that term from the law of nature.

This division of law Carneades passed over altogether. For he divided all law into the law of nature and the law of particular countries. Nevertheless if undertaking to treat of the body of law which is maintained between states—for he added a statement in regard to war and things acquired by means of war—he would surely have been obliged to make mention of this law.

Wrongly, moreover, does Carneades ridicule justice as folly. For since, by his own admission, the national who in his own country obeys its laws is not foolish, even though, out of

regard for that law, he may be obliged to forgo certain things
advantageous for himself, so that nation is not foolish which
does not press its own advantage to the point of disregarding
the laws common to nations. The reason in either case is the
same. For just as the national, who violates the law of his
country in order to obtain an immediate advantage, breaks
down that by which the advantages of himself and his posterity are for all future time assured, so the state which transgresses the laws of nature and of nations cuts away also the
bulwarks which safeguard its own future peace. Even if no
advantage were to be contemplated from the keeping of the
law, it would be a mark of wisdom, not of folly, to allow
ourselves to be drawn towards that to which we feel that our
nature leads. . . .

We may readily admit the truth of the saying that right is
that which is acceptable to the stronger; so that we may
understand that law fails of its outward effect unless it has a
sanction behind it. In this way Solon accomplished very great
results, as he himself used to declare,

> By joining force and law together,
> Under a like bond.

Nevertheless law, even though without a sanction, is not
entirely void of effect. For justice brings peace of conscience,
while injustice causes torments and anguish, such as Plato
describes, in the breast of tyrants. Justice is approved, and
injustice condemned, by the common agreement of good men.
But, most important of all, in God injustice finds an enemy,
justice a protector. . . .

Many hold, in fact, that the standard of justice which they
insist upon in the case of individuals within the state is inapplicable to a nation or the ruler of a nation. The reason for
the error lies in this, first of all, that in respect to law they
have in view nothing except the advantage which accrues
from it, such advantage being apparent in the case of citizens
who, taken singly, are powerless to protect themselves. But
great states, since they seem to contain in themselves all
things required for the adequate protection of life, seem not to
have need of that virtue which looks toward the outside, and
is called justice.

But that law is not founded on expediency alone, there is
no state so powerful that it may not some time need the help
of others outside itself, either for purposes of trade, or even to
ward off the forces of many foreign nations united against it.
In consequence we see that even the most powerful peoples

and sovereigns seek alliances, which are quite devoid of significance according to the point of view of those who confine law within the boundaries of states. Most true is the saying, that all things are uncertain the moment men depart from law.

If no association of men can be maintained without law, surely also that association which binds together the human race, or binds many nations together, has need of law; this was perceived by him who said that shameful deeds ought not to be committed even for the sake of one's country. . . .

The causes which determine the characterization of a war as lawful or unlawful Ayala did not touch upon. Gentili outlined certain general classes, in the manner which seemed to him best; but he did not so much as refer to many topics which have come up in notable and frequent controversies.

We have taken all pains that nothing of this sort escape us; and we have also indicated the sources from which conclusions are drawn, whence it would be an easy matter to verify them, even if any point has been omitted by us. . . .

First of all, I have made it my concern to refer the proofs of things touching the law of nature to certain fundamental conceptions which are beyond question, so that no one can deny them without doing violence to himself. For the principles of that law, if only you pay strict heed to them, are in themselves manifest and clear, almost as evident as are those things which we perceive by the external senses; and the senses do not err if the organs of perception are properly formed and if the other conditions requisite to perception are present. . . .

In order to prove the existence of this law of nature, I have, furthermore, availed myself of the testimony of philosophers, historians, poets, finally also of orators. Not that confidence is to be reposed in them without discrimination; for they were accustomed to serve the interests of their sect, their subject, or their cause. But when many at different times, and in different places, affirm the same thing as certain, that ought to be referred to a universal cause; and this cause, in the lines of inquiry which we are following, must be either a correct conclusion drawn from the principles of nature, or common consent. The former points to the law of nature; the latter, to the law of nations.

The distinction between these kinds of law is not to be drawn from the testimonies themselves (for writers everywhere confuse the terms law of nature and law of nations), but from the character of the matter. For whatever cannot be deduced from certain principles by a sure process of reasoning, and yet is clearly observed everywhere, must have its origin in the free will of man.

These two kinds of law, therefore, I have always particularly sought to distinguish from each other and from municipal law. Furthermore, in the law of nations I have distinguished between that which is truly and in all respects law, and that which produces merely a kind of outward effect simulating that primitive law, as, for example, the prohibition to resist by force, or even the duty of defence in any place by public force, in order to secure some advantage, or for the avoidance of serious disadvantages. How necessary it is, in many cases, to observe this distinction, will become apparent in the course of our work. . . .

Human law is either municipal law, or broader in scope than municipal law, or more restricted than municipal law.

Municipal law is that which emanates from the civil power. The civil power is that which bears sway over the state. The state is a complete association of free men, joined together for the enjoyment of rights and for their common interest.

The law which is narrower in scope than municipal law, and does not come from the civil power, although subject to it, is of varied character. It comprises the commands of a father, of a master, and all other commands of a similar character.

The law which is broader in scope than municipal law is the law of nations; that is the law which has received its obligatory force from the will of all nations, or of many nations. I added 'of many nations' for the reason that, outside of the sphere of the law of nature, which is also frequently called the law of nations, there is hardly any law common to all nations. Not infrequently, in fact, in one part of the world there is a law of nations which is not such elsewhere, as we shall at the proper time set forth in connection with captivity and postliminy.

The proof for the law of nations is similar to that for unwritten municipal law; it is found in unbroken custom and the testimony of those who are skilled in it. The law of nations, in fact, as Dio Chrysostom well observes, 'is the creation of time and custom.' And for the study of it the illustrious writers of history are of the greatest value to us.

(Extracts from the Prolegomena and Book I, xiv.)

HOBBES AND SPINOZA

By the 17th century, practical statesmen and political thinkers alike recognized the need for civil order and obedience, despite private belief and personal morality, so as to end the civil and religious wars. The concept of sovereignty needed no theological justification. It became purely secular, related to the ultimate power of the people. The two leading exponents of this view were Hobbes and Spinoza.

Hobbes, (1588–1679), was born with "natural timidity" in the year of the Spanish Armada, became a tutor in aristocratic households, a friend of Bacon and a partisan of the Royalist cause, and in 1640 fled to France, where he spent 11 years in exile. In 1642, he published *De Cive*, a discussion of the purpose and extent of civil power, and in 1651 *Leviathan*. The immediate result for Hobbes was not reward, but disappointment and anxiety. Neither the French court and clergy, nor the royalist émigrés appreciated it. Hobbes fled back to London.

Hobbes had been appalled by the anarchic situation produced by the civil war in England, the execution of Charles I, and by the religious doctrinal disputes. *Leviathan,* attempting to explain the creation and preservation of an authority that would end such anarchy, is the most logical, systematic treatise in British political theory. He attempted to create a political structure and principles on Euclidean geometric lines, to deduce a system of rules from the known inclinations of men.

The basis for agreement between men was not their common possession of reason; the skepticism of Erasmus and Montaigne had equated reason with individual opinion. Any valid explanation of society and government must take account of the real nature of man. Man was the creator of his society. He asserted himself as far as his power allowed him, according to natural right. Man was motivated by his appetites, desires, fear and self-interest, seeking pleasure and avoiding pain. What he called good was simply the object of his appetite or desire. His main desire, and the most important of natural laws, was self-preservation and the avoidance of violent death. This was the root of all right and morality.

Since the powers men had were essentially equal, there was natural strife as men sought to satisfy their desires. To escape this intolerable situation, where every individual lived for himself, and to obtain peace and order, men agreed to form a society. They surrendered their rights of self-assertion in order to set up a power capable of enforcing its authority. Men escaped from the perilous state of nature, gave up natural rights to defend themselves, made a social contract, and created a sovereign. Order was secured by this sovereign.

The possession of power was justified not by appeal to tradition, divine right or heredity, but in utilitarian fashion. Society and the state were artificial, deliberate human creations, the products of individual wills. Unity had been created by voluntary action. Hobbes' conception of the social order was naturalistic, non-Christian and based on man as the measure of his own good.

The actions of individuals created the sovereign state. Then law and justice were created by the sovereign. No conditions were imposed on the sovereign; disobedience was not permissible. The state power was that "mortal god to which we owe under the immortal God our peace and defense." All were subject to the sovereign. Subjects "shine no more than stars in the presence of the sun." Corporations, which might disturb unity, "were worms in the entrails of a natural man."

Sovereign power was considerable, but this was always better than civil war, "the dissolute condition of masterless men." Liberty was the absence of external restraints, and depended on the silence of the law. Religion, too, must be controlled by the state, and help secure the state, or the social order would be destroyed through ignorant, credulous, passionate men. Over half of the Leviathan is about religion, but Hobbes' real interest in it was as a possible source of civil discord, and as an instrument of power. He was competely Erastian—the sovereign was the "supreme pastor"—opposed to both papal intervention and the Church of Rome.

Hobbes created a powerful sovereign, but no totalitarian monster. The sovereign, like everyone else, was afraid of death, and therefore tried to satisfy the needs of subjects in order to avoid this end. The actions of the state were to be limited. Concerning the absence of economic regulation, Hobbes may have been the first liberal. The state was powerful, but only to secure order and security, not for self-glorification. The attention of the sovereign was confined to the outward behavior of man; he could not control man's private beliefs. And as an ultimate weapon, an individual could resist if his life were in danger, for the sovereign would not be performing the function for which he existed.

Hobbes had given up the idea of a general good; good was the object of men's desires. He had denied the Aristotelian concept of the social nature of man. He had constructed an absolutist state from its atomistic, individual parts. He had refused to allow the sovereign to be restrained by natural law. He had disposed of any theological justification of power. To answer Hobbes became a major preoccupation of succeeding writers. His influence waned, but it was restored with the Utilitarians in the 19th century.

Spinoza

A similar thesis, with subtle variations, was elaborated by Spinoza (1632–1677). Born in Amsterdam of Portuguese Jews, Spinoza left his synagogue and gave up his inheritance. He worked at grinding and polishing lenses, an occupation responsible for his early death from consumption. His *Tractatus Theologico-Politicus* was published anonymously in 1670, and his *Tractatus Politicus* posthumously.

Like Hobbes, he showed how men could be made to live in settled peace in spite of instability and enmity, how men, "even when led by passion, may still have fixed and stable laws." This task required dispassionate, logical, scientific study, in which morality and religion played little part. The study of power was the key to the understanding of politics and society. Politics was almost the art of applied psychology, for stability could be obtained through institutions based on experience and the behavior of men.

The state resulted from the desires of men to escape the condition of war in the state of nature, and to seek self-preservation. Out of rational self-interest a contract created a sovereign power. But men never surrendered all their rights so that they became sheep. The wise sovereign promoted the interest of all his subjects, and tried to obtain "a union or agreement of minds." A powerful ruler had been set up, but in practice he was limited by the fear he felt of his subjects.

Spinoza's natural law theory was one in which God was equated with universal nature, and in which natural right was equated with the power of nature. The laws regulating the natural man were dictates of reason. Spinoza stressed, more than Hobbes, the value of reason and its exercise. A political organization, therefore, should allow man the freest possible use of his reason. A satisfactory state provided not only security, but intellectual freedom. It would not suppress opinion, since there was a need for enlightened citizens. The enlightened man was preferable to the man with an inadequate understanding of his conditions and at the mercy of his emotions.

Spinoza advocated toleration, religious freedom, and separation of church and state, attacking religious superstition, which supported persecution and intolerance.

HOBBES
Leviathan

The Nature of Man

. . . That which men desire, they are also said to LOVE: and to HATE those things for which they have aversion. So that desire and love are the same thing; save that by desire, we always signify the absence of the object; by love, most commonly the presence of the same. So also by aversion, we signify the absence; and by hate, the presence of the object.

Of appetites and aversions, some are born with men; as appetite of food, appetite of excretion, and exoneration, which may also and more properly be called aversions, from somewhat they feel in their bodies; and some other appetites, not many. The rest, which are appetites of particular things, proceed from experience, and trial of their effects upon themselves or other men. For of things we know not at all, or believe not to be, we can have no further desire, than to taste and try. But aversion we have for things, not only which we know have hurt us, but also that we do not know whether they will hurt us, or not. . . .

And because the constitution of a man's body is in continual mutation, it is impossible that all the same things should always cause in him the same appetites, and aversions: much less can all men consent, in the desire of almost any one and the same object.

But whatsoever is the object of any man's appetite or desire, that is it which he for his part calleth *good:* and the object of his hate and aversion, *evil;* and of his contempt, *vile* and *inconsiderable.* For these words of good, evil, and contemptible, are ever used with relation to the person that useth them: there being nothing simply and absolutely so; nor any common rule of good and evil, to be taken from the nature of the objects themselves; but from the person of the man, where there is no commonwealth; or, in a commonwealth, from the person that representeth it; or from an arbitrator or judge, whom men disagreeing shall by consent set up, and make his sentence the rule thereof.

The passions that most of all cause the difference of wit, are principally, the more or less desire of power, of riches, of knowledge, and of honour. All which may be reduced to the first, that is, desire of power. For riches, knowledge, and honour, are but several sorts of power.

And therefore, a man who has no great passion for any of these things; but is, as men term it, indifferent; though he may be so far a good man, as to be free from giving offence; yet he cannot possibly have either a great fancy, or much judgment. For the thoughts are to the desires, as scouts, and spies, to range abroad, and find the way to the things desired. . . .

. . . the felicity of this life, consisteth not in the repose of a mind satisfied. For there is no such *finis ultimus*, utmost aim, nor *summun bonum,* greatest good, as is spoken of in the books of the old moral philosophers. Nor can a man any more live, whose desires are at an end, than he, whose senses and imaginations are at a stand. Felicity is a continual progress of the desire, from one object to another; the attaining of the former, being still but the way to the latter. The cause whereof is, that the object of man's desire, is not to enjoy once only, and for one instant of time; but to assure for ever, the way of his future desire. And therefore the voluntary actions, and inclinations of all men, tend, not only to the procuring, but also to the assuring of a contented life; and differ only in the way: which ariseth partly from the diversity of passions, in divers men; and partly from the difference of the knowledge, or opinion each one has of the causes, which produce the effect desired.

So that in the first place, I put for a general inclination of all mankind, a perpetual and restless desire of power after power, that ceaseth only in death. And the cause of this, is not always that a man hopes for a more intensive delight, than he has already attained to; or that he cannot be content with a moderate power: but because he cannot assure the power and means to live well, which he hath present, without the acquisition of more. And from hence it is, that kings, whose power is greatest, turn their endeavours to the assuring

t at home by laws, or abroad by wars: and when that is done,
here succeedeth a new desire; in some, of fame from new
conquest; in others, of ease and sensual pleasure; in others, of
admiration, or being flattered for excellence in some art, or
other ability of the mind.

Competition of riches, honour, command, or other power,
inclineth to contention, enmity, and war: because the way of
one competitor, to the attaining of his desire, is to kill, subdue, supplant, or repel the other. Particularly, competition of
praise, inclineth to a reverence of antiquity. For men contend
with the living, not with the dead; to these ascribing more
than due, that they may obscure the glory of the other.

Desire of ease, and sensual delight, disposeth men to obey a
common power: because by such desires, a man doth abandon the protection that might be hoped for from his own
industry, and labour. Fear of death, and wounds, disposeth to
the same; and for the same reason. On the contrary, needy
men, and hardy, not contented with their present condition; as
also, all men that are ambitious of military command, are
inclined to continue the causes of war; and to stir up trouble
and sedition: for there is no honour military but by war; nor
any such hope to mend an ill game, as by causing a new
shuffle.

Desire of knowledge, and arts of peace, inclineth men to
obey a common power: for such desire, containeth a desire of
leisure; and consequently protection from some other power
than their own.

. . . And they that make little, or no inquiry into the
natural causes of things, yet from the fear that proceeds from
the ignorance itself, of what it is that hath the power to do
them much good or harm, are inclined to suppose, and feign
unto themselves, several kinds of powers invisible; and to
stand in awe of their own imaginations; and in time of distress
to invoke them; as also in the time of an expected good success, to give them thanks; making the creatures of their own
fancy, their gods. By which means it hath come to pass, that
from the innumerable variety of fancy, men have created in
the world innumerable sorts of gods. And this fear of things
invisible, is the natural seed of that, which every one in himself calleth religion; and in them that worship, or fear that
power otherwise than they do, superstition.

And this seed of religion, having been observed by many;
some of those that have observed it, have been inclined
thereby to nourish, dress, and form it into laws; and to add to
it of their own invention, any opinion of the causes of future

events, by which they thought they should be best able to govern others, and make unto themselves the greatest use of their powers.

(Extracts from Part I, chapters 6, 8, 11, 12.)

The State of Nature

Nature hath made men so equal, in the faculties of the body, and mind; as that though there be found one man sometimes manifestly stronger in body, or of quicker mind than another; yet when all is reckoned together, the difference between man, and man, is not so considerable, as that one man can thereupon claim to himself any benefit, to which another may not pretend, as well as he. For as to the strength of body, the weakest has strength enough to kill the strongest, either by secret machination, or by confederacy with others, that are in the same danger with himself.

And as to the faculties of the mind, setting aside the arts grounded upon words, and especially that skill of proceeding upon general, and infallible rules, called science; which very few have, and but in few things; as being not a native faculty, born with us; nor attained, as prudence, while we look after somewhat else, I find yet a greater equality amongst men, than that of strength. For prudence, is but experience; which equal time, equally bestows on all men, in those things they equally apply themselves unto. That which may perhaps make such equality incredible, is but a vain conceit of one's own wisdom, which almost all men think they have in a greater degree, than the vulgar; that is, than all men but themselves, and a few others, whom by fame, or for concurring with themselves, they approve. For such is the nature of men, that howsoever they may acknowledge many others to be more witty, or more eloquent, or more learned; yet they will hardly believe there be many so wise as themselves; for they see their own wit at hand, and other men's at a distance. But this proveth rather that men are in that point equal, than unequal. For there is not ordinarily a greater sign of the equal distribution of any thing, than that every man is contented with his share.

From this equality of ability, ariseth equality of hope in the attaining of our ends. And therefore if any two men desire the same thing, which nevertheless they cannot both enjoy, they become enemies; and in the way to their end, which is principally their own conservation, and sometimes their delectation only, endeavour to destroy, or subdue one another.

. . . And from this diffidence of one another, there is no

way for any man to secure himself, so reasonable, as anticipation; that is, by force, or wiles, to master the persons of all men he can, so long, till he see no other power great enough to endanger him: and this is no more than his own conservation requireth, and is generally allowed. . . .

Again, men have no pleasure, but on the contrary a great deal of grief, in keeping company, where there is no power able to over-awe them all. For every man looketh that his companion should value him, at the same rate he sets upon himself: and upon all signs of contempt, or undervaluing, naturally endeavours, as far as he dares, (which amongst them that have no common power to keep them in quiet, is far enough to make them destroy each other), to extort a greater value from his contemners, by damage; and from others, by the example.

So that in the nature of man, we find three principal causes of quarrel. First, competition: secondly, diffidence; thirdly, glory.

The first, maketh men invade for gain; the second, for safety; and the third, for reputation. The first use violence, to make themselves masters of other men's persons, wives, children, and cattle; the second, to defend them; the third, for trifles, as a word, a smile, a different opinion, and any other sign of undervalue, either direct in their persons, or by reflection in their kindred, their friends, their nation, their profession, or their name.

Hereby it is manifest, that during the time men live without a common power to keep them all in awe, they are in that condition which is called war; and such a war, as is of every man, against every man. For WAR, consisteth not in battle only, or the act of fighting; but in a tract of time, wherein the will to contend by battle is sufficiently known: and therefore the notion of *time*, is to be considered in the nature of war; as it is in the nature of weather. For as the nature of foul weather, lieth not in a shower or two of rain; but in an inclination thereto of many days together: so the nature of war, consisteth not in actual fighting; but in the known disposition thereto, during all the time there is no assurance to the contrary. All other time is PEACE.

Whatsoever therefore is consequent to a time of war, where every man is enemy to every man; the same is consequent to the time, wherein men live without other security, than what their own strength, and their own invention shall furnish them withal. In such condition, there is no place for industry; because the fruit thereof is uncertain: and consequently no culture of the earth; no navigation, nor use of the commodities that may be imported by sea; no commodious building; no instruments of moving, and removing, such things as require much force; no knowledge of the face of the earth; no account of time; no arts; no letters; no society; and which is worst of all, continual fear, and danger of violent death; and the life of man, solitary, poor, nasty, brutish, and short.

It may seem strange to some man, that has not well weighed these things; that nature should thus dissociate, and render men apt to invade, and destroy one another: and he may therefore, not trusting to this inference, made from the passions, desire perhaps to have the same confirmed by experience. Let him therefore consider with himself, when taking a journey, he arms himself, and seeks to go well accompanied; when going to sleep, he locks his doors; when even in his house he locks his chests; and this when he knows there be laws, and public officers, armed, to revenge all injuries shall be done him; what opinion he has of his fellow-subjects, when he rides armed; of his fellow citizens, when he locks his doors; and of his children, and servants, when he locks his chests. Does he not there as much accuse mankind by his actions, as I do by my words? But neither of us accuse man's nature in it. The desires, and other passions of man, are in themselves no sin. No more are the actions, that proceed from those passions, till they know a law that forbids them: which till laws be made they cannot know: nor can any law be made, till they have agreed upon the person that shall make it.

It may peradventure be thought, there was never such a time, nor condition of war as this; and I believe it was never generally so, over all the world: but there are many places, where they live so now. For the savage people in many places of America, except the government of small families, the concord whereof dependeth on natural lust, have no government at all; and live at this day in that brutish manner, as I said before. Howsoever, it may be perceived what manner of life there would be, where there were no common power to fear, by the manner of life, which men that have formerly lived under a peaceful government, use to degenerate into, in a civil war.

But though there had never been any time, wherein particular men were in a condition of war one against another; yet in all times, kings, and persons of sovereign authority, because of their independency, are in continual jealousies, and in the state and posture of gladiators; having their weapons pointing, and their eyes fixed on one another; that is, their forts, garrisons, and guns upon the frontiers of their kingdoms; and continual spies upon their neighbours; which is a posture of war. But because they uphold thereby, the industry of their subjects; there does not follow from it, that misery, which accompanies the liberty of particular men.

To this war of every man, against every man, this also is consequent; that nothing can be unjust. The notions of right and wrong, justice and injustice have there no place. Where there is no common power, there is no law: where no law, no injustice. Force, and fraud, are in war the two cardinal virtues. Justice, and injustice are none of the faculties neither of the body, nor mind. If they were, they might be in a man that were alone in the world, as well as his senses, and passions. They are qualities, that relate to men in society, not in solitude. It is consequent also to the same condition, that there be no propriety, no dominion, no *mine* and *thine* distinct; but only that to be every man's, that he can get: and for so long, as he can keep it. And thus much for the ill condition, which man by mere nature is actually placed in; though with a possibility to come out of it, consisting partly in the passions, partly in his reason.

The passions that incline men to peace, are fear of death; desire of such things as are necessary to commodious living; and a hope by their industry to obtain them. And reason suggesteth convenient articles of peace, upon which men may be drawn to agreement. These articles, are they, which otherwise are called the Laws of Nature.

(Extract from Part I, Chapter 13.)

The Social Contract

THE RIGHT OF NATURE, which writers commonly call *jus naturale*, is the liberty each man hath, to use his own power, as he will himself, for the preservation of his own nature; that is to say, of his own life; and consequently, of doing any thing, which in his own judgment, and reason, he shall conceive to be the aptest means thereunto.

BY LIBERTY, is understood, according to the proper signification of the word, the absence of external impediments: which impediments, may oft take away part of a man's power to do what he would; but cannot hinder him from using the power left him, according as his judgment, and reason shall dictate to him.

A LAW OF NATURE, *lex naturalis*, is a precept or general rule, found out by reason, by which a man is forbidden to do that, which is destructive of his life, or taketh away the means of preserving the same; and to omit that, by which he thinketh it may be best preserved. For though they that speak of this subject, use to confound *jus,* and *lex,* right and *law:* yet they ought to be distinguished; because RIGHT, consisteth in liberty to do, or to forbear: whereas LAW, determineth, and bindeth to one of them: so that law, and right, differ as much, as obligation, and liberty; which in one and the same matter are inconsistent.

And because the condition of man is a condition of war of every one against every one; in which case every one is governed by his own reason; and there is nothing he can make use of, that may not be a help unto him, in preserving his life against his enemies; it followeth, that in such a condition, every man has a right to every thing; even to one another's body. And therefore, as long as this natural right of every man to every thing endureth, there can be no security to any man, how strong or wise soever he be, of living out the time, which nature ordinarily alloweth men to live. And consequently it is a precept, or general rule of reason, *that every man, ought to endeavour peace, as far as he has hope of obtaining it; and when he cannot obtain it, that he may seek, and use, all helps, and advantages of war.* The first branch of which rule, containeth the first, and fundamental law of nature; which is, *to seek peace, and follow it.* The second, the sum of the right of nature; which is, *by all means we can, to defend ourselves.*

From this fundamental law of nature, by which men are commanded to endeavour peace, is derived this second law; *that a man be willing, when others are so too, as far-forth, as for peace, and defence of himself he shall think it necessary, to lay down this right to all things; and be contented with so much liberty against other men, as he would allow other men against himself.* For as long as every man holdeth this right, of doing anything he liketh; so long are all men in the condition of war. But if other men will not lay down their right, as well as he; then there is no reason for any one, to divest himself of his: for that were to expose himself to prey, which no man is bound to, rather than to dispose himself to peace. This is that law of the Gospel; *whatsoever you require that others should do to you, that do ye to them.*

To *lay down* a man's *right* to anything, is to *divest* himself of the *liberty,* of hindering another of the benefit of his own right to the same.

Whensoever a man transferreth his right, or renounceth it; it is either in consideraton of some right reciprocally transferred to himself; or for some other good he hopeth for thereby. For it is a voluntary act: and of the voluntary acts of every man, the object is some *good to himself.* And therefore there be some rights, which no man can be understood by any words, or other signs, to have abandoned, or transferred. As first a man cannot lay down the right of resisting them, that assault him by force, to take away his life; because he cannot be understood to aim thereby, at any good to himself. The same may be said of wounds, and chains, and imprisonment; both because there is no benefit consequent to such patience; as there is to the patience of suffering another to be wounded, or imprisoned: as also because a man cannot tell, when he seeth men proceed against him by violence whether they intend his death or not. And lastly the motive, and end for which this renouncing, and transferring of right is introduced, is nothing else but the security of a man's person, in his life, and in the means of so preserving life, as not to be weary of it. And therefore if a man by words, or other signs, seem to despoil himself of the end, for which those signs were intended; he is not to be understood as if he meant it, or that it was his will; but that he was ignorant of how such words and actions were to be interpreted.

The mutual transferring of right, is that which men call CONTRACT.

There is difference between transferring of right to the thing; and transferring, or tradition, that is delivery of the thing itself. For the thing may be delivered together with the translation of the right; as in buying and selling with ready-money; or exchange of goods, or lands: and it may be delivered some time after.

Again, one of the contractors, may deliver the thing contracted for on his part, and leave the other to perform his part at some determinate time after, and in the mean time be trusted; and then the contract on his part, is called PACT, or COVENANT: or both parts may contract now, to perform here after: in which cases, he that is to perform in time to come, being trusted, his performance is called *keeping of promise,* or faith; and the failing of performance, if it be voluntary, *violation of faith.*

(Extract from Part I, Chapter 14.)

Laws of Nature

From that law of nature, by which we are obliged to transfer to another, such rights, as being retained, hinder the peace of mankind, there followeth a third; which is this, *that men perform their covenants made:* without which, convenants are in vain, and but empty words; and the right of all men to all things remaining, we are still in the condition of war.

And in this law of nature, consisteth the fountain and original of JUSTICE. For where no covenant hath preceded, there hath no right been transferred, and every man has right to every thing; and consequently, no action can be unjust. But when a covenant is made, then to break it is *unjust:* and the definition of INJUSTICE, is no other than *the not performance of covenant.* And whatsoever is not unjust, is *just.*

The laws of nature are immutable and eternal; for injustice, ingratitude, arrogance, pride, iniquity, acception of persons, and the rest, can never be made lawful. For it can never be that war shall preserve life, and peace destroy it.

The same laws, because they oblige only to a desire, and endeavour, I mean an unfeigned and constant endeavour, are easy to be observed. For in that they require nothing but endeavour, he that endeavoureth their performance, fulfilleth them; and he that fulfilleth the law, is just.

And the science of them, is the true and only moral philosophy. For moral philosophy is nothing else but the science of what is *good,* and *evil,* in the conversation, and society of mankind. *Good,* and *evil,* are names that signify our appetites, and aversions; which in different tempers, customs, and doctrines of men, are different: and divers men, differ not only in their judgment, on the senses of what is pleasant, and unpleasant to the taste, smell, hearing, touch, and sight; but also of what is conformable, or disagreeable to reason, in the actions of common life. Nay, the same man, in divers times, differs from himself; and one time praiseth, that is, calleth good, what another time he dispraiseth, and calleth evil: from whence arise disputes, controversies, and at last war. And therefore so long as a man is in the condition of mere nature, which is a condition of war, as private appetite is the measure of good, and evil: and consequently all men agree on this, that peace is good, and therefore also the way, or means of peace, which, as I have shewed before, are *justice, gratitude, modesty, equity, mercy,* and the rest of the laws of nature, are good; that is to say, *moral virtues;* and their contrary *vices,* evil.

These dictates of reason men used to call by the name of laws, but improperly: for they are but conclusions, or theorems concerning what conduceth to the conservation and defence of themselves; whereas law, properly, is the word of him, that by right hath command over others. But yet if we consider the same theorems, as delivered in the word of God, that by right commandeth all things; then are they properly called laws.

(Extract from Part I, chapter 15.)

Political Power

The greatest of human powers, is that which is compounded of the powers of most men, united by consent, in one person, natural, or civil, that has the use of all their powers depending on his will; such as is the power of a commonwealth. . . .

A multitude of men, are made *one* person, when they are by one man, or one person, represented; so that it be done with the consent of every one of that multitude in particular. For it is the *unity* of the representer, not the *unity* of the represented, that maketh the person *one*. And it is the representer that beareth the person, and but one person: and *unity*, cannot otherwise be understood in multitude.

And because the multitude naturally is not *one*, but *many*; they cannot be understood for one; but many authors, of every thing their representative saith, or doth in their name; every man giving their common representer, authority from himself in particular; and owning all the actions the representer doth, in case they give him authority without stint: otherwise, when they limit him in what, and how far he shall represent them, none of them owneth more than they gave him commission to act.

And if the representative consist of many men, the voice of the greater number, must be considered as the voice of them all. For if the lesser number pronounce, for example, in the affirmative, and the greater in the negative, there will be negatives more than enough to destroy the affirmatives; and thereby the excess of negatives, standing uncontradicted, are the only voice the representative hath.

The final cause, end, or design of men, who naturally love liberty, and dominion over others, in the introduction of that restraint upon themselves, in which we see them live in commonwealths, is the foresight of their own preservation, and of a more contented life thereby; that is to say, of getting themselves out from that miserable condition of war, which is necessarily consequent to the natural passions of men, when there is no visible power to keep them in awe, and tie them by fear of punishment to the performance of their convenants, and observation of the laws of nature.

For the laws of nature, as *justice, equity, modesty, mercy,* and, in sum, *doing to others, as we would be done to* of themselves, without the terror of some power, to cause them to be observed, are contrary to our natural passions, that carry us to partiality, pride, revenge, and the like. And covenants, without the sword, are but words, and of no strength to secure a man at all. Therefore notwithstanding the laws of nature (which every one hath then kept, when he has the will to keep them, when he can do it safely) if there be no power erected, or not great enough for our security; every man will, and may lawfully rely on his own strength and art, for caution against all other men. . . .

The only way to erect such a common power, as may be able to defend them from the invasion of foreigners, and the injuries of one another, and thereby to secure them in such sort, as that by their own industry, and by the fruits of the earth, they may nourish themselves and live contentedly; is, to confer all their power and strength upon one man, or upon one assembly of men, that may reduce all their wills, by plurality of voices, unto one will: which is as much as to say, to appoint one man, or assembly of men, to bear their person; and every one to own, and acknowledge himself to be author of whatsoever he that so beareth their person, shall act, or cause to be acted, in those things which concern the common peace and safety; and therein to submit their wills, every one to his will, and their judgments, to his judgment. This is more than consent, or concord; it is a real unity of them all, in one and the same person, made by covenant of every man with every man, in such manner, as if every man should say to every man, *I authorize and give up my right of governing myself, to this man, or to this assembly of men, on this condition, that thou give up thy right to him, and authorize all his actions in like manner.* This done, the multitude so united in one person, is called a COMMONWEALTH, in Latin CIVITAS. This is the generation of that great LEVIATHAN, or rather, to speak more reverently, of that *mortal god,* to which we owe under the *immortal God,* our peace and defence. For by this authority, given him by every particular man in the commonwealth, he hath the use of so much power and strength conferred on him, that by terror thereof, he is enabled to form the wills of them all, to peace at home, and mutual aid against their enemies abroad. And in him consisteth the essence of the commonwealth; which, to define it, is *one person, of whose acts a great multitude, by mutual covenants one with another, have made themselves every one the author, to the end he may use the strength and means of them all, as he shall think expedient, for their peace and common defence.*

And he that carrieth this person, is called SOVEREIGN, and said to have *sovereign power;* and every one besides, his SUBJECT.

The attaining to this sovereign power, is by two ways. One,

by natural force; as when a man maketh his children, to submit themselves, and their children to this government, as being able to destroy them if they refuse; or by war subdueth his enemies to his will, giving them their lives on that condition. The other, is when men agree amongst themselves, to submit to some man, or assembly of men voluntarily, on confidence to be protected by him against all others. This latter, may be called a political commonwealth, or commonwealth by *institution;* and the former, a commonwealth by *acquisition.* And first, I shall speak of a commonwealth by institution.

A *commonwealth* is said to be *instituted* when a *multitude* of men do agree, and *covenant, every one, with every one,* that to whatsoever *man,* or *assembly of men,* shall be given by the major part, the *right to present* the person of them all, that is to say, to be their *representative;* every one, as well he that *voted for it,* as he that *voted against it,* shall *authorize* all the actions and judgments, of that man, or assembly of men, in the same manner, as if they were his own, to the end, to live peaceably amongst themselves, and be protected against other men.

From this institution of a commonwealth are derived all the *rights,* and *faculties* of him, or them, on whom the sovereign power is conferred by the consent of the people assembled.

First, because they covenant, it is to be understood, they are not obliged by former covenant to any thing repugnant hereunto. And consequently they that have already instituted a commonwealth, being thereby bound by covenant, to own the actions and judgments of one, cannot lawfully make a new covenant, amongst themselves, to be obedient to any other, in any thing whatsoever, without his permission. And therefore, they that are subjects to a monarch, cannot without his leave cast off monarchy, and return to the confusion of a disunited multitude; nor transfer their person from him that beareth it, to another man, or other assembly of men: for they are bound, every man to every man, to own, and be reputed author of all, that he that already is their sovereign, shall do, and judge fit to be done: so that any one man dissenting, all the rest should break their covenant made to that man, which is injustice: and they have also every man given the sovereignty to him that beareth their person; and therefore if they depose him, they take from him that which is his own, and so again it is injustice. Besides, if he that attempteth to depose his sovereign, be killed, or punished by him for such attempt, he is author of his own punishment, as being by the institution, author of all his sovereign shall do:

and because it is injustice for a man to do any thing, for which he may be punished by his own authority, he is also upon that title, unjust. And whereas some men have pretended for their disobedience to their sovereign, a new covenant, made, not with men, but with God; this also is unjust: for there is no covenant with God, but by mediation of somebody that representeth God's person; which none doth but God's lieutenant, who hath the sovereignty under God. But this pretence of covenant with God, is so evident a lie, even in the pretenders' own consciences, that it is not only an act of an unjust, but also of a vile, and unmanly disposition.

The opinion that any monarch receiveth his power by covenant, that is to say, on condition, proceedeth from want of understanding this easy truth, that covenants being but words and breath, have no force to oblige, contain, constrain, or protect any man, but what it has from the public sword; that is, from the united hands of that man, or assembly of men that hath the sovereignty, and whose actions are avouched by them all, and performed by the strength of them all, in him united. . . .

And whether a man be of the congregation, or not; and whether his consent be asked, or not, he must either submit to their decrees, or be left in the condition of war he was in before; wherein he might without injustice be destroyed by any man whatsoever.

. . . No man that hath sovereign power can justly be put to death, or otherwise in any manner by his subjects punished. For seeing every subject is author of the actions of his sovereign; he punisheth another for the actions committed by himself.

So that it appeareth plainly, to my understanding, both from reason, and Scripture, that the sovereign power, whether placed in one man, as in monarchy, or in one assembly of men, as in popular, and aristocratical commonwealths, is as great, as possibly men can be imagined to make it. And though of so unlimited a power, men may fancy many evil consequences, yet the consequences of the want of it, which is perpetual war of every man against his neighbour, are much worse. The condition of man in this life shall never be without inconveniences; but there happeneth in no commonwealth any great inconvenience, but what proceeds from the subject's disobedience, and breach of those covenants, from which the commonwealth hath its being. And whosoever thinking sovereign power too great, will seek to make it less, must subject himself, to the power, that can limit it; that is to say, to a greater.

The greatest objection is, that of the practice; when men ask, where, and when, such power has by subjects been acknowledged. But one may ask them again, when, or where has there been a kingdom long free from sedition and civil war. In those nations, whose commonwealths have been long-lived, and not been destroyed but by foreign war, the subjects never did dispute of the sovereign power. But howsoever, an argument from the practice of men, that have not sifted to the bottom, and with exact reason weighed the causes, and nature of commonwealths, and suffer daily those miseries, that proceed from the ignorance thereof, is invalid. For though in all places of the world, men should lay the foundation of their houses on the sand, it could not thence be inferred, that so it ought to be. The skill of making, and maintaining commonwealths, consisteth in certain rules, as doth arithmetic and geometry; not, as tennis-play, on practice only: which rules, neither poor men have the leisure, nor men that have had the leisure, have hitherto had the curiosity, or the method to find out.

(Extracts from Part I, chapters 10, 16; Part II, chapters 17 and 18.)

Liberty and Law

LIBERTY, or FREEDOM, signifieth, properly, the absence of opposition; by opposition, I mean external impediments of motion. . . .

A FREEMAN, *is he, that in those things, which by his strength and wit he is able to do, is not hindered to do what he has a will to* . . . from the use of the word *free-will*, no liberty can be inferred of the will, desire, or inclination, but the liberty of the man; which consisteth in this, that he finds no stop, in doing what he has the will, desire, or inclination to do.

Fear and liberty are consistent. . . . And generally all actions which men do in commonwealths, for *fear* of the law, are actions, which the doers had *liberty* to omit.

Liberty, and *necessity* are consistent . . . in the actions which men voluntarily do: which, because they proceed from their will, proceed from *liberty;* and yet, because every act of man's will, and every desire, and inclination proceedeth from some cause, and that from another cause, in a continual chain, whose first link is in the hand of God the first of all causes, proceed from *necessity.* . . .

But as men, for the attaining of peace, and conservation of themselves thereby, have made an artificial man, which we call a commonwealth; so also have they made artificial chains, called *civil laws*, which they themselves, by mutual covenants, have fastened at one end, to the lips of that man, or assembly, to whom they have given the sovereign power; and at the other end to their own ears. These bonds, in their own nature but weak, may nevertheless be made to hold, by the danger, though not by the difficulty of breaking them. . . .

. . . The laws are of no power to protect them, without a sword in the hands of a man, or men, to cause those laws to be put in execution. The liberty of a subject, lieth therefore only in those things, which in regulating their actions, the sovereign hath prætermitted: such as is the liberty to buy, and sell, and otherwise contract with one another; to choose their own abode, their own diet, their own trade of life, and institute their children as they themselves think fit; and the like.

Nevertheless we are not to understand, that by such liberty, the sovereign power of life and death, is either abolished, or limited . . . nothing the sovereign representative can do to a subject, on what pretence soever, can properly be called injustice, or injury; because every subject is author of every act the sovereign doth; so that he never wanteth right to any thing, otherwise, than as he himself is the subject of God, and bound thereby to observe the laws of nature.

. . . To come now to the particulars of the true liberty of a subject; that is to say, what are the things, which though commanded by the sovereign, he may nevertheless, without injustice, refuse to do; we are to consider, what rights we pass away, when we make a commonwealth; or, which is all one, what liberty we deny ourselves, by owning all the actions, without exception, of the man, or assembly we make our sovereign. For in the act of our *submission*, consisteth both our *obligation*, and our *liberty;* which must therefore be inferred by arguments taken from thence; there being no obligation on any man, which ariseth not from some act of his own; for all men equally, are by nature free. And because such arguments, must either be drawn from the express words, *I authorize all his actions*, or from the intention of him that submitteth himself to his power, which intention is to be understood by the end for which he so submitteth; the obligation, and liberty of the subject, is to be derived, either from those words, or others equivalent; or else from the end of the institution of sovereignty, namely, the peace of the subjects within themselves, and their defence against a common enemy.

. . . [Subjects have liberty to defend their own bodies, and are not bound to hurt themselves or to be a soldier]. . . . As for other liberties, they depend on the silence of the law. In cases where the sovereign has prescribed no rule, there the subject hath the liberty to do, or forbear, according to his own discretion. And therefore such liberty is in some places more, and in some less; and in some times more, in other times less, according as they that have the sovereignty shall think most convenient.

The obligation of subjects to the sovereign, is understood to last as long, and no longer, than the power lasteth, by which he is able to protect them. For the right men have by nature to protect themselves, when none else can protect them, can by no covenant be relinquished. The sovereignty is the soul of the commonwealth; which once departed from the body, the members do no more receive their motion from it. The end of the obedience is protection; which, wheresoever a man seeth it, either in his own, or in another's sword, nature applieth his obedience to it, and his endeavour to maintain it. And though sovereignty, in the intention of them that make it, be immortal; yet is it in its own nature, not only subject to violent death, by foreign war; but also through the ignorance, and passions of men, it hath in it, from the very institution, many seeds of a natural mortality, by intestine discord.

(Extract from Part II, chapter 21.)

The Sovereign Power

. . . And as the power, so also the honour of the sovereign, ought to be greater, than that of any, or all the subjects. For in the sovereignty is the fountain of honour. The dignities of lord, earl, duke, and prince are his creatures. As in the presence of the master, the servants are equal, and without any honour at all; so are the subjects, in the presence of the sovereign. And though they shine some more, some less, when they are out of his sight; yet in his presence, they shine no more than the stars in the presence of the sun.

But a man may here object, that the condition of subjects is very miserable . . . not considering that the state of man can never be without some incommodity or other; and that the greatest, that in any form of government can possibly happen to the people in general, is scarce sensible in respect of the miseries, and horrible calamities, that accompany a civil war, or that dissolute condition of masterless men, without subjection to laws, and a coercive power to tie their hands from rapine and revenge: nor considering that the greatest pressure of sovereign governors, proceedeth not from any delight, or profit they can expect in the damage or weakening of their subjects, in whose vigour, consisteth their own strength and glory; but in the restiveness of themselves, that unwillingly contributing to their own defence, make it necessary for their governors to draw from them what they can in time of peace, that they may have means on any emergent occasion, or sudden need, to resist, or take advantage on their enemies. . . .

. . . But the rights, and consequences of sovereignty, are the same in both. His power cannot, without his consent, be transferred to another: he cannot forfeit it: he cannot be accused by any of his subjects, of injury: he cannot be punished by them: he is judge of what is necessary for peace; and judge of doctrines: he is sole legislator; and supreme judge of controversies; and of the times, and occasions of war, and peace: to him it belongeth to choose magistrates, counsellors, commanders, and all other officers, and ministers; and to determine of rewards, and punishments, honour, and order.

By civil laws, I understand the laws, that men are therefore bound to observe, because they are members, not of this, or that commonwealth in particular, but of a commonwealth. For the knowledge of particular laws belongeth to them, that profess the study of the laws of their several countries; but the knowledge of civil law in general, to any man. . . .

. . . And first it is manifest, that law in general, is not counsel, but command; nor a command of any man to any man; but only of him, whose command is addressed to one formerly obliged to obey him.

Which considered, I define civil law in this manner. CIVIL LAW, *is to every subject, those rules, which the commonwealth hath commanded him, by word, writing, or other sufficient sign of the will, to make use of, for the distinction of right, and wrong; that is to say, of what is contrary, and what is not contrary to the rule.* . . .

The legislator in all commonwealths, is only the sovereign, be he one man, as in a monarchy, or one assembly of men, as in a democracy, or aristocracy . . . none can abrogate a law made, but the sovereign; because a law is not abrogated, but by another law, that forbiddeth it to be put in execution.

The sovereign of a commonwealth, be it an assembly, or one man, is not subject to the civil laws. For having power to make, and repeal laws, he may when he pleaseth, free himself from that subjection, by repealing those laws that trouble him, and making of new; and consequently he was free before.

. . . The law of nature is a part of the civil law in all

commonwealths of the world. Reciprocally also, the civil law is a part of the dictates of nature. For justice, that is to say, performance of covenant, and giving to every man his own, is a dictate of the law of nature. But every subject in a commonwealth, hath covenanted to obey the civil law; either one with another, as when they assemble to make a common representative, or with the representative itself one by one, when subdued by the sword they promise obedience, that they may receive life; and therefore obedience to the civil law is part also of the law of nature. Civil, and natural law are not different kinds, but different parts of law; whereof one part being written, is called civil the other unwritten, natural.

. . . It is not that *juris prudentia*, or wisdom of subordinate judges; but the reason of this our artificial man the commonwealth, and his command, that maketh law: and the commonwealth being in their representative but one person, there cannot easily arise any contradiction in the laws; and when there doth, the same reason is able, by interpretation, or alteration, to take it away. In all courts of justice, the sovereign, which is the person of the commonwealth, is he that judgeth: the subordinate judge, ought to have regard to the reason, which moved his sovereign to make such law, that his sentence may be according thereunto; which then is his sovereign's sentence; otherwise it is his own, and an unjust one.

. . . The *diseases* of a commonwealth, that proceed from the poison of seditious doctrines, where of one is, *That every private man is judge of good and evil actions.* This is true in the condition of mere nature, where there are no civil laws; and also under civil government, in such cases as are not determined by the law. But otherwise, it is manifest, that the measure of good and evil actions, is the civil law; and the judge the legislator, who is always representative of the commonwealth. From this false doctrine, men are disposed to debate with themselves, and dispute the commands of the commonwealth; and afterwards to obey, or disobey them, as in their private judgments they shall think fit; whereby the commonwealth is distracted and *weakened.*

Another doctrine repugnant to civil society, is, that *whatsoever a man does against his conscience, is sin;* and it dependeth on the presumption of making himself judge of good and evil. For a man's conscience, and his judgment is the same thing, and as the judgment, so also the conscience may be erroneous. Therefore, though he that is subject to no civil law, sinneth in all he does against his conscience, because he has no other rule to follow but his own reason; yet it is not so with him that lives in a commonwealth; because the law is the public conscience, by which he hath already undertaken to be guided. Otherwise in such diversity, as there is of private consciences, which are but private opinions, the commonwealth must needs be distracted, and no man dare to obey the sovereign power, further than it shall seem good in his own eyes.

To the care of the sovereign, belongeth the making of good laws. But what is a good law? By a good law, I mean not a just law: for no law can be unjust. The law is made by the sovereign power, and all that is done by such power, is warranted, and owned by every one of the people; and that which every man will have so, no man can say is unjust. It is in the laws of a commonwealth, as in the laws of gaming: whatsoever the gamesters all agree on, is injustice to none of them. A good law is that, which is *needful*, for the *good of the people*, and withal *perspicuous*.

For the use of laws, which are but rules authorized, is not to bind the people from all voluntary actions; but to direct and keep them in such motion, as not to hurt themselves by their own impetuous desires, rashness or indiscretion; as hedges are set, not to stop travellers, but to keep them in their way. And therefore a law that is not needful, having not the true end of a law, is not good. A law may be conceived to be good, when it is for the benefit of the sovereign; though it be not necessary for the people; but it is not so. For the good of the sovereign and people, cannot be separated. It is a weak sovereign, that has weak subjects; and a weak people, whose sovereign wanteth power to rule them at his will. Unnecessary laws are not good laws; but traps for money: which where the right of sovereign power is acknowledged, are superfluous; and where it is not acknowledged, insufficient to defend the people.

. . . But seeing a commonwealth is but one person, it ought also to exhibit to God but one worship; which then it doth, when it commandeth it to be exhibited by private men, publicly. And this is public worship; the property whereof, is to be *uniform:* for those actions that are done differently, by different men, cannot be said to be a public worship. And therefore, where many sorts of worship be allowed, proceeding from the different religion of private men, it cannot be said there is any public worship, nor that the commonwealth is of any religion at all.

And because a commonwealth hath no will, nor makes no laws, but those that are made by the will of him, or them that have the sovereign power; it followeth that those attributes which the sovereign ordaineth, in the worship of God, for signs of honour, ought to be taken and used for such, by private men in their public worship.

For when Christian men, take not their Christian sovereign, for God's prophet; they must either take their own dreams, for the prophecy they mean to be governed by, and the tumour of their own hearts for the Spirit of God; or they must suffer themselves to be led by some strange prince; or by some of their fellow-subjects, that can bewitch them, by slander of the government, into rebellion, without other miracle to confirm their calling, than sometimes an extraordinary success and impunity; and by this means destroying all laws, both divine and human, reduce all order, government, and society, to the first chaos of violence and civil war.

. . . The right of judging what doctrines are fit for peace, and to be taught the subjects, is in all commonwealths inseparably annexed to the sovereign power civil, whether it be in one man, or in one assembly of men. For it is evident to the meanest capacity, that men's actions are derived from the opinions they have of the good or evil, which from those actions redound unto themselves; and consequently, men that are once possessed of an opinion, that their obedience to the sovereign power will be more hurtful to them than their disobedience, will disobey the laws, and thereby overthrow the commonwealth, and introduce confusion and civil war; for the avoiding whereof, all civil government was ordained.

And therefore Christian kings are the supreme pastors of their people, and have power to ordain what pastors they please, to teach the Church, that is, to teach the people committed to their charge.

. . . The members of every commonwealth depend only on the sovereign, which is the soul of the commonwealth; which failing, the commonwealth is dissolved into a civil war, no one man so much as cohering to another, for want of a common dependence on a known sovereign; just as the members of the natural body dissolve into earth, for want of a soul to hold them together. Therefore there is nothing in this similitude, from whence to infer a dependence of the laity on the clergy, or of the temporal officers on the spiritual; but of both on the civil sovereign; which ought indeed to direct his civil commands to the salvation of souls; but is not therefore subject to any but God himself.

(Extracts from Part II, chapters 18, 26, 29, 30, 31, 36, 42.)

SPINOZA

Tractatus Theologico-Politicus and Tractatus Politicus

Natural Right and the State

. . . Nature has sovereign right to do anything she can; in other words, her right is co-extensive with her power. The power of nature is the power of God, which has sovereign right over all things . . . it follows that every individual has sovereign right to do all that he can; in other words, the rights of an individual extend to the utmost limits of his power as it has been conditioned. Now it is the sovereign law and right of nature that each individual should endeavour to preserve itself as it is, without regard to anything but itself; therefore this sovereign law and right belongs to every individual, namely, to exist and act according to its natural conditions.

The natural right of the individual man is thus determined, not by sound reason, but by desire and power. All are not naturally conditioned so as to act according to the laws and rules of reason; nay, on the contrary, all men are born ignorant, and before they can learn the right way of life and acquire the habit of virtue, the greater part of their life, even if they have been well brought up, has passed away. Nevertheless, they are in the meanwhile bound to live and preserve themselves as far as they can by the unaided impulses of desire. Nature has given them no other guide, and has denied them the present power of living according to sound reason; so that they are no more bound to live by the dictates of an enlightened mind, than a cat is bound to live by the laws of the nature of a lion.

Whatsoever, therefore, an individual . . . thinks useful for himself, whether led by sound reason or impelled by the passions, that he has a sovereign right to seek and to take for himself as he best can, whether by force, cunning, entreaty, or any other means; consequently he may regard as an enemy anyone who hinders the accomplishment of his purpose.

. . . Men must necessarily come to an agreement to live together as securely and well as possible if they are to enjoy as a whole the rights which naturally belong to them as individuals, and their life should be no more conditioned by the force and desire of individuals, but by the power and will of the whole body. This end they will be unable to attain if desire be their only guide (for by the laws of desire each man is drawn in a different direction); they must, therefore, most firmly decree and establish that they will be guided in everything by reason (which no will dare openly to repudiate lest he should be taken for a madman), and will restrain any desire which is injurious to a man's fellows, that they will do to all as they would be done by, and that they will defend their neighbour's rights as their own.

. . . If each individual hands over the whole of his power to the body politic, the latter will then possess sovereign natural right over all things; that is, it will have sole and unquestioned dominion, and everyone will be bound to obey, under pain of the severest punishment. A body politic of this kind is called a Democracy, which may be defined as a society which wields all its power as a whole. The sovereign power is not restrained by any laws, but everyone is bound to obey it in all things; such is the state of things implied when men either tacitly or expressly handed over to it all their power of self-defence, or in other words, all their right. For if they had wished to retain any right for themselves, they ought to have taken precautions for its defence and preservation; as they have not done so, and indeed could not have done so without dividing and consequently ruining the state, they placed themselves absolutely at the mercy of the sovereign power; and, therefore, having acted as reason and necessity demanded, they are obliged to fulfill the commands of the sovereign power, however absurd these may be, else they will be public enemies, and will act against reason, which urges the preservation of the state as a primary duty. For reason bids us choose the lesser of two evils. . . .

. . . Action in obedience to orders does take away freedom in a certain sense, but it does not, therefore, make a man a slave, all depends on the object of the action. If the object of the action be the good of the state, and not the good of the agent, the latter is a slave and does himself no good; but in a Commonwealth and Dominion . . . where the weal of the whole people, and not that of the ruler, is the supreme law, obedience to the sovereign power does not make a man a slave, of no use to himself, but a subject. Therefore, that state is the freest whose laws are founded on sound reason, so that every member of it may, if he will, be free; that is, live with full consent under the entire guidance of reason.

. . . No one can ever so utterly transfer to another his power and, consequently, his rights, as to cease to be a man; nor can there ever be a power so sovereign that it can carry out every possible wish. It will always be vain to order a subject to hate what he believes brings him advantage, or to love what brings him loss, or not to be offended at insults, or not to wish to be free from fear, or a hundred other things of the sort, which necessarily follow from the laws of human nature.

. . . That the preservation of a state chiefly depends on the subjects' fidelity and constancy in carrying out the orders they receive, is most clearly taught both by reason and experience; how subjects ought to be guided so as best to preserve their fidelity and virtue is not so obvious. All, both rulers and ruled, are men, and prone to follow after their lusts. The fickle disposition of the multitude almost reduces those who have experience of it to despair, for it is governed solely by emotions, not by reason: it rushes headlong into every enterprise, and is easily corrupted either by avarice or luxury: everyone thinks himself omniscient and wishes to fashion all things to his liking, judging a thing to be just or unjust, lawful or unlawful, according as he thinks it will bring him profit or loss: vanity leads him to despise his equals, and refuse their guidance: envy of superior fame or fortune (for such gifts are never equally distributed) leads him to desire and rejoice in his neighbour's downfall.

. . . To guard against all these evils, and form a dominion where no room is left for deceit; to frame our institutions so that every man, whatever his disposition, may prefer public right to private advantage, this is the task and this the toil.

(Extracts from *Tractatus Theologico-Politicus,* chapters 16 and 17.)

. . . Men are more led by blind desire, than by reason: and therefore the natural power or right of human beings should be limited, not by reason, but by every appetite, whereby they are determined to action, or seek their own preservation. I, for my part, admit, that those desires, which arise not from reason, are not so much actions as passive affections (*passiones*) of man. But as we are treating here of the universal power or right of nature, we cannot here recognize any distinction between desires, which are engendered in us by reason, and those which are engendered by other causes; since the latter, as much as the former, are effects of nature, and display the natural impulse, by which man strives to continue in existence . . . man . . . is part of nature, and everything . . . ought to be referred to the power of nature . . .

. . . So long as the natural right of man is determined by the power of every individual, and belongs to everyone, so long it is a nonentity, existing in opinion rather than fact, as there is no assurance of making it good. And it is certain that the greater cause of fear every individual has, the less power, and consequently the less right, he possesses. To this must be added, that without mutual help men can hardly support life and cultivate the mind. And so our conclusion is, that that natural right, which is special to the human race, can hardly be conceived, except where men have general rights and combine to defend the possession of the lands they inhabit and cultivate, to protect themselves, to repel all violence, and to live according to the general judgment of all. For the more there are that combine together, the more right they collectively possess.

. . . Every citizen depends not on himself, but on the commonwealth, all whose commands he is bound to execute, and has no right to decide, what is equitable or iniquitous, just or unjust. But, on the contrary, as the body of the dominion should, so to speak, be guided by one mind, and consequently the will of the commonwealth must be taken to the will of all; what the state decides to be just and good must be held to be so decided by every individual. And so, however iniquitous the subject may think the commonwealth's decisions, he is none the less bound to execute them.

. . . Reason altogether teaches to seek peace, and peace cannot be maintained, unless the commonwealth's general laws be kept unbroken. And so, the more a man is guided by reason, the more he is free, the more constantly he will keep the laws of the commonwealth, and execute the commands of the supreme authority, whose subject he is. Furthermore, the civil state is naturally ordained to remove general fear, and prevent general sufferings, and therefore pursues above everything the very end, after which everyone, who is led by reason, strives, but in the natural state strives vainly.

. . . Wherefore, if a man who is led by reason, has sometimes to do by the commonwealth's order what he knows to be repugnant to reason, that harm is far compensated by the good, which he derives from the existence of a civil state. For it is reason's own law, to choose the less of two evils.

. . . As in the state of nature the man who is led by reason is most powerful and most independent, so too that commonwealth will be most powerful and most independent, which is founded and guided by reason. For the right of the commonwealth is determined by the power of the multitude, which is led, as it were, by one mind. But this unity of mind can in no wise be conceived, unless the commonwealth pursues chiefly the very end, which sound reason teaches is to the interest of all men. . . .

. . . Such things, as no one can be induced to do by rewards or threats, do not fall within the rights of the commonwealth.

For instance, by reason of his faculty of judgment, it is in no man's power to believe.

. . . Thirdly and lastly, it comes to be considered, that those things are not so much within the commonwealth's right, which cause indignation in the majority. For it is certain, that by the guidance of nature men conspire together, either through common fear, or with the desire to avenge some common hurt; and as the right of the commonwealth is determined by the common power of the multitude, it is certain that the power and right of the commonwealth are so far diminished, as it gives occasion for many to conspire together.

(Extracts from *Tractatus Politicus,* chapters 2 and 3.)

Freedom of the Citizen

. . . No man's mind can possibly lie wholly at the disposition of another, for no one can willingly transfer his natural right of free reason and judgment, or be compelled so to do. For this reason government which attempts to control minds is accounted tyrannical, and it is considered an abuse of sovereignty and a usurpation of the rights of subjects, to seek to prescribe what shall be accepted as true, or rejected as false, or what opinions should actuate men in their worship of God. All these questions fall within man's natural right, which he cannot abdicate even with his own consent.

. . . However unlimited, therefore, the power of a sovereign may be, however implicitly it is trusted as the exponent of law and religion, it can never prevent men from forming judgments according to their intellect, or being influenced by any given emotion. It is true that it has the right to treat as enemies all men whose opinions do not, on all subjects, entirely coincide with its own; but we are not discussing its strict rights, but its proper course of action. I grant that it has the right to rule in the most violent manner, and to put citizens to death for every trivial causes, but no one supposes it can do this with the approval of sound judgment. Nay, inasmuch as such things cannot be done without extreme peril to itself, we may even deny that it has the absolute power to do them, or, consequently, the absolute right; for the rights of the sovereign are limited by his power.

Since, therefore, no one can abdicate his freedom of judgment and feeling; since every man is by indefeasible natural right the master of his own thoughts, it follows that men thinking in diverse and contradictory fashions, cannot, without disastrous results, be compelled to speak only according to the dictates of the supreme power. Not even the most experienced, to say nothing of the multitude, know how to keep silence. Men's common failing is to confide their plans to others, though there be need for secrecy, so that a government would be most harsh which deprived the individual of his freedom of saying and teaching what he thought; and would be moderate if such freedom were granted. . . .

. . . The ultimate aim of government is not to rule, or restrain, by fear, nor to exact obedience, but contrariwise, to free every man from fear, that he may live in all possible security; in other words, to strengthen his natural right to exist and work without injury to himself or others.

No, the object of government is not to change men from rational beings into beasts or puppets, but to enable them to develop their minds and bodies in security, and to employ their reason unshackled; neither showing hatred, anger, or deceit, nor watched with the eyes of jealousy and injustice. In fact, the true aim of government is liberty.

. . . Since men's free judgments are very diverse, each one thinking that he alone knows everything, and although complete unanimity of feeling and speech is out of the question, it is impossible to preserve peace, unless individuals abdicate their right of acting entirely on their own judgment. Therefore, the individual justly cedes the right of free action, though not of free reason and judgment; no one can act against the authorities without danger to the state, though his feelings and judgment may be at variance therewith; he may even speak against them, provided that he does so from rational conviction, not from fraud, anger, or hatred, and provided that he does not attempt to introduce any change on his private authority.

For instance, supposing a man shows that a law is repugnant to sound reason, and should therefore be repealed; if he submits his opinion to the judgment of the authorities (who, alone, have the right of making and repealing laws), and meanwhile acts in nowise contrary to that law, he has deserved well of the state, and has behaved as a good citizen should; but if he accuses the authorities of injustice, and stirs up the people against them, or if he seditiously strives to abrogate the law without their consent, he is a mere agitator and rebel.

Thus we see how an individual may declare and teach what he believes, without injury to the authority of his rulers, or to the public peace; namely, by leaving in their hands the entire power of legislation as it affects action, and by doing nothing against their laws, though he be compelled often to act in contradiction to what he believes, and openly feels, to be best.

(Extract from *Tractatus Theologico-Politicus*, chapter 20.)

The Best State

. . . That dominion is the best, where men pass their lives in unity, and the laws are kept unbroken. For it is certain, that seditions, wars, and contempt or breach of the laws are not so much to be imputed to the wickedness of the subjects, as to the bad state of a dominion. For men are not born fit for citizenship, but must be made so. Besides, men's natural passions are everywhere the same; and if wickedness more prevails, and more offences are committed in one commonwealth than in another, it is certain that the former has not enough pursued the end of unity, nor framed its laws with sufficient forethought; and that, therefore, it has failed in making quite good its right as a commonwealth. . . .

. . . That commonwealth, whose peace depends on the sluggishness of its subjects, that are led about like sheep, to learn but slavery, may more properly be called a desert than a commonwealth. . . .

. . . A free multitude is guided more by hope than fear; a conquered one, more by fear than hope: inasmuch as the former aims at making use of life, the latter but at escaping death. The former, I say, aims at living for its own ends, the latter is forced to belong to the conqueror; and so we say that this is enslaved, but that free.

. . . Yet if slavery, barbarism, and desolation are to be called peace, men can have no worse misfortune. No doubt there are usually more and sharper quarrels between parents and children, than between masters and slaves; yet it advances not the art of housekeeping, to change a father's right into a right of property, and count children but as slaves. Slavery then, not peace, is furthered by handing over to one man the whole authority. For peace, as we said before, consists not in mere absence of war, but in a union or agreement of minds.

(Extracts from *Tractatus Politicus*, chapters 5 and 6.)

SECTION XII

THE DEVELOPMENT
OF CONSTITUTIONALISM

Not all British thinkers took such an exalted view of state power as did Hobbes. Concerned as they were with the need for order, they were still eager to put limits on state authority. The idea of restriction by law, by constitutionalism, was developed by Coke, Harrington, Hooker and Locke.

Coke

Sir Edward Coke (1552–1634), ambitious politician, rival of Bacon in politics as in love, inquisitorial attorney general of Elizabeth, who prosecuted the mighty Essex and Raleigh, the latter with great brutality, chief justice under James I, who had defied the King and then recanted, contributed to the idea of control over arbitrary power.

Both as chief justice of the King's Bench, and as a member of the House of Commons, he opposed the claim of James to divine right. For Coke, the law limited royal authority. With Coke, "the common law took flesh." Neither the King nor Parliament was superior to the law. "In many cases the law will control acts of Parliament and sometimes adjudge them to be utterly void." He resurrected Magna Carta and retranslated it. "No man," he wrote, "shall be imprisoned except by due process of the common law, the native, English law." The moving spirit behind the Petition of Right of 1628, he pleaded against weakening the "foundation of laws," or the building would fall.

Harrington

While Hobbes stood aloof and contemptuous from the problems of Cromwellian England, James Harrington (1611–

1677) threw himself into the fray. Not only in his book, *The Commonwealth of Oceana* in 1656, but in political pamphlets, the formation of clubs, and even a small pressure group in Parliament, he urged the need for certain constitutional devices to prevent absolute government. These included a written constitution, the secret ballot, rotation in public office, and, since he was aware of the relation between wealth and political power, an agrarian law to limit the amount of landed wealth a subject might possess. Above all, Harrington argued for a system of checks and balances. This would be obtained through two elected assemblies, a senate merely debating and proposing measures, and a larger popular assembly, which would vote on them. Oligarchy would therefore be avoided, and no single party could monopolize power. With prophetic insight, he declared, "A commonwealth consisting of a party will be in perpetual labor of her own destruction."

Harrington had great faith in governmental forms, believing that the right machinery would distill "the refined spirit of a nation." From this machinery would follow good laws, military strength and prosperity. "Give us good orders, and they will make us good men." Ever since the days of the early colonies, Harrington has been an attractive and influential writer in the United States.

Hooker

Richard Hooker (1155?–1600), fellow of Oxford and parish priest, wrote the first four books of his *Laws of Ecclesiastical Polity* between 1593 and 1597, reviewing the dispute in the Anglican Church and attempting to justify the persecution of nonconformists. But he went far beyond this propaganda task.

He argued that the universe was pervaded by laws which were rational, and could be found and understood by men's reason. Reason supplemented divine revelation, as natural law —discovered through reason—supplemented divine law. Instead of simply the eternal law of God, there were a series of different kinds of law: natural law, laws of the angels, and human laws which were based on reason. Good laws were the dictates of right reason; their justice depended on conformity to natural law.

Through reason, men understood the need for society. Society was the result of a social contract, philosophic and moral rather than historical. The ruler must act in the public interest, and observe law. Government, as well as society itself, was based on consent, given either by an individual or by his representatives or ancestors. But belonging to a state implied obedience to the laws, "the deed of the whole body politic." This obedience included ecclesiastical as well as secular laws, for disobedience to both would undermine society. The Anglican Church and its laws were the laws of God and of reason; they were to be guarded by the ruler. Laws might be changed, but only by "the authors themselves," not by individual or group opposition.

In Hooker can be traced a diversity of intellectual debts. He fused Aristotle's social nature of man, the Stoic universal law, the Christian view of governmental institutions as the remedy for sin, Rome's concept of sovereignty, feudal contractual relations, and the Conciliar view of community authority. He combined theories of sovereignty and the rule of law. The king's power was based on and limited by law, and the authority of the "whole entire body" of the community. Yet it is not clear how the limits were to be enforced.

Locke

From Hooker—for him always "the judicious Hooker"—John Locke drew his ideas on law and his view of government as a delegated power responsible to the whole community. Locke (1632–1704), the son of a lawyer who had fought for Parliament in the Civil War, became physician in 1666 to the prominent politician Ashley, later Earl of Shaftesbury. The latter introduced him to the political world, and its occupational and geographical hazards. During one of his periods of political exile, he lived in Holland, becoming acquainted with William of Orange, soon to ascend the British throne in 1689 as William III. In 1690, he published his *Essay Concerning Human Understanding* and the *Two Treatises of Civil Government*.

Locke's whole political thinking was a generalization about the value of the 1688 Revolution. Neither glorious nor a revolution, the transfer of power to William III introduced the idea of limited monarchy in an age weary of civil war and of persecution, in a period when colonial expansion and a banking system were both developing. Locke's little read *First Treatise* was an attack on the divine right and heredity concepts of Filmer. His *Second Treatise* was, in effect, a tacit reply to Hobbes.

In all his fields of inquiry—politics, education, theology and philosophy—Locke emphasized the importance of reason, toleration and moderation. Knowledge was not innate, nor revealed, nor did it rest on authority. It consisted of seeing relations among ideas derived from sense experience. Because of the limitation of the human understanding, one could talk only about probability, not about certainty. But this did not imply a need for an absolute power such as Hobbes advocated.

The state of nature was not a state of strife, but was based on law, reason and equality. Natural law, a rational law, sought the peace and preservation of all mankind; the natural rights of men were life, liberty and property, respected by all. But the inconveniences of the state of nature led to the formation of a political society. For Hobbes, any state was better than anarchy. For Locke, the state of nature was not worse than the worst government, and therefore the state must produce certain benefits, and "a standing rule to live by." The social contract was made for safe and peaceful living, and secure enjoyment of property. It was a contract made among equals to create a society, and then between the society created and the ruler. Power came from the people; rulers were agents acting for the common good. Law was rooted in common consent, which in practice meant majority will, not unanimity. Supreme power, the power of the whole community, was found in the will of society as expressed in law having the sanction of the majority, and executed by agents.

Not only did Locke stress consent as the basis of political power. He also suggested restraints on the power of the majority, to prevent violation of laws of nature, property rights, the inalienable rights of men, or anything in the fundamental compact. The function of the state was limited to stated purposes. Power was held in trust and government ought to be dissolved if it was not serving the purpose for which it had been established. Rebellion was justified, but only after a long train of abuses, not over every little mismanagement.

An eclectic writer, Locke joined together what may seem to be conflicting concepts: the supremacy of parliament, legislative supremacy, majority rule, the consent of the governed, law as a standing rule. He was aware of the connection between property and power. The citizen was the man of property, even if his property might be limited. Political rights were not bestowed on the propertyless. Political systems were organized by and liberty preserved by a separation of powers among the legislative, executive and federative branches. Locke was not a democrat in the contemporary sense, but he has probably been the most influential philosopher of democratic constitutionalism.

HARRINGTON
The Commonwealth of Oceana

The Economic Basis of Politics

. . . Government (to define it *de jure* or according to ancient prudence) is an art whereby a civil society of men is instituted and preserved upon the foundation of common right or interest; it is the empire of laws and not of men.

And government (to define it *de facto* or according to modern prudence) is an art whereby some man, or some few men, subject a city or a nation and rule it according to his or their private interest, which, because the laws in such cases are made according to the interest of a man, or of some few families, may be said to be the empire of men and not of laws.

. . . To go my own way and yet to follow the ancients, the principles of governments are twofold: internal, or the "goods of the mind"; and external, or the "goods of fortune." The goods of the mind are natural or acquired virtues, as wisdom, prudence, and courage, etc. The goods of fortune are riches. There be goods also of the body, as health, beauty, strength; but these are not to be brought to account upon this score, because if a man or an army acquire victory or empire it is more from their discipline, arms, and courage than from their natural health, beauty, or strength, [which is seen in the fact] that a people conquered may have more of natural strength, beauty, and health, and yet find little remedy. The principles of government, then, are in the goods of the mind or in the goods of fortune. To the goods of the mind [corresponds] authority; to the goods of fortune, power or empire. . . .

Lands, or the parts and parcels of a territory, are held by the proprietor or proprietors, lord or lords of it, in some proportion; and such (except it be in a city that has little or no land and whose revenue is in trade) as in the proportion or balance of dominion or property in land, such is the nature of the empire.

If one man be sole landlord of a territory, or overbalance the people, for example, three parts in four, he is *Grand Signior:* for so the Turk is called from his property; and his empire is absolute monarchy.

If the few or a nobility, or a nobility with the clergy be landlords, or overbalance the people unto the like proportion, it makes the Gothic balance, and the empire is mixed monarchy, as that of Spain, Poland, and late of Oceana.

And if the whole people be landlords, or hold the lands so divided among them that no one man or number of men within the compass of the few or aristocracy overbalance them, the empire (without the interposition of force) is a commonwealth. . . .

As first, where a nobility holds half the property, or about that proportion, and the people the other half; in which case, without altering the balance, there is no remedy but the one must eat out the other, as the people did the nobility in Athens, and the nobility the people in Rome. Secondly, when a prince holds about half the dominion and the people the other half, which was the case of the Roman emperors, planted partly upon their military colonies and partly upon the Senate and the people, the government becomes a very shambles both of the princes and the people. Somewhat of this nature are certain governments at this day which are said to subsist by confusion. In this case, to fix the balance is to entail misery; but, in the three former, not to fix it is to loose the government. . . . This kind of law fixing the balance in lands is called "Agrarian," and was first introduced by God himself, who divided the land of Canaan unto his people by lots, and is of such virtue that wherever it has held, that government has not altered except by consent, as in that unparalleled example of the people of Israel when, being in liberty, they would needs choose a king. But without an Agrarian, government, whether monarchical, aristocratical, or popular, has no long lease.

For dominion, personal or in money, it may now and then stir up a Melius or a Manlius which, if the commonwealth be not provided with some kind of dictatorian power, may be dangerous, though it has been seldom or never successful: because unto property producing empire, it is required that it should have some certain root or foothold which, except in land, it cannot have, being otherwise, as it were, upon the wing.

Nevertheless, in such cities as subsist most by trade and have little or no land, as Holland and Genoa, the balance of treasure may be equal to that of land in the cases mentioned.

But Hobbes . . . has caught hold of the public sword, to which he reduces all manner and matter of government, as where he affirms this opinion (that any monarch receives his power by covenant, that is to say, upon conditions) "to proceed from the not understanding the easy truth that covenants, being but words and breath, have no power to oblige, contain, constrain, or protect any man, [save] what they have from the public sword." But, as he said of the law: that without this sword it is but paper, so might he have thought of this sword, that without a hand it is but cold iron. The hand which holds this sword is the militia of a nation, and the militia of a nation is either an army in the field or ready for the field upon occasion. But an army is a beast that has a great belly and must be fed; wherefore this will come unto what pastures you have, and what pastures you have will come unto the balance of property, without which the public sword is but a name or mere spit-frog. Wherefore, to set that which Hobbes says of arms and of contracts a little straighter, he that can graze this beast with the great belly as the Turk does his timariots may well deride him that imagines he received his power by covenant or is obliged unto any such toy: it being in *this* case only that covenants are but words and breath. But if the property of the nobility stocked with their tenants and retainers be the pasture of that beast, the ox knows his master's crib, and it is impossible for a king in such a constitution to reign otherwise than by covenant; or if he break it, it is words that come to blows.

By what has been said, it should seem that we may lay aside further disputes of the public sword, or of the right of the militia, which, be the government what it will or let it change how it can, is inseparable from the overbalance in dominion. Nor, if otherwise stated by the law or custom, as in the commonwealth of Rome . . . where the people having the sword the nobility came to have the overbalance, avails it to other end than destruction. For, as a building swaying from the foundation must fall, so the law swaying from reason, and the militia from the balance of dominion [must also fall]. And so much for the balance of national or domestic empire which is in dominion.

Laws and Restraints

. . . The soul of man (whose life or motion is perpetual contemplation or thought) is the mistress of two potent rivals, the one reason, the other passion, that are in continual suit. And according as she gives up her will to these or either of them is the felicity or misery which man partakes in this mortal life.

For as whatever was passion in the contemplation of a man, being brought forth by his will into action, is vice and the bondage of sin, so whatever was reason in the contemplation of man, being brought forth by his will into action, is virtue and freedom of soul.

Again, as those actions of a man that were sin acquire unto

himself repentance or shame, and affect others with scorn or pity, so those actions of a man that are virtue acquire unto himself honor, and upon others *authority*.

Now government is no other than the soul of a city or nation. Wherefore that which was reason in the debate of a commonwealth, being brought forth by the result, must be virtue. And [in] as much as the soul of a city or nation is the sovereign power, her virtues must be law. But the government whose *law* is *virtue*, and whose *virtue* is *law*, is the same whose *empire* is *authority*, and whose *authority* is *empire*.

Again, if the liberty of a man consist in the empire of his reason, the absence whereof would betray him unto the bondage of his passions, then the liberty of a commonwealth consists in the empire of her laws, the absence whereof would betray her unto the lusts of tyrants. And these I conceive to be the principles upon which Aristotle and Livy (injuriously accused by Hobbes for not writing out of nature) have grounded their assertion that a "commonwealth is an empire of laws and not of men." But they must not carry it so. "For," says Hobbes, "the liberty whereof there is so frequent and honorable mention in the histories and philosophy of the ancient Greeks and Romans, and the writings and discourses of those that from them have received all their learning in the politics, is not the liberty of particular men, but the liberty of the commonwealth."

He might as well have said that the estates of particular men in a commonwealth are not the riches of particular men but the riches of the commonwealth, for equality of estates causes equality of power, and equality of power is the liberty not only of the commonwealth but of every man. . . .

. . . But seeing they that make the laws in commonwealths are but men, the main question seems to be how a commonwealth comes to be an empire of laws and not of men; or how the debate or result of a commonwealth is so sure to be according unto reason, seeing they who debate and they who resolve be but men. . . .

For be it so that reason is nothing but interest, there be divers interests and so divers reasons.

As first, there is *private reason* which is the interest of a private man.

Secondly, there is *reason of state*, which is the interest . . . of the ruler or rulers; that is to say, of the prince, of the nobility, or of the people.

Thirdly, there is that reason which is *the interest of mankind* or of the whole.

. . . And if reason be nothing else but interest, and the

interest of mankind be the right interest, then the reason of mankind must be right reason. Now compute well, for if the *interest of popular government* come the nearest unto the *interest of mankind,* then the *reason of popular government* must come the nearest unto *right reason.* . . .

. . . An equal commonwealth is such a one as is equal, both in the balance and foundation in the superstructures; that is to say, in her Agrarian Law and in her rotation.

An *equal Agrarian* is a perpetual law establishing and preserving the balance of dominion by such a distribution that no one man or number of men within the compass of the few or aristocracy can come to overpower the whole people by their possessions in lands.

As the Agrarian answers to the foundation, so does rotation to the superstructures.

Equal rotation is equal vicissitude in government, or succession unto magistracy conferred for such convenient terms, enjoying equal vacations, as take in the whole body by parts succeeding others through the *free election* or suffrage of the people.

The contrary whereunto is prolongation of magistracy which, trashing the wheel of rotation, destroys the life or natural motion of a commonwealth. . . .

An equal commonwealth (by that which has been said) *is a government established upon an equal Agrarian, arising into the superstructures or three orders: the senate debating and proposing, the people resolving, and the magistracy executing by an equal rotation through the suffrage of the people given by the ballot.* For though rotation may be without the ballot, and the ballot without rotation, yet the ballot not only as to the ensuing Model includes both, but is by far the most equal way; for which cause under the name of the ballot I shall hereafter understand both that and rotation too. . . .

HOOKER
Laws of Ecclesiastical Polity

The Laws of Reason

Where understanding therefore needeth, in those things Reason is the director of man's Will by discovering in action what is good. For the Laws of well-doing are the dictates of right Reason. . . . There is that light of Reason, whereby good may be known from evil, and which discovering the same rightly is termed right.

The Will notwithstanding doth not incline to have or do that which Reason teacheth to be good, unless the same do also teach it to be possible. For albeit the Appetite, being more general, may wish any thing which seemeth good, be it never so impossible; yet for such things the reasonable Will of man doth never seek. Let Reason teach impossibility in any thing, and the Will of man doth let it go; a thing impossible it doth not affect, the impossibility thereof being manifest.

. . . The universal consent of men is the perfectest and strongest in this kind, which comprehendeth only the signs and tokens of goodness. Things casual do vary, and that which a man doth but chance to think well of cannot still have the like hap. Wherefore although we know not the cause, yet thus much we may know; that some necessary cause there is, whensoever the judgments of all men generally or for the most part run one and the same way, especially in matters of natural discourse. For of things necessarily and naturally done there is no more affirmed but this, "They keep either always or for the most part one tenure." The general and perpetual voice of men is as the sentence of God himself. For that which all men have at all times learned, Nature herself must needs have taught; and God being the author of Nature, her voice is but his instrument. By her from Him we receive whatsoever in such sort we learn.

. . . A Law is properly that which Reason in such sort defineth to be good that it must be done. And the Law of Reason or human Nature is that which men by discourse of natural Reason have rightly found out themselves to be all for ever bound unto in their actions.

Laws of Reason have these marks to be known by. Such as keep them resemble most lively in their voluntary actions that very manner of working which Nature herself doth necessarily observe in the course of the whole world. The works of Nature are all behoveful, beautiful, without superfluity or defect; even so theirs, if they be framed according to that which the Law of Reason teacheth. Secondly, those Laws are investigable by Reason, without the help of Revelation supernatural and divine. Finally, in such sort they are investigable that the knowledge of them is general, the world hath always been acquainted with them. It is not agreed upon by one, or two, or few, but by all. Which we may not so understand, as if every particular man in the whole world did know and confess whatsoever the Law of Reason doth contain; but this Law is such that being proposed no man can reject it as unreasonable and unjust. Again, there is nothing in it but any man (having natural perfection of wit and ripeness of judgment) may by labour and travail find out. And to conclude, the general principles thereof are such, as it is not easy to find men ignorant of them. Law rational therefore, which men commonly use to call the Law of Nature, meaning thereby the Law which human Nature knoweth itself in reason universally bound unto, which also for that cause may be termed most fitly the Law of Reason; this Law, I say, comprehendeth all those things which men by the light of their natural understanding evidently know, or at leastwise may know, to be beseeming or unbeseeming, virtuous or vicious, good or evil for them to do.

Civil Society

. . . We see then how nature itself teacheth laws and statutes to live by. The laws which have been hitherto mentioned do bind men absolutely even as they are men, although they have never any settled fellowship, never any solemn agreement amongst themselves what to do or not to do. But forasmuch as we are not by ourselves sufficient to furnish ourselves with competent store of things needful of such a life as our nature doth desire, a life fit for the dignity of man; therefore to supply those defects and imperfections which are in us living single and solely by ourselves, we are naturally induced to seek communion and fellowship with others. This was the cause of men's uniting themselves at the first in politic Societies, which societies could not be without Government, nor Government without a distinct kind of Law from that which hath been already declared. Two foundations there are which bear up public societies; the one, a natural inclination, whereby all men desire sociable life and fellowship; the other, an order expressly or secretly agreed upon touching the manner of their union in living together. The latter is that which we call the Law of a Commonweal, the very soul of a politic body, the parts whereof are by law animated, held together, and set on work in such actions, as the common good requireth. Laws politic, ordained for external order and regiment amongst men, are never framed as they should be, unless presuming the will of man to be inwardly obstinate, rebellious, and averse from all obedience unto the sacred laws of his nature; in a word, unless presuming man to be in regard of his depraved mind little better than a wild beast, they do accordingly provide notwithstanding so to frame his outward actions, that they be no hinderance unto the common good for which societies are instituted: unless they do this, they are not perfect. . . .

All men desire to lead in this world a happy life. That life is led most happily, wherein all virtue is exercised without impediment or let.

... We all make complaint of the iniquity of our times: not unjustly; for the days are evil. But compare them with those times wherein there were no civil societies, with those times wherein there was as yet no manner of public regiment established, with those times wherein there were not above eight persons righteous living upon the face of the earth; and we have surely good cause to think that God hath blessed us exceedingly, and hath made us behold most happy days.

To take away all such mutual grievances, injuries, and wrongs, there was no way but only by growing unto composition and agreement amongst themselves, by ordaining some kind of government public, and by yielding themselves subject thereunto; that unto whom they granted authority to rule and govern, by them the peace, tranquillity, and happy estate of the rest might be procured. Men always knew that when force and injury was offered they might be defenders of themselves; they knew that howsoever men may seek their own commodity, yet if this were done with injury unto others it was not to be suffered, but by all men and by all good means to be withstood; finally they knew that no man might in reason take upon him to determine his own right, and according to his own determination proceed in maintenance thereof, inasmuch as every man is towards himself and them whom he greatly affecteth partial; and therefore that strifes and troubles would be endless, except they gave their common consent all to be ordered by some whom they should agree upon: without which consent there were no reason that one man should take upon him to be lord or judge over another; because, although there be according to the opinion of some very great and judicious men a kind of natural right in the noble, wise, and virtuous, to govern them which are of servile disposition; nevertheless for manifestation of this their right, and men's more peaceable contentment on both sides, the assent of them who are to be governed seemeth necessary.

... All public regiment of what kind soever seemeth evidently to have risen from deliberate advice, consulation, and composition between men, judging it convenient and behoveful; there being no impossibility in nature considered by itself, but that men might have lived without any public regiment. Howbeit, the corruption of our nature being presupposed, we may not deny but that the Law of Nature doth now require of necessity some kind of regiment; so that to bring things unto the first course they were in, and utterly to take away all kind of public government in the world, were apparently to overturn the whole world.

The case of man's nature standing therefore as it doth, some kind of regiment the Law of Nature doth require; yet the kinds thereof being many, Nature tieth not to any one, but leaveth the choice as a thing arbitrary. At the first when some certain kind of regiment was once approved, it may be that nothing was then further thought upon for the manner of governing, but all permitted unto their wisdom and discretion which were to rule; till by experience they found this for all parts very inconvenient, so as the thing which they had devised for a remedy did indeed but increase the sore which it should have cured. They saw that to live by one man's will became the cause of all men's misery. This constrained them to come unto laws, wherein all men might see their duties beforehand, and know the penalties of transgressing them. If things be simply good or evil, and withal universally so acknowledged, there needs no new law to be made for such things.

. . . And because the greatest part of men are such as prefer their own private good before all things, even that good which is sensual before whatsoever is most divine; and for that the labour of doing good, together with the pleasure arising from the contrary, doth make men for the most part slower to the one and proner to the other, then that duty prescribed them by law can prevail sufficiently with them: therefore unto laws that men do make for the benefit of men it hath seemed always needful to add rewards, which may more allure unto good than any hardness deterreth from it, and punishments, which may more deter from evil than any sweetness thereto allureth. Wherein as the generality is natural, *virtue rewardable and vice punishable;* so the particular determination of the reward or punishment belongeth unto them by whom laws are made. . . .

In laws, that which is natural bindeth universally, that which is positive not so. To let go those kind of positive laws which men impose upon themselves, as by vow unto God, contract with men, or such like. . . . Laws do not only teach what is good, but they enjoin it, they have in them a certain constraining force. And to constrain men unto any thing inconvenient doth seem unreasonable. Most requisite therefore it is that to devise laws which all men shall be forced to obey none but wise men be admitted. Laws are matters of principal consequence; men of common capacity and but ordinary judgment are not able . . . to discern what things are fittest for each kind and state of regiment. We cannot be ignorant how much our obedience unto laws dependeth upon this point. . . . They presume that the law doth speak with all indifferency; that the law hath no side-respect to their persons; that the law is as it were an oracle proceeded from wisdom and understanding.

Howbeit laws do not take their constraining force from the quality of such as devise them, but from that power which doth give them the strength of laws . . . the power of making laws whereby to govern God hath over all: and by the natural law, whereunto he hath made all subject the lawful power of making laws to command whole politic societies of men belongeth so properly unto the same entire societies, that for any prince or potentate of what kind soever upon earth to exercise the same of himself, and not either by express commission immediately and personally received from God, or else by authority derived at the first from their consent upon whose persons they impose laws, it is no better than mere tyranny.

Laws they are not therefore which public approbation hath not made so. But approbation not only they give who personally declare their assent by voice sign or act, but also when others do it in their names by right originally at the least derived from them. As in parliaments, councils, and the like assemblies, although we be not personally ourselves present, notwithstanding our assent is by reason of others agents there in our behalf. And what we do by others, no reason but that it should stand as our deed, no less effectually to bind us than if ourselves had done it in person. In many things assent is given, they that give it not imagining they do so, because the manner of their assenting is not apparent . . . that which hath been received long sithence and is by custom now established, we keep as a law which we may not transgress; yet what consent was ever thereunto sought or required at our hands?

Of this point therefore we are to note, that sith men naturally have no full and perfect power to command whole politic multitudes of men, therefore utterly without our consent we could in such sort be at no man's commandment living. And to be commanded we do consent, when that society whereof we are part hath at any time before consented, without revoking the same after by the like universal agreement. Wherefore as any man's deed past is good as long as himself continueth; so the act of a public society of men done five hundred years sithence standeth as theirs who presently are of the same societies, because corporations are immortal; we were then alive in our predecessors, and they in their successors do live still. Laws therefore human, of what kind soever, are available by consent.

If here it be demanded how it cometh to pass that this being common unto all laws which are made, there should be found even in good laws so great variety as there is; we must note the reason hereof to be the sundry particular ends, whereunto the different disposition of that subject or matter, for which laws are provided, causeth them to have a special respect in making laws . . . law-makers must have an eye to the place where, and to the men amongst whom; one kind of laws cannot serve for all kinds of regiment; where the multitude beareth sway, laws that shall tend unto preservation of that state must make common smaller offices to go by lot, for fear of strife and division likely to arise . . . if the helm of chief government be in the hands of a few of the wealthiest, then laws providing for continuance thereof must make the punishment of contumely and wrong offered unto any of the common sort sharp and grievous. . . .

Now as the learned in the laws of this land observe, that our statutes sometimes are only the affirmation or ratification of that which by common law was held before; so here it is not to be omitted that generally all laws human, which are made for the ordering of politic societies, be either such as establish some duty whereunto all men by the law of reason did before stand bound; or else such as make that a duty now which before was none. The one sort we may for distinction's sake call "mixedly," and the other "merely" human. That which plain or necessary reason bindeth men unto may be in sundry considerations expedient to be ratified by human law . . . this very thing is cause sufficient why duties belonging unto each kind of virtue, albeit the Law of Reason teach them, should notwithstanding be prescribed even by human law. Which law in this case we term *mixed*, because the matter whereunto it bindeth is the same which reason necessarily doth require at our hands, and from the Law of Reason it differeth in the manner of binding only. For whereas men before stood bound in conscience to do as the Law of Reason teacheth, they are now by virtue of human law become constrainable, and if they outwardly transgress, punishable. As for laws which are *merely* human, the matter of them is any thing which reason doth but probably teach to be fit and convenient; so that till such time as law hath passed amongst men about it, of itself it bindeth no man. . . .

. . . Laws whether mixedly or merely human are made by politic societies; some, only as those societies are civilly united; some, as they are spiritually joined and make such a body as we call the Church. . . . Almighty God hath graciously endued our nature, and thereby enabled the same to find out both those laws which all men generally are for ever bound to observe, and also such as are most fit for their behoof, who lead their lives in any ordered state of government.

LOCKE

The Second Treatise of Civil Government

The State of Nature

Political power I take to be a right of making laws with penalties of death and, consequently, all less penalties for the regulating and preserving of property, and of employing the force of the community in the execution of such laws, and in the defence of the commonwealth from foreign injury, and all this only for the public good.

. . . We must consider what state all men are naturally in, and that is a state of perfect freedom to order their actions and dispose of their possessions and persons as they think fit, within the bounds of the law of nature, without asking leave or depending upon the will of any other man.

A state also of equality, wherein all the power and jurisdiction is reciprocal, no one having more than another; there being nothing more evident than that creatures of the same species and rank, promiscuously born to all the same advantages of nature and the use of the same faculties, should also be equal one amongst another without subordination or subjection. . . .

. . . The state of nature has a law of nature to govern it which obliges every one; and reason, which is that law, teaches all mankind who will but consult it that, being all equal and independent, no one ought to harm another in his life, health, liberty, or possessions; men being all the workmanship of one omnipotent and infinitely wise Maker . . . they are his property whose workmanship they are, made to last during his, not one another's, pleasure; and being furnished with like faculties, sharing all in one community of nature, there cannot be supposed any such subordination among us that may authorize us to destroy another, as if we were made for one another's uses as the inferior ranks of creatures are for ours. Every one, as he is bound to preserve himself and not to quit his station wilfully, so by the like reason, when his own preservation comes not in competition, ought he, as much as he can, to preserve the rest of mankind, and may not, unless it be to do justice to an offender, take away or impair the life, or what tends to the preservation of life: the liberty, health, limb, or goods of another.

And that all men may be restrained from invading others' rights and from doing hurt to one another, and the law of nature be observed which willeth the peace and preservation of all mankind, the execution of the law of nature is, in that state, put into every man's hands, whereby everyone has a right to punish the transgressors of that law to such a degree as may hinder its violation.

And thus in the state of nature one man comes by a power over another; but yet no absolute or arbitrary power to use a criminal, when he has got him in his hands, according to the passionate heats or boundless extravagancy of his own will; but only . . . what is proportionate to his transgression. In transgressing the law of nature, the offender declares himself to live by another rule than that of reason and common equity, which is that measure God has set to the actions of men for their mutual security; and so he becomes dangerous to mankind. . . .

. . . Civil government is the proper remedy for the inconveniences of the state of nature, which must certainly be great where men may be judges in their own case. . . . Much better than absolute monarchy is the state of nature, wherein men are not bound to submit to the unjust will of another; and if he that judges, judges amiss in his own or any other case, he is answerable for it to the rest of mankind.

. . . Men living together according to reason, without a common superior on earth with authority to judge between them, is properly the state of nature. But force, or a declared design of force, upon the person of another, where there is no common superior on earth to appeal to for relief, is the state of war. . . . Want of a common judge with authority puts all men in a state of nature; force without right upon a man's person makes a state of war both where there is, and is not, a common judge.

. . . To avoid this state of war—wherein there is no appeal but to heaven, and wherein every the least difference is apt to end, where there is no authority to decide between the contenders—is one great reason of men's putting themselves into society and quitting the state of nature; for where there is an authority, a power on earth from which relief can be had by appeal, there the continuance of the state of war is excluded, and the controversy is decided by that power. . . .

The natural liberty of man is to be free from any superior power on earth, and not to be under the will or legislative authority of man, but to have only the law of nature for his rule. The liberty of man in society is to be under no other legislative power but that established by consent in the commonwealth; nor under the dominion of any will or restraint of any law, but what that legislative shall enact according to the trust put in it. . . . Freedom of men under government is to have a standing rule to live by, common to every one of that society and made by the legislative power erected in it, a liberty to follow my own will in all things where the rule prescribes not, and not to be subject to the inconstant, uncertain, unknown, arbitrary will of another man; as freedom of nature is to be under no other restraint but the law of nature.

This freedom from absolute, arbitrary power is so necessary to and closely joined with a man's preservation that he cannot part with it but by what forfeits his preservation and life together; for a man not having the power of his own life cannot by compact or his own consent enslave himself to any one, nor put himself under the absolute arbitrary power of another to take away his life when he pleases.

Property

. . . Though the earth and all inferior creatures be common to all men, yet every man has a property in his own person; this nobody has any right to but himself. The labour of his body and the work of his hands, we may say, are properly his. Whatsoever then he removes out of the state that nature hath provided and left it in, he hath mixed his labour with, and joined to it something that is his own, and thereby makes it his property. It being by him removed from the common state nature hath placed it in, it hath by this labour something annexed to it that excludes the common right of other men. For this labour being the unquestionable property of the labourer, no man but he can have a right to what that is once joined to, at least where there is enough and as good left in common for others.

. . . It is allowed to be his goods who hath bestowed his labour upon it, though before it was the common right of every one. . . .

. . . The same law of nature that does by this means give us property does also bound that property, too. As much as any one can make use of to any advantage of life before it spoils, so much he may by his labour fix a property in; whatever is beyond this is more than his share, and belongs to others. Nothing was made by God for man to spoil or destroy. . . .

. . . As much land as a man tills, plants, improves, cultivates, and can use the product of, so much is his property. He by his labour does, as it were, enclose it from the common.

. . . The measure of property nature has well set by the extent of men's labour and the conveniences of life. No man's labour could subdue or appropriate all, nor could his enjoyment consume more than a small part; so that it was impossible for any man, this way, to entrench upon the right of another, or acquire to himself a property to the prejudice of his neighbour, who would still have room for as good and as large a possession—after the other had taken out his—as before it was appropriated. This measure did confine every man's possession to a very moderate proportion. . . . The same rule of propriety, viz., that every man should have as much as he could make use of, would hold still in the world without straitening anybody, since there is land enough in the world to suffice double the inhabitants, had not the invention of money and the tacit agreement of men to put a value on it introduced —by consent—larger possessions and a right to them. . . .

. . . It is plain that men have agreed to a disproportionate and unequal possession of the earth, they having, by a tacit and voluntary consent, found out a way how a man may fairly possess more land than he himself can use the product of, by receiving in exchange for the overplus gold and silver which may be hoarded up without injury to any one, these metals not spoiling or decaying in the hands of the possessor. This partage of things in an inequality of private possessions men have made practicable out of the bounds of society and without compact, only by putting a value on gold and silver, and tacitly agreeing in the use of money; for, in governments, the laws regulate the right of property, and the possession of land is determined by positive constitutions.

Civil Society

Though I have said . . . "that all men by nature are equal," I cannot be supposed to understand all sorts of equality. Age or virtue may give men a just precedency; excellency of parts and merit may place others above the common level; birth may subject some, and alliance or benefits others, to pay an observance to those whom nature, gratitude, or other respects may have made it due; and yet all this consists with the equality which all men are in, in respect of jurisdiction or dominion one over another, which was the equality I there spoke of as proper to the business in hand, being that equal right that every man hath to his natural freedom, without being subjected to the will or authority of any other man.

. . . Law, in its true notion, is not so much the limitation as the direction of a free and intelligent agent to his proper interest, and prescribes no farther than is for the general good of those under that law. Could they be happier without it, the law, as a useless thing, would of itself vanish; and that ill deserves the name of confinement which hedges us in only from bogs and precipices. So that, however it may be mistaken, the end of law is not to abolish or restrain but to preserve and enlarge freedom; for in all the states of created beings capable of laws, where there is no law, there is no freedom. For liberty is to be free from restraint and violence from others, which cannot be where there is not law; but freedom is not, as we are told: a liberty for every man to do what he lists—for who could be free, when every other man's humour might domineer over him?—but a liberty to dispose and order as he lists his person, actions, possessions, and his whole property, within the allowance of those laws under which he is, and therein not to be subject to the arbitrary will of another, but freely follow his own.

. . . The freedom then of man, and liberty of acting according to his own will, is grounded on his having reason which is able to instruct him in that law he is to govern himself by, and make him know how far he is left to the freedom of his own will. To turn him loose to an unrestrained liberty before he has reason to guide him is not the allowing him the privilege of his nature to be free, but to thrust him out amongst brutes and abandon him to a state as wretched and as much beneath that of a man as theirs. . . .

. . . There being always annexed to the enjoyment of land a submission to the government of the country of which that land is a part, it has been commonly supposed that a father could oblige his posterity to that government of which he himself was a subject, and that his compact held them; whereas it, being only a necessary condition annexed to the land and the inheritance of an estate which is under that government, reaches only those who will take it on that condition, and so in no natural tie or engagement but a voluntary submission; for every man's children, being by nature as free as himself or any of his ancestors ever were, may, whilst they are in that freedom, choose what society they will join themselves to, what commonwealth they will put themselves under. But if they will enjoy the inheritance of their ancestors, they must take it on the same terms their ancestors had it and submit to all the conditions annexed to such a possession. By this power, indeed, fathers oblige their children to obedience to themselves even when they are past minority, and most commonly, too, subject them to this or that political power. . . .

God, having made man such a creature that in his own judgment it was not good for him to be alone, put him under strong obligations of necessity, convenience, and inclination to drive him into society, as well as fitted him with understanding and language to continue and enjoy it. . . .

. . . Because no political society can be, nor subsist, without having in itself the power to preserve the property and, in order thereunto, punish the offences of all those of that society, there and there only is political society where every one of the members hath quitted his natural power, resigned it up into the hands of the community in all cases that excludes him not from appealing for protection to the law established by it. And thus, all private judgment of every particular member being excluded, the community comes to be umpire by settled standing rules, indifferent and the same to all parties, and by men having authority from the community for the execution of those rules, decides all the differences that may happen between any members of that society concerning any matter of right, and punishes those offences which any member hath committed against the society with such penalties as the law has established; whereby it is easy to discern who are, and who are not, in political society together. Those who are united into one body and have a common established law and judicature to appeal to, with authority to decide controversies between them and punish offenders, are in civil society one with another; but those who have no such common appeal, I mean on earth, are still in the state of nature, each being, where there is no other, judge for himself and executioner, which is, as I have before shown it, the perfect state of nature.

[Every man] has given a right to the commonwealth to employ his force for the execution of the judgments of the commonwealth, whenever he shall be called to it; which, indeed, are his own judgments, they being made by himself or his representative. And herein we have the original of the legislative and executive power of civil society which is to judge by standing laws. . . .

Whenever, therefore, any number of men are so united into one society as to quit every one his executive power of the law of nature and to resign it to the public, there and there only is a political or civil society. And this is done wherever any number of men, in the state of nature, enter into society to make one people, one body politic, under one supreme government, or else when any one joins himself to, and incorporates with, any government already made; for hereby he authorizes the society or, which is all one, the legislative thereof, to make laws for him as the public good of the society shall require, to the execution whereof his own assistance, as to his own degrees, is due. And this puts men out of the state of nature into that of a commonwealth by setting up a judge on earth, with authority to determine all the controversies and redress the injuries that may happen to any member of the commonwealth; which judge is the legislative, or magistrate appointed by it. And wherever there are any number of men, however associated, that have no such decisive power to appeal to, there they are still in the state of nature.

. . . The end of civil society (is) to avoid and remedy these inconveniences of the state of nature which necessarily follow from every man being judge in his own case, by setting up a known authority to which everyone of that society may appeal upon any injury received or controversy that may arise and which everyone of the society ought to obey. . . .

In absolute monarchies, indeed, as well as other governments of the world, the subjects have an appeal to the law and judges to decide any controversies and restrain any violence that may happen betwixt the subjects themselves, one amongst another. . . .

. . . If it be asked, what security, what fence is there, in such a state, against the violence and oppression of this absolute ruler, the very question can scarce be borne. They are ready to tell you that it deserves death only to ask after safety Betwixt subject and subject, they will grant, there must be measures, laws, and judges, for their mutual peace and security; but as for the ruler, he ought to be absolute and is above all such circumstances; because he has power to do more hurt and wrong, it is right when he does it. To ask how you may be guarded from harm or injury on that side where the strongest hand is to do it, is presently the voice of faction and rebellion, as if when men, quitting the state of nature entered into society, they agreed that all of them but one should be under the restraint of laws, but that he should still retain all the liberty of the state of nature, increased with power and made licentious by impunity. This is to think that men are so foolish that they take care to avoid what mischief may be done them by polecats or foxes, but are content, nay think it safety, to be devoured by lions.

The Social Contract

Men being by nature all free, equal, and independent, no one can be put out of this estate and subjected to the political power of another without his own consent. The only way whereby any one divests himself of his natural liberty, and puts on the bonds of civil society, is by agreeing with other men to join and unite into a community for their comfortable, safe, and peaceable living one amongst another, in a secure enjoyment of their properties and a greater security against any that are not of it. . . .

. . . When any number of men have, by the consent of every individual, made a community, they have thereby made that community one body, with a power to act as one body, which is only by the will and determination of the majority. . . .

. . . And thus every man, by consenting with others to make one body politic under one government, puts himself under an obligation to every one of that society to submit to the determination of the majority, and to be concluded by it; or else this original compact, whereby he with others incorporates into one society, would signify nothing, and be no compact, if he be left free and under no other ties than he was in before in the state of nature. . . .

. . . Where the majority cannot conclude the rest, there they cannot act as one body, and consequently will be immediately dissolved again.

Whosoever, therefore, out of a state of nature unite into a community must be understood to give up all the power necessary to the ends for which they unite into society to the majority of the community, unless they expressly agreed in any number greater than the majority. And this is done by barely agreeing to unite into one political society, which is all the compact that is, or needs be, between the individuals that enter into or make up a commonwealth. . . .

. . . The son cannot ordinarily enjoy the possessions of his father but under the same terms his father did, by becoming a member of the society; whereby he puts himself presently under the government he finds there established as much as any other subject of that commonwealth. . . .

. . . There is a common distinction of an express and a tacit consent which will concern our present case. Nobody doubts but an express consent of any man entering into any society makes him a perfect member of that society, a subject of that government. The difficulty is, what ought to be looked upon as a tacit consent, and how far it binds,—*i.e.*, how far any one shall be looked upon to have consented and thereby submitted to any government, where he has made no expressions of it at all. And to this I say that every man that hath any possessions or enjoyment of any part of the dominions of any government doth thereby give his tacit consent and is as far forth obliged to obedience to the laws of that government, during such enjoyment, as anyone under it; whether this his possession be of land to him and his heirs for ever, or a lodging only for a week, or whether it be barely travelling freely on the highway; and, in effect, it reaches as far as the very being of anyone within the territories of that government.

. . . Whenever the owner, who has given nothing but such a tacit consent to the government, will, by donation, sale, or otherwise, quit the said possession, he is at liberty to go and incorporate himself into any other commonwealth, or to agree with others to begin a new one *in vacuis locis,* in any part of the world they can find free and unpossessed. Whereas he that has once, by actual agreement and any express declaration, given his consent to be of any commonwealth is perpetually and indispensably obliged to be and remain unalterably a subject to it, and can never be again in the liberty of the state of nature, unless by any calamity the government he was under comes to be dissolved, or else by some public act cuts him off from being any longer a member of it. . . .

Nothing can make any man so (subjects or members of that commonwealth) but his actually entering into it by positive engagement and express promise and compact.

The End of Society and Government

If man in the state of nature be so free, if he be absolute lord of his own person and possessions, equal to the greatest and subject to nobody, why will he part with his freedom why will he give up his empire and subject himself to the dominion and control of any other power? . . . Though in the state of nature he hath such a right, yet the enjoyment of it is very uncertain and constantly exposed to the invasion of others; for all being kings as much as he, every man his equal and the greater part no strict observers of equity and justice the enjoyment of the property he has in this state is very unsafe, very unsecure. This makes him willing to quit a condition which, however free, is full of fears and continual dangers; and it is not without reason that he seeks out and is willing to join in society with others who are already united, or have a mind to unite, for the mutual preservation of their lives, liberties, and estates, which I call by the general name "property."

The great and chief end, therefore, of men's uniting into commonwealths and putting themselves under government is the preservation of their property. To which in the state of nature there are many things wanting:

First, There wants an established, settled, known law, received and allowed by common consent to be the standard of right and wrong and the common measure to decide all controversies between them; for though the law of nature be plain and intelligible to all rational creatures, yet men, being biased by their interest as well as ignorant for want of studying it, are not apt to allow of it as a law binding to them in the application of it to their particular cases.

Secondly, In the state of nature there wants a known and indifferent judge with authority to determine all differences according to the established law; for every one in that state being both judge and executioner of the law of nature, men being partial to themselves, passion and revenge is very apt to carry them too far and with too much heat in their own cases, as well as negligence and unconcernedness to make them too remiss in other men's.

Thirdly, in the state of nature, there often wants power to back and support the sentence when right, and to give it due execution. They who by any injustice offend will seldom fail, where they are able, by force, to make good their injustice; such resistance many times makes the punishment dangerous and frequently destructive to those who attempt it.

The power of doing whatsoever he thought fit for the preservation of himself and the rest of mankind, he gives up to be regulated by laws made by the society, so far forth as the preservation of himself and the rest of that society shall require; which laws of the society in many things confine the liberty he had by the law of nature.

The power of punishing he wholly gives up, and engages his natural force to assist the executive power of the society, as the law thereof shall require. . . .

Men . . . enter into society . . . the better to preserve himself, his liberty and property—. . . the power of the society, or legislative constituted by them, can never be supposed to extend farther than the common good. . . . And so whoever has the legislative or supreme power of any commonwealth is bound to govern by established standing laws, promulgated and known to the people, and not by extemporary decrees; by indifferent and upright judges who are to decide controversies by those laws; and to employ the force of the community at home only in the execution of such laws, or abroad to prevent or redress foreign injuries, and secure the community from inroads and invasion. And all this to be directed to no other end but the peace, safety, and public good of the people.

The Legislative Power

The great end of men's entering into society being the enjoyment of their properties in peace and safety, and the great instrument and means of that being the laws established in that society, the first and fundamental positive law of all commonwealths is the establishing of the legislative power. . . . This legislative is not only the supreme power of the commonwealth, but sacred and unalterable in the hands where the community have once placed it; nor can any edict of anybody else, in what form soever conceived or by what power soever backed, have the force and obligation of a law which has not its sanction from that legislative which the public has chosen and appointed; for without this the law could not have that which is absolutely necessary to its being a law: the consent of the society over whom nobody can have a power to make laws, but by their own consent and by authority received from them. . . .

. . . Though it (the legislative) be the supreme power in every commonwealth; yet:

First, It is not, nor can possibly be, absolutely arbitrary over the lives and fortunes of the people . . . the legislative power . . . the utmost bounds of it, is limited to the public good of the society. It is a power that hath no other end but preservation, and therefore can never have a right to destroy, enslave, or designedly to impoverish the subjects.

Secondly, The legislative or supreme authority cannot assume to itself a power to rule by extemporary, arbitrary decrees, but is bound to dispense justice and to decide the rights of the subject by promulgated, standing laws, and known authorized judges. . . . Men give up all their natural power to the society which they enter into, and the community put the legislative power into such hands as they think fit with this trust, that they shall be governed by declared laws, or else their peace, quiet, and property will still be at the same uncertainty as it was in the state of nature. . . .

Thirdly, The supreme power cannot take from any man part of his property without his own consent; for the preservation of property being the end of government and that for which men enter into society, it necessarily supposes and requires that the people should have property. . . . Hence it is a mistake to think that the supreme or legislative power of any commonwealth can do what it will, and dispose of the estates of the subject arbitrarily, or take any part of them at pleasure.

. . . Governments cannot be supported without great charge, and it is fit every one who enjoys his share of the protection should pay out of his estate his proportion for the maintenance of it. But still it must be with his own consent—*i.e.*, the consent of the majority, giving it either by themselves or their representatives chosen by them. . . .

Fourthly, The legislative cannot transfer the power of making laws to any other hands; for it being but a delegated power from the people, they who have it cannot pass it over to others. . . .

These are the bounds which the trust that is put in them by the society and the law of God and nature have set to the legislative power of every commonwealth, in all forms of government:

First, They are to govern by promulgated established laws, not to be varied in particular cases, but to have one rule for rich and poor, for the favourite at court and the countryman at plough.

Secondly, These laws also ought to be designed for no other end ultimately but the good of the people.

Thirdly, They must not raise taxes on the property of the people without the consent of the people, given by themselves or their deputies. And this properly concerns only such governments where the legislative is always in being, or at least where the people have not reserved any part of the legislative to deputies to be from time to time chosen by themselves.

Fourthly, The legislative neither must nor can transfer the power of making laws to anybody else, or place it anywhere but where the people have.

The Separation of Powers

The legislative power is that which has a right to direct how the force of the commonwealth shall be employed for preserving the community and the members of it. But . . . there is no need that the legislative should be always in being, not having always business to do. And it may be too great a temptation to human frailty, apt to grasp at power, for the same persons who have the power of making laws to have also in their hands the power to execute them, whereby they may exempt themselves from obedience to the laws they make, and suit the law, both in its making and execution, to their own private advantage, and thereby come to have a distinct interest from the rest of the community contrary to the end of society and government. . . .

But because the laws that are at once and in a short time made have a constant and lasting force and need a perpetual execution or an attendance thereunto; therefore, it is necessary there should be a power always in being which should see to the execution of the laws that are made and remain in force. And thus the legislative and executive power come often to be separated.

There is another power in every commonwealth. . . . The whole community is one body in the state of nature in respect of all other states or persons out of its community.

This, therefore, contains the power of war and peace, leagues and alliances, and all the transactions with all persons and communities without the commonwealth, and may be called "federative." . . .

These two powers, executive and federative, though they be really distinct in themselves, yet one comprehending the execution of the municipal laws of the society within itself upon all that are parts of it, the other the management of the security and interest of the public without, with all those that it may receive benefit or damage from, yet they are always almost united. And though this federative power in the well or ill management of it be of great moment to the commonwealth, yet it is much less capable to be directed by antecedent, standing, positive laws than the executive, and so must necessarily be left to the prudence and wisdom of those whose hands it is in to be managed for the public good. . . .

. . . It is almost impracticable to place the force of the commonwealth in distinct and not subordinate hands, or the executive and federative power be placed in persons that might act separately, whereby the force of the public would be under different commands, which would be apt some time or other to cause disorder and ruin.

The Power of the People

Though in a constituted commonwealth, standing upon its own basis and acting according to its own nature, that is, acting for the preservation of the community, there can be but one supreme power which is the legislative, to which all the rest are and must be subordinate, yet, the legislative being only a fiduciary power to act for certain ends, there remains still in the people a supreme power to remove or alter the legislative when they find the legislative act contrary to the trust reposed in them; for all power given with trust for the attaining an end being limited by that end, whenever that end is manifestly neglected or opposed, the trust must necessarily be forfeited and the power devolve into the hands of those that gave it, who may place it anew where they shall think best for their safety and security. And thus the community perpetually retains a supreme power of saving themselves from the attempts and designs of anybody, even of their legislators, whenever they shall be so foolish or so wicked as to lay and carry on designs against the liberties and properties of the subject; for no man or society of men having a power to deliver up their preservation, or consequently the means of it, to the absolute will and arbitrary dominion of another, whenever any one shall go about to bring them into such a slavish condition, they will always have a right to preserve what they have no a power to part with, and to rid themselves of those who invade this fundamental, sacred, and unalterable law of self-preservation for which they entered into society. And thus the community may be said in this respect to be always the supreme power, but not as considered under any form of government, because this power of the people can never take place till the government be dissolved.

. . . Allegiance being nothing but an obedience according to law which, when he (the supreme executive) violates, he has no right to obedience nor can claim it otherwise than as the public person invested with the power of the law, and so is to be considered as the image, phantom, or representative of the commonwealth, acted by the will of the society, declared in its laws, and thus he has no will, no power, but that of the law. But when he quits this representation, this public will, and acts by his own private will, he degrades himself and is but a single private person without power and without will that has no right to obedience—the members owing no obedience but to the public will of the society. . . .

. . . Using force upon the people without authority, and contrary to the trust put in him that does so, is a state of war with the people who have a right to reinstate their legislative in the exercise of their power; for having erected a legislative with an intent they should exercise the power of making laws, either at certain set times or when there is need of it, when they are hindered by any force from what is so necessary to the society, and wherein the safety and preservation of the people consists, the people have a right to remove it by force. In all states and conditions, the true remedy of force without authority is to oppose force to it. The use of force without authority always puts him that uses it into a state of war, as the aggressor, and renders him liable to be treated accordingly.

. . . And where the body of the people, or any single man, is deprived of their right, or is under the exercise of a power without right and have no appeal on earth, then they have a liberty to appeal to heaven whenever they judge the cause of sufficient moment. And, therefore, though the people cannot be judge so as to have by the constitution of that society any superior power to determine and give effective sentence in the case, yet they have, by a law antecedent and paramount to all positive laws of men, reserved that ultimate determination to themselves which belongs to all mankind, where there lies no appeal on earth—viz., to judge whether they have just cause to make their appeal to heaven. And this judgment they cannot part with, it being out of a man's power so to submit himself to another as to give him a liberty to destroy him, God and nature never allowing a man so to abandon himself as to neglect his own preservation; and since he cannot take away his own life, neither can he give another power to take it. Nor let any one think this lays a perpetual foundation for disorder; for this operates not till the inconvenience is so great that the majority feel it and are weary of it and find a necessity to have it amended. . . .

The Possibility of Resistance

. . . May the commands, then, of a prince be opposed? May he be resisted as often as any one shall find himself aggrieved, and but imagine he has not right done him? This will unhinge and overturn all polities, and, instead of government and order, leave nothing but anarchy and confusion.

To this I answer that force is to be opposed to nothing but to unjust and unlawful force. . . .

. . . That which makes the community and brings men out of the loose state of nature into one politic society is the agreement which everybody has with the rest to incorporate and act as one body, and so be one distinct commonwealth. The usual and almost only way whereby this union is dissolved is the inroad of foreign force making a conquest upon them. . . . Whenever the society is dissolved, it is certain the government of that society cannot remain. . . .

. . . Besides this overturning from without, governments are dissolved from within:

First, When the legislative is altered. Civil society being a state of peace amongst those who are of it, from whom the state of war is excluded by the umpirage which they have provided in their legislative for the ending all differences that may arise amongst any of them, it is in their legislative that the members of a commonwealth are united and combined together into one coherent living body. This is the soul that gives form, life, and unity to the commonwealth; from hence the several members have their mutual influence, sympathy, and connexion; and, therefore, when the legislative is broken or dissolved, dissolution and death follows; for the essence and union of the society consisting in having one will, the legislative, when once established by the majority, has the declaring and, as it were, keeping of that will. . . .

. . . There is one way more whereby such a government may be dissolved, and that is when he who has the supreme executive power neglects and abandons that charge, so that the laws already made can no longer be put in execution. This is demonstratively to reduce all to anarchy, and so effectually to dissolve the government . . . and the people become a confused multitude, without order or connexion. . . . Where the laws cannot be executed, it is all one as if there were no laws; and a government without laws is, I suppose, a mystery in politics, inconceivable to human capacity and inconsistent with human society.

In these and the like cases, when the government is dissolved, the people are at liberty to provide for themselves by erecting a new legislative, differing from the other by the change of persons or form, or both, as they shall find it most for their safety and good. . . .

. . . There is, therefore, secondly, another way whereby governments are dissolved, and that is when the legislative or the prince, either of them, act contrary to their trust. . . .

. . . When they endeavour to invade the property of the subject, and to make themselves or any part of the community masters or arbitrary disposers of the lives, liberties, or fortunes of the people.

. . . By this breach of trust they forfeit the power the people had put into their hands for quite contrary ends, and it devolves to the people who have a right to resume their original liberty, and by the establishment of a new legislative, such as they shall think fit, provide for their own safety and security, which is the end for which they are in society. . . .

. . . The people generally ill-treated, and contrary to right, will be ready upon any occasion to ease themselves of a burden that sits heavy upon them. . . .

. . . Such revolutions happen not upon every little mismanagement in public affairs. Great mistakes in the ruling part, many wrong and inconvenient laws, and all the slips of human frailty will be borne by the people without mutiny or murmur. But if a long train of abuses, prevarications, and artifices, all tending the same way, make the design visible to the people, and they cannot but feel what they lie under and see whither they are going, it is not to be wondered that they should then rouse themselves and endeavour to put the rule into such hands which may secure to them the ends for which government was at first erected, and without which ancient names and specious forms are so far from being better that they are much worse than the state of nature or pure anarchy —the inconveniences being all as great and as near, but the remedy farther off and more difficult.

. . . But if they who say "it lays a foundation for rebellion" mean that it may occasion civil wars or intestine broils, to tell the people they are absolved from obedience when illegal attempts are made upon their liberties or properties . . . they may as well say, upon the same ground, that honest men may not oppose robbers or pirates, because this may occasion disorder or bloodshed. If any mischief come in such cases, it is not to be charged upon him who defends his own right, but on him that invades his neighbour's. . . .

. . . It is true such men may stir whenever they please, but it will be only to their own just ruin and perdition; for till the mischief be grown general, and the ill designs of the rulers become visible, or their attempts sensible to the greater part, the people who are more disposed to suffer than right themselves by resistance are not apt to stir. The examples of particular injustice or oppression of here and there an unfortunate man, moves them not. . . .

. . . The common question will be made: "Who shall be judge whether the prince or legislative act contrary to their trust? . . . To this I reply: The people shall be judge; for who shall be judge whether his trustee or deputy acts well and according to the trust reposed in him but he who deputes him and must, by having deputed him, have still a power to discard him when he fails in his trust?

. . . If a controversy arise betwixt a prince and some of the people in a matter where the law is silent or doubtful, and the thing be of great consequence, I should think the proper umpire in such a case should be the body of the people. . . .

. . . To conclude, the power that every individual gave the society when he entered into it can never revert to the individuals again as long as the society lasts, but will always remain in the community, because without this there can be no community, no commonwealth, which is contrary to the original agreement; so also when the society hath placed the legislative in any assembly of men, to continue in them and their successors with direction and authority for providing such successors, the legislative can never revert to the people whilst that government lasts, because having provided a legislative with power to continue for ever, they have given up their political power to the legislative and cannot resume it. But if they have set limits to the duration of their legislative and made this supreme power in any person or assembly only temporary, or else when by the miscarriages of those in authority it is forfeited, upon the forfeiture, or at the determination of the time set, it reverts to the society, and the people have a right to act as supreme and continue the legislative in themselves, or erect a new form, or under the old form place it in new hands, as they think good.

SECTION XIII

VICO AND HUME

In the early 18th century, two writers of widely differing backgrounds and interests were discussing the possibility of a science of politics and of history: Vico in Italy and Hume in England.

Vico

Giovanni Battista Vico (1668–1744) lived most of his life in Naples, a poverty-stricken teacher. His book, *The New Science,* initially appeared in 1725 and was published in a definitive edition in 1744, after having been rewritten twice. He admired Bacon as "a universal man in theory and practice," and Grotius, who had "embraced in a system of universal law the whole of philosophy and philology." Vico attempted to emulate them, to establish a universal concept of knowledge, and to provide a history of the development of all nations.

In *The New Science,* Vico tried to bring together history and philosophy, fact and theory, to form an integrated conception of mankind. The book was a comprehensive investigation into the origins and development of human culture. It was a forerunner of much of the later discussion of comparative law, and philosophy of history. Vico was the first European writer (in this the Arabic Ibn Khaldun had preceded him) to show the interrelationships of society, culture and personality. He analyzed the systematic cultural differences in different historical periods, and showed that these differences might be arranged in sequences.

In Homer, he found a set of ideas, "a heroic poetic logic." From this starting point, Vico was able to divide history into three stages: divine, heroic and human. He could conclude that the working of Divine Providence led "to the great city of the Nations founded and governed by God."

There are two particularly interesting concepts in Vico: the law of ebb and flow, and the role of Providence in the life of man. The first idea, the process of history seen as a regular alternation between progress and regression in upward spiral movement, helped lead to the Enlightenment idea of progress, though Vico himself did not reach this conclusion. The second concept illustrated the influence of God working through purely human means, usually whole nations, to bring about His design for mankind. Freedom and individuality existed, even if God was omniscient.

Vico was an interesting precursor of the 19th century. In his attack on Cartesianism—its application of the geometric method to all the sciences, and its neglect of poetic language and the imagination—and on materialism, his stress on religious impulses, and his emphasis on society rather than the individual, Vico heralded the 19th-century idealist movement.

Hume

David Hume (1711–1776) wrote his *Treatise of Human Nature*, which "fell dead born from the press," in 1739, his *Enquiry concerning Human Understanding* in 1749, and his *Political Discourses* in 1752. He wrote no systematic work on politics, but his essays and philosophical works are full of valuable insights into political problems.

The foundation of a science of politics was based on discussion of political behavior through empirical statements and logical relationships. Facts were known from observation, not from reason; reason could not decide on the existence of facts. A science of politics could be developed on the basis of such observation married to historical knowledge. But it would be a modest science: "The world is still too young to fix many general truths in politics." All rules were deliberately made to deal with human needs, and so were rules of convenience, not of logic or morality. Hume attacked the contract theory because it was historically false and logically invalid as an explanation of the formation of society. Society had not been made by a voluntary agreement, but was the result of convenience, and the needs and passions of men.

To understand society, one had to examine the principles of human nature. The passions—violent and calm, including benevolence as well as self-interest—were the determining factors in man's conduct. Reason was the slave, not the master, of the passions. Moreover, custom, rather than reason, was the great guide of human life. If there were laws of nature, they were the result of human experience.

Political institutions were the deposit of historical experience, and so ought not to be changed. Hume brought a gentle skepticism to political inquiry. No one ought to be fanatical about any abstract theory of government. In his discussion of parties, Hume argued the distinction between those extremist groups that were a threat to the system, and those that were moderate and therefore desirable.

This skepticism did not prevent Hume from making normative judgments. He was a conservative with an aristocratic bias, believing that the best political regime was obtained in a society where men of property exercised political power. His skepticism suggested only that judgments be based on empirical research rather than abstract reason, by analysis rather than theological or obscurantist theory. Hume, like Aristotle, is the great model of cool, dispassionate, but interested observation of political phenomena.

VICO

The New Science

The Role of Providence in History

. . . Providence ordered certain groupings of a monarchical form, under fathers (equivalent to Princes), superior in virility, maturity and virtue. These fathers, pious, chaste and strong, in the state which must be called "of nature" (which was the same as the family state), must have formed the first natural orders. Since they were settled on the land and could no longer save their lives by running away, they had to defend themselves and their families by killing the wild animals that attacked them and to find sustenance by tilling the earth and sowing grain, which made for the preservation of the nascent human race.

Meanwhile, great numbers of men, impious in their disrespect for the gods, shameless in their sexual practices and indeed so wicked as to have intercourse with their mothers and daughters, wandered, weak and solitary, through the plains and valleys. In the long run, their nefarious common ownership of personal property and women gave rise to violent combat, and the defeated ran to seek refuge with the fathers, who by sheltering them extended their family kingdom to this inferior group of "clients." Their rule was based on the heroic virtues: piety, because they worshiped divinity, although they knew no better than to divide it into a plurality of gods such as could be grasped by their limited apprehension; temperance, because they kept to one woman, whom they had taken in a religious ceremony for a lifelong companion; physical strength, by which they killed wild animals and tilled the earth, and finally, magnanimity, which meant that they gave help to the weak and those in danger. These were, then, the Herculean commonwealths, in which pious, wise, chaste, strong and magnanimous leaders cast down the proud and defended the weak, in true civilized fashion.

But finally, the fathers, made great by the religion and virtue of their ancestors and the labors of their clients, began to violate the natural order, which is that of justice, by bearing down harshly on those whom they should have protected until finally these clients rebelled against them. But since, without order (which means without God), human society cannot endure, Providence led the fathers to unite with the most closely related orders against the rebels. In order to pacify them, they set up the first agrarian law in the world, which gave them beneficial possession or usufruct of the fields, without permanent legal title. Thus the first cities came into being, based on reigning orders of nobles. And when the natural order, which was based on accord with the condition of nature, on superiority of kind, sex, age, and virtue, failed, Providence raised up a civil order to go with the cities. And first of all, in close accord with nature, it was decreed that by virtue of nobility (which could derive only from religiously celebrated marriages), and hence also of heroism, the nobles should reign over the plebeians (who did not marry under the same religious auspices). Now that the divine reigns (in which families had been governed by divine auspices) were no more and the heroic form of government called heroes to rule, the basis of the commonwealth was the heroic orders' custody of religion, and through this religion all laws and rights belonged to the heroes alone. But since such nobility had become a gift of fortune, Providence raised the order of fathers, venerable on account of their age, to dominion among the nobles. The most spirited and robust among them emerged as kings who led the rest and formed them into orders to resist and hold down the clients who had rebelled against them. But with the passage of years and the development of the human mind, the plebeians began to see through the vanity of this so-called heroism. They realized that they partook of the same human nature as the nobles and wanted to enter the civil orders of the cities. Since eventually the people was to become sovereign, Providence caused the plebeians to wage a long struggle with the nobles over piety and religion, that is, over the transmission of the auspices, together with their public and private rights, to the new class which laid claim to them. Concern for piety and religion, then, made the people sovereign in the cities. In this respect the people of ancient Rome outdistanced all others and hence came to have world dominion. In any case, as the natural order was mingled more and more with the civil orders, the people's commonwealths were born. In them everything had to be brought into balance and, in order that blind chance should not rule, Providence ordained that a man's financial status, as determined by the census, should be the yardstick of his fitness for public office. Thus the industrious and not the lazy, the savers and not the spendthrifts, the magnanimous not the petty, in short, the rich, possessed of virtue or the idea of virtue, rather than the vice-ridden poor were considered the most fitted to govern. From such commonwealths, composed of people whose desire for justice caused them to frame universally good and hence just laws, there came a philosophy intrinsically designed to shape heroes and hence concerned with truth. Providence thus ordained because virtuous actions were no longer inspired by religious beliefs, and only philosophy could explain the meaning of virtue in such a way that if men were not virtuous they might at least be ashamed of vice. And out of philosophy Providence allowed the flowering of eloquence, which in commonwealths endowed with such good laws could not but espouse the cause of justice and thus further promote good lawmaking. . . .

But the commonwealths were gradually corrupted, and so were the philosophies; skepticism became the rule and learned fools attacked truth. A false eloquence came into being, ready to support either side of a debated cause. There was an abuse of eloquence (like that practiced by the tribunes of the Plebs in ancient Rome) and people chose to use their riches not merely to preserve their social standing but to attain power. Civil wars created disorder, and the commonwealths lapsed from perfect liberty into the worst form of tyranny, that is, anarchy, or the unbridled license of so-called free peoples.

To this great disease of cities Providence applies one of the three remedies, in the following order.

First it arranges for a man like Augustus Caesar to rise up among the people and establish himself as monarch, to take by force of arms all the orders and laws which were born of liberty but proved powerless to regulate it. On the other hand, the very form of the monarchic state is to contain the mon-

arch's unlimited will and power within the natural limitations
of the people's religion and liberty. For no monarchy that
fails to satisfy the people can endure.

Next, if Providence does not find such a remedy within the
people it seeks one outside. Since people so far corrupted have
already become slaves to their passions—luxury, effeminacy,
avarice, envy, and pride—and because of their dissolute life
have sunk into the vices of slaves, Providence decrees that
they should be suubject, by natural law, to other and stronger
nations which conquer them by force of arms and hold them
as provinces. From which process there shine out two great
truths of nature: first, that he who cannot govern himself
must be governed by another and, second, that the fittest not
only survive but also govern.

But if a people suffers from such dire disease that it can
neither settle upon a monarch of its own nor does any
stronger nation come to conquer and eventually conserve it,
then Providence imposes a radical cure. For such men, like
animals, have fallen into the way of thinking each one of his
own interest, and into such sensitivity, or rather pride, that
they take offense at nothing, and even in the midst of the
greatest festivity, when they are crowded closest together, they
are spiritually alone, each one unable to agree with his neighbor because he is so intent upon his own pleasure. By dint of
factionalism and desperate civil wars they make the cities into
jungles and the jungles into cavemen's dwellings. Only long
centuries of benightedness will disprove the specious philosophical subtleties which have made them more barbarian in
their thinking than they ever were, in more primitive times,
under the dominion of their senses. For, when untutored, they
displayed a sort of generous savagery, which could be met
with either flight or accommodation, but when intellectually
corrupted their savagery cloaked with fine words and embraced the deadliness of its intentions. Peoples which have
reached this degree of conscious wickedness are so stunned by
Providence's drastic cure that they are no longer sensitive to
the delicacies, pleasures and pomps of life, but aware only of
the bare necessities of living. The few survivors in a land of
plenty quite naturally amend their behavior; they return to old-
time simplicity and the cult of religion, faith and truth, which
are the natural foundations of justice and the ornaments and
beauties of God's eternal order.

. . . This is the great city of the nations, founded and
governed by God. Lycurgus, Solon and the decemvirs have
been extolled as legislators because it has heretofore been
believed that their wise ordinances were responsible for the

glories of Sparta, Athens and Rome, three cities preeminent in civic virtues. And yet these were of short duration and small extent compared to the universe of peoples, builded on such laws and ordinances that even in corruption it assumes governmental forms which allow it to endure. Must we not say that this is the counsel of a superhuman wisdom? . . .

Men themselves have made this world of nations . . . and yet it seems to have issued from a mind quite different, often contrary and always superior to the particular ends which men have meant to achieve, turning them to larger purposes and indeed employing them for the human race's preservation. Men, for instance, meant to satisfy their bestial desires and abandon their offspring, and instead they found themselves devising the chaste institution of marriage, that cornerstone of the family. The fathers, as we have seen, started to abuse their paternalistic power over their clients and dependents, and they wound up by making them subject to the civil powers which gave birth to cities. The reigning orders of nobles meant to take advantage of their lordly power over the plebeians and they found themselves obedient to the laws which created popular liberty. Free peoples wanted to free themselves from the restraint of their laws and they fell into the hands of monarchs. Monarchs sought to strengthen their position by leading their people into vice, and by so doing they prepared them to submit to the dominion of other and stronger lands. Whole nations attempted to lose themselves and a few survivors fled for safety to the wilderness whence, like Phoenixes, they arose to a new life. That which accomplished all this was mind, for men did it with intelligence; it was not fate, for they did it by choice; it was not chance, for it invariably led to the same results.

And so the facts contradict Epicurus, and his followers, Hobbes and Machiavelli, all of whom believe in chance, and Zeno and Spinoza who believe in fate. On the contrary, the facts support the opposite school of political philosophy, whose prince is the divine Plato, who asserts that Providence rules the affairs of men. . . . For in this work we have shown that, thanks to Providence, the most primitive governments had their entire being in religion, which was the basis of the family state, that heroic or aristocratic civil governments had the same religious foundation, then, when it comes to popular governments, that religion helped men to attain them and, finally, that in a monarchic state, religion must be the buckler of princes. If a people loses its religion it has no other basis for social life, no shield with which to defend itself, no fount of wisdom, no foundation, not even a form to shape its existence.

. . . For religion alone induces men to do good works, and this through the intermediary of the senses, since the virtuous maxims of the philosophers serve only to provide eloquence with the means of persuading the senses to do their duty. But there is an essential difference between our true Christian religion and all the other false ones. In ours divine grace works for an infinite and eternal good, which cannot fall under the dominion of the senses, and in consequence the mind moves the senses to deeds of virtue. Whereas the false religions have finite and perishable ends, both in this life and the next (where they anticipate a paradise of sensual pleasures), and hold that the senses must incline the mind to do good works.

But Providence, through the order of civil things treated in this book, makes itself apparent to us in three ways: first, by marvel; second, by veneration (such as all learned men feel for the unmatchable wisdom of the ancients), and third, by the ardent desire with which they strove to seek and attain it. These are, indeed, three lights of Providence's divinity; they aroused in the ancients the three admirable sentiments we have described above, which were later corrupted by the vanity of scholars and also of nations. The fact is that all wise men admire, venerate and seek to unite themselves to the infinite wisdom of God.

From all that has been discussed in this work we may conclude that this science of ours is inseparably bound up with the study of piety, and that if a man is not pious he cannot be wise.

(Extracts from the Conclusion.)

HUME

Interest and Political Obligation

Nothing appears more surprising to those who consider human affairs with a philosophical eye than the easiness with which the many are governed by the few and the implicit submission with which men resign their own sentiments and passions to those of their rulers. When we inquire by what means this wonder is affected, we shall find that, as force is always on the side of the governed, the governors have nothing to support them but opinion. It is, therefore, on opinion only that government is founded, and this maxim extends to the most despotic and most military governments as well as to the most free and most popular. The sultan of Egypt or the emperor of Rome might drive his harmless subjects like brute beasts against their sentiments and inclination. But he must, at least, have led his *mamelukes* or *praetorian bands*, like men, by their opinion.

Opinion is of two kinds, to wit, opinion of *interest* and opinion of *right*. By opinion of interest I chiefly understand the sense of general advantage which is reaped from government, together with the persuasion that the particular government which is established is equally advantageous with any other that could easily be settled. When this opinion prevails among the generality of a state or among those who have the force in their hands, it gives great security to any government.

Right is of two kinds: right to *power* and right to *property*. What prevalence opinion of the first kind has over mankind may easily be understood by observing the attachment which all nations have to their ancient government and even to those names which have had the sanction of antiquity. Antiquity always begets the opinion of right; and whatever disadvantageous sentiments we may entertain of mankind, they are always found to be prodigal both of blood and treasure in the maintenance of public justice. There is, indeed, no particular in which, at first sight, there may appear a greater contradiction in the frame of the human mind than the present. When men act in a faction, they are apt, without shame or remorse, to neglect all the ties of honor and mortality in order to serve their party; and yet, when a faction is formed upon a point of right or principle, there is no occasion where men discover a greater obstinacy and a more determined sense of justice and equity. The same social disposition of mankind is the cause of these contradictory appearances.

It is sufficiently understood that the opinions or right to property is of moment in all matters of government. A noted author has made property the foundation of all government, and most of our political writers seem inclined to follow him in that particular. This is carrying the matter too far, but still it must be owned that the opinion of right to property has a great influence in this subject.

Upon these three opinions, therefore, of public *interest*, of *right to power*, and of *right to property*, are all governments founded and all authority of the few over the many. There are, indeed, other principles which add force to these and determine, limit, or alter their operation, such as *self-interest*, *fear*, and *affection*. But still we may assert that these other principles can have no influence alone, but suppose the antecedent influence of those opinions above mentioned. They are, therefore, to be esteemed the secondary, not the original, principles of government.

For, *first*, as to *self-interest*, by which I mean the expectation of particular rewards, distinct from the general protection which we receive from government, it is evident that the magistrate's authority must be antecedently established, at least be hoped for, in order to produce this expectation. The prospect of reward may augment his authority with regard to some particular persons, but can never give birth to it with regard to the public. Men naturally look for the greatest favors from their friends and acquaintance, and, therefore, the hopes of any considerable number of the state would never center in any particular set of men if these men had no other title to magistracy and had no separate influence over the opinions of mankind. The same observation may be extended to the other two principles of *fear* and *affection*. No man would have any reason to *fear* the fury of a tyrant if he had no authority over any but from fear, since, as a single man, his bodily force can reach but a small way, and all the farther power he possesses must be founded either on our own opinion or on the presumed opinion of others. And though *affection* to wisdom and virtue in a *sovereign* extends very far and has great influence, yet he must antecedently be supposed invested with a public character; otherwise the public esteem will serve him in no stead; nor will his virtue have any influence beyond a narrow sphere.

A government may endure for several ages, though the balance of power and the balance of property do not coincide. This chiefly happens where any rank or order of the state has acquired a large share in the property, but, from the originial constitution of the government, has no share in the power. Under what pretense would any individual of that order assume authority in public affairs? As men are commonly much attached to their ancient government, it is not to be expected that the public would ever favor such usurpations. But where the original constitution allows any share of power, though small, to an order of men who possess a large share of property, it is easy for them gradually to stretch their authority and bring the balance of power to coincide with that of property. This has been the case with the House of Commons in England.

. . . When men, from their early education in society, have become sensible of the infinite advantages that result from it and have besides acquired a new affection to company and conversation, and when they have observed that the principal disturbance in society arises from those goods which we call external and from their looseness and easy transition from one person to another, they must seek for a remedy by putting these goods as far as possible on the same footing with the fixed and constant advantages of the mind and body. This can be done after no other manner than by a convention entered into by all the members of the society to bestow stability on the possession of those external goods and leave everyone in the peaceable enjoyment of what he may acquire by his fortune and industry. By this means everyone knows what he may safely possess, and the passions are restrained in their partial and contradictory motions. Nor is such a restraint contrary to these passions, for if so it could never be entered into nor maintained; but it is only contrary to their heedless and impetuous movement. Instead of departing from our own interest or from that of our nearest friends by abstaining from the possessions of others, we cannot better consult both these interests than by such a convention, because it is by that means we maintain society, which is so necessary to their well-being and subsistence as well as to our own.

This convention is not of the nature of a *promise;* for even promises themselves, as we shall see afterward, arise from human conventions. It is only a general sense of common interest, which sense all the members of the society express to one another and which induces them to regulate their conduct by certain rules. I observe that it will be for my interest to leave another in the possession of his goods *provided* he will act in the same manner with regard to me. He is sensible of a like interest in the regulation of his conduct. When this common sense of interest is mutually expressed and is known to both, it produces a suitable resolution and behavior. And this may properly enough be called a convention or agreement betwixt us. . . .

After this convention concerning abstinence from the possessions of others is entered into, and everyone has acquired a stability in his possessions, there immediately arise the ideas of *justice* and *injustice*, as also those of *property, right,* and *obligation*. The latter are altogether unintelligible without first understanding the former. Our property is nothing but those goods whose constant possession is established by the laws of society—that is, by the laws of justice. Those, therefore, who make use of the words *"property,"* or *"right,"* or *"obligation"* before they have explained the origin of justice, or even make use of them in that explication, are guilty of a very gross fallacy and can never reason upon any solid foundation. A man's property is some object related to him. This relation is not natural but moral, and founded on justice. It is very preposterous, therefore, to imagine that we can have any idea of property without fully comprehending the nature of justice and showing its origin in the artifice and contrivance of men. The origin of justice explains that of property. The same artifice gives rise to both. As our first and most natural sentiment of morals is founded on the nature of our passions and gives the preference to ourselves and friends above strangers, it is impossible there can be naturally any such thing as a fixed right or property, while the opposite passions of men impel them in contrary directions and are not restrained by any convention or agreement.

No one can doubt that the convention for the distinction of property and for the stability of possession is of all circumstances the most necessary to the establishment of human society, and that after the agreement for the fixing and observing of this rule there remains little or nothing to be done toward settling a perfect harmony and concord. . . .

. . . This *state of nature*, therefore, is to be regarded as a mere fiction, not unlike that of the *golden age* which poets have invented, only with this difference, that the former is described as full of war, violence, and injustice, whereas the latter is painted out to us as the most charming and most peaceable condition that can possibly be imagined. The seasons in that first age of nature were so temperate, if we may believe the poets, that there was no necessity for men to provide themselves with clothes and houses as a security against the violence of heat and cold. The rivers flowed with wine and milk, the oaks yielded honey, and nature spontaneously produced her greatest delicacies. Nor were these the chief advantages of that happy age. The storms and tempests were not alone removed from nature, but those more furious tempests were unknown to human breasts which now cause such uproar and engender such confusion. Avarice, ambition, cruelty, selfishness were never heard of; cordial affection, compassion, sympathy were the only movements with which the human mind was yet acquainted. Even the distinction of *mine* and *thine* was banished from that happy race of mortals, and carried with them the very notions of property and obligation, justice and injustice.

. . . I have already observed that justice takes its rise from human conventions, and that these are intended as a remedy to some inconveniences which proceed from the concurrence of certain *qualities* of the human mind with the *situation* of external objects. The qualities of the mind are *selfishness* and *limited generosity;* and the situation of external objects is their *easy change,* joined to their *scarcity* in comparison of the wants and desires of men. . . .

If men were supplied with everything in the same abundance, or if *everyone* had the same affection and tender regard for *everyone* as for himself, justice and injustice would be equally unknown among mankind.

Here then is a proposition which, I think, may be regarded as certain, *that it is only from the selfishness and confined generosity of man, along with the scanty provision nature has made for his wants, that justice derives its origin.* . . .

(Extracts from *Of the First Principles of Government,* and *Of the Origin of Justice and Property.*)

The Social Contract

. . . When we consider how nearly equal all men are in their bodily force, and even in their mental powers and faculties, till cultivated by education, we must necessarily allow that nothing but their own consent could at first associate them together and subject them to any authority. The people, if we trace government to its first origin in the woods and deserts, are the source of all power and jurisdiction, and voluntarily, for the sake of peace and order, abandoned their native liberty and receive laws from their equal and companion. The conditions upon which they were willing to submit were either expressed or were so clear and obvious that it might well be esteemed superfluous to express them. If this, then, be meant by the *original contract,* it cannot be denied that all government is, at first, founded on a contract and that the most ancient rude combinations of mankind were formed chiefly by that principle. In vain are we asked in what records this charter of our liberties is registered. It was not written on parchment, nor yet on leaves or barks of trees. It preceded the use of writing and all the other civilized arts of life. But we trace it plainly in the nature of man and in the equality, or something approaching equality, which we find in all the individuals of that species. The force which now prevails, and which is founded on fleets and armies, is plainly political and derived from authority, the effect of established government. A man's natural force consists only in the vigor of his limbs and the firmness of his courage, which could never subject multitudes to the command of one. Nothing but their own consent and their sense of the advantages resulting from peace and order could have had that influence.

Yet even this consent was long very imperfect and could not be the basis of a regular administration. . . . No compact or agreement, it is evident, was expressly formed for general submission, an idea far beyond the comprehension of savages. Each exertion of authority in the chieftain must have been particular and called forth by the present exigencies of the case. The sensible utility resulting from his interposition made these exertions become daily more frequent; and their frequency gradually produced a habitual and, if you please to call it so, a voluntary and therefore precarious acquiescence in the people.

But philosophers who have embraced a party—if that be not a contradiction in terms—are not content with these concessions. They assert not only that government in its earliest infancy arose from consent, or rather the voluntary acquiescence of the people, but also that, even at present, when it has attained its full maturity, it rests on no other foundation. They affirm that all men are still born equal and owe allegiance to no prince or government unless bound by the obligation and sanction of a *promise*. And as no man, without some equivalent, would forego the advantages of his native liberty and subject himself to the will of another, this promise is always understood to be conditional and imposes on him no obligation, unless he meet with justice and protection from his sovereign. These advantages the sovereign promises him in return; and if he fail in the execution, he has broken on his part the articles of engagement, and has thereby freed his subject from all obligations to allegiance. . . .

But would these reasoners look abroad into the world, they would meet with nothing that in the least corresponds to their ideas or can warrant so refined and philosophical a system. On the contrary, we find everywhere princes who claim their subjects as their property and assert their independent right of sovereignty from conquest or succession. We find also everywhere subjects who acknowledge this right in their prince and suppose themselves born under obligations of obedience to the certain sovereign, as much as under the ties of reverence and duty to certain parents. . . . Obedience or subjection becomes so familiar that most men never make any inquiry about its origin or cause, more than about the principle of gravity, resistance, or the most universal laws of nature. Or if curiosity ever move them, as soon as they learn that they themselves and their ancestors have, for several ages, or from time immemorial, been subject to such a form of government or such a family, they immediately acquiesce and acknowledge their obligation to allegiance. Were you to preach, in most parts of the world, that political connections are founded altogether on voluntary consent or a mutual promise, the magistrate would soon imprison you as seditious for loosening the ties of obedience, if your friends did not before shut you up as delirious for advancing such absurdities. It is strange that an act of the mind which every individual is supposed to have formed, and after he came to the use of reason too—otherwise it could have no authority—that this act, I say, should be so much unknown to all of them that over the face of the whole earth there scarcely remain any traces or memory of it.

But the contract on which government is founded is said to be the *original contract,* and consequently may be supposed too old to fall under the knowledge of the present generation. If the agreement by which savage men first associated and conjoined their force be here meant, this is acknowledged to be real; but being so ancient and being obliterated by a thousand changes of government and princes, it cannot now be supposed to retain any authority. If we would say anything to the purpose, we must assert that every particular government which is lawful and which imposes any duty of allegiance on the subject was at first founded on consent and a voluntary compact. . . .

Almost all the governments which exist at present, or of which there remains any record in story, have been founded originally either on usurpation or conquest or both, without any pretense of a fair consent or voluntary subjection of the people. . . .

The face of the earth is continually changing by the increase of small kingdoms into great empires, by the dissolution of great empires into smaller kingdoms, by the planting of colonies, by the migration of tribes. Is there anything discoverable in all these events but force and violence? Where is the mutual agreement or voluntary association so much talked of? . . .

In reality there is not a more terrible event than a total dissolution of government, which gives liberty to the multitude and makes the determination or choice of a new establishment depend upon a number which nearly approaches to that of the body of the people. . . .

It is in vain to say that all governments are or should be at first founded on popular consent as much as the necessity of human affairs will admit. . . . I maintain that human affairs will never admit of this consent, seldom of the appearance of it; but that conquest or usurpation—that is, in plain terms, force—by dissolving the ancient governments, is the origin of almost all the new ones which were ever established in the world. And that in the few cases where consent may seem to have taken place, it was commonly so irregular, so confined, or so much intermixed either with fraud or violence that it cannot have any great authority. . . .

. . . Were all men possessed of so perfect an understanding as always to know their own interests, no form of government had ever been submitted to but what was established on consent and was fully canvassed by every member of the society. But this state of perfection is likewise much superior to human nature. Reason, history, and experience show us that all political societies have had an origin much less accurate and regular; and were one to choose a period of time when the people's consent was the least regarded in public transactions, it would be precisely on the establishment of a new government. In a settled constitution their inclinations are often consulted, but during the fury of revolutions, conquests, and public convulsions, military force or political craft usually decides the controversy. . . .

Should it be said that, by living under the dominion of a prince which one might leave, every individual has given a *tacit* consent to his authority and promised him obedience, it may be answered that such an implied consent can only have place where a man imagines that the matter depends on his choice. But where he thinks—as all mankind do who are born under established governments—that by his birth he owes allegiance to a certain prince or certain form of government, it would be absurd to infer a consent or choice which he expressly in this case renounces and disclaims.

Can we seriously say that a poor peasant or artisan has a free choice to leave his country when he knows no foreign language or manners and lives from day to day by the small wages which he acquires? We may as well assert that a man, by remaining in a vessel, freely consents to the dominion of the master, though he was carried on board while asleep and must leap into the ocean and perish the moment he leaves her.

. . . A small degree of experience and observation suffices to teach us that society cannot possibly be maintained without the authority of magistrates, and that this authority must soon fall into contempt where exact obedience is not paid to it. The observation of these general and obvious interests is the source of all allegiance and of that moral obligation which we attribute to it.

. . . We shall only observe, before we conclude, that though an appeal to general opinion may justly, in the speculative sciences of metaphysics, natural philosophy, or astronomy, be deemed unfair and inconclusive, yet in all questions with regard to morals, as well as criticism, there is really no other standard by which any controversy can ever be decided. And nothing is a clearer proof that a theory of this kind is erroneous than to find that it leads to paradoxes repugnant to the common sentiments of mankind and to the practice and opinion of all nations and all ages. . . .

(Extract from *Of the Original Contract.*)

The Role of Custom, and Genial Skepticism

. . . Wherever the repetition of any particular act or operation produces a propensity to renew the same act or operation without being impelled by any reasoning or process of the understanding, we always say that this propensity is the effect of *custom.* By employing that word we pretend not to have given the ultimate reason of such a propensity. We only point out a principle of human nature which is universally acknowledged, and which is well known by its effects. Perhaps we can push our inquiries no further or pretend to give the cause of this cause, but must rest contented with it as the ultimate principle which we can assign of all our conclusions from experience . . . no man, having seen only one body move after being impelled by another, could infer that every other body will move after a like impulse. All inferences from experience, therefore, are effects of custom, not of reasoning.

Custom, then, is the great guide of human life. It is that principle alone which renders our experience useful to us and makes us expect, for the future, a similar train of events with those which have appeared in the past. Without the influence of custom we should be entirely ignorant of every matter of fact beyond what is immediately present to the memory and senses. We should never know how to adjust means to ends or to employ our natural powers in the production of any effect. There would be an end at once of all action as well as of the chief part of speculation. . . .

. . . All the philosophy in the world, and all the religion, which is nothing but a species of philosophy, will never be able to carry us beyond the usual cause of experience or give us measures of conduct and behavior different from those which are furnished by reflections on common life. No new fact can ever be inferred from the religious hypothesis, no event foreseen or foretold, no reward or punishment expected or dreaded, beyond what is already known by practice and observation . . . nor have the political interests of society any connection with the philosophical disputes concerning metaphysics and religion. . . .

Though I should allow your premises, I must deny your conclusion. You conclude that religious doctrines and reasonings *can* have no influence on life because they *ought* to have no influence, never considering that men reason not in the same manner you do, but draw many consequences from the belief of a divine existence and suppose that the Deity will inflict punishments on vice and bestow rewards on virtue beyond what appear in the ordinary course of nature. Whether this reasoning of theirs be just or not is no matter. Its influence on their life and conduct must still be the same. And those who attempt to disabuse them of such prejudices may, for aught I know, be good reasoners, but I cannot allow them to be good citizens and politicians, since they free men from one restraint upon their passions and make the infringement of the laws of society in one respect more easy and secure.

After all, I may perhaps agree to your general conclusion in favor of liberty, though upon different premises from those on which you endeavor to found it. I think that the state ought to tolerate every principle of philosophy, nor is there an instance that any government has suffered in its political interests by such indulgence. There is no enthusiasm among philosophers; their doctrines are not very alluring to the people, and no restraint can be put upon their reasonings but what must be of dangerous consequence to the sciences, and even to the state, by paving the way for persecution and oppression in points where the generality of mankind are more deeply interested and concerned.

All probable arguments are built on the supposition that there is conformity betwixt the future and the past, and therefore [he] can never prove it. This conformity is a *matter of fact,* and if it must be proved will admit of no proof but from experience. But our experience in the past can be a proof of nothing for the future but upon a supposition that there is a resemblance betwixt them. This, therefore, is a point which can admit of no proof at all, and which we take for granted without any proof.

We are determined by *custom* alone to suppose the future conformable to the past. . . .

It is not, therefore, reason which is the guide of life, but custom. That alone determines the mind in all instances to suppose the future conformable to the past. However easy this step may seem, reason would never, to all eternity, be able to make it. . . .

. . . No matter of fact can be proved but from its cause or effect. Nothing can be known to be the cause of another but by experience. We can give no reason for extending to the future our experience in the past, but are entirely determined by custom when we conceive an effect to follow from its usual cause. But we also believe an effect to follow, as well as conceive it. This belief joins no new idea to the conception. It only varies the manner of conceiving and makes a difference to the feeling or sentiment. Belief, therefore, in all matters of fact arises only from custom and is an idea conceived in a peculiar *manner*.

The same thing extends to the operations of the mind. Whether we consider the influence of the will in moving our body or in governing our thought, it may safely be affirmed that we could never foretell the effect merely from the consideration of the cause, without experience. And even after we have experience of these effects, it is custom alone, not reason, which determines us to make it the standard of our future judgments. When the cause is presented, the mind, from habit, immediately passes to the conception and belief of the usual effect. This belief is something different from the conception. It does not, however, join any new idea to it. It only makes it be felt differently, and renders it stronger and more lively.

. . . All that has been said tends to give us a notion of the imperfections and narrow limits of human understanding. Almost all reasoning is there reduced to experience, and the belief which attends experience is explained to be nothing but a peculiar sentiment or lively conception produced by habit. Nor is this all; when we believe anything of *external* existence or suppose an object to exist a moment after it is no longer perceived, this belief is nothing but a sentiment of the same kind. . . . Upon the whole we assent to our faculties and employ our reason only because we cannot help it. Philosophy would render us entirely Pyrrhonian, were not nature too strong for it.

Through this whole book there are great pretensions to new discoveries in philosophy; but if anything can entitle the author to so glorious a name as that of an "inventor," it is the use he makes of the principle of the association of ideas, which enters into most of his philosophy. Our imagintion has a great authority over our ideas, and there are no ideas that are different from each other which it cannot separate and join and compose into all the varieties of fiction. But notwithstanding the empire of the imagination, there is a secret tie or union among particular ideas which causes the mind to conjoin them more frequently together and makes the one, upon its appearance, introduce the other. Hence arises what we call the *apropos* of discourse; hence the connection of writing; and hence that thread or chain of thought which a man naturally supports even in the loosest *reverie*. These principles of association are reduced to three, viz., "resemblance"—a picture naturally makes us think of the man it was drawn for; "contiguity"—when St. Dennis is mentioned, the idea of Paris naturally occurs: "causation"—when we think of the son we are apt to carry our attention to the father. It will be easy to conceive of what vast consequence these principles must be in the science of human nature if we consider that so far as regards the mind these are the only links that bind the parts of the universe together or connect us with any person or object exterior to ourselves. For as it is by means of thought only that anything operates upon our passions, and as these are the only ties of our thoughts, they are really *to us* the cement of the universe, and all the operations of the mind must, in a great measure, depend on them.

(Extracts from *An Enquiry Concerning Human Understanding* and *An Abstract of a Treatise of Human Nature*.)

Political Parties

. . . As much as legislators and founders of states ought to be honored and respected among men, as much ought the founders of sects and factions to be detested and hated, because the influence of faction is directly contrary to that of laws. Factions subvert government, render laws impotent, and beget the fiercest animosities among men of the same nation, who ought to give mutual assistance and protection to each other. And what should render the founders of parties more odious is the difficulty of extirpating these weeds when once they have taken root in any state. They naturally propagate themselves for many centuries, and seldom end but by the total dissolution of that government in which they are sown. . . .

Factions may be divided into *personal* and *real*, that is, into factions founded on personal friendship or animosity among such as compose the contending parties and into those founded on some real difference of sentiment or interest. The reason of this distinction is obvious, though I must acknowledge that parties are seldom found pure and unmixed, either of the one kind or the other. . . .

. . . Nothing is more usual than to see parties which have begun upon a real difference continue even after that difference is lost. When men are once enlisted on opposite sides, they contract an affection to the persons with whom they are united and an animosity against their antagonists, and these passions they often transmit to their posterity. . . .

Parties from *principle,* especially abstract speculative principle, are known only to modern times and are, perhaps, the most extraordinary and unaccountable phenomenon that has yet appeared in human affairs . . . where the difference of principle is attended with no contrariety of action, but everyone may follow his own way without interfering with his neighbor, as happens in all religious controversies, what madness, what fury can beget such an unhappy and such fatal division? . . . But such is the nature of the human mind that it always lays hold on every mind that approaches it, and as it is wonderfully fortified by a unanimity of sentiments, so it is shocked and disturbed by any contrariety. Hence the eagerness which most people discover in a dispute, and hence their impatience of opposition even in the most speculative and indifferent opinions.

This principle, however frivolous it may appear, seems to have been the origin of all religious wars and divisions. . . .

To abolish all distinctions of party may not be practicable, perhaps not desirable in a free government. The only dangerous parties are such as entertain opposite views with regard to the essentials of government, the succession of the crown, or the more considerable privileges belonging to the several members of the constitution; where there is no room for any compromise or accommodation, and where the controversy may appear so momentous as to justify even an opposition by arms to the pretensions of antagonists. . . .

. . . The only rule of government, they might have said, known and acknowledged among men is use and practice; reason is so uncertain a guide that it will always be exposed to doubt and controversy; could it ever render itself prevalent over the people, men had always retained it as their sole rule of conduct; they had still continued in the primitive unconnected state of nature without submitting to political government, whose sole basis is not pure reason, but authority and precedent. Dissolve these ties, you break all the bonds of civil society and leave every man at liberty to consult his private interest by those expedients which his appetite, disguised under the appearance of reason, shall dictate to him. The spirit of innovation is in itself pernicious, however favorable its particular object may sometimes appear—a truth so obvious that the popular party themselves are sensible of it and therefore cover their encroachments on the crown by the plausible pretense of their recovering the ancient liberties of the people. . . .

. . . But the people must not pretend because they can, by their consent, lay the foundations of government, that therefore they are to be permitted at their pleasure to overthrow and subvert them. There is no end of these seditious and arrogant claims.

. . . The greater moderation we now employ in representing past events, the nearer shall we be to produce a full coalition of the parties and an entire acquiescence in our present establishment. Moderation is of advantage to every establishment; nothing but zeal can overturn a settled power, and an overactive zeal in friends is apt to beget a like spirit in antagonists. The transition from a moderate opposition against an establishment to an entire acquiescence in it is easy and insensible.

. . . There are enough to zealots on both sides who kindle up the passions of their partisans and, under pretense of public good, pursue the interests and ends of their particular faction. For my part I shall always be more fond of promoting moderation than zeal, though perhaps the surest way of producing moderation in every party is to increase our zeal for the public. Let us therefore try, if it be possible from the foregoing doctrine, to draw a lesson of moderation with regard to the parties into which our country is at present divided, at the same time that we allow not this moderation to abate the industry and passion with which every individual is bound to pursue the good of his country.

(Extracts from *Of Parties in General, Of the Coalition of Parties*, and *That Politics May Be Reduced to a Science*.)

FRENCH THOUGHT IN THE LATE 17TH AND 18TH CENTURIES

The first half of the 17th century was a period in which English writing on politics was of the most significance and influence. In the latter part of the century, France again became the center of political discussion. Political problems engaged the attention of religious reformers, aristocratic writers, administrators, teachers of princes, and two important groups of writers, the first concerned primarily with economic problems, and the second with toleration and civil liberties.

The Education of Princes

The 17th century in France was marked by religious controversy, between the Jesuits and Jansenists, between Bossuet and Fénelon, as well as between Catholics and Huguenots. Disputes of this kind led to the *Pastoral Letters* of the Huguenot theologian Jurieu (1637–1713). Written in Rotterdam and smuggled into France, the letters argued the Lockean case for toleration, on the grounds that all power belonged to the people and was held on trust by rulers. The disputes also produced the *Dictionary* of Bayle (1647–1706), admired by Jefferson, as well as the Philosophes. The *Dictionary*, a compilation of somewhat diffuse articles on a wide variety of subjects, was to be immensely influential through its advocacy of toleration and its use of genial indecency as a method of attacking religious superstition, magic and authority.

But it was with the function and powers of absolute monarchy that most of the writing was concerned. The literature was essentially one of indictment or defense of the absolute monarch, Louis XIV. It was produced by aristocrats like the Duc de Saint-Simon, arguing the need for constitutional restraints on the king, and by administrators like Vaubon and

Bois-Guillebert, advocating the need for administrative reorganization and economic reform. Three important writers contributed to this literature, which lasted until the Revolution, on the functions and duties of sovereigns: Bossuet, Fénelon and La Bruyère.

Jacques Bossuet (1627–1704), the effective preacher at the Royal Chapel, famous for his eloquent and forceful funeral orations, became tutor to the dauphin in 1670. As part of his tutorial function, he wrote in 1679 *La Politique Tirée de L'Écriture Sainte*. Bossuet, the influential ecclesiastic and the vigorous polemicist who was the center of a number of religious disputes, was probably the last major writer to draw all his propositions and proofs from the words of the Scriptures. His premise, based on his close study of Hobbes, was that men had surrendered their power to the sovereign in return for security and order. His book was a eulogy of absolute government which was divine and unchallengeable. Yet the absolute ruler was neither arbitrary nor irresponsible, for he was responsible to God, and he was obliged to rule in the best interests of his citizens.

Fénelon (1651–1714), whose promising career was checked as a result of his bitter theological quarrel with Bossuet, became tutor to the Duke of Burgundy in 1689. Ten years later he published *Télémaque*, the story of the wanderings of Telemachus, accompanied by Mentor, in search of his father Ulysses. The description and analysis of different countries provided the opportunity for sharp criticism of the French monarch and institutions by contrast. Fénelon argued against despotism, saying that kings did not rule simply by the will of God, but through the will of the people. He advocated monarchical reform, aid to the poor, the end of the impoverishment of the country, and the beginning of a national system of education.

La Bruyère (1645–1696), a friend of Bossuet, was recommended by the latter to be history teacher and later "gentleman-in-waiting" to the Duke of Bourbon. Living with the Condé family and thus gaining experience of aristocratic behavior, in 1688 he wrote his *Characters*, a series of reflections, maxims and aphorisms. With gentle irony and tolerance, he exposed the errors of the *ancien regime*, its tyranny and its selfishness, in a number of charming essays.

The Physiocrats

The Physiocrats were an informal group of writers concerned with economic problems. All rejected the idea of mercantilism, which had become the rationale for increasing aggressiveness by centralized states. Mercantilism involved strong control by the state over industry and trade, protective tariffs, taxation, the acquisition of precious metals, a larger navy, and the building of a colonial empire. The objective was the fostering of manufacturing and commerce, and a favorable balance of payments.

The Physiocrats—a group including Quesnay, Mirabeau, Dupont de Nemours, Mercier de la Rivière, and having Turgot as an ally—called themselves the "economists." The more familiar name was bestowed upon them because of their advocacy of "physiocracy," government of all society through the system of natural law.

The most familiar, influential and typical of their works was the *Tableau Economique* of Quesnay, physician to Madame de Pompadour. Mirabeau, in his over-enthusiastic praise of the book, compared it in importance with the other two great discoveries of the world, the discovery of writing and the invention of money. Quesnay wanted to find the eternal, natural laws of wealth, taking it for granted that such laws had the same character as physical laws. He held that all wealth was produced by nature. In opposition to the mercantilists, who had belittled agriculture in their desire to stimulate manufactures, Quesnay argued that only argiculture was productive. The need was to multiply the sources of wealth, agricultural produce. This could be done by freeing agriculture from restrictions, ending monopolies and by complete freedom of trade, internal and external. Controls were unnecessary since the individual knew his own interest best, and acted in accordance with the laws of nature. A single tax on agricultural production would be enough to produce the revenue needed for the expenses of government. Taxes and loans were otherwise to be avoided.

Here was a philosophy emphasizing the rights of property and individual liberty for the 18th century landlord. It was based on the assumption of a harmony of interests underlying the whole economy, in which each person acted as a rational creature according to immutable, unbreakable laws. The state would encourage a system of education which would teach the fundamental principles of natural law. Through this teaching, agricultural production would be stimulated, the cost of living reduced, sufficient revenue produced, and revolution warded off. Politically, the Physiocrats supported hereditary monarchy assisted by an enlightened public opinion.

Turgot attempted to act according to the lines laid down. In 1776 he abolished the guilds, the *corvée*—the compulsory labor system—and tried to introduce a single tax on land. But his dismissal in the same year ended all hope of the Physiocratic ideas being put into practice.

The group, in essence, founded the study of economics, divorcing it from politics, and turning attention from the study of commerce to the analysis of production. It was this analysis, together with their discussion of surplus profit and their idea that political institutions resulted from economic and social behavior, that led Marx to praise the Physiocrats as "the true fathers of modern economics."

The Philosophes

A second, more influential, group of French writers was the Philosophes, a group which counted Diderot, Voltaire, Holbach, Helvétius, D'Alembert and Grimm as its members, and Montesquieu and Rousseau as its associates at different times.

The mounting political, social and economic problems in mid-18th century France captured the attention of this group. With superb skill in a variety of literary forms, they continued the devastating attacks of Bayle on superstition and intolerance. Influenced by the advance in science, and especially by the example of Newton, they collected facts in all spheres of knowledge. They dealt with the arts and sciences simply, providing a coherent and comprehensible account of the essential nature of a subject. If the group had little original to say, it said everything with immense enthusiasm and energy. If the members attacked religious superstition and fanaticism, they were, in the main, deists rather than atheists; they retained God as the mechanic of a well-designed universe. Above all, they were influential. A measure of their success is shown in La Tour's portrait of Madame de Pompadour, where *L'Esprit des Lois* and the *Encyclopedia* rest beside her.

Voltaire (1694–1778), historian, playwright and satirist, the gamin with inexhaustible literary fertility, the Bernard Shaw of the 18th century, wrote on all subjects with incisive clarity and dazzling simplicity. He mounted his most caustic attack on the Church, advocating the importance of reason, and of the toleration of all beliefs, religious and secular. His defense of the Protestant Calas, unjustly accused of murder, still echoes down the ages as a stirring example of the intellectual defending the persecuted. There were contradictions in Voltaire's voluminous writings—on parliamentary government, absolute monarchy, the "canaille"—but his main objectives remained constant: civil liberties, a rational law, toleration and a Church deprived of wealth and power.

Diderot (1713–84), was the editor of the *Encyclopédie*, the great 35-volume work of rational inquiry into all subjects, to which all the Philosophes contributed. To ensure the publication of the work, he fought against the Establishment of the day: Church, courts, university, censorship and the state. A gifted, sensitive journalist, his theater and art criticisms were extraordinarily modern, the latter being deliberately imitated by Baudelaire. He wrote no work specifically on politics— "many a fine page, but no one fine work"—but everything he wrote was concerned, in one way or another, with the need for toleration.

Helvétius (1715–1771), wealthy tax-farmer, of German origin, wrote his *De l'Esprit* in 1758. Though the book was burned by the public hangman and Helvétius publicly recanted, his views remained unchanged, as his posthumous works showed. Helvétius, aiming to be "the Newton of politics," sought for a single principle to explain social behavior. He found it in man's self-interested pursuit of pleasure and the avoidance of pain. This was the key to the motives and ends of men, since consciousness was derived from sensation and was the same in all men. The art of legislation, and the way to make men happy, was to create a system in which the ends of justice, public good, and the greatest happiness of the greatest number, were obtained more easily. By a process of manipulation, punishments and rewards, and education, men could be socially conditioned and forced to be just to one another. Helvétius provided an early version of both the concept of utilitarianism and of a technocratic elite, adjusting men to a predetermined harmony.

Holbach (1723–1789), whose salon became a meeting place for the group, wrote his *Le Système de la Nature* in 1770. He argued that the social freedom of man depended on intellectual freedom, and this meant substituting naturalism for theism. He advised, "Study nature and learn her laws." All good action came from the study of science through observation and experience, not from prejudice or supernatural explanations. Religion had caused intolerance, persecution and superstition. Without it, there might be satisfactory legislation and an improved educational system.

The Philosophes possessed in common, in varying degrees, belief in reason as the means by which to solve human problems. This belief was not a simple naïveté or abstract rationalism, but was well tempered with sentiment. The Philosophes looked to nature as the source of justice and virtue. They all attacked religious fanaticism and dogma in order to end ignorance and superstition. They could hardly foresee that political fanaticism might be greater and more destructive than religious. They tended, with some reservations, to think of man as naturally good, of man's progress toward perfection as natural, in the good society to be created. Optimistically, the devil was thrown out of court, or at least until the Lisbon Earthquake resulting in the ruin of the city and perhaps 20,000 dead, dispelled any complacency on this score.

In general, the Philosophes were interested in civil liberties and constitutional restraints rather than in political equality, in good enlightened government rather than free government, in the absence of privileges and fair taxation rather than a democratic regime, in a rational, humane system of law rather than economic regulation, in an intellectual elite rather than fraternity, and above all, in toleration.

In general, the Philosophes were interested in civil liberties and constitutional restraints rather than in political equality, in good enlightened government rather than free government, in the absence of privileges and fair taxation rather than a democratic regime, in a rational, humane system of law rather than economic regulation, in an intellectual elite rather than fraternity, and above all, in toleration.

Montesquieu (1689–1755) inherited the office of magistrate in his native Bordeaux, but was more interested in writing about law than practicing it. In 1734 he wrote the *Persian Letters*, a critical and at times biting satire on French politics; in 1748 he published *L'Esprit des Lois*. The book, written over a twenty-year period, is less a systematic treatise than a series of reflections on a variety of topics, including Italian and English opera, the burning of Jews, Negro slavery, the nature of citizens of Moscow.

Though Vico wrote in similar, if obscure, fashion, Montesquieu was really the founder of the modern historical method and of sociological jurisprudence. Political institutions and laws, including the laws governing change, were to be studied by both fact and theory, by empirical research and by "nature" and "reason." All laws were "the relations which necessarily flow from the nature of things." Each law was conditioned by its relation to the physical environment, and religious and social phenomena and behavior. The essential principle behind institutions held them together, and demonstrated the interrelationship of facts; a change in one part of the structure inevitably produced a change in another.

Montesquieu's central thesis was the relativity of law, and the view that laws and constitutions were less significant than the spirit behind them and the desire to operate them well or badly. His approach is relativistic, in that there was no one solution or regime applicable to all countries, that there was more than one way of being civilized, that the regime of a country depended on time, physical conditions, climate and traditions of each country, and had to be judged by its adaptation to those conditions.

The spirit of an institution or law was understood by examining it in all its inter-relations. Therefore, the informing spirit of different political systems would be different: in democracy, it would be virtue; in aristocracy it would be moderation; in monarchy, honor; and in despotism, fear. All laws would be derived from these principles.

It was his discussion of political liberty and the separation of powers that made Montesquieu a familiar and influential political thinker. The Founding Fathers referred more often to Book XI, which discusses these topics, than to the rest of the work altogether. Whether Montesquieu interpreted correctly or not the British system that he took as his model is still open to dispute, but the effect of his analysis was to help shape future political systems.

He established what is now the orthodox method of discussing governmental organization. Governmental powers were of three kinds: legislative, executive and judicial. If any two of these powers were exercised by the same person or group, a threat to liberty would exist. The ideal system, providing maximum liberty, existed where the law was made by one body, executed by a different one, and ruled on by a third, each of the three groups containing different personnel as well as exercising different functions. In France, political liberty would be aided by the existence of the *parlements*, serving as the *dépôt des lois*, knowing and opposing what was contrary to the law, and by intermediary bodies—between the central government and the people—which would maintain tradition and check central power.

Montesquieu shared, with the rest of the Philosophes, a dislike of clericalism, slavery and despotism, a demand for humane civil and criminal law, and a recognition of the need for tax reform. Yet he was unjustly suspect to most of the group through their misunderstanding of his attitude to law and to establish creeds and institutions. His book was an implicit attack on the concepts of natural rights, utility and the social contract, since for him all these ideas falsely assumed the existence of an abstract man, similar under all conditions. His thinking was to influence the writing of the

United States Constitution as well as to dominate the early part of the French Revolution.

BOSSUET

Politics Drawn from Holy Scriptures
(La Politique Tirée de l'Ecriture Sainte)

The Absolute Monarch

Monarchy is the most common, the oldest, and the most natural form of government. Every state began with monarchy, and almost all have remained in that form of government. . . . Men are all born subjects, and by nature are accustomed not only to obey, but also to having only one leader. Monarchy is the best system. If it is the most natural, it is consequently the most durable and the strongest. It is also the most opposed to that division that is the worst evil of states and the most certain cause of their ruin.

Of all forms of monarchy, the best is heredity where succession is in the male line and in order of seniority. Hereditary monarchy has three main advantages which make it the best government. First, it is the most natural form and perpetuates itself. Secondly, it is the type of government which makes its leaders care most for the preservation of the state. The prince who works for his state works for his children. . . . Thirdly, the dignity of the royal families, who are loved and respected, is not the object of ambition and jealousy. . . .

We have established by the Scriptures that royalty has its origin in divinity itself. God chose the monarchical and hereditary state as the most natural and the most durable. . . . We have found that, by order of Divine Providence, monarchy was from its origin the most comfortable to the will of God, as declared by the Scriptures. . . .

There are four essential characteristics or qualities of royal authority: it is sacred, it is paternal, it is absolute, it is subject to reason. . . .

God establishes kings as his ministers, and reigns over peoples through them. . . . All power comes from God. . . . Princes act as ministers of God and as His lieutenants on earth. . . . The royal throne is not the throne of a man, but the throne of God himself. . . .

The person of kings is sacred; they are the representatives of divine majesty, deputed by Providence to execute its designs. . . . Princes must be obeyed according to religion and to conscience. . . .

Kings must respect their own power, and use it only for the

public good. Their power coming from on high, they must not think they can use it at their own will. They must exercise it with fear and restraint, as something from God for which they must render account. . . .

Kings therefore must tremble in exercising the power given them by God, and understand how horrible a sacrilege it is to abuse a power coming from God. . . . They must govern as God commands, in a manner that is noble, disinterested, and kindly, in a divine way.

Kings take the place of God who is the true father of mankind. The king is the father of his people, and goodness is his most natural character. . . . The prince is not born for himself, but for his people . . . He must attend to the needs of the people: the tyrant is concerned for himself only. The government must be gentle, not like a lion, not oppressing subjects and servants. Princes are made to be loved. . . .

To make the term "absolute government" odious, many incorrectly confuse it with arbitrary government, which is quite different. . . .

The prince is not accountable to anyone for his orders. Without absolute authority, he can neither do good nor repress evil. It is necessary that his power is such that no one can hope to escape it. When the prince has judged, there can be no other judgment. The prince can correct himself when he knows he has acted badly; but, when challenged, there can be no other remedy except his own authority. . . . There is no "coactive force" against the prince. A "coactive force" is a power to compel and execute what is ordered legitimately . . . To the prince alone belongs legitimate command: to him alone belongs also the "coactive force" . . . In the state, only the prince is armed: otherwise, all is in confusion and the state will fall into anarchy . . . The prince has the sovereign authority of judging and control of all the forces of the state. . . .

To the prince only belongs the general care of the people. This is the first principle and the basis of all others. He controls all public affairs, appointments, the armed forces, decrees and ordinances, marks of distinction. All power is dependent on his, all assemblies on his authority. For the good of the state, all power is in the hands of one person . . . Otherwise, the state will be divided. The public peace will be ruined, for no one can serve two masters. . . . There is nothing better than to allow all the power of the state to he who has the most interest in the conservation of and the greatness of the state itself.

Yet, kings are not freed from the laws. . . . They are subject, as are others, to the equity of the laws. They must be just and must give their people an example of protecting justice. But they are not subject to the penalties of the laws. . . . The people must submit peacefully to the authority of the prince. If the impatient people are stirred up, and do not wish to remain quiet under royal authority, the fire of division will begin and will consume the hedge with all the other trees, that is, the king and the people. If the great power, the royal power, falls, all the other powers will be overthrown, and the whole state will be reduced to ashes. Royal authority must be invincible. If there is in the state some authority capable of stopping or obstructing the exercise of public power, no one is safe.

Government is a work of reason and intelligence. . . . The king must be the soul and the intelligence of the state. . . . The prince must understand governmental and business matters, must be familiar with his times, must know men, must know himself, must know both internal and external conditions. His principal book is the world; he must be attentive to all that happens around him in order to profit by it.

Majesty is the image of the greatness of God in the prince. The prince, as prince, is not an individual: he is a public person. All the state is in him; the will of all the people is contained in his. As all perfection and virtue are united in God, so all the powers of individuals are united in the person of the prince. What grandeur that a single man contains in himself. . . .

The power of God is felt in an instant from one end of the earth to the other: royal power acts in the same manner in the whole kingdom. This power controls the kingdom as God controls the world. If God withdrew His hand, the world would fall into nothingness. If authority ceased in the kingdom, all would be in confusion. Consider the prince in his office. From there are issued the orders that unify magistrates and captains, citizens and soldiers, provinces and armies on land and sea. It is the image of God. Order, justice, tranquility in the whole kingdom: that is the natural effect of the authority of the prince . . . The majesty of the prince is so great that it must be borrowed from God who gives it to the prince for the good of the people for whom it is good to be constrained by a superior force.

Kings, exercise your power boldly, for it is divine and salutary for mankind. But exercise it with humility. It comes to you from an outside source. It leaves you feeble, mortal, sinners, and it burdens you before God with a greater responsibility. It is necessary to serve the state as the prince understands it, for in him lies the reason that leads the state.

Those who think to serve the state otherwise than in serving and obeying the prince, attribute to themselves a part of royal authority. They disturb the public peace, and the cooperation of all the parts with the head. . . .

The life of the prince is regarded as the health of all the people: it is why each is careful of the life of the prince, as of his own, and more than his own. . . . A good subject loves his prince as the public welfare, as the health of all the state, as the air he breathes, as the light of his eyes, as his life, and even more than his life. . . .

Subjects must owe the prince complete obedience. If the prince is not obeyed promptly, public order will be disturbed, and there will no longer be harmony or peace in the state . . . Whoever disobeys the public power is judged worthy of death. God has made kings and princes his lieutenants on earth in order to render their authority sacred and inviolable. . . . There is nothing more founded on the word of God than that obedience is due to legitimate authority, according to religion and conscience. There is only one exception to the obedience owed a prince, and that is if he commands anything against God. God must be obeyed rather than men. . . .

There is another type of government, arbitrary government, which is not found with us or in perfectly civilised states. Four conditions accompany this kind of government. First, the subject peoples are born slaves, serfs; among them there are no free people. Secondly, no one possesses property. All things belong to the prince, and there is no inheritance from father to son. Thirdly, the prince has the right to dispose, at his discretion, not only of the goods, but also of the lives of his subjects. And fourthly, there is no law except his will.

This system of arbitrary government is barbarous and odious. Absolute government is different from this. It is absolute in its ability to compel, for there is no power capable of forcing the sovereign, who in this sense is independent of all human authority. But this is not arbitrary government because all is subject to the judgment of God. Also, everyone has legitimate possession of his own property.

FENELON
Télémaque

The Duties of a Ruler

I inquired in what the authority of the king consisted; and Mentor answered: "His authority over the subject is absolute, but the authority of the law is absolute over him. His power to do good is unlimited, but he is restrained from doing evil. The laws have put the people into his hands as the most valuable deposit, upon condition that he shall treat them as his children. It is the intent of the law that the wisdom and equity of one man shall be the happiness of many, and not that the wretchedness and slavery of many should gratify the pride and luxury of one. The king ought to possess nothing more than the subject, except what is necessary to alleviate the fatigue of his station, and impress upon the minds of the people a reverence of that authority by which the laws are executed. Moreover, the king should indulge himself less, as well in case as in pleasure, and should be less disposed to the pomp and the pride of life than any other man; he ought not to be distinguished from the rest of mankind by the greatness of his wealth, or the variety of his enjoyments, but by superior wisdom, more heroic virtue, and more splendid glory. Abroad he ought to be the defender of his country, by commanding her armies; and at home, the judge of his people, distributing justice among them, improving their morals, and increasing their felicity. It is not for himself that the gods have intrusted him with royalty: he is exalted above individuals, only that he may be the servant of the people; to the public he owes all his time, all his attention, and all his love; he deserves dignity only in proportion as he gives up private enjoyments for the public good.

"The proof of abilities in a king, as the supreme governor of others, does not consist in doing every thing himself: to attempt it is a poor ambition; and to suppose that others will believe it can be done, an idle hope. In government, the king should not be the body, but the soul; by his influence, and under his direction, the hands should operate, and the feet should walk. He should conceive what is to be done, but he should appoint others to do it. His abilities will appear in the conception of his designs, and especially in the choice of his instruments. He should never stoop to their function, nor suffer them to aspire to his. Neither should he trust them implicitly; he ought to examine their proceedings, and be equally able to detect a want of judgment or integrity. He governs well who discerns the various characters and abilities of men, and employs them to administer government under him, in departments that are exactly suited to their talents. The perfection of supreme government consists in the governing of those that govern. He that presides, should try, restrain, and correct them; he should encourage, raise, change, and displace them; he should keep them forever under his eye, and in his hand; but, to make the minute particulars of their subordinate departments objects of personal application, indicates meanness and suspicion, and fills the mind with petty anxieties, that leave it neither time nor liberty for designs that are worthy of royal attention. To form great designs, the mind must be free and tranquil; no intricacies of business must embarrass or perplex, no subordinate objects must divide the attention. A mind that is exhausted upon minute particulars, resembles the lees of wine, that have neither flavor nor strength. A king that busies himself in doing the duty of his servants, is always determined by present appearances, and never extends his view to futurity; he is always absorbed by the business of the day that is passing over him; and this being his only object, it acquires an undue importance, which, if compared with others, it would lose. The mind that admits but one object at a time, must naturally contract; and it is impossible to judge well of any affair, without considering many, comparing them with each other, and ranging them in a certain order, by which their relative importance will appear. He that neglects this rule in government, resembles a musician, who should content himself with the discovery of melodious tones, one by one, and never think of combining or harmonizing them into music, which would not only gratify the ear, but affect the heart. Or he may be compared to an architect, who should fancy the powers of his art exhausted, by heaping together large columns, and great quantities of stone curiously carved, without considering the proportion of his building, or the arrangement of his ornaments. Such an artist, when he was building a saloon, would not reflect that a suitable staircase should be added; and when he was busy upon the body of the building, he would forget the court-yard and the portal. His work would be nothing more than a confused assemblage of parts, not suited to each other, nor concurring to form a whole. . . .

". . . The government of a kingdom requires a certain harmony like music, and just proportions like architecture.

"The presiding mind, the genius that governs the State, is he who, doing nothing, causes all to be done; who meditates, contrives, looks forward to the future, and back to the past; who sees relative proportions, arranges all things in order, and provides for remote contingencies; who keeps himself in perpetual exercise to wrestle with fortune, as the swimmer struggles with a torrent; and whose mind is night and day upon the stretch, that, anticipating all events, nothing may be left to chance.

"Do you think, my dear Telemachus, that a great painter is

incessantly toiling that he may dispatch his work with the greater expedition? No: such drudgery and constraint would quench all the fire of imagination; he would no longer work like a genius, for the genius works as he is impelled by the power of fancy, in sudden, vigorous, but irregular sallies. Does the genius spend his time in grinding colors and preparing pencils? No: he leaves that to others who are yet in the rudiments of his art. He reserves himself for the labors of the mind; he transfers his ideas to the canvas in bold and glowing strokes, which give dignity to his figures, and animate them not only with life but passion. His mind teems with the thoughts and sentiments of the heroes he is to represent; he is carried back to the ages in which they lived, and to the circumstances in which they were placed. But with this fervid enthusiasm he possesses also a judgment that restrains and regulates it, so that his whole work, however bold and animated, is perfectly consonant with propriety and truth. And can it be imagined that less elevation of genius, less effort of thought, is necessary to make a great king than a good painter? Let us therefore conclude that the province of a king is to think, to form great designs, and to make choice of men properly qualified to carry them into execution."

Those who know the principles of government, and can distinguish the characters of men, know what is to be expected from them, and how to obtain it; they know, at least, whether the persons they employ are, in general, proper instruments to execute their designs, and whether they conceive and adopt their views with sufficient precision and abilities to carry them into effect. Besides, as their attention is not divided by embarrassing particulars, they keep the great object steadily in view, and can always judge whether they are approaching it. If they are sometimes deceived, it is in accidental and trifling matters that are not essential to the principal design.

(Extracts from Book XVII.)

MONTESQUIEU

The Spirit of the Laws
(L'Esprit des Lois)

The Relativity of Law

Law in general is human reason, inasmuch as it governs all the inhabitants of the earth: the political and civil laws of each nation ought to be only the particular cases in which human reason is applied.

They should be adapted in such a manner to the people for whom they are framed that it should be a great chance if those of one nation suit another.

They should be in relation to the nature and principle of each government: whether they form it, as may be said of politic laws; or whether they support it, as in the case of civil institutions.

They should be in relation to the climate of each country, to the quality of its soil, to its situation and extent, to the principal occupation of the natives, whether husbandmen, huntsmen, or shepherds: they should have relation to the degree of liberty which the constitution will bear; to the religion of the inhabitants, to their inclinations, riches, numbers, commerce, manners, and customs. In fine, they have relations to each other, as also to their origin, to the intent of the legislator, and to the order of things on which they are established; in all of which different lights they ought to be considered. . . .

These relations I shall examine, since all these together constitute what I call the Spirit of Laws.

I have not separated the political from the civil institutions, as I do not pretend to treat of laws, but of their spirit . . . this spirit consists in the various relations which the laws may bear to different objects.

(Extract from Book I, chapter 3.)

The Principles of Different Systems

There are three species of government: republican, monarchical, and despotic. In order to discover their nature, it is sufficient to recollect the common notion, which supposes three definitions, or rather three facts: that a republican government is that in which the body, or only a part of the people, is possessed of the supreme power; monarchy, that in which a single person governs by fixed and established laws; a despotic government, that in which a single person directs everything by his own will and caprice. . . .

. . . There is this difference between the nature and principle of government, that the former is that by which it is constituted, the latter that by which it is made to act. One is its particular structure, and the other the human passions which set it in motion.

Now, laws ought no less to relate to the principle than to the nature of each government.

There is no great share of probity necessary to support a

monarchical or despotic government. The force of laws in one, and the prince's arm in the other, are sufficient to direct and maintain the whole. But in a popular state, one spring more is necessary, namely, virtue.

. . . For it is clear that in a monarchy, where he who commands the execution of the laws generally thinks himself above them, there is less need of virtue than in a popular government, where the person intrusted with the execution of the laws is sensible of his being subject to their direction.

Clear is it also that a monarch who, through bad advice or indolence, ceases to enforce the execution of the laws, may easily repair the evil; he has only to follow other advice, or to shake off this indolence. But when, in a popular government, there is a suspension of the laws, as this can proceed only from the corruption of the republic, the state is certainly undone.

. . . When virtue is banished, ambition invades the minds of those who are disposed to receive it, and avarice possesses the whole community. The objects of their desires are changed; what they were fond of before has become indifferent; they were free while under the restraint of laws, but they would fain now be free to act against law. . . .

. . . As virtue is necessary in a popular government, it is requisite also in an aristocracy. True it is that in the latter it is not so absolutely requisite. . . .

. . . An aristocratic government has an inherent vigor, unknown to democracy. The nobles form a body, who by their prerogative, and for their own particular interest, restrain the people; it is sufficient that there are laws in being to see them executed.

But easy as it may be for the body of the nobles to restrain the people, it is difficult to restrain themselves. Such is the nature of this constitution, that it seems to subject the very same persons to the power of the laws, and at the same time to exempt them.

Now such a body as this can restrain itself only in two ways; either by a very eminent virtue, which puts the nobility in some measure on a level with the people, and may be the means of forming a great republic; or by an inferior virtue, which puts them at least upon a level with one another, and upon this their preservation depends.

Moderation is therefore the very soul of this government; a moderation, I mean, founded on virtue, not that which proceeds from indolence and pusillanimity.

In monarchies policy effects great things with as little virtue as possible. Thus in the nicest machines, art has reduced the number of movements, springs and wheels.

The state subsists independently of the love of our country of the thirst of true glory, of self-denial, of the sacrifice of our dearest interests, and of all those heroic virtues which we admire in the ancients, and to us are known only by tradition

The laws supply here the place of those virtues; they are by no means wanted, and the state dispenses with them: an action performed here in secret is in some measure of no consequence.

. . . Honor, that is, the prejudice of every person and rank supplies the place of the political virtue of which I have been speaking, and is everywhere her representative: here it is capable of inspiring the most glorious actions, and, joined with the force of laws, may lead us to the end of government as well as virtue itself.

Hence, in well-regulated monarchies, they are almost all good subjects, and very few good men; for to be a good man a good intention is necessary, and we should love our country not so much on our own account, as out of regard to the community.

. . . Honor sets all the parts of the body politic in motion and by its very action connects them; thus each individual advances the public good, while he only thinks of promoting his own interest. . . .

. . . As virtue is necessary in a republic, and in a monarchy honor, so fear is necessary in a despotic government. . . .

. . . A moderate government may, whenever it pleases, and without the least danger, relax its springs. It supports itself by the laws, and by its own internal strength. But when a despotic prince ceases for one single moment to uplift his arm, when he cannot instantly demolish those whom he has intrusted with the first employments, all is over: for as fear, the spring of this government, no longer subsists, the people are left without a protector.

It is in a republican government that the whole power of education is required. The fear of despotic governments naturally arises of itself amidst threats and punishments; the honor of monarchies is favored by the passions, and favor them in its turn; but virtue is a self-renunciation, which is ever arduous and painful.

This virtue may be defined as the love of the laws and of our country. As such love requires a constant preference of public to private interest, it is the source of all private virtues; for they are nothing more than this very preference itself.

This love is peculiar to democracies. In these alone the government is intrusted to private citizens. Now, a government is like every thing else: to preserve it we must love it.

. . . A love of the republic in a democracy is a love of the democracy; as the latter is that of equality.

A love of the democracy is likewise that of frugality. Since every individual ought here to enjoy the same happiness and the same advantages, they should consequently taste the same pleasures and form the same hopes, which cannot be expected but from a general frugality.

The love of equality in a democracy limits ambition to the sole desire, to the sole happiness, of doing greater services to our country than the rest of our fellow-citizens. . . .

. . . The good sense and happiness of individuals depend greatly upon the mediocrity of their abilities and fortunes. Therefore, as a republic, where the laws have placed many in a middling station, is composed of wise men, it will be wisely governed; as it is composed of happy men, it will be extremely happy.

. . . In monarchies and despotic governments, nobody aims at equality; this does not so much as enter their thoughts; they all aspire to superiority. People of the very lowest condition desire to emerge from their obscurity, only to lord it over their fellow-subjects.

It is the same with respect to frugality. To love it, we must practise and enjoy it. . . .

A true maxim it is, therefore, that in order to love equality and frugality in a republic, these virtues must have been previously established by law.

. . . All inequality in democracies ought to be derived from the nature of the government, and even from the principle of equality. For example, it may be apprehended that people who are obliged to live by their labor would be too much impoverished by a public employment, or neglect the duties attending it; that artisans would grow insolent, and that too great a number of freemen would overpower the ancient citizens. In this case the equality in a democracy may be suppressed for the good of the state. But this is only an apparent equality; for a man ruined by a public employment would be in a worse condition than his fellow-citizens; and this same man, being obliged to neglect his duty, would reduce the rest to worse condition than himself, and so on.

As equality of fortunes supports frugality, so the latter maintains the former. These things, though in themselves different, are of such a nature as to be unable to subsist separately; they reciprocally act upon each other; if one withdraws itself from a democracy, the other surely follows it.

True is it that when a democracy is founded on commerce, private people may acquire vast riches without a corruption of morals. This is because the spirit of commerce is naturally attended with that of frugality, economy, moderation, labor, prudence, tranquillity, order, and rule. So long as this spirit subsists, the riches it produces have no bad effect. The mischief is, when excessive wealth destroys the spirit of commerce, then it is that the inconveniences of inequality begin to be felt. . . .

. . . The preservation of the ancient customs is a very considerable point in respect to manners. Since a corrupt people seldom perform any memorable actions, seldom establish societies, build cities, or enact laws; on the contrary, since most institutions are derived from people whose manners are plain and simple, to keep up the ancient customs is the way to preserve the original purity of morals.

Besides, if by some revolution the state has happened to assume a new form, this seldom can be effected without infinite pains and labor, and hardly ever by idle and debauched persons. Even those who had been the instruments of the revolution were desirous it should be relished, which is difficult to compass without good laws. Hence it is that ancient institutions generally tend to reform the people's manners, and those of modern date to corrupt them. . . .

. . . The spirit of moderation is what we call virtue in an aristocracy; it supplies the place of the spirit of equality in a popular state.

As the pomp and splendor with which kings are surrounded form a part of their power, so modesty and simplicity of manners constitute the strength of an aristocratic nobility.

. . . In aristocratic governments there are two principal sources of disorder: excessive inequality between the governors and the governed; and the same inequality between the different members of the body that governs. From these two inequalities, hatreds and jealousies arise, which the laws ought ever to prevent or repress. . . .

. . . The laws should likewise forbid the nobles all kinds of commerce: merchants of such unbounded credit would monopolize all to themselves. Commerce is a profession of people who are upon an equality; hence among despotic states the most miserable are those in which the prince applies himself to trade.

Cardinal Richelieu advises monarchs to permit no such

things as societies or communities that raise difficulties upon every trifle. If this man's heart had not been bewitched with the love of despotic power, still these arbitrary notions would have filled his head.

The bodies intrusted with the deposition of the laws are never more obedient than when they proceed slowly, and use that reflection in the prince's affairs which can scarcely be expected from the ignorance of a court, or from the precipitation of its councils.

. . . It rarely happens that the states of the kingdom are entirely corrupted: the prince adheres to these; and the seditious, who have neither will nor hopes to subvert the government, have neither power nor will to dethrone the prince.

In these circumstances men of prudence and authority interfere; moderate measures are first proposed, then complied with, and things at length are redressed; the laws resume their vigor, and command submission. . . .

. . . When the savages of Louisiana are desirous of fruit, they cut the tree to the root, and gather the fruit. This is an emblem of despotic government.

The principle of despotic government is fear; but a timid, ignorant, and faint-spirited people have no occasion for a great number of laws.

Everything ought to depend here on two or three ideas; hence there is no necessity that any new notions should be added. . . .

. . . As fear is the principle of despotic government, its end is tranquillity; but this tranquillity cannot be called a peace: no, it is only the silence of those towns which the enemy is ready to invade. . . .

. . . After what has been said, one would imagine that human nature should perpetually rise up against despotism. But, notwithstanding the love of liberty, so natural to mankind, notwithstanding their innate detestation of force and violence, most nations are subject to this very government. This is easily accounted for. To form a moderate government, it is necessary to combine the several powers; to regulate, temper, and set them in motion; to give, as it were, ballast to one, in order to enable it to counterpoise the other. This is a masterpiece of legislation, rarely produced by hazard, and seldom attained by prudence. On the contrary, a despotic government offers itself, as it were, at first sight; it is uniform throughout; and as passions only are requisite to establish it, this is what every capacity may reach.

(Extracts from Book II, chapter 1; Book III, chapters 1, 3–7, 9; Book V, chapters 3–5, 7, 8, 10, 11, 13, 14.)

The Corruption of the Principles of the Three Governments

The corruption of every government generally begins with that of its principles.

The principle of democracy is corrupted not only when the spirit of equality is extinct, but likewise when they fall into a spirit of extreme equality, and when each citizen would fain be upon a level with those whom he has chosen to command him. Then the people, incapable of bearing the very power they have delegated, want to manage everything themselves, to debate for the senate, to execute for the magistrate, and to decide for the judges.

When this is the case, virtue can no longer subsist in the republic. . . .

. . . Aristocracy is corrupted if the power of the nobles becomes arbitrary: when this is the case, there can no longer be any virtue either in the governors or the governed.

If the reigning families observe the laws, it is a monarchy with several monarchs, and in its own nature one of the most excellent; for almost all these monarchs are tied down by the laws. But when they do not observe them, it is a despotic state swayed by a great many despotic princes. . : .

. . . An aristocracy may maintain the full vigor of its constitution if the laws be such as are apt to render the nobles more sensible of the perils and fatigues than of the pleasure of command: and if the government be in such a situation as to have something to dread, while security shelters under its protection, and uncertainty threatens from abroad. . . .

. . . As democracies are subverted when the people despoil the senate, the magistrates, the judges of their functions, so monarchies are corrupted when the prince insensibly deprives societies or cities of their privileges. In the former case the multitude usurp the power, in the latter it is usurped by a single person. . . .

. . . It is natural for a republic to have only a small territory; otherwise it cannot long subsist. In an extensive republic there are men of large fortunes, and consequently of less moderation. . . .

. . . The public good is sacrificed to a thousand private views; it is subordinate to exceptions, and depends on accidents. In a small one, the interest of the public is more obvious, better understood, and more within the reach of every citizen; abuses have less extent, and, of course, are less protected.

. . . A monarchical state ought to be of moderate extent.

Were it small, it would form itself into a republic; were it very large, the nobility, possessed of great estates, far from the eye of the prince, with a private court of their own, and secure, moreover, from sudden executions by the laws and manners of the country—such a nobility, I say, might throw off their allegiance, having nothing to fear from too slow and too distant a punishment. . . .

. . . A large empire supposes a despotic authority in the person who governs. It is necessary that the quickness of the prince's resolutions should supply the distance of the places they are sent to; that fear should prevent the remissness of the distant governor or magistrate; that the law should be derived from a single person, and should shift continually, according to the accidents which incessantly multiply in a state in proportion to its extent.

If it be, therefore, the natural property of small states to be governed as a republic, of middling ones to be subject to a monarch, and of large empires to be swayed by a despotic prince; the consequence is, that in order to preserve the principles of the established government, the state must be supported in the extent it has acquired, and that the spirit of this state will alter in proportion as it contracts or extends its limits.

(Extracts from Book VIII, chapters 1, 2, 5, 6, 16, 17, 19, 20.)

Political Liberty

It is true that in democracies the people seem to act as they please; but political liberty does not consist in an unlimited freedom. In governments, that is, in societies directed by laws, liberty can consist only in the power of doing what we ought to will, and in not being constrained to do what we ought not to will.

We must have continually present to our minds the difference between independence and liberty. Liberty is a right of doing whatever the laws permit, and if a citizen could do what they forbid he would be no longer possessed of liberty, because all his fellow-citizens would have the same power.

Democratic and aristocratic states are not in their own nature free. Political liberty is to be found only in moderate governments; and even in these it is not always found. It is there only when there is no abuse of power. But constant experience shows us that every man invested with power is apt to abuse it, and to carry his authority as far as it will go. Is it not strange, though true, to say that virtue itself has need of limits?

To prevent this abuse, it is necessary from the very nature of things that power should be a check to power. A government may be so constituted, as no man shall be compelled to do things to which the law does not oblige him, nor forced to abstain from things which the law permits.

Though all governments have the same general end, which is that of preservation, yet each has another particular object. Increase of dominion was the object of Rome; war, that of Sparta; religion, that of the Jewish laws; commerce, that of Marseilles; public tranquillity, that of the laws of China; navigation, that of the laws of Rhodes; natural liberty, that of the policy of the Savages; in general, the pleasures of the prince, that of despotic states; that of monarchies, the prince's and the kingdom's glory; the independence of individuals is the end aimed at by the laws of Poland, thence results the oppression of the whole.

One nation there is also in the world that has for the direct end of its constitution political liberty and that is England.

. . . In every government there are three sorts of power: the legislative; the executive in respect to things dependent on the law of nations; and the executive in regard to matters that depend on the civil law. . . .

. . . The latter we shall call the judiciary power, and the other simply the executive power of the state.

The political liberty of the subject is a tranquillity of mind arising from the opinion each person has of his safety. In order to have this liberty, it is requisite the government be so constituted as one man need not be afraid of another.

When the legislative and executive powers are united in the same person, or in the same body of magistrates, there can be no liberty; because apprehensions may arise, lest the same monarch or senate should enact tyrannical laws, to execute them in a tyrannical manner.

Again, there is no liberty, if the judiciary power be not separated from the legislative and executive. Were it joined with the legislative, the life and liberty of the subject would be exposed to arbitrary control; for the judge would be then the legislator. Were it joined to the executive power, the judge might behave with violence and oppression.

There would be an end of everything, were the same man or the same body, whether of the nobles or of the people, to exercise those three powers, that of enacting laws, that of executing the public resolutions, and that of trying the causes of individuals.

. . . Many of the princes of Europe, whose aim has been levelled at arbitrary power, have constantly set out with uniting in their own persons all the branches of magistracy, and all the great offices of state. . . .

. . . The judiciary power ought not to be given to a standing senate; it should be exercised by persons taken from the body of the people at certain times of the year, and consistently with a form and manner prescribed by law, in order to erect a tribunal that should last only so long as necessity requires.

By this method the judicial power, so terrible to mankind, not being annexed to any particular state or profession, becomes, as it were, invisible. People have not then the judges continually present to their view; they fear the office, but not the magistrate. . . .

. . . The other two powers may be given rather to magistrates or permanent bodies, because they are not exercised on any private subject; one being no more than the general will of the state, and the other the execution of that general will.

But though the tribunals ought not to be fixed, the judgments ought; and to such a degree as to be ever conformable to the letter of the law. Were they to be the private opinion of the judge, people would then live in society, without exactly knowing the nature of their obligations. . . .

. . . As in a country of liberty, every man who is supposed a free agent ought to be his own governor; the legislative power should reside in the whole body of the people. But since this is impossible in large states, and in small ones is subject to many inconveniences, it is fit the people should transact by their representatives what they cannot transact by themselves. . . .

The great advantage of representatives is, their capacity of discussing public affairs. For this the people collectively are extremely unfit, which is one of the chief inconveniences of a democracy.

It is not at all necessary that the representatives who have received a general instruction from their constituents should wait to be directed on each particular affair, as is practised in the diets of Germany. True it is that by this way of proceeding the speeches of the deputies might with greater propriety be called the voice of the nation; but, on the other hand, this would occasion infinite delays; would give each deputy a power of controlling the assembly; and, on the most urgent and pressing occasions, the wheels of government might be stopped by the caprice of a single person. . . .

. . . The people ought to have no share in the government but for the choosing of representatives, which is within their reach. For though few can tell the exact degree of men's capacities, yet there are none but are capable of knowing in general whether the person they choose is better qualified than most of his neighbors. . . .

. . . The executive power ought to be in the hands of a monarch, because this branch of government, having need of despatch, is better administered by one than by many: on the other hand, whatever depends on the legislative power is oftentimes better regulated by many than by a single person.

But if there were no monarch, and the executive power should be committed to a certain number of persons selected from the legislative body, there would be an end then of liberty; by reason the two powers would be united, as the same persons would sometimes possess, and would be always able to possess, a share in both.

Were the legislative body to be a considerable time without meeting, this would likewise put an end to liberty. For of two things one would naturally follow: either that there would be no longer any legislative resolutions, and then the state would fall into anarchy; or that these resolutions would be taken by the executive power, which would render it absolute. . . .

. . . Were the executive power not to have a right of restraining the encroachments of the legislative body, the latter would become despotic; for as it might arrogate to itself what authority it pleased, it would soon destroy all the other powers.

But it is not proper, on the other hand, that the legislative power should have a right to stay the executive. For as the execution has its natural limits, it is useless to confine it; besides, the executive power is generally employed in momentary operations. . . .

. . . But if the legislative power in a free state has no right to stay the executive, it has a right and ought to have the means of examining in what manner its laws have been executed. . . .

. . . But whatever may be the issue of that examination, the legislative body ought not to have a power of arraigning the person, nor, of course, the conduct, of him who is intrusted with the executive power. His person should be sacred, because as it is necessary for the good of the state to prevent the legislative body from rendering themselves arbitrary, the moment he is accused or tried there is an end of liberty. . . .

. . . Though, in general, the judiciary power ought not to be united with any part of the legislative, yet this is liable to three exceptions, founded on the particular interest of the party accused.

The great are always obnoxious to popular envy. . . . The nobility, for this reason, ought not to be cited before the ordinary courts of judicature, but before that part of the legislature which is composed of their own body.

It is possible that the law, which is clear sighted in one sense, and blind in another, might, in some cases, be too severe . . . it belongs to its (the legislative's) supreme authority to moderate the law in favor of the law itself, by mitigating the sentence.

It might also happen that a subject intrusted with the administration of public affairs may infringe the rights of the people, and be guilty of crimes which the ordinary magistrates either could not or would not punish . . . in order to preserve the dignity of the people and the security of the subject, the legislative part which represents the people must bring in its charge of impeachment before the legislative part which represents the nobility, who have neither the same interests nor the same passions. . . .

. . . The executive power, pursuant of what has been already said, ought to have a share of the legislature by the power of rejecting; otherwise it would soon be stripped of its prerogative. But should the legislative power usurp a share of the executive, the latter would be equally undone.

If the prince were to have a part in the legislature by the power of resolving, liberty would be lost. But as it is necessary he should have a share in the legislature for the support of his own prerogative, this share must consist in the power of rejecting. . . .

. . . Here, then, is the fundamental constitution of the government we are treating of. The legislative body being composed of two parts, they check one another by the mutual privilege of rejecting. They are both restrained by the executive power, as the executive is by the legislative.

These three powers should naturally form a state of repose or inaction. But as there is a necessity for movement in the course of human affairs, they are forced to move, but still in concert.

As the executive power has no other part in the legislative than the privilege or rejecting, it can have no share in the public debates. It is not even necessary that it should propose, because as it may always disapprove of the resolutions that shall be taken, it may likewise reject the decisions on those proposals which were made against its will. . . .

Were the executive power to determine the raising of public money, otherwise than by giving its consent, liberty would be at an end; because it would become legislative in the most important point of legislation.

If the legislative power was to settle the subsidies, not from year to year, but forever, it would run the risk of losing its liberty, because the executive power would be no longer dependent; and when once it was possessed of such a perpetual right, it would be a matter of indifference whether it held it of itself or of another. The same may be said if it should come to a resolution of intrusting, not an annual, but a perpetual command of the fleets and armies to the executive power.

To prevent the executive power from being able to oppress, it is requisite that the armies with which it is intrusted should consist of the people, and have the same spirit as the people, as was the case at Rome till the time of Marius. To obtain this end, there are only two ways, either that the persons employed in the army should have sufficient property to answer for their conduct to their fellow-subjects, and be enlisted only for a year, as was customary at Rome; or if there should be a standing army, composed chiefly of the most despicable part of the nation, the legislative power should have a right to disband them as soon as it pleased; the soldiers should live in common with the rest of the people; and no separate camp, barracks, or fortress should be suffered.

When once an army is established, it ought not to depend immediately on the legislative, but on the executive power; and this from the very nature of the thing, its business consisting more in action than in deliberation. . . .

(Extracts from Book XI, chapters 3–6.)

Climate and the Laws

If it be true that the temper of the mind and the passions of the heart are extremely different in different climates, the laws ought to be in relation both to the variety of those passions and to the variety of those tempers.

People are more vigorous in cold climates. Here the action of the heart and the reaction of the extermities of the fibres are better performed, the temperature of the humors is greater, the blood moves more freely towards the heart, and reciprocally the heart has more power. This superiority of strength must produce various effects; for instance, a greater boldness, that is, more courage; a greater sense of superiority, that is, less desire of revenge; a greater opinion of security, that is, more frankness, less suspicion, policy, and cunning. In short, this must be productive of very different tempers. Put a man into a close, warm place, and for the reasons above given he will feel a great faintness. If under this circumstance you propose a bold enterprise to him, I believe you will find him very little disposed towards it; his present weakness will throw him into despondency; he will be afraid of everything, being in a state of total incapacity. The inhabitants of warm countries are, like old men, timorous; the people in cold countries are, like young men, brave. . . .

In cold countries they have very little sensibility for pleasure; in temperate countries, they have more; in warm countries, their sensibility is exquisite. As climates are distinguished by degrees of latitude, we might distinguish them also in some measure by those of sensibility. I have been at the opera in England and in Italy, where I have seen the same pieces and the same performers; and yet the same music produces such different effects on the two nations; one is so cold and phlegmatic, and the other so lively and enraptured, that it seems almost inconceivable.

It is the same with regard to pain, which is excited by the laceration of some fibre of the body. . . . You must flay a Muscovite alive to make him feel.

. . . The heat of the climate may be so excessive as to deprive the body of all vigor and strength. Then the faintness is communicated to the mind; there is no curiosity, no enterprise, no generosity of sentiment; the inclinations are all passive; indolence constitutes the utmost happiness; scarcely any punishment is so severe as mental employment; and slavery is more supportable than the force and vigor of mind necessary for human conduct.

. . . If to that delicacy of organs which renders the eastern nations so susceptible of every impression you add likewise a sort of indolence of mind, naturally connected with that of the body, by means of which they grow incapable of any exertion or effort, it is easy to comprehend that when once the soul has received an impression it cannot change it. This is the reason that the laws, manners, and customs, even those which seem quite indifferent, such as their mode of dress, are the same to this very day in eastern countries as they were a thousand years ago.

. . . Fertile provinces are always of a level surface, where the inhabitants are unable to dispute against a stronger power; they are then obliged to submit; and when they have once submitted, the spirit of liberty cannot return; the wealth of the country is a pledge of their fidelity. But in mountainous districts, as they have but little, they may preserve what they have. The liberty they enjoy, or, in other words, the government they are under, is the only blessing worthy of their defence. It reigns, therefore, more in mountainous and rugged countries than in those which nature seems to have most favored.

The mountaineers preserve a more moderate government, because they are not so liable to be conquered. They defend themselves easily, and are attacked with difficulty; ammunition and provisions are collected and carried against them with great expense, for the country furnishes none. It is, then, a more arduous, a more dangerous, enterprise to make war against them; and all the laws that can be enacted for the safety of the people are there of least use.

. . . Mankind are influenced by various causes: by the climate, by the religion, by the laws, by the maxims of government, by precedents, morals, and customs; whence is formed a general spirit of nations.

In proportion as, in every country, any one of these causes acts with more force, the others in the same degree are weakened. Nature and the climate rule almost alone over the savages; customs govern the Chinese; the laws tyrannize in Japan; morals had formerly all their influence at Sparta; maxims of government, and the ancient simplicity of manners, once prevailed at Rome. . . .

. . . It is the business of the legislature to follow the spirit of the nation, when it is not contrary to the principles of government; for we do nothing so well as when we act with freedom, and follow the bent of our natural genius.

. . . We have said that the laws were the particular and precise institutions of a legislator, and manners and customs the institutions of a nation in general. Hence it follows that when these manners and customs are to be changed, it ought not to be done by laws; this would have too much the air of tyranny: it would be better to change them by introducing other manners and other customs.

Thus when a prince would make great alterations in his kingdom, he should reform by law what is established by law, and change by custom what is settled by custom; for it is very bad policy to change by law what ought to be changed by custom.

. . . The empire of the climate is the first, the most powerful, of all empires. . . . Nations are in general very tenacious of their customs; to take them away by violence is to render them unhappy: we should not therefore change them, but engage the people to make the change themselves.

(Extracts from Book XIV, chapters 1, 2, 4; Book XVIII, chapters 2, 4, 5, 14.)

SELECTED BIBLIOGRAPHY

->>->>->>->>->>->>->>->>

I. *The Greeks*

E. Barker, *Greek Political Theory: Plato and His Predecessors* (London, 1918).
————, *The Political Thought of Plato and Aristotle* (London, 1906).
G. L. Dickinson, *The Greek View of Life* (2nd ed., London, 1898).
M. I. Finley, *Democracy, Ancient and Modern* (London, 1973).
G. Glotz, *The Greek City* (London, 1929).
T. R. Glover, *Democracy in the Ancient World* (London, 1927).
D. Grene, *Man in His Pride* (Chicago, 1950).
W. K. Guthrie, *The Greeks and Their Gods* (Boston, 1955).
M. Hammond, *City-State and World State* (Cambridge, 1951).
E. A. Havelock, *The Liberal Temper in Greek Politics* (London, 1957).
T. Irwin, *Plato's Moral Theory: The Early and Middle Dialogues* (Oxford, 1977).
W. Jaeger, *Paideia, The Ideals of Greek Culture* (3 vols., New York, 1939).
J. W. Jones, *The Law and Legal Theory of the Greeks* (Oxford, 1956).
H. Kitto, *The Greeks* (London, 1951).
G. R. Morrow, *Plato's Cretan City* (Princeton, 1960).
K. Popper, *The Open Society and Its Enemies* (London, 1945).

T. L. Thorson, ed., *Plato: Totalitarian or Democrat?* (Englewood Cliffs, 1963).

E. Voeglin, *The World of the Polis* (Baton Rouge, 1956).

———, *Plato and Aristotle* (Baton Rouge, 1957).

J. Wild, *Plato's Theory of Man* (Cambridge, 1946).

E. M. and N. Wood, *Class Ideology and Ancient Political Theory* (New York, 1978).

A. Zimmern, *The Greek Commonwealth* (Oxford, 1922).

II.   Hellenism and Roman Stoicism

E. V. Arnold, *Roman Stoicism* (Cambridge, 1911).

E. Barker, *From Alexander to Constantine* (Oxford, 1956).

N. W. De Witt, *Epicurus and His Philosophy* (Minneapolis, 1954).

W. S. Ferguson, *Hellenistic Athens* (London, 1911).

G. Grote, *History of Greece* (London, 1883).

R. Hicks, *Stoic and Epicurean* (London, 1910).

J. A. O. Larsen, *Representative Government in Greek and Roman History* (Berkeley, 1955).

A. Momigliano, *Alien Wisdom: The Limits of Hellenization* (Cambridge, 1975).

G. Murray, *The Stoic Philosophy* (London, 1915).

M. Reesor, *The Political Theory of the Old and Middle Stoa* (New York, 1951).

W. W. Torn and G. T. Griffith, *Hellenistic Civilization* (3rd ed., London, 1952).

E. Zeller, *Stoics, Epicureans and Sceptics* (London, 1880).

III.   Rome

F. E. Adcock, *Roman Political Ideas and Practice* (Ann Arbor, 1959).

J. B. Bury, *History of the Later Roman Empire* (London, 1923).

R. W. and A. J. Carlyle, *A History of Mediaeval Political Theory in the West* (6 vols., New York, 1909–36).

M. L. Clarke, *The Roman Mind* (London, 1956).

F. R. Cowell, *Cicero and the Roman Republic* (London, 1948).

S. Dill, *Roman Society in the Last Century of the Western Empire* (London, 1898).

K. von Fritz, *The Theory of the Mixed Constitution in Antiquity* (New York, 1954).

H. Hill, *The Roman Middle Class in the Republican Period* (Oxford, 1952).

L. Homo, *Roman Political Institutions* (London, 1929).

C. H. McIlwain, *The Growth of Political Thought in the West* (New York, 1932).

H. H. Schullard, *Roman Politics 220–150 B.C.* (Oxford, 1951).

F. Schulz, *Principles of Roman Law* (Oxford, 1936).

R. E. Smith, *The Failure of the Roman Republic* (Cambridge, 1955).

R. Syme, *The Roman Revolution* (Oxford, 1939).

F. W. Walbank, *A Historical Commentary on Polybius* (Oxford, 1957).

IV. Early Christianity

R. H. Barrow, *Introduction to St. Augustine, The City of God* (London, 1950).

N. H. Baynes, *The Political Ideas of St. Augustine's City of God* (London, 1936).

P. R. L. Brown, *Augustine of Hippo: A Biography* (Berkeley, 1967).

C. N. Cochrane, *Christianity and Classical Culture* (Oxford, 1940).

G. Combes, *La Doctrine Politique de Saint Augustine* (Paris, 1927).

H. Deane, *The Political and Social Ideas of St. Augustine* (New York, 1963).

J. N. Figgis, *The Political Aspects of the City of God* (London, 1921).

M. L. W. Laistner, *Christianity and Pagan Culture in the Later Roman Empire* (Ithaca, 1951).

H. Lietzmann, *The Era of the Christian Fathers* (New York, 1952).

H. Marrou, *Saint Augustine* (New York, 1957).

A. Momigliano, ed., *The Conflict Between Paganism and Christianity in the 4th Century* (Oxford, 1963).

H. R. Niebuhr, *Christ and Culture* (New York, 1951).

E. Troeltsch, *The Social Teaching of the Christian Churches* (2 vols., New York, 1931).

H. A. Wolfson, *The Philosophy of the Church Fathers* (Cambridge, 1956).

ʹ. Medieval Life and Thought

H. Adams, *Mont-Saint-Michel and Chartres* (Boston, 1913).

G. Barraclough, *The Medieval Empire* (London, 1950).

N. H. Baynes and H. St. L. Moss, *Byzantium* (Oxford, 1948).

C. Dawson, *Religion and the Rise of Western Culture* (London, 1950).

O. Gierke, *Political Theories of the Middle Ages* (Cambridge, 1900).

E. Gilson, *History of Christian Philosophy in the Middle Ages* (London, 1955).

B. Jarrett, *Social Theories of the Middle Ages* (Boston, 1926).

E. Jenks, *Law and Politics in the Middle Ages* (New York, 1898).

W. O. Ker, *The Dark Ages* (Edinburgh, 1956).

F. Kern, *Kingship and Law in the Middle Ages* (Oxford, 1939).

G. Leff, *Medieval Thought* (London, 1958).

H. Pirenne, *Economic and Social History of Medieval Europe* (London, 1936).

S. Runciman, *The Eastern Schism* (Oxford, 1956).

H. O. Taylor, *The Medieval Mind* (Cambridge, 1938).

———, *The Classical Heritage of the Middle Ages* (New York, 1901).

G. Tellenbach, *Church, State and Christian Society at the Time of the Investiture Contest* (Oxford, 1940).

P. Vinogradoff, *Roman Law in Medieval Europe* (London, 1909).

———, *The Growth of the Manor* (2nd ed., New York, 1951).

VI.   *The Two Realms: The Last Phase*

A. Black, *Monarchy and Community* (Cambridge, 1970).

F. C. Copleston, *Aquinas* (London, 1956).

A. P. d'Entreves, *The Medieval Contribution to Political Thought* (Oxford, 1939).

A. Gewirth, *Marsilius of Padua* (New York, 1951).

T. Gilby, *The Political Thought of Aquinas* (Chicago, 1958)

E. H. Kantorowicz, *The King's Two Bodies* (Princeton, 1957).

E. Lewis, *Medieval Political Ideas* (New York, 1954).

J. B. Morrall, *Gerson and the Great Schism* (London, 1960).

D. J. O'Connor, *Aquinas and Natural Law* (New York, 1968).

I. Origo, *The Merchant of Prato* (London, 1957).

P. E. Sigmund, *Nicolas of Cusa and Medieval Political Thought* (Cambridge, 1963).

Q. Skinner, *The Foundations of Modern Political Thought* (2 vols., New York, 1978).

B. Tierney, *Foundations of the Conciliar Theory* (Cambridge, 1955).

W. Ullmann, *The Growth of Papal Government in the Middle Ages* (London, 1955).

————, *A Short History of the Papacy in the Middle Ages* (London, 1972).

H. Waddell, *The Wandering Scholars* (7th ed., London, 1947).

VII. *The Renaissance*

J. W. Allen, *A History of Political Thought in the 16th Century* (London, 1928).

S. Anglo, *Machiavelli: A Dissection* (New York, 1970).

H. Baron, *The Crisis of the Early Italian Renaissance* (Princeton, 1955).

S. M. Benians, *From Renaissance to Revolution* (New York, 1923).

J. Burckhardt, *The Civilization of the Renaissance in Italy* (2nd ed., New York, 1945).

H. Butterfield, *The Statecraft of Machiavelli* (London, 1940).

F. Chabod, *Machiavelli and the Renaissance* (London, 1958).

W. K. Ferguson, *The Renaissance in Historical Thought* (Boston, 1948).

J. N. Figgis, *Studies in Political Thought from Gerson to Grotius* (Cambridge, 1907).

M. Fleischer, ed. *Machiavelli and the Nature of Political Thought* (New York, 1972).

A. H. Gilbert, *Machiavelli's "Prince" and Its Forerunners* (Durham, 1938).

F. Gilbert, *Machiavelli and Guicciardini: Politics and History in 16th Century Florence* (Princeton, 1965).

M. R. Gilmore, *The World of Humanism* (New York, 1952).

H. Haydn, *The Counter-Renaissance* (New York, 1950).

J. H. Hexter, *The Vision of Politics on the Eve of the Reformation* (New York, 1973).

G. Mattingly, *Renaissance Diplomacy* (London, 1955).

F. Meinecke, *Machiavellianism* (New Haven, 1957).

A. Parel, ed., *The Political Calculus: Essays on Machiavelli's Philosophy* (Toronto, 1972).

J. G. A. Pocock, *The Machiavellian Moment* (Princeton, 1975).

L. Strauss, *Thoughts on Machiavelli* (Glencoe, 1958).

D. Weinstein, *Savonarola and Florence: Prophecy and Patriotism in the Renaissance* (Princeton, 1970).

VIII.   The Reformation

J. W. Allen, *English Political Thought, 1603–44* (London, 1938).

J. Atkinson, *Martin Luther and the Birth of Protestantism* (Harmondsworth, 1968).

C. Beard, *The Reformation of the 16th Century* (London, 1927).

E. Erikson, *Young Man Luther* (New York, 1958).

R. H. Fife, *The Revolt of Martin Luther* (New York, 1957).

H. J. Grimm, *The Reformation Era, 1500–1600* (New York, 1954).

K. Holl, *The Cultural Significance of the Reformation* (New York, 1959).

A. Hyma, *Renaissance to Reformation* (Grand Rapids, 1951).

J. T. McNeill, *The History and Character of Calvinism* (New York, 1954).

R. H. Murray, *Erasmus and Luther* (London, 1920).

F. M. Powicke, *The Reformation in England* (London, 1949).

C. Read, *Social and Political Forces in the English Reformation* (Houston, 1953).

G. Ritter, *Luther: His Life and Work* (New York, 1963).

E. G. Schweibert, *Luther and His Times* (St. Louis, 1950).

P. Smith, *The Age of the Reformation* (New York, 1920).

M. Spinka, *Advocates of Reform* (Philadelphia, 1953).

R. H. Tawney, *Religion and the Rise of Capitalism* (New York, 1954).

B. L. Woolf, ed., *Reformation Writings of Luther* (London, 1952).

IX.   The Right of Resistance

F. Braudel, *The Mediterranean and the Mediterranean World in the Age of Philip II* (New York, 1972).

B. S. Capp, *The Fifth Monarchy Men* (London, 1972).

F. Church, *The Italian Reformers* (New York, 1932).

G. Dodge, *The Political Theory of the Huguenots of the Dispersion* (New York, 1947).

O. Gierke, *Natural Law and the Theory of Society* (Cambridge, 1934).

G. P. Gooch, *Political Thought from Bacon to Halifax* (London, 1929).

W. Haller, *The Rise of Puritanism* (New York, 1938).

C. Hill, *The World Turned Upside Down* (London, 1972).

P. Janelle, *The Catholic Reformation* (Milwaukee, 1949).

O. Jaszi and J. D. Lewis, *Against the Tyrant* (Glencoe, 1957).

D. Kelley, *François Hotman: A Revolutionary's Ordeal*, (Princeton, 1973).

M. M. Knappen, *Tudor Puritanism* (Chicago, 1939).

C. Morris, *Political Thought in England: Tyndale to Hooker* (New York, 1953).

R. H. Murray, *The Political Consequences of the Reformation* (Boston, 1926).

J. W. Thompson, *The Wars of Religion in France* (Chicago, 1909).

M. Walzer, *The Revolution of the Saints* (New York, 1972).

A. S. P. Woodhouse, ed., *Puritanism and Liberty* (Chicago, 1938).

X. Sovereignty and Divine Right

F. I. Baumer, *The Early Tudor Theory of Kingship* (New Haven, 1940).

G. R. Elton, *England Under the Tudors* (London, 1955).

J. N. Figgis, *The Divine Right of Kings* (Cambridge, 1896).

J. H. Franklin, *Jean Bodin and the Rise of Absolutist Theory* (Cambridge, 1973).

J. W. Gough, *Fundamental Law in English Constitutional History* (Oxford, 1955).

J. H. Hexter, *The Reign of King Pym* (Cambridge, 1941).

J. E. A. Jolliffe, *Angevin Kingship* (London, 1955).

W. K. Jordan, *The Development of Religious Toleration in England* (Cambridge, 1932).

P. King, *The Ideology of Order* (London, 1974).

J. Mattern, *Concepts of the State, Sovereignty, and International Law* (Baltimore, 1928).

G. L. Mosse, *The Struggle for Sovereignty in England* (East Lansing, 1950).

J. U. Neff, *Cultural Foundations of Industrial Civilisation* (Cambridge, 1958).

A. F. Pollard, *Factors in Modern History* (London, 1907).

J. B. Scott, *The Spanish Origin of International Law* (London, 1934).

K. Thomas, *Religion and the Decline of Magic* (New York, 1971).

F. D. Wormuth, *The Royal Prerogative, 1603–49* (Ithaca, 1939).

XI.   *Hobbes and Spinoza*

J. Bowle, *Hobbes and His Critics* (London, 1951).

J. Dunner, *Spinoza and Western Democracy* (New York, 1955).

D. P. Gauthier, *The Logic of Leviathan* (Oxford, 1969).

M. M. Goldsmith, *Hobbes's Science of Politics* (New York, 1966).

W. H. Greenleaf, *Order, Empiricism and Politics* (London, 1964).

C. B. Macpherson, *The Political Theory of Possessive Individualism: Hobbes to Locke* (London, 1964).

R. P. McKeon, *The Philosophy of Spinoza* (New York, 1928).

H. A. Myers, *The Spinoza-Hegel Paradox* (Ithaca, 1944).

R. Peters, *Hobbes* (London, 1956).

R. Polin, *Politique et philosophie chez Hobbes* (Paris, 1953).

F. Pollock, *Spinoza* (London, 1880).

L. Strauss, *The Political Philosophy of Hobbes* (Chicago, 1952).

―――――, *Persecution and the Art of Writing* (Glencoe, 1952).

H. Warrennder, *The Political Philosophy of Hobbes* (Oxford, 1957).

H. A. Wolfson, *The Philosophy of Spinoza* (Cambridge, 1934).

XII.   *The Development of Constitutionalism*

C. Blitzer, *An Immortal Commonwealth: The Political Thought of James Harrington* (New Haven, 1960).

C. D. Bowen, *The Lion and the Throne* (Boston, 1957).

M. W. Cranston, *Locke* (New York, 1957).

E. T. Davies, *The Political Ideas of Richard Hooker* (London, 1948).

M. Downs, *James Harrington* (Boston, 1977).

J. Dunn, *The Political Thought of John Locke* (New York, 1969).

J. H. Franklin, *John Locke and the Theory of Sovereignty* (Cambridge, 1978).

G. P. Gooch, *English Democratic Ideas in the Seventeenth Century* (2nd ed., Cambridge, 1927).

J. W. Gough, *John Locke's Political Philosophy* (2nd ed., Oxford, 1973).

D. G. James, *The Life of Reason: Hobbes, Locke, Bolingbroke* (London, 1949).

S. Lamprecht, *The Moral and Political Philosophy of Locke* (New York, 1918).

H. J. Laski, *Political Thought in England from Locke to Bentham* (London, 1920).

C. H. McIlwain, *The High Court of Parliament and Its Supremacy* (New Haven, 1910).

P. Munz, *The Place of Hooker in the History of Thought* (London, 1952).

H. F. Russell-Smith, *Harrington and His Oceana* (Cambridge, 1914).

M. Salvadori, ed., *Locke and Liberty* (London, 1960).

M. Seliger, *The Liberal Politics of John Locke* (New York, 1968).

L. Strauss, *Natural Right and History* (Chicago, 1953).

F. D. Wormuth, *The Origins of Modern Constitutionalism* (New York, 1949).

J. W. Yolton, *John Locke and the Way of Ideas* (London, 1956).

———, ed., *John Locke: Problems and Perspectives* (Cambridge, 1969).

XIII. *Vico and Hume*

I. Berlin, *Vico and Herder* (London, 1976).

J. B. Black, *The Art of History* (London, 1926).

H. Cairns, *Legal Philosophy from Plato to Hegel* (Baltimore, 1949).

R. Caponigri, *Time and Idea* (Chicago, 1953).

R. G. Collingwood, *The Idea of History* (Oxford, 1946).

B. Croce, *The Philosophy of Vico* (London, 1913).

D. J. Greene, *The Politics of Samuel Johnson* (New Haven, 1960).

M. H. Fisch and T. G. Bergin, eds., *The Autobiography of Vico* (Ithaca, 1944).

E. Halevy, *The Growth of Philosophic Radicalism* (London, 1928).

P. Hazard, *The European Mind* (New Haven, 1953).

F. L. Lucas, *The Art of Living* (London, 1959).

J. A. Passmore, *Hume's Intentions* (Cambridge, 1952).

C. Robbins, *The Eighteenth Century Commonwealth Man* (Cambridge, 1959).

W. G. Ross, *Human Nature and Utility in Hume's Social Philosophy* (Garden City, 1942).

L. Stephen, *History of English Thought in the Eighteenth Century* (2nd ed., London, 1881).

C. Vaughan, *Studies in the History of Political Philosophy* (Manchester, 1925).

F. Vaughan, *The Political Philosophy of Vico* (The Hague, 1972).

W. H. Walsh, *An Introduction to the Philosophy of History* (London, 1951).

E. Wilson, *To the Finland Station* (New York, 1953).

B. Willey, *The 18th Century Background* (London, 1940).

XIV. *French Thought in the Late 17th and 18th Centuries*

E. Auerbach, *Mimesis* (New York, 1957).

C. Becker, *The Heavenly City of the 18th Century Philosophers* (New Haven, 1932).

H. N. Brailsford, *Voltaire* (London, 1935).

E. Cassirer, *The Philosophy of the Enlightenment* (Princeton, 1951).

A. Cherel, *Fénelon au XVIII Siècle en France* (Paris, 1917).

L. G. Crocker, *Diderot's Chaotic Order* (Princeton, 1974).

L. Dimier, *Bossuet* (Paris, 1917).

L. Ducros, *Les Encyclopedistes* (Paris, 1900).

P. Gay, *Voltaire's Politics* (Princeton, 1959).

G. Havens, *The Age of Ideas* (New York, 1955).

P. Hazard, *European Thought in the 18th Century* (New Haven, 1954).

M. Hulliung, *Montesquieu and the Old Regime* (Berkeley, 1976).

F. Lange, *The History of Materialism* (London, 1925).

A. G. Martimort, *Le Gallicanisme de Bossuet* (Paris, 1953).

B. K. Martin, *French Liberal Thought in the 18th Century* (London, 1929).

T. L. Pangle, *Montesquieu's Philosophy of Liberalism* (Chicago, 1973).

H. Robinson, *Bayle the Sceptic* (New York, 1931).

M. Roustan, *Pioneers of the French Revolution* (Boston, 1926).

H. Sée, *Les Idées Politiques en France au XVII*ᵉ *Siècle* (Paris, 1923).

———, *Les Idées Politiques en France au XVIII*ᵉ *Siècle* (Paris, 1920).

A. Strugnell, *Diderot's Politics* (The Hague, 1973).

H. Taine, *The Origins of Contemporary France* (New York, 1876).

F. Venturi, *Utopia and Reform in the Enlightenment* (Cambridge, 1971).

A. Wilson, *Diderot* (New York, 1972).

INDEX

-»»-»»-»»-»»-»»-»»-»»-»»

INDEX

Absolutism, 412–13

Abstract of a Treatise of Human Nature, An, 409

Acton, Lord, 15, 178

Admonition to England and Scotland to call them to Repentence, 264

Anti-clericalism, 226–28

Antigone, 25, 30–34

Aquinas, St. Thomas, 15, 142, 177–78, 263; authority, 207–209; kingship, 207–10; law: esesnce of, 196–98, eternal, 200–201, human, 205–207, natural, 201–203, types, 198–200; tyranny, 209–10, 290–92

Aristotle, 14, 17, 20, 28–30, 177, 180, 181, 183, 187–88, 190, 197, 277, 291, 328, 359, 364; association, political, 64–72; citizen, good, 75–78; citizenship, 72–82; constitutions, 78–82, 93–96; government, 96–101; kingship, 90–92, 272; law, 90–92; man, good, 75–78; politics, 92–93, 288; power, political, 87–90; rule, paternal, 71–72; slavery, 24, 67–71; sovereignty, 84–87; state, 65–67

Assassination. *See* Resistance

Association, political, 64–72. *See also* Commonwealth, Social organization, Society, *and* State

Augustine, Saint, 141–43, 177; commonwealth, 155–56; justice, 155–56; two cities, 149–55; universe, 146–49

Aurelius, Marcus. *See* Marcus Aurelius

Authority: dual, 158–60; political, 207–209; secular, 238–46

Barclay, William, 264, 265, 301, 302

Baudelaire, Pierre C., 105

Bayle, Pierre, 412, 415

Bellarmine, Robert, 265–66, 298–300

Bodin, Jean, 17, 19, 218, 301–302, 304–13

Boniface VIII, 175, 178

Bossuet, Jacques, 412, 413, 419–22

Brutus, Stephen J., 263, 266–72; kings, 269–72; people, powers of, 269–72; resistance, 266–68

Calvin, John, 234–35, 236–37; government, 255–59; liberty, 250–54; obedience, 259–62; rulers, 249–50

Christianity, 359; early, 140–56; liberty, 250–54

Church, consent in, 211–14

Cicero, 122–23, 142; justice, 136–39; reason, right, 135–36; state, mixed, 131–33, 274, 276

Citizen: freedom of, 354–56; good, 75–78

City of God, The, 142, 143, 146–56

Civil society: Hooker, 367–72; Locke, 375–78; Suarez, 287–98

Civitas Dei, 143

Climate, 438–40

Coalition of Parties, Of the, 411

Commonwealth: Augustine, 155–56; John of Salisbury, 169–74; nature of, 169–74, 276–78. *See also* Association, Social organization, Society, *and* State

Commonwealth of Oceana, The, 358, 361–65

Commonwealth, On the, 122–23, 131–33, 135–36, 136–37

Commonwealth, The, 131–33

Community, 288–90

Concordantia Catholica, 211–14

Consent, in church, 211–14

Constance, Church Council of, 179

Constitutionalism, 263, 272–80, 357–89

Constitutions: Aristotle, 78–82, 93–96; classification, 78–82; mixed, 125–31; Polybius, 125–31; practicable, 93–96; types, 93–96

Corinthians, 144, 244–45, 300

Cusa, Nicholas of. *See* Nicholas of Cusa

Custom, role of, 406–409

Dante, 175–76, 302; world government, 180–87

Defense of Liberty against Tyrants, A, 263, 266–72

Defensor Pacis, 176, 187–94

Dialogus, 195

Diderot, Denis, 415–16

Discourses, 216–17, 224–28

Divine right, 302–303; James I, 313–19

Duties, On, 123, 131, 135

Duties, 144–46

Ecclesiastica Potestate, De, 194–195

Economists, 414. *See also* Physiocrats

Egidius Romanus, 175, 194–95

Enquiry concerning Human Understanding, An, 391, 409

Ephesians, 241

Epicureanism, 103

Equality, 143–44

Esprit, De l', 416

Esprit des Lois, L', 415, 417, 425–40

Essay concerning Human Understanding, 359

Family, 51–54, 288–91

Fénelon, François, 412, 413, 422–25

Feudal system, 157–58, 161–66

First Principles of Government, Of the, 397–402

Fortescue, John, 14, 218–19, 229–32, 277–78

Francogallia, 263–64, 272–80

Freedom: of citizen, 354–56; *New Testament*, 143

French monarchy, 272–80

Galatians, 143–44, 146, 239

Gentili, Alberico, 303, 324

God and Political Duty, On, 249–62

Governance of England, The, 218

Government: Aristotle, 96–101; branches of, 96–101; Calvin, 255–59; corruption, 432–33; deliberative, 96–98; executive, 98–100; Hotman, 272–80; judicial, 100–101; Montesquieu, 425–33; need for, 255–59; purpose, 380–89; Suarez, 287–98; types, 426–31; world, 180–87

Grotius, Hugo, 14, 19, 303–304, 319–25, 390

Harrington, James, 357–58, 361–65; laws and restraints, 363–65; politics, economic basis of, 361–63

Hellenism, 102

Hobbes, Thomas, 14, 16, 17, 326–28, 329–49, 357, 360, 362–63, 364, 413; laws of nature, 337–38; liberty and law, 343–45; man, nature of, 329–32; political power, 339–43; social contract, 335–37; sovereign power, 345–49; state of nature, 332–35

Hooker, Richard, 357, 358–59, 365–72; civil society, 367–72; laws of reason, 365–67

Hotman, Francois, 263–64, 272–80

Human law, 203–207

Hume, David, 391–92, 397–411; custom, role of, 406–408; interest, 397–402; obligation, 400–401; political parties, 409–11; social contract, 402–406

Institutes of the Christian Religion, 236, 249–62

Interest, 397–402

International law, 124, 303–304, 319–25

Italy, 228–29

James I, 264, 265, 302, 357; divine right, 313–19; speech of 1609, 317–18; speech of 1616, 318–19

John of Salisbury, 160; commonwealth, 169–74; prince, 166–69

Jure Belli ac Pacis, De, 303, 319–25

Jure Regni apud Scotos, De, 264

Justice: Aristotle, 82–90; Augustine, 155–56; Cicero, 136–39

King: Aquinas, 207–10; Aristotle, 90–92; authority, 207–209; divine right, 301–303, 313–19; elected, 269–70; Fénelon, 422–25; Hotman, 272–80; James I, 313–19; Suarez, 293–97. See also Monarch, Prince, and Ruler

Kingship. See King

Kingship and the Education of a King, On, 264–65

La Bruyère, Jean de, 413

Laudibus Legum Anglie, De, 218, 229–32

Law: Aquinas, 196–201; Aristotle, 90–92; Cicero, 133–35; civil, 123; climate, 438–40; essence, 196–98; eternal, 200–201; Harrington, 363–65; Hobbes, 337–38; Hooker, 365–67; human, 203–207; international, 124, 303–304, 319–25; liberty,

Law: Aquinas (*continued*) 343–45; Marsiglio, 187–90; Montesquieu, 425–26; of nations, 124; of nature, 124, 133–35, 201–203; of reason, 365–67; restraints, 363–65; Roman, 123–25; rule of, 90–92; types, 198–200; validity of, 187–90

Law and God the Lawgiver, On, 265, 287–98

Laws, 27, 131, 134–35, 137–39

Laws of Ecclesiastical Polity, 358, 365–72

Laws, On, 123

Legibus, De, 123

Legibus, ac Deo legislatore, De, 265

Leviathan, 326, 329–49

Liberty: Calvin, 250–54; Christian, 250–54; Hobbes, 343–45; Montesquieu, 433–38; political, 433–38

Locke, John, 14, 15, 17, 19, 357, 359–60; civil society, 375–78; government, 380–89; legislative power, 382–83; power of the people, 384–86; property, 374–75; resistance, 386–89; separation of powers, 383–84; social contract, 379–80; society, 380–89; state of nature, 372–74; toleration, 412

Luther, Martin, 235–36; princes, duties of, 246–49; secular authority, 238–46

Machiavelli, Niccolò, 14, 17, 19, 215–17; anti-clericalism, 226–28; Italy, liberation of, 228–29; politics, art of, 219–24; religion, 224–26

Man: good, 75–78; nature of, 329–32

Marcus Aurelius, 105, 113–19, 309

Mariana, Juan de, 264–65, 280–87

Marsiglio of Padua, 14, 175, 176, 302; law, 190–91; order, 191–92; *regnum* and *sacerdotium,* 192–94; rulers, 190–91; unity, 191–92

Marx, Karl, 15, 18, 103, 415

Matthew, 145, 242, 243–44, 299

Mediaeval Institutions, 161–66

Meditations, 105, 113–19

Middle Ages, 157–74

Monarch, 419–22. *See also* King, Prince *and* Ruler

Monarchia, De, 175, 180–87

Monarchy: Bossuet, 419–20; Dante, 180–85; Fortescue, 229–32; Hotman, 272–80; limited, 229–32; need for, 180–85

Montesquieu, Charles, 218, 415, 417–18; climate, 438–40; governments, 425–33; law, 425–26, 438–40; liberty, 433–38

Nation-state, 217–19

Nations, law of, 124

Nature: law of, 124, 337–38; right of, 350–54; state of, 332–35, 372–74

New Science, The, 390, 392–97

New Testament, 143–46

Nicholas of Cusa, 14, 179, 211–14

Obedience, 259–62

Obligations: *New Testament,* 144–46; political, 397–402

Ockham, William of. *See* William of Ockham

Open Letter Concerning the Hard Book Against the Peasants, An, 245–46

Order, 191–92

Original Contract, Of the, 402–406

Origin of Justice and Property, Of the, 401–402

Padua, Marsiglio of. *See* Marsiglio of Padua

Parlement of Paris, 279

Parliament: in nation-state, 218–19; powers of, 232–33, 279

Peace, 180–85

People, power of, 384–86

Philosopher-king, 62–64

Philosophers: as kings, 54–59; value of, 59–62

Philosophes, 415–19

Physiocrats, 413–15. *See also* Economists

Plato, 14, 20, 23, 26–28, 123; family, 51–54; philosopher-king, 62–64; philosophers, 54–59, value of, 59–62; rulers, 37–41, 277; rules, function of, 41–43; social organization, 34–37; soul, 47–49; state, 43–47; women, 50–51

Policraticus, 160, 166–74

Polis. *See* Association, Commonwealth, Social organization, Society, *and* State

Political parties, 409–11

Political philosophy, 13–21

Political power: Aristotle, 87–90; Hobbes, 339–43

Politics: art of, 219–24; economic basis of, 361–63; Machiavelli, 219–24; nature of, 92–93

Politics, 28–29, 64–101, 181, 187, 188, 190, 197, 198, 272, 288

Politiques, 301, 302

Politique Tirée de L'Écriture Sainte, 413, 419–22

Polybius, 121–22, 125–31, 274

Pope: Bellarmine, 298–300; power of, 194–95, 295–300; Romanus, 194–95

Power: legislative, 382–83; of the people, 384–86; political, 87–90, 339–43; Pope, 194–95, 295–300; separation of, 383–84; sovereign, 345–49

Power of the Pope in Temporal Affairs, The, 298–300

Prince: duties of, 246–49; education, 412–13; John of Salisbury, 166–69; Luther, 246–49; nature of, 166–68. *See also* King, Monarch, *and* Ruler

Prince, The, 216, 217, 219–24, 228–29

Property, 374–75

Providence, role of, 392–97

Reason, 135–36

Reformation, 234–62

Rege et Regis Institutione, De, 264–65, 280–87

Regnum and *sacerdotium*, 158–60, 178, 192–94

Religion, 224–26; law and, 287–98

Renaissance, 215–33

Representation: beginnings of, 164–66; ideas of, 178–79; Rome, 123–24, 125

Republic, 26, 27, 28, 34–64, 123, 274, 276

Republica Anglorum, De, 218, 232–33

Resistance, 234–35; Brutus, 266–69; Catholic belief, 264–66; legitimacy of, 266–67; Locke, 386–89; possibility of, 386–89; by private persons, 267–69; Protestant belief, 263–64; right of, 263–300

Right of nature, 350–54

Right reason and nature, 135–36

Romans, 144, 238, 239, 240, 241

Rome, 120–39, 272, 275–76

Rule, paternal, 71–72

Ruler: duties of, 422–25; Marsiglio, 190–91; minister of God, 249; Plato, 37–41; restraints, 190–91; right to choose, 195–96; William of Ockham, 195–96. *See also* King, Monarch, *and* Prince

Rules, function, 41–43

Sacerdotium. See Regnum and sacerdotium

Saint-Simon, Duke de, 412

Salisbury, John of. *See* John of Salisbury

Second Treatise of Civil Government, 372–89

Secular authority: divine nature of, 238–43; extent of, 243–46

Secular Authority, to What Extent It Should Be Obeyed, 238–45, 246–49

Seneca, 105, 106–13, 276

Separation of powers, 383–84

Six Books of the Republic, The, 301, 304–13

Skepticism, 406–409

Slavery, 124; Aristotle, 24, 67–71; Paul, 141

Smith, Thomas, 218–19, 232–33

Social contract: Hobbes, 335–37; Hume, 402–406; Locke, 379–80

Social organization, 34–37. *See also* Association, Commonwealth, Society, *and* State

Society: civil, 375–78; community, 288–91; estates, 273–74; Hooker, 367–72; purpose, 380–89. *See also* Association, Commonwealth, Social organization, *and* State

Socrates, 24, 26

Sophists, 25–26

Sophocles, 25, 30–34

Soul, 47–49

Sovereignty, 301–302, 345–49; Aristotle, 84–87; Bodin, 304–13; external, 303–304; popular, 269–72; Rome, 124–25

Spinoza, Baruch, 15, 19, 328–29; freedom, 354–56; right of nature, 350–54; state, 350–54; best, 356

State: Aristotle, 65–67; autonomy of, 185–87; best, 356; Cicero, 131–33; composition of, 43–47; Dante, 185–87; justice in, 82–90; mixed, 131–33; nation-, 217–19; of nature, 372–74; Spinoza, 316–19. *See also* Association, Commonwealth, Social organization, *and* Society

Statesmen's Book, The, 166–74

Stephenson, Carl, 161–66

Stoicism, 123–24, 159, 359; Hellenistic, 103–104; Marcus Aurelius, 113–19; Ro-

Stoicism (*continued*)
man, 104–105; Seneca, 106–13
Suarez, Francisco, 265, 287–98
Summa Theologica, The, 15, 196–200
Systematic Politics, 264
Système de la Nature, Le, 416

Télémaque, 413, 422–25
Timothy, 144, 145–46, 239
Toleration, 412
Tractatus Politicus, 328, 352–54, 356
Tractatus Theologico-Politicus, 328, 350–52, 354–56
True Law of Free Monarchies, The, 302, 313–17
Two Cities, The, 149–55
Two Treatises of Civil Government, 359

Tyranny, 209–10, 272–73
Tyrant: John of Salisbury, 166–69; Mariana, 280–87; right to destroy, 280–87

Unity: Dante, 180–85; Marsiglio, 191–92
Universal History, 121–22, 125–31
Universe, 146–49

Vico, Giovanni B., 390–91, 392–97, 417
Vindiciae contra Tyrannos, 263, 266–72
Virgil, Polydore, 277

William of Ockham, 175, 176, 195–96
Women, 50–51
World government, 180–87